CLASSICS
from a
FRENCH
KITCHEN

CLASSICS
from a
FRENCH KITCHEN

Delicious, simple recipes, both ancient and modern, together with savory history and gastronomic lore in the grand tradition of the cuisine of France

ELIANE AMÉ-LEROY CARLEY

Foreword by Paul Bocuse
Illustrations by Ann W. Gibb

Crown Publishers, Inc. ⚜ *New York*

To my parents,
who taught me to know
and to love
French cuisine
and
to my children,
Robert and Viviane,
for their endless support

Published by Crown Publishers, Inc.,
One Park Avenue, New York, New York 10016,
and simultaneously in Canada by General Publishing Company Limited
Manufactured in the United States of America
Library of Congress Cataloging in Publication Data
Carley, Eliane Amé-Leroy.
Classics from a French kitchen.
Bibliography: p.
Includes index.
1. Cookery, French.   I. Title.
TX719.C285 1983   641.5944   82-18311
ISBN: 0-517-54919-0
Book design by Camilla Filancia
10 9 8 7 6 5 4 3 2 1
First Edition

CONTENTS

❧ ❧ ❧

FOREWORD

Madame Eliane Amé-Leroy Carley, whom I had the keen pleasure of meeting in the United States, is not only a writer of great talent, but also a scholar regarding gastronomic matters and a true *fine fourchette,* and it pleases me to salute her warmly here.

It gives me, therefore, great pleasure to preface this remarkable work, which is the result of many years of meticulous research.

It is a beautiful book that will make even more people appreciate our cuisine, its savory history, its eating customs, and its illustrious recipes, some of which were given to the author's mother by the celebrated Auguste Escoffier.

The reader should know that Madame A. L. Carley was reared in the midst of state secrets and in an atmosphere of fine food. Her father, in fact, was French Ambassador and Chef de Cabinet to Aristide Briand at the League of Nations, at a time when the white tablecloths of my venerated master Fernand Point, whose friend he was, did more for peace than the green carpets of the international meetings!

Moreover, her uncle, the great historian Maxime Leroy, member of l'Institut, unceasingly initiated the young Eliane in what he considered a necessary discipline, but too often neglected: the culinary history of our ancestors, so particularly revealing in the whole evolution of a race based on the civilization of wine.

Last, let us not forget that if the nobility of the sword has vanished and it now appears sensible to place the spit above the blade, it is up to our cooks to preserve the panache of France during these difficult times.

So be it! Good appetite, dear readers.   PAUL BOCUSE

ACKNOWLEDGMENTS

I am grateful for the generous help I have received from many sources over the last thirteen years, while this book was being written. To all who have assisted me so willingly with my research, I wish to express my gratitude and appreciation.

Frère Antoine Bru, Bibliothécaire de l'Abbaye de Port-du-Salut, Entrammes, J. C. Augar, Chef du Service de l'Information de la Préfecture de Paris; Roger Berthon, Président de la Société des Amis du Vieux Saint-Germain, Saint-Germain-en-Laye; Alescondre Bertrande, Membre de l'Institut et Conservateur du Musée de Saint-Germain; La Bibliothèque Nationale, Paris; H. Bompaire, de la Maison Moët et Chandon, Épernay; Carmen Caselli-Desmarais and Béryl LeMoyne, librarians of the Bibliothèque de la Ville de Montréal, Canada; Le Syndicat d'Initiative de Castelnaudary; J. Chaix, Propriétaire de l'Hôstellerie de l'Abbaye de la Celle, La Celle; Jacques Charles, Membre de la Société Archéologique et Historique de l'Orléanais, Serquigny; Conservatoire National des Arts et Métiers, Paris; J. Corbière, Compagnie Gervais Danone, Paris; Hervé Cras, Chef du Service d'Études du Musée de la Marine, Paris; Henri Denier, Archiviste de la Ville de Rouen; Joseph Donon, founder and President of Les Amis d'Escoffier Fondation, Inc., Middletown, Rhode Island; C. Fontanon, Centre de Documentation d'Histoire des Techniques, Paris; Raymond Grangier, Chef de Cuisine of the S.S. *France;* P. Gras, Conservateur de la Bibliothèque Publique de Dijon; H. Jabeneau, Directeur du Pavillon Henri IV, Saint-Germain-en-Laye; Elisha Keeler, reference librarian of the Darien Library, Connecticut, who was able to locate rare materials from the Library of Congress, from various public libraries, and from many university libraries; J. Koscher, Le Proviseur du Lycée d'Enseignement Technologique et Professionel d'Hôtellerie et de Tourisme de Strasbourg; Christian Lelièvre, la Chambre Régionale de Commerce et d'Industrie de Provence; Jacques Médecin, Monsieur le Maire de la Ville de Nice; Les Archives Municipales de Metz, France; my sister, Josette, and her husband, Doctor Charles Milsom, Paris; Musée de l'Art Culinaire, Fondation A. Escoffier, Villeneuve-Loubet; Margaret J. Oaksford, librarian of the School of Hotel Administration, Cornell University, Ithaca, New York; Joan Grant Obermayer, Darien, Connecticut; M. Pagola, Le Musée Basque, Bayonne; P. Pauchard, Hôtel de France, Nantua; Bernard Savouret, Conservateur des Archives de la Ville de Dijon; Barbara Feret Schuman and Eileen de Vries, librarians of the Culinary Institute of America, Hyde Park, New York; L. Tossard, Le Grand Maître de la Tripière d'Or, Caen; Mapie de Toulouse-Lautrec, Paris; Louis Vaudable, Maxim's, Paris; M. Vidal, head pastry chef of the S.S. *France;* Danielle Wattel, Darien, Connecticut; and with special gratitude to my editor, Ruth Buchan.

PREFACE

Every country has two kinds of cooking. Its own and the French. Why? Because French cooking offers unparalleled taste sensations from recipes which, through the centuries, have been refined to a point of perfection.

To savor fully a delectable French dish, one should know its background, which is linked so closely through all of France's history. It is an added dimension that opens a renewed appreciation of French cooking and its contribution to other cuisines.

When Escoffier said, "To write the history of the food habits of a nation is to paint a picture of its civilization," he could have added that to know French cuisine is to understand the soul of France.

My aim is to point out the colorful circumstances from which our classic recipes have evolved, covering many centuries—from 90 B.C., when Lucullus prepared an omelet made with an ostrich egg, to the relatively recent time of the first soufflé. Not only the dishes themselves, but many little-known, fascinating stories, based on fourteen years of searching for documentation from reliable sources, make one appreciate more fully the creation of these recipes.

As with living art, French cooking, which has contributed so magnificently to the glory and renown of France, is not at a standstill, but will continue to move forward. Thus, we are looking to new aspects and dimensions in the enjoyment of France's culinary art, but without forgetting our heritage.

I hope this book will be welcomed by all who have an awareness and interest in the many facets of French gastronomy.

Experience the pleasure of cooking as the French do, and you will make these recipes your friends.

1. ON DINING

In tracing the customs of eating and serving food, one discovers many interesting and curious facts, outstanding among them the habit of eating in the bath. It seems that from the Middle Ages through the Renaissance, it was a popular custom for a man and a woman to share a bath accompanied by a meal and music. They sat on low stools in the bathtub and small tables were set beside or over the tub. The ladies wore only an elaborate headdress! This practice was attributed to the scarcity of hot water.

The happiest custom, and one we could well reinstate, was the practice of singing during meals. For many centuries, up to the eighteenth, this habit prevailed at the court and in the homes of well-to-do families. The songs were called *vaudeville.*

Before the eighteenth century there was no special room for eating. In most homes the kitchen, always a large room with an imposing chimney, was also the eating place. On festive occasions the living room was used. Even at Versailles, there were no dining rooms. Louis XIV would eat in public in the Hall of Mirrors, the better for all to see. Indeed, official state dinners are still held there today.

It was the custom at that time for men of nobility to wear their hats at mealtime. They removed them only when making a toast.

After her marriage to Henri II in 1533, Catherine de Médicis, bringing with her the customs of her native Florence, was instrumental in having the women of France return to the table. For the last hundred years, since the reign of Louis XI, the ladies had been banished to their rooms, where mush was served to them, "because the motion of their jaws deforms the shape of their faces and so coarsens their natural beauty."

Eating utensils developed slowly as customs changed and circumstances demanded. It was the fashionable lords at the court of Henri III, who wore the voluminous, starched collars of the period, who started to use forks to protect their collars. At first the fork was considered a ridiculous and dangerous instrument. The two long, sharp tines continually wounded tongues and lips. Forks were not generally accepted until the eighteenth century. Even Louis XIV, dining at Versailles, never got used to eating with a fork. He used three of his fingers because it was considered poor table manners to eat with all five.

The *tranchoir* was a thick piece of unleavened bread that served as a plate until the sixteenth century. It absorbed the meat juices. This was also eaten or put aside to give to the poor. It was not until the seventeenth century that soup plates and spoons and individual plates appeared.

Ever since the time of Charlemagne the tablecloth has been an important part of dining in France, and during the Middle Ages it took on a symbolic importance. To share someone's tablecloth meant that the guest was considered an equal; if the guest was not accepted, the host would be served on the tablecloth and the guest was given an individual place mat.

During the latter part of the Middle Ages, napkins were worn on the left shoulder and over the left arm (as is still the custom of waiters in some restaurants). During the Renaissance, napkins were worn over the voluminous collars. The expression "It's difficult to make both ends meet" developed because it was so hard to tie the napkins. The art of folding napkins was very important, and each guest was given one of a different shape, representing a bird, a fruit, a fish, or a chicken. Earlier, as shown in paintings and tapestries of feasts, guests wiped their hands on the short coats of the ever-present hounds, or if there were no dogs nearby, on the edge of the tablecloth.

During the same period in China, they used napkins made of asbestos. Marco Polo reported that "when they become dirty, they are bleached by being put in the fire and become as white as snow."

As for serving the foods, the custom at the French court and in the upper-class homes was to have all the dishes of each course brought to the table at the same time. The meal was presented on very wide tables in a lavish display of symmetrical arrangements of food, embellished with beautiful golden ornaments.

Generally there were three courses, each consisting of numerous dishes. The first course was placed on the table before the guests were seated. They then indicated to the *maître d'hôtel* what dish they wanted. This was called *service à la française.*

It was all changed when Prince Kourakine, Ambassador of the Czar, came to Paris in 1810. He introduced a new system of serving food. The dishes were brought from the kitchen, served one at a time to each guest, and then returned to the pantry. This was called *service à la russe.* This innovation was adopted almost overnight, and spoken of at the time with great excitement. This style of service is still followed, and gone are the decorative *pièces montées* (set pieces) as well as the art of carving at the table before marveling guests.

The dining customs of France shift and change but the respect for, and love of, good food remains firm. Perhaps the following menus will help you entertain and enjoy food the French way.

MENUS
⚜ ⚜ ⚜

A good meal should be as harmonious as a symphony
and as well built as a Romanesque cathedral.
—FERNAND POINT

• *Special Evenings* •

ELEGANT DINNER FOR TWO

Soupe Germiny   Sorrel Soup
Pintadeaux Braisés à l'Orange   Braised Cornish Game Hens
with Orange
Pommes de Terre Paille   Shoestring Potatoes
Salade Verte   Mixed Green Salad
Melon aux Fraises au Cointreau   Melon with Strawberries flavored
with Cointreau liqueur

SPRING DINNER PARTY FOR SIX

Bisque de Crevettes   Shrimp Bisque
Rôti de Veau à la Parisienne avec Fonds d'Artichauts à la Barigoule
Parisian Veal Roast with Stuffed Artichoke Bottoms
Pommes de Terre Noisette   Potato Balls in Butter
Salade Verte   Mixed Green Salad
Fromages   Cheeses
Profiteroles au Chocolat   Cream Puffs with Chocolate Sauce

SUMMER FORMAL BUFFET

Oeufs en Gelée   Eggs in Aspic
Mousse de Saumon   Salmon Mousse
Salade Parisienne   Parisian Salad (mixed vegetables
with lobster and mayonnaise)
Pâté en Croûte   Pâté in Crust
Chaud-Froid de Volaille   Breast of Chicken, Chaud-Froid
Sandwiches Assortis   Assorted Sandwiches
Croquembouche   Pyramid of Caramelized Cream Puffs
Baba au Rhum
Petits Fours
Fruits Rafraîchis au Champagne   Fruits in Champagne

WINTER DINNER PARTY FOR EIGHT

Potage Crème à la Dubarry   Cream of Cauliflower Soup
Noisettes d'Agneau Béarnaise   Noisettes of Lamb
with Béarnaise Sauce
Pommes de Terre Paille   Shoestring Potatoes
Endives Braisées   Braised Endive
Salade Mimosa
Petits Choux Saint-Honoré   Caramelized Cream Puffs

RÉVEILLON (CHRISTMAS EVE)

Petits Vol-au-Vents aux Huîtres   Small Patty Shells with Oysters
Dindonneau Farci aux Marrons   Roast Turkey Stuffed
with Chestnuts
Céleris en Branches Braisées   Braised Celery
Salade de Carentan   Bibb Lettuce with Endive, Apple,
Walnuts, Seasoning, and *Crème Fraîche*

ON DINING

Bûche de Noël   Yule Log
Bombe aux Framboises   Molded Raspberry Ice Cream

INFORMAL DINNER

Mouclade   Mussels with Curry and Cream
Poulet Grillé, Sauce Diable   Grilled Chicken with Deviled Sauce
Haricots Verts au Beurre   Green Beans with Butter
Fromage de Roquefort   Roquefort Cheese
Poires au Vin   Pears in Red Wine

WINTER DINNER PARTY FOR SIX

Soufflés d'Huîtres   Oyster Soufflés
Noisettes de Porc à la Tourangelle
Noisettes of Pork with Prunes and Cream
Riz au Gras   Rice au Gras
Salade d'Endive et Betterave   Endive and Beet Salad
Fromage de Brie   Brie Cheese
Crème Renversée au Caramel au Rhum   Caramel Custard with Rum

DINNER FOR TEN

Coquilles Saint-Jacques à la Parisienne   Parisian Scallops
Filet de Boeuf avec Pommes de Terre   Beef Fillet with Potatoes
Asperges en Branches, Sauce Mousseline   Asparagus with
Mousseline Sauce
Salade d'Endive et Cresson   Endive and Watercress Salad
Riz à l'Impératrice   Rice Pudding
with Glacéed Fruits and Apricot Sauce

SUMMER DINNER PARTY

Soupe de Cresson (froide)   Watercress Soup (chilled)
Coulibiac de Saumon, Sauce Smitane   Pâté of Salmon with Rice,
Herbs, Hard-Cooked Eggs and Mushrooms, with Sour Cream
Sauce
Salade Verte   Mixed Green Salad
Mousse au Citron (et aux fraises)   Lemon Mousse (with strawberries)

• *Informal Occasions* •

SIMPLE LUNCHEON NEAR THE POOL

Bouchées Feuilletées aux Anchois   Anchovies in Pastry Rounds
Assiette de Crudités ou *Salade Niçoise*
Plate of Raw Vegetables, Vinaigrette Sauce, or Salade Niçoise
Mousse Glacée à l'Ananas   Frozen Pineapple Mousse
Petits Fours

PICNIC

Tomates Surprise   Tomato Surprise (with ham and
hard-cooked eggs)
Pâté en Croûte   Pâté in Crust
Salade de Pommes de Terre (au cresson)   French Potato Salad
(with watercress)
Fromages   Cheeses
Fraises au Fromage Blanc   Strawberries with Fresh White Cheese

SIMPLE DINNER AT THE SEASHORE

Soupe des Pêcheurs   Fishermen's Soup
Avocats Farcis au Roquefort   Roquefort-Stuffed Avocados
Fruits de Saison   Fruits of the Season

SUPPER AFTER THE THEATER

Crème de Palourdes   Cream of Clam Soup
Oeufs Brouillés Cannelons   Scrambled Eggs with Truffles
Salade de Pamplemousses et d'Oranges
Grapefruit and Orange Fruit Bowl

COLD SUMMER DINNER ON THE TERRACE

Crème de Cerfeuil Froide   Cream of Chervil Soup (cold)
Poulet en Gelée   Chicken in Aspic
Macédoine de Légumes   Mixed Vegetable Salad
Fromages   Cheeses
Fraises Melba   Strawberries with Melba Sauce

ON DINING

A P R È S - S K I   D I N N E R

Cassoulet   Beans with Pork, Sausage, and Goose
Salade Verte   Mixed Green Salad
Fromages   Cheeses
Charlotte Russe aux Abricots   Charlotte Russe with Apricots
Tous les Fruits   Fresh Fruits

• *Daytime Entertaining* •

L U N C H E O N   F O R   F O U R

Oeufs en Gelée   Eggs in Aspic
Filets de Sole à la Florentine   Sole with Spinach and Cheese Sauce
Fromages   Cheeses
Mousse au Café   Coffee Mousse
Tuiles aux Amandes   Almond Wafers

S U N D A Y   C O U N T R Y   W E E K E N D   L U N C H E O N

Hors-d'Oeuvre Assortis   Assorted Hors-d'oeuvre
Gigot à la Bretonne   Leg of Lamb Breton Style
Salade Verte   Mixed Green Salad
Plateau de Fromages   Tray of Cheeses
Tarte aux Fraises   Strawberry Tart

E A S T E R   L U N C H E O N

Quenelles de Poisson   Fish Quenelles
Jambon au Madère   Ham with Madeira Sauce
Épinards en Branche   Leaf Spinach
Salade Verte   Mixed Green Salad
Fromages   Cheeses
Mousse Glacée à l'Ananas   Frozen Pineapple Mousse

BRIDGE PARTY

Velouté de Tomates Provençale   Tomato Velouté
Croque-Monsieur (garnis de cresson)
Toasted Ham and Cheese Sandwich (with watercress)
Parfait au Café   Coffee Parfait

TEA PARTY

Petits Sandwiches Assortis   Assorted Finger Sandwiches
Tarte Feuilletée aux Poires (à l'orange)   Caramelized Pear Pie (with
orange glaze)
Éclairs au Café   Coffee Éclairs
Choux à la Crème   Cream Puffs
Biscuit Roulé   Jelly Roll

✦ *For the Family* ✦

FAMILY DINNER

Potage Crécy   Cream of Carrot Soup
Poulet à l'Ivoire   Poached Chicken with Cream Sauce
Salade Fontaine   Fontaine Salad
Fromages   Cheeses
Poires Hélène   Pears Hélène

MEATLESS DINNER FOR FOUR

Potage de Poireaux à la Crème   Cream of Leek Soup
Omelette aux Champignons   Mushroom Omelet
Tomates à la Provençale   Tomatoes with Garlic and Bread Crumbs
Fromage de Camembert   Camembert Cheese
Tarte Galette Feuilletée aux Pommes   Apple Pie with Puff Pastry

◆ ◆ ◆

King Edward VII asked Escoffier after a splendid meal if it was
true that he never tasted the food he prepared.

Escoffier replied, "Yes," and pointed to his nose. He sniffed
and added, "No need!"

2. *Les Hors-d'Oeuvre et les Petites Entrées*
HORS-D'OEUVRE AND LUNCHEON DISHES

⚜ ⚜ ⚜

After one cocktail, worse yet, two, the palate can no longer distinguish a bottle of Château Mouton-Rothschild from a bottle of ink.
—FERNAND POINT

Hors-d'oeuvre are exactly what the word implies: something outside the main part of a regular meal, or something extra served at the beginning. In the United States, *hors-d'oeuvre* are generally served as nibbles with cocktails, but they hold a much more important place in French cuisine, as we shall see.

Serving *hors-d'oeuvre* is a very old custom. Even menus from the Roman empire list *hors-d'oeuvre* such as oysters and sliced eggs with anchovies. In the sixteenth century, Rabelais described a menu offered to Pantagruel that could be served today. Three of the six *hors-d'oeuvre* included were caviar, salted tuna, and olives.

During the Siege of Paris in 1870, when any kind of food was at a premium and animals, even pets, were not safe in the street, the famous restaurant Voisin would not hear of doing without the traditional *hors-d'oeuvre* for the *Réveillon* (Christmas Eve dinner). And so, in addition to the radishes and sardines (procured from whatever secret source they had found), stuffed donkey head was served! One by one, all the animals of the zoo met more or less the same fate, during that desperate period.

Again during the World War I food shortage, we learn of the importance of *hors-d'oeuvre* by reading a decree in the *Journal Officiel* (February 15, 1917): "No restaurant may serve more than four *hors-d'oeuvre* per person."

In France, *hors-d'oeuvre* are served at table before the noontime meal, the main meal of the day. It is interesting to find that, just as the British call their midmorning snack "elevenses" after the time of the day it is eaten, the French spoke of their main meal as, at

9

first, *decimer*, from *decima*, the Latin word for ten, the hour at which they ate. This word evolved into *disner* and finally became *dîner*. The word is still used but the time has changed a bit, from ten o'clock to twelve or one.

Hors-d'oeuvre are generally limited in number to five, arranged attractively in shallow dishes, called *raviers*. An appetizing choice might include *champignons à la Grecque* (Greek-style mushrooms), *salade de tomates* (tomato salad), *rillettes* (potted pork) or sliced salami, *oeufs mollets cressonnières* (soft-cooked eggs with watercress), and radishes served with crusty French bread and a dish of cold small curls of unsalted butter. (A dab of butter and a pinch of salt are delicious on a crisp radish.)

Curnonsky, "the prince of the gastronomes," whose real name was Maurice-Edmond Sailland, describes *hors-d'oeuvre* in his book *La Table et l'Amour* (1950): "*Hors-d'oeuvre* in France are loved and rightly so—on condition that they remain what they are supposed to be: amusing appetizers destined to create a bit of pleasant atmosphere. *Hors-d'oeuvre* must not be such that one cannot eat after they have been served. Therefore, it is wise to limit the number."

In some cases these recipes do not give a number of servings. How many each recipe will serve depends on the number and type of *hors-d'oeuvre* included and on the individual appetite.

Cocktail d'Huîtres

OYSTER COCKTAIL

2 pints shelled oysters   *4 to 6 servings*
½ cup white wine
2 tablespoons tarragon vinegar
Coarse salt and white pepper
3 tablespoons finely minced shallots
½ cup Crème Fraîche (see Index) or sour cream
Boston lettuce, shredded
Fresh parsley or chives, finely minced
Rye toast

1. Place oysters in a pan with the white wine, vinegar, coarse salt and white pepper to taste. Bring to a boil and simmer for exactly 1 minute. Remove the oysters.

2. Add the shallots to the wine mixture and boil until mixture is reduced to about 3 tablespoons. Add the oysters and chill for at least 1 hour.

3. Combine the oysters with the *crème fraîche*. Place on plates

lined with the Boston lettuce. Sprinkle with parsley or chives. Serve with thin buttered rye toast.

◆ UNDER THE COOK'S HAT ◆

Use a special knife with a solid blade to open oysters. Hold the oyster in a cloth to protect your hand. Insert the knife between the shells at the back to break the hinge, then turn the knife sideways to separate the shells. Loosen the oyster from the shell with the blunt side of the blade.

Another infallible method for opening oysters that is safer than a knife in unskilled hands is this: Preheat the oven to 350°F.; place the oysters on a baking sheet and heat in the oven for 5 minutes. Prepare a tray of crushed ice. Remove the oysters from the oven and place them on the ice, covering them with a little ice. Or place them on a chilled tray in the freezer for 5 minutes immediately after being in the oven. The muscles of the oysters slacken and they open by themselves.

◆ ◆ ◆

In early times strolling Parisian merchants selling olives used to shout:

Quiconque mange des olives
Chaque jour de chaque saison,
Vit aussi vieux que les solives
De la plus solide maison.

Whoever eats olives
Every day of each season,
Survives as long as the beams
Of the best built house.

Olives aux Anchois

OLIVES STUFFED WITH ANCHOVY

3 ounces Gervais or cream cheese
1 tablespoon anchovy paste
½ teaspoon lemon juice
Salt and white pepper
36 large green or black olives, pitted

1. Mash the Gervais or cream cheese with the anchovy paste. Add lemon juice, and salt and pepper to taste. Blend thoroughly.

2. Stuff the olives with the cream mixture, using a pastry bag fitted with a small plain tube. Serve chilled.

Assiette de Crudités

PLATE OF RAW VEGETABLES

This is an especially appetizing start for a light luncheon. The *assiette de crudités* is composed of small amounts of the following ingredients, attractively arranged:

Shredded carrots, radishes, slices of hard-cooked egg each topped by an anchovy, sliced raw mushrooms, cooked beets cut into strips, sliced tomatoes, olives, and sprigs of watercress. Sprinkle with a flavored Vinaigrette (see Index).

◆ ◆ ◆

Until Voltaire's time, an artichoke bottom was called *cul d'artichaut*. (*Cul* is a crude word for bottom.) Voltaire thought the term was shocking and replaced it with *fond d'artichaut*, a more refined name that is still used today.

Fonds d'Artichauts Marinés

MARINATED ARTICHOKE BOTTOMS

Marinated artichoke hearts or bottoms make good *hors-d'oeuvre* or garnishes for fish or meat. They can be combined with any one of several accompaniments to suit your taste.

Make a recipe of Vinaigrette (see Index) and let the cooked artichokes (see Artichokes in Index) marinate in it for 30 minutes. Add one of the following:

• A spoonful of Mixed Vegetable Salad (see Index) on each artichoke.

• Crab meat mixed with Anchovy Mayonnaise (see Index). Serve chilled on Boston lettuce leaves.

• Or quarter the artichoke hearts and combine with Rémoulade Sauce (see Index); serve in a dish lined with Boston lettuce leaves.

Avocats Farcis au Roquefort

ROQUEFORT-STUFFED AVOCADOS

3 ripe avocados, chilled   *6 servings*
Lemon juice
2 ounces Roquefort cheese, at room temperature
1½ cups sour cream, at room temperature
Salt
Paprika
Walnuts (optional)

1. Cut the avocados into halves and remove the pits and skin.
2. Brush avocado flesh with lemon juice to prevent darkening.
3. Mix the cheese, sour cream, and salt to taste. Fill the avocados with this mixture with a spoon or, even better, pipe it in from a pastry bag fitted with a decorative tube. Dust with a little paprika on top for color. Coarsely chopped walnuts may be added to the filling before spooning it into the avocado.

Poireaux Vinaigrette

LEEKS WITH VINAIGRETTE

Serve as an *hors-d'oeuvre* or salad course.

6 medium-size whole leeks, with most of the green removed
Salt

VINAIGRETTE DRESSING
6 tablespoons oil
2½ tablespoons cider vinegar
Salt and freshly ground pepper
Dijon mustard

2 hard-cooked egg yolks, crumbled

1. Cook the leeks in salted water until tender, about 20 minutes. Drain thoroughly.
2. Prepare the vinaigrette dressing: Mix together oil, vinegar, seasonings and mustard to taste.
3. Marinate the leeks in the vinaigrette, and chill for 2 hours.
4. Just before serving, sprinkle crumbled egg yolk over the leeks.

• *Garnishes* •

Use your artistic sense to enhance the appearance of the *hors-d'oeuvre* with colorful garnishes such as tiny geometric designs made of pimientos or truffles; fresh parsley, whole or minced; a few sprigs of watercress; olives; and slices of grooved lemons.

Grooved lemon slices are prepared with a special knife with a hooked blade which removes strips of the rind at regular intervals. The lemon is grooved from stem to blossom end, then sliced crosswise. This method is called *citron cannelé* (grooved lemon). For a decorative touch, place a slice of pimiento-stuffed olive in the center of each lemon slice.

A combination of some of the following vegetable *hors-d'oeuvre*, arranged individually on shallow serving dishes or *raviers*, would make an attractive display.

Fernand Point decrees that whatever garnish is used with a dish it should match as a tie matches a suit.

Champignons à la Grecque

GREEK-STYLE MUSHROOMS

Serve at room temperature in the winter and cold in the summer.

1 pound small mushrooms · *4 servings*
¾ cup white wine or white vermouth
¾ cup beef broth
1 beef bouillon cube, crushed
1½ tablespoons lemon juice
Bouquet garni (1 bay leaf, ½ teaspoon thyme, 2 parsley sprigs)
4 shallots, minced
4 large garlic cloves, halved
4 tablespoons olive oil
Salt and pepper
1 tablespoon tomato paste
Fresh parsley, minced
Lemon slices, grooved and cut into halves

1. Cut the mushroom stems off level with the caps.
2. Place all of the ingredients except the tomato paste, parsley and lemon slices in a pan. Bring to a fast boil for 5 minutes, then add the tomato paste and cook for another 5 minutes.
3. Remove mushrooms with a perforated spoon and set aside.

Reduce the sauce over high heat for a few minutes, until thickened. Remove *bouquet garni*. Return mushrooms to sauce. Cool.

4. Serve in a *ravier* with a sprinkling of parsley. Garnish with the lemon slices.

◆   *Variation*   ◆

Artichokes prepared *à la grecque* are also delicious. Substitute 8 very small cooked artichokes for the mushrooms in the basic recipe.

Salade de Betteraves

BEET SALAD

Serve as one of several *hors-d'oeuvre*.

1 pound oven-baked or canned beets, julienned or diced

VINAIGRETTE DRESSING
2 tablespoons tarragon vinegar
3 tablespoons olive oil
1 small onion, finely minced
1 garlic clove, finely minced
2 tablespoons finely minced fresh parsley
Salt and freshly ground pepper

Combine the beets and vinaigrette dressing. Serve chilled.

Salade de Chou Rouge

RED CABBAGE SALAD

Serve as one of several *hors-d'oeuvre*.

1 very small head of red cabbage, finely shredded
⅓ cup wine vinegar
3 tablespoons peanut oil
Salt and freshly ground pepper
2 tablespoons finely chopped onion
Fresh parsley, chopped
Fresh chervil, chopped

1. Parboil the shredded cabbage in boiling water for 1 minute. Drain thoroughly.

2. Place the cabbage in a bowl. Pour the wine vinegar over the hot cabbage; stir well. Marinate for 10 minutes. Drain excess vinegar from the bowl.

3. Add the peanut oil, salt and pepper to taste, and onion. Sprinkle with parsley and chervil.

Concombres à la Crème
CUCUMBERS WITH CREAM

Serve as one of several *hors-d'oeuvre*.

2 cucumbers, peeled
Fresh lemon juice
½ cup Crème Fraîche (see Index) or sour cream
Fresh tarragon or chives, snipped
Salt and white pepper

1. Cut the cucumbers lengthwise into halves. Scrape out the seeds with a spoon and cut halves into thin slices.

2. Mix the cucumbers with lemon juice to taste. Add the *crème fraîche*, tarragon or chives, and salt and white pepper to taste.

3. Decorate with more tarragon or chives. Serve very cold.

Lentilles Vinaigrette
LENTILS WITH VINAIGRETTE

Serve as one of several *hors-d'oeuvre*.

1 cup dried lentils
1 small onion, cut into halves
½ bay leaf
Pinch of ground cloves
Salt

VINAIGRETTE DRESSING
5 tablespoons peanut oil
2 tablespoons wine vinegar or lemon juice
1 tablespoon minced parsley
1 tablespoon minced shallot or onion
Salt and pepper

1. Wash the lentils under cold running water. Drain and place in a pan. Cover the lentils with 2 inches of cold water.

2. Add the onion, bay leaf, cloves, and salt to taste. Bring to a boil, then simmer uncovered for about 30 minutes, or until the lentils are just tender. Drain thoroughly and transfer to a bowl. Discard the onion and bay leaf.

3. Prepare vinaigrette dressing, adding seasoning to taste.

4. While the lentils are still tepid, toss gently with the dressing. Chill before serving, in a *ravier* or a shallow dish.

Salade de Champignons
RAW MUSHROOM SALAD

This salad brings out all the delicate flavor of the mushrooms, with their scent of the forest.

½ pound mushrooms, thinly sliced   *2 servings*
2 tablespoons fresh lemon juice
⅓ cup Crème Fraîche (see Index)
2 tablespoons snipped chives
Salt and white pepper
Watercress

1. Combine first 4 ingredients, with seasoning to taste. Mix well.
2. Serve on a bed of watercress leaves.

Salade de Tomates
TOMATO SALAD

1. Blanch tomatoes for about 10 seconds. Remove the skins.

2. Slice tomatoes very thin. Arrange in a *ravier* or shallow dish, in overlapping rows. Cover with Vinaigrette Dressing (see Index).

3. Sprinkle with chopped fresh chervil and tarragon. A little chopped onion or some snipped chives may be added.

Tomates Surprise
TOMATO SURPRISE

These tomatoes can be served as an *hors-d'oeuvre*.

1. Make 6 or 7 slices from stem to bottom almost all the way through firm ripe oval-shaped tomatoes. The tomatoes will look like accordions. Season with salt between the slices and invert the tomatoes on a rack to drain for 30 minutes.

2. Spread each tomato slice generously with mayonnaise. Alternate shaped pieces of boiled ham or tongue with thin slices of hard-cooked egg between slices of each tomato.

3. Press the slices together to reshape tomatoes. Remove excess mayonnaise and sprinkle with finely chopped parsley and snipped chives. Serve chilled, garnished with watercress.

◆ UNDER THE COOK'S HAT ◆

The French method of slicing a tomato: Use a serrated blade and cut vertically to the base of the tomato. This minimizes the loss of juice and helps the slices retain their shape.

Petites Tomates Fourrées au Fromage

CHERRY TOMATOES STUFFED WITH CREAM CHEESE

1. Cut off a thin slice at the stem end of each cherry tomato. Remove some of the pulp with a small pointed knife or a melon-baller. Sprinkle each one with salt and set upside down to drain.

2. Mash Gervais or cream cheese with just enough heavy cream to soften. Add snipped chives, salt and white pepper to taste.

3. Fill the tomatoes with the cheese mixture, using a teaspoon or a pastry bag fitted with a star tube.

◆ *Variation* ◆

Mix Gervais or cream cheese with Roquefort cheese to taste. Omit the chives.

Oeufs en Gelée

EGGS IN ASPIC

Oeufs en gelée is the traditional start of a French luncheon. The eggs can be poached or *mollet* (soft-cooked with a slightly runny center).

1. Poach small eggs, then place them in a bowl of cold water to cool. Drain the eggs with a slotted spoon. Trim the whites to a uniform roundness.

2. Make a Quick Aspic (see Index).

3. Pour enough aspic into individual molds to coat them with a ⅛-inch-thick layer. Chill until aspic is almost set. If aspic hardens too much, it will unmold in layers, with some adhering to the mold.

4. In the bottom of the mold, on top of the almost set aspic, center one of the following decorations: a truffle slice; 2 leaves of fresh tarragon blanched for 1 minute; or a small lozenge of boiled ham. (The decorations should be chilled first, and dipped into almost solidified aspic.) Pour another layer of aspic over the decorations and chill until almost set.

5. Place an egg on the chilled aspic and fill the mold to the brim with more of the syrupy aspic. Chill for several hours. Unmold just before serving.

◆ UNDER THE COOK'S HAT ◆

To unmold, pass a knife around the mold. Dip the mold into hot water for a few seconds, invert on the serving plate, and give a few hard raps on the bottom of the mold.

Oval metal molds for eggs in aspic with a capacity of ½ cup can be bought in stores specializing in cookware or in department stores.

Oeufs à la Rémoulade
HARD-COOKED EGGS WITH RÉMOULADE SAUCE

This simple egg preparation is a classic *hors-d'oeuvre* served in many French restaurants.

1. Slice hard-cooked eggs with an egg slicer. Slightly overlap the slices in a *ravier* lined with Boston lettuce leaves.

2. Make a Rémoulade Sauce (see Index) and thin it with a little cream to a spreading consistency. Spoon over the eggs and sprinkle with chopped fresh parsley or snipped chives.

Oeufs Mollets Cressonnières
SOFT-COOKED EGGS IN WATERCRESS MAYONNAISE

Oeufs mollets literally translated means half-soft eggs. The eggs are cooked only to the point where the whites are set and the yolks are soft around the edges but still runny in the center. This recipe is one of the favorite ways in French cookery for preparing eggs.

4 large eggs, at room temperature   *4 servings*
1 bunch of watercress
1 cup freshly made Mayonnaise (see Index)
Lemon juice
1 to 2 tablespoons heavy cream

1. Lower the eggs carefully into boiling water and simmer for 6½ minutes. Plunge immediately into cold water to stop the cooking. Crush the eggshell in several places and remove the shells. Rinse eggs in cold water and chill.

2. Chop the watercress leaves and stems very fine in a parsley mincer, or with a sharp knife. Blend with the mayonnaise. Add lemon juice to taste, and just enough cream to give the sauce a good spreading consistency.

3. Slice the eggs lengthwise into halves. Cover with the watercress mayonnaise. Serve in a *ravier* or shallow dish.

◆   *Variation*   ◆

A combination of 3 tablespoons minced parsley and 3 tablespoons snipped chives mixed with a little tarragon can be substituted for the watercress.

Rillettes

POTTED PORK

One of the specialties of Touraine is *rillettes,* shredded pork cooked in its own fat and served cold. It is one of the oldest recipes, and was mentioned as *rilles* in Rabelais's books. The best *rillettes* come from Tours. Serve as an *hors-d'oeuvre* with French bread and a Vouvray wine.

½ pound fresh pork fat, cut into small cubes   *3 to 4 cups*
2½ pounds fresh ham or pork roast, cut into 2-inch pieces
Salt and freshly ground pepper
½ bay leaf
¼ teaspoon thyme
1 medium-size onion, chopped
¾ cup water
¼ cup dry white wine or dry vermouth (optional)
Lard, melted

1. Place all ingredients except the wine and lard in a large heavy-bottomed pot. Cover and barely simmer for 6 to 7 hours, or until all liquid has evaporated and the meat is tender. Stir frequently and do not let the meat brown or sizzle. About 30 minutes before the meat is done, add the wine and finish the cooking uncovered.

2. Remove the bay leaf and any bones. Mash the pork with a fork until shredded. Place in small earthenware pots. Seal with melted lard and store in a cool place. Remove lard before serving.

Croûte Briarde
FRENCH BREAD WITH BRIE

1. Mash a large piece of Brie cheese, crust removed, with a fork. Blend in unsalted butter (use half as much butter as cheese). Season with salt and white pepper to taste.

2. Cut a baguette of French bread into 4-inch pieces, then cut each section lengthwise into halves.

3. Spread the Brie-butter mixture on the cut sides of the bread. Place under the broiler until golden.

Serve with a chilled fruity white wine.

Fromage Triple Crème aux Herbes
TRIPLE CREAM CHEESE WITH HERBS

This preparation can be made very quickly with cream cheese but Yogurt Cheese (see Index) is preferable.

8 ounces cream cheese or yogurt cheese,   *4 servings*
    at room temperature
½ cup heavy cream
¼ teaspoon salt
White pepper
½ teaspoon tarragon vinegar
1 teaspoon finely minced parsley
¼ garlic clove, finely minced

1. Mash the cheese until soft. Beat the heavy cream until stiff. Combine the whipped cream and cheese until smooth.

2. Add the salt, pepper to taste, vinegar, parsley, and garlic, blending well.

3. Chill for several hours, but serve at room temperature.

Canapés
CANAPÉ BASES

This is the easiest and quickest method for making a large quantity of deliciously crisp bases for canapés.

    1. Remove the crust from 6 slices of good-quality firm white sandwich bread. Cut into triangles, large circles, or other shapes.
    2. Butter the bread very generously on one side. Place on a nonstick baking sheet in the upper rack of a preheated 350°F. oven. Toast for about 3 minutes, or until the underneath side is golden brown. Turn the bread over with a spatula and bake for another 2 minutes, until the bread underneath is golden brown.

Canapés de Caviar
CAVIAR CANAPÉS

    1. Butter each 1½-inch round canapé base (preceding recipe) and cover with a thin layer of caviar. Sprinkle with a little lemon juice.
    2. Serve on a plate lined with a paper doily.

Canapés de Palourdes
CLAM CANAPÉS

These canapés are very simple to make and are always a success.

    1 can (8 ounces) minced clams
8 ounces cream cheese, at room temperature
1 teaspoon minced shallot or onion
1 to 2 tablespoons heavy cream
Salt and white pepper
Canapé Bases (see Index)

    1. Drain the clams, retaining 1 tablespoon of the juice.
    2. Blend the cream cheese, clams, reserved juice, shallot, cream, and seasonings to taste.
    3. Spread the clam mixture on canapé bases and bake in a preheated 375°F. oven until tops are golden.

♦ U N D E R T H E C O O K ' S H A T ♦

This creamy clam mixture makes an excellent filling for raw endive leaves cut into 1½-inch pieces.

The clam mixture can be prepared several hours in advance and stored in the refrigerator until time to use.

Canapés aux Crabes
CRAB CANAPÉS

4 tablespoons unsalted butter, softened
⅓ cup freshly grated Parmesan cheese
⅓ cup freshly grated Swiss cheese
¼ cup heavy cream
Salt and freshly ground black pepper
Pinch of cayenne pepper
1 cup cooked fresh or canned crab
Canapé Bases (see Index), cut into 1½-inch rounds

1. Cream the butter with the cheeses, cream, and salt and peppers to taste. Combine with the crab. Chill for 1 hour.

2. Just before serving, place a heaping teaspoon of the crab mixture on each canapé. Place under the broiler until golden. Serve hot.

Canapés aux Sardines
SARDINE CANAPÉS

1. Remove skin and bones from canned sardines.

2. Combine the sardines with an equal volume of soft unsalted butter. Mash until the mixture has the consistency of thick cream. Season with lemon juice, salt and pepper.

3. Spread on Canapé Bases (see Index) and top with finely minced parsley.

Canapés aux Crevettes
SHRIMP CANAPÉS

3 tablespoons unsalted butter
3 shallots, chopped
½ pound mushrooms, stems removed and caps thinly sliced
1 pound small raw shrimps, shelled

1 teaspoon anchovy paste
1 tablespoon lemon juice
1½ tablespoons flour
½ cup heavy cream
Salt and freshly ground pepper
Canapé Bases (see Index)
⅓ cup grated Parmesan cheese
Butter for dotting
Watercress

1. Melt 3 tablespoons butter in a skillet and add the shallots. When soft, add the mushrooms, shrimps, anchovy paste and lemon juice. Cook over medium heat for about 3 minutes.

2. Sprinkle the flour over the mixture, stirring well. Add the cream and cook until the mixture thickens. Season with salt and pepper to taste and simmer for a few minutes.

3. Spoon the mixture onto the canapé bases. Sprinkle with cheese and dot with butter. Place the canapés under a preheated broiler until golden. Garnish with a few sprigs of watercress.

◆   *Variation*   ◆

Double the proportions and serve the eggs in the center of a rice ring, as a filling for *vol-au-vent*, or as a filling for crêpes.

Croque-Monsieur

TOASTED HAM AND CHEESE SANDWICH

Croque-Monsieur, a popular French toasted sandwich, makes an excellent *hors-d'oeuvre* or simple luncheon. It is similar to the *tranche de l'homme* (slice of man) made of toast, sliced cheese, and ham that was customarily eaten by peasants and hunters for breakfast.

1. Butter a thin slice of good-quality white sandwich bread. Cover with a very thin slice of Gruyère cheese. Add a thin slice of boiled ham and another thin slice of Gruyère. Top it all with a slice of bread buttered on the inside. Trim all four sides.

2. Melt Clarified Butter (see Index) in a large frying pan. Fry the sandwich, covered, over low heat. When golden brown on both sides, cut into triangles or small squares. Garnish with a few sprigs of watercress sprinkled with lemon juice.

◆ UNDER THE COOK'S HAT ◆

In France, you could substitute an aged Saint-Paulin cheese for the Gruyère, but since that is unavailable here, a good Tilsit is a fine substitute.

Pain Bagnat
MEDITERRANEAN SANDWICH

This savory sandwich—a specialty of Provence, particularly of the area near Nice—literally means "bathed bread" (with olive oil), in the Provençal dialect. It is best eaten in the sun with a chilled rosé wine from Provence.

1. Cut a long, crusty loaf of French bread into 8-inch lengths. Cut each piece lengthwise into halves. Remove some of the soft insides from both the top and bottom slices.
2. Brush both sides with a good olive oil. Rub the bread with a garlic clove split in several places.
3. Cover the bottom layers with sliced red tomatoes, green peppers, rings of red onions, a few anchovies, and pitted black Mediterranean olives. Hard-cooked eggs are sometimes added.
4. Sprinkle with Vinaigrette (see Index). Cover with the top layer of bread, pressing the halves together lightly.

◆ *Variation* ◆

Brush the slices of bread with oil and garlic, then toast lightly under a broiler until golden before proceeding with the filling.

Bouchées Feuilletées aux Anchois
ANCHOVIES IN PASTRY ROUNDS

Bouchée means "a mouthful." These tiny *hors-d'oeuvre* are eaten in one bite.

PASTRY   *Makes about 24*
4 ounces unsalted butter, chilled
1 cup flour
½ teaspoon salt
½ cup small-curd, country-style cottage cheese
1 tablespoon water, or more as needed

2 cans (2 ounces each) rolled fillets of anchovies with capers
1 egg yolk, mixed with 1½ teaspoons water

1. Make the pastry: Dip the butter into the flour and, with a small knife, chip off small pieces the size of big peas. Continue until all the butter is chipped off. (This step prevents the morsels of butter from sticking to each other.) Work the mixture lightly to break the butter into smaller pieces.

2. Add salt, cottage cheese, and 1 tablespoon water, or more if needed. Quickly shape the dough into a ball. Place in a bowl and cover with plastic wrap. Chill for 1 hour, then let stand at room temperature for 10 minutes before using.

3. Drain the anchovies and place on a paper towel.

4. Dust the dough and rolling pin with flour. Roll the dough to ⅛-inch thickness on a lightly floured surface. Let the dough rest for 15 minutes.

5. For each *bouchée*, cut 2 pastry circles with a sharp fluted cookie cutter. The circles should be about 1½ inches across. Form a ball with the trimmings from the circles. Let the dough stand for 10 minutes, then reroll and cut more circles.

6. Place half of the pastry circles on a baking sheet. Place a rolled anchovy fillet in the center of each one. Brush the remaining circles with water and place each one, damp side down, on the circles with anchovies. Press well around the edges with a fork to seal.

7. Brush the tops of the *bouchées* with the egg-yolk mixture. Do not let the egg drip down the sides. Bake in a preheated 375°F. oven for 15 minutes, or until rounds are golden and well puffed. Serve hot.

◆   *Variations*   ◆

The *bouchées* can be filled with ground smoked ham, small shrimps, a cube of excellent cheese, or a slice of sausage.

Petits Vol-au-Vents aux Huîtres

SMALL PATTY SHELLS WITH OYSTERS

1. Prepare small Vol-au-Vents (see Index).

2. Simmer a pint of shelled oysters in their own liquor until the edges begin to curl (about 5 minutes). Drain and reserve their liquor for the sauce.

3. Make a thick Sauce Normande (see Index) with the oyster liquor.

4. Just before serving, fill the patty shells with the oysters and sauce. Cover with the pastry tops and bake in a 400°F. oven until heated through.

Petits Choux à la Sardine

SARDINE PUFFS

PASTRY PUFFS   *Makes about 30*

½ cup water
4 tablespoons unsalted butter
Pinch of salt
½ cup all-purpose flour, sifted
3 eggs

FILLING

1 can (3¾ ounces) boneless and skinless sardines
1 teaspoon lemon juice
1 cup heavy cream
Salt and freshly ground pepper

1. Preheat oven to 425°F.
2. Make the pastry: In a medium-size saucepan, bring water, butter, and salt to a fast boil. Remove from the heat and add the flour all at once. Stir vigorously with a wooden spoon. Return the saucepan to low heat for 2 to 3 minutes, beating until the batter leaves the sides of the pan and forms a smooth, shiny ball.
3. Put the batter in a bowl and beat in 1 egg until well blended. Beat in the second and third eggs in the same way. Beat until the dough is elastic and stringy.
4. Fill a pastry bag with a ½-inch round tube with the *choux* paste. If you do not have a pastry bag, use a teaspoon to shape the paste into little balls the size of large cherries. Place the balls about 2 inches apart on baking sheets. Flatten by pressing lightly with wet fingertips.
5. Bake at 425°F. for about 20 minutes, until golden and well puffed. Turn off the oven for 5 to 10 minutes. Cool on a rack. Remove tops with a serrated knife.
6. While the puffs are cooling, prepare the filling: Mash the sardines to a purée with the lemon juice. Whip the cream until stiff. Season with salt and pepper. Combine the cream and sardine purée and blend thoroughly.
7. Fill the small puffs, using a pastry bag or a small spoon.

◆　*Variations*　◆

Other good savory fillings for *petits choux* are a purée of smoked salmon combined with whipped cream, prepared as in the sardine recipe; chopped cooked shrimps with finely minced celery bound with homemade mayonnaise and seasoned with lemon juice and Dijon mustard; or chopped chicken with Mayonnaise Chantilly (see Index). See also following recipe for Cheese Puffs.

Petits Choux au Fromage

CHEESE PUFFS

Pastry Puffs (preceding recipe)　　　　*Makes about 30*
1 egg yolk, mixed with 1 teaspoon water
8 ounces cream cheese
⅓ cup heavy cream
Salt and white pepper
Pinch of cayenne pepper
1 cup grated Gruyère cheese

1. Prepare the pastry puffs as directed. Brush with the egg-yolk mixture before baking.
2. While the puffs are cooling, prepare the filling: In a small saucepan, mash the cream cheese with the cream. Season with salt, white pepper and cayenne pepper. Stir over medium heat; when the mixture is bubbling, fold in the Gruyère.
3. Fill the puffs with the hot mixture. Reheat them in the oven and serve at once, piled in a mound.

Petites Crêpes Fourrées au Roquefort

SMALL CRÊPES WITH ROQUEFORT

CRÊPE BATTER　　　　　　　　　　*Makes 24*
1 cup flour
2 eggs
¼ teaspoon salt
½ cup milk
2 tablespoons unsalted butter, melted

FILLING
4 ounces Roquefort cheese
8 ounces Petit-Suisse or cream cheese
½ cup shelled walnuts, finely chopped

1 tablespoon Cognac (optional)
Salt and freshly ground pepper

1. Combine the batter ingredients, blending thoroughly. Refrigerate. Let stand for 1 hour.

2. Make very small crêpes, two or three at a time, in a crêpe pan or a nonstick skillet. Drop 1 tablespoon of batter for each one. Turn the pan quickly to spread the batter into 2-inch circles. Cook until golden underneath, then turn the crêpes over and cook for another minute.

3. Mash the cheeses together. Add the walnuts and Cognac. Heat in a small pan until hot and creamy. Add salt and pepper to taste.

4. Spread the Roquefort cream almost to the border of the crêpes. Roll and serve immediately, or keep hot in a warm oven.

Quiche Lorraine

QUICHE LORRAINE

Quiche Lorraine, a very old dish which goes back to the sixteenth century, comes from the provinces of Lorraine and Alsace, and was originally made with bread dough. It became more refined and now is made with a *pâte brisée,* or even more elegantly with *pâte feuilletée.*

The quiches were traditionally served the first of May to announce springtime. Of huge proportions, they were served in the middle of a meal. The original *Küche* does not contain cheese.

The name *quiche* comes from the word *Küche* in the Alsatian dialect and means pie. But a pie should not be called a quiche unless it is made in the traditional way of Alsace or Lorraine.

Different parts of France have their own "pies," the *flamiche* made with leeks, from the provinces of Burgundy and Picardy, and the *pissaladière* from Provence, made with onions and anchovies.

This quiche uses the traditional bread dough, easy to make and more compatible with the filling.

QUICHE DOUGH (for a 9- to 10-inch French pie pan)
½ tablespoon dry yeast
⅓ cup lukewarm water
2 tablespoons bacon fat
1¾ cups unbleached flour, sifted
½ teaspoon salt
Butter for pan

FILLING

¾ pound slab bacon, or 4 slices of bacon, half-inch-thick, cut
    into cubes

¼ pound Swiss Gruyère cheese, grated

3 whole eggs

2 extra egg yolks

1½ cups heavy cream

Salt and pepper

¼ teaspoon grated nutmeg

2 tablespoons unsalted butter

1. Fry the bacon in a large skillet until golden but not crisp. Set aside.

2. Prepare the dough: Dissolve the yeast in the water and let mixture develop for 5 minutes. Add 2 tablespoons bacon fat from the skillet. Stir thoroughly. Add the flour and salt, stirring with a fork until flour is absorbed by the liquid. On a flat surface, work the dough quickly until smooth, adding a little flour if too sticky. Make a ball of the flour, place in a lightly oiled bowl, cover, and let it rise in a warm spot until double in bulk, about 45 minutes.

3. Flatten the dough into a round shape. Roll into a very thin circle, then transfer the dough to a buttered French pie pan. Press into the pan, making sure there are no breaks in the dough. Make a crinkled edge with your fingers, or run the rolling pin over the top of the pie pan to remove excess dough.

4. Spread the cooked bacon on the dough, pressing a few pieces into the dough so they will not float while baking. Sprinkle the cheese over the bacon.

5. Mix the whole eggs, egg yolks, cream, salt and pepper to taste and the nutmeg. Pour half of the filling into the dough-lined pan. Place in a preheated 375°F. oven, then pour in the rest of the filling. Dot with butter. Bake for 10 minutes. Reduce the heat to 325°F. and bake for another 15 to 20 minutes, or until the custard is set and golden brown on top. Serve hot.

◆   *Variations*   ◆

For an elegant meal, bake a pie shell of Puff Pastry (see Index) and follow the preceding recipe.

The bacon can be replaced with Polish ham.

Add 2 tablespoons minced onion to the bacon when almost golden, for a flavorful addition.

Quiche à l'Oignon Alsacienne

ONION QUICHE FROM ALSACE

This pie is a delicious regional dish from Alsace, where onions are very popular. Alsace is one of the few places in France where bacon is used. Ham can be substituted or a combination of the two can be used. In this recipe, *pâte brisée* takes the place of the bread dough.

> 1¼ cups minced onions
> 7 tablespoons unsalted butter
> ½ cup flour, less 1 tablespoon
> 2 cups milk
> Salt and pepper
> Nutmeg
> 2 egg yolks
> 1 cup slab bacon, cut into ¼-inch sticks
> Tart Pastry (see Index)

1. Sauté the onions in 4 tablespoons of the butter until lightly golden, and reserve.

2. Melt the other 3 tablespoons of the butter in a saucepan. Add the flour and cook until well blended. Add the milk, salt and pepper to taste, and a pinch of grated nutmeg. Simmer for 10 minutes, stirring occasionally.

3. Off the heat, add the egg yolks and the reserved onions. Taste for seasoning.

4. Place the bacon in boiling water for 3 minutes. Drain and pat dry in a towel.

5. Line a 10-inch fluted French pie tin with the tart pastry. Fill with the egg-onion mixture, which should reach three-quarters of the way up the side. Scatter the bacon on top. Bake in a preheated 450°F. oven for 20 to 25 minutes. Serve very hot.

Pissaladière

ONION AND ANCHOVY PIE

Pissaladière, a famous pie from Nice that is cousin to the pizza, derives its name from *pissala* (anchovies, in the Provençal dialect). Usually bought at a bakery, this large pie shell is filled with cooked onions, anchovy fillets arranged lattice-fashion on top, and studded with black olives. This beautiful and delicious pie is often taken on picnics or fishing trips.

Bread dough is the traditional basis for the crust.

BREAD DOUGH
2 tablespoons solid shortening
½ cup hot water
.3 ounce fresh yeast or 1½ teaspoons active dry yeast
¼ teaspoon malt syrup
1¾ cups flour
½ teaspoon salt

FILLING
6 tablespoons good olive oil, or as needed
3 large Bermuda onions, thinly sliced
Bouquet garni (1 bay leaf, 1 sprig thyme, 3 parsley sprigs, tied
    together)
3 garlic cloves
Salt
2 ounces anchovy fillets, each split into halves
18 small Italian or Greek black olives, pitted
Freshly ground pepper

1. Prepare the dough: Combine the shortening and water in a bowl and stir until shortening is melted. When the water is tepid, add the yeast and malt syrup. Let stand for 5 minutes. Stir well. Add the flour and salt. Stir with a spoon to make a ball; the dough will be sticky and soft. Place dough in a lightly oiled bowl in a warm spot and let it rise until double in bulk, about 45 minutes.

2. Prepare the filling: Heat olive oil in a skillet. Add the onions, *bouquet garni* and garlic. Season sparingly with salt. Cook slowly for about 45 minutes, until onions are tender and uniform in color, but without browning. Remove the *bouquet garni* and garlic. Set onions aside.

3. Turn out the dough onto a floured surface. Punch down, then roll out into a circle large enough to fit a 12-inch pizza pan that has been lightly oiled. If the dough pulls back, let it rest for a few minutes. Using a pastry wheel, trim any excess dough, leaving a 1-inch overhang. Tuck this underneath the outer edge of the dough to form a slightly raised border.

4. Spread the lukewarm onions on the dough. Arrange the anchovy fillets in the traditional lattice design over the onions. Place an olive in each square in the lattice. Let the dough rise again until double in bulk.

5. Bake in a preheated 400°F. oven for 15 minutes, or until the dough is cooked. Season with pepper, and serve immediately.

Saucisse de Veau en Vinaigrette
VEAL SAUSAGE WITH VINAIGRETTE DRESSING

Serve as one of several *hors-d'oeuvre*.

VINAIGRETTE DRESSING
2 tablespoons minced shallots
2 tablespoons unsalted butter
3 tablespoons dry white wine or vermouth
1 tablespoon vinegar
3 tablespoons oil
Salt and freshly ground pepper
3 boiled *Weisswürste* (veal sausages), thinly sliced
Boston lettuce leaves
3 tablespoons finely minced parsley

1. Prepare the vinaigrette dressing. In a small pan, slowly cook the shallots in the butter until wilted. Add the wine and cook until evaporated to approximately 2 teaspoons. Add the vinegar, oil and seasoning to taste. Chill.

2. To serve, overlap the slices of sausage in a *ravier* lined with leaves of Boston lettuce.

3. Pour the vinaigrette on the sausage and sprinkle with parsley.

P Â T É S
⚜ ⚜ ⚜

Bécasse! à vous, Monsieur! dit-on de mon côté:
J'ajuste: l'oiseau tombe . . . O l'excellent pâté!
Car pour le bon chasseur tout gibier est exquis,
Et qui dit le contraire en ignore le prix.

There's a woodcock! Your turn, Sir! says my companion:
I aim: the bird falls . . . to make an excellent pâté!
To the keen hunter all game is exquisite,
Who denies it shows ignorance of the reward.
—D. CORDIER, *Journal des chasseurs*, 1913

Hunting has been a favorite pastime of the French from the days of the Gauls to the present. In peacetime, the medieval barons would put aside their military outfits only to put on hunting gear, and they were almost prouder of their hunting exploits than of their war deeds. Many châteaus in the Ile-de-France or Touraine, such as Amboise, were built as hunting lodges for the kings and their courts, so great was their passion for hunting. The resulting game would end up on the roasting spits or in pâtés.

An Italian Ambassador named Lippomano, while traveling in France in 1557, wrote: "In France, *pâtisserie*, which is meat cooked in a crust, is enjoyed more than anywhere. In cities, and even in villages, you find *pâtissiers* who sell them ready to eat, or which need only to be cooked." At that time *pâtisserie* meant *pâté en croûte* and not sweet pastry, as sugar was unknown and honey was the only sweetener. *Pâtissiers* were extremely prosperous in the Middle Ages because pâté, being so easy to eat, was in demand. The fork was introduced in France only at the beginning of the seventeenth century, and even then was used only by the nobility. While pâtés may have been refined through the years, they remain fundamentally the same.

Pâté, a word that comes from pâte or dough, and terrines, crustless pâtés named for the earthenware dishes in which they are baked, have always had an important place in French cooking. Today's *charcuterie* (or cooked meat) windows still display tempting pâtés in crust or terrines with sparkling aspic. Forcemeat or *farce fine* for making pâté can usually be bought in these shops. The pâté takes its name from the principal meat or fish, which makes up about half the volume of the forcemeat.

A *pâté en croûte* or a terrine is a great asset to one's culinary repertoire. Serve one at a very special picnic, buffet, or elegant dinner, before or after the main course.

Terrine Maison
COUNTRY PÂTÉ

¾ pound veal, ground three times, preferably through
    your own grinder
¾ pound calf's liver, ground
½ pound fresh pork fat, cut into tiny cubes
½ cup white wine
¼ cup Port wine
½ teaspoon crumbled dried thyme

½ teaspoon ground allspice
1 tablespoon salt
½ pound Polish ham, finely chopped with a knife
2 eggs, well beaten
¼ cup shallots, finely chopped
3 tablespoons finely chopped onion
1 small garlic clove, minced
Pepper
Several thin slices of fresh pork fat
Thin slices of bacon
2 bay leaves

1. Combine thoroughly, in a large china or pottery bowl, the veal, liver, cubed pork fat, wines, thyme, allspice and salt. Cover and refrigerate for at least 3 hours.

2. Add the ham, eggs, shallots, onion, garlic, and pepper to taste. Stir the mixture until light and well blended.

3. Line a 1½-quart terrine or glass baking pan with thin strips of pork fat, pounded thin between 2 pieces of wax paper.

4. Spoon the mixture into the terrine, pressing it down to fill all spaces. Smooth the top. Cover with a layer of bacon slices slightly overlapping, and top with the bay leaves. Seal with aluminum foil and cover with the top.

5. Place the terrine in a large baking pan set on the middle shelf of the oven. Pour enough boiling water into the pan to reach one-third of the way up the sides of the terrine. Bake in a preheated 350°F. oven for 1½ hours, or until the fat and juices have risen to the top of the terrine and are clear yellow.

6. Remove the terrine from the oven. Empty the baking pan of its water. Place the terrine back in it. Place a piece of heavy cardboard on top of the foil, slightly smaller than the terrine, and several heavy objects as a weight, such as canned goods, up to 3 to 4 pounds. When the pâté is cool, remove the weight and chill the pâté for at least 12 hours, preferably longer.

Serve from the terrine in thick slices with crusty French bread, or Melba toast, and a robust red wine.

◆ UNDER THE COOK'S HAT ◆

To serve the pâté in aspic, unmold it and remove the layer of pork fat and bacon. Wash the terrine and pour in a thin layer, about ⅛ inch, of aspic flavored with Port wine. When almost firm, replace the pâté in the mold. Pour enough aspic around and over it to encase it completely. Chill for several hours, until the aspic is firm. The pâté can be kept under refrigeration this way for a week.

Pâté en Croûte

PÂTÉ IN CRUST

This pâté does not require a mold. It is a wonderful picnic dish, garnished with watercress or parsley. Serve with tomatoes filled with Mixed Vegetable Salad (see Index).

½ pound Polish ham, finely diced   *6 to 8 servings*
¾ pound fresh pork fat from a pork loin, cut into ¼-inch dice
2 pounds pork loin, ground twice
2 onions, finely minced
3 shallots, finely minced
1 garlic clove, finely minced
1 bay leaf, pulverized
½ teaspoon ground thyme
3 tablespoons unsalted butter
½ teaspoon ground allspice
2 tablespoons finely minced parsley
Salt and pepper
¾ cup dry white wine
3 tablespoons Cognac
2 whole eggs, slightly beaten
1 recipe Puff Pastry (see Index)
1 egg yolk, beaten with 1 teaspoon water

1. Place the ham, pork fat, and ground pork in a pottery bowl.
2. In a small skillet sauté the onions, shallots, garlic, bay leaf, and thyme in the butter for 2 to 3 minutes, until onions are soft. When cool, add to the meat mixture.
3. Add the allspice, parsley, salt and pepper to taste, wine, and Cognac; mix thoroughly. Cover the bowl with plastic wrap and chill for 2 hours or overnight.
4. Bring the mixture to room temperature before mixing in the 2 whole eggs.
5. Cut off one-third of the puff pastry dough and roll it into a rectangle 7 by 16 inches. Transfer the dough to a baking sheet 11 by 18 inches. Cover with wax paper. Roll remaining dough into a rectangle 9 by 18 inches. Place over the smaller rectangle, cover with wax paper, and chill for 30 minutes.

6. Lift the larger rectangle of dough off the baking sheet. Reserve.

7. Place the meat mixture on the smaller rectangle, shaping into a long loaf. Leave about 2 inches of dough all around, then lift the sides of the dough up against the meat, brushing the outside of the dough with water. Cover the meat and dough with the larger rectangle of pastry, tucking under on all sides.

8. Brush the pâté with the egg yolk and water mixture, except for ¼ inch around the base so the dough can rise. Decorate the pâté with a crisscross design with the back of a knife, being careful not to break through the dough. Or add decorative pastry cutouts brushed beforehand with beaten egg white.

9. Bake the pâté in a preheated 400°F. oven for 45 minutes. Cover the pâté loosely with a piece of aluminum foil to prevent it from getting too brown. Reduce the heat to 350°F. and bake for 45 minutes longer. Serve at room temperature. Cut the pâté into ¾-inch-thick slices.

◆ ◆ ◆

King Jean Le Bon decreed in 1531 that the sale of stale pâté was prohibited. If the pâté was more than one day old, the owner of the *pâtisserie* was fined and the pâté was burned in front of his shop.

◆ *Aspic* ◆

Aspic is the common name for a lavender-flavored herb (spike lavender) that was originally used in the preparation of jelly, and from this, aspic as we know it gets its name.

It was at the turn of the nineteenth century that the creative chef Carême realized that gelatin opened new horizons in decorating and glamorizing food; he was the first to develop it and use it extensively.

Aspic, with its sparkling clear, amber color, elegantly dresses cold dishes. Nothing is more festive than a ham, pâté, or mousse on a silver dish, decorated with aspic; or sliced cold roast beef or canapés coated with a brilliant aspic—prepared in advance, yet retaining all its color and quality for one or two days.

To make an aspic, a base of consommé, well flavored with Port wine, Madeira wine, or Cognac, is needed. Preparing a classic aspic is a tedious task that can be minimized by using the following method.

QUICK ASPIC

¼ teaspoon dried tarragon
⅓ cup minced onion
2 egg whites (to clarify aspic)
Salt and pepper
⅓ cup dry white wine
4 cups Beef Stock (see Index) or canned beef broth
1½ envelopes unflavored gelatin
3 tablespoons Port or Madeira wine, or Cognac

1. In a large pan combine all the ingredients except the gelatin and wine or Cognac. Sprinkle the stock with gelatin and bring to the boiling point, whisking it constantly with a back-and-forth motion across the center of the pan. (A circular motion will cloud the aspic.) When the boiling point is reached, remove the pan from the heat and let stand for 15 minutes.

2. Strain the stock slowly through several thicknesses of cheesecloth. Do not stir or move the bowl or it will become cloudy. When strained, or about 1 hour later, add the wine or Cognac.

3. Set the bowl in a pan of cracked ice and stir the aspic to prevent it from setting around the edges. When syrupy, it is ready to be used.

♦   U N D E R   T H E   C O O K ' S   H A T   ♦

A fine aspic should be clear and quivery, but not rubbery.

To glaze a mold use 1 tablespoon of unflavored gelatin to 1½ cups of stock. For aspic decoration use 1 tablespoon of gelatin to 2 cups of stock. For jellied soups use 1 tablespoon of gelatin to 3 cups of liquid.

♦   ♦   ♦

In her book *César Ritz: Host to the World* (1938), Marie Louise Ritz reported this conversation between Ritz and Escoffier:

> At teatime, I complained about the toast in Escoffier's hearing. "Toast is never thin enough to suit me," I said. "Can't you do something about it?"
>
> As usual, Escoffier and Ritz took such a remark with absolute seriousness. They discussed the problem of thin toast. "Why not," said Ritz, "toast the thin slices of bread once, then cut it through again and again toast it?" And with Escoffier he retired to the kitchens to see if it could not be done. The result was Escoffier's

justly famous Toast Melba. When they brought out on the lawn a plate full of thin, crisp, curled wafers, Escoffier said, "Behold. A new dish, and it is called Toast Marie." But as I ate it I tried to think up another name. Marie was far too anonymous to suit me.

During that year Melba had returned from America very ill. She was staying at the Savoy, where she was a much-indulged invalid. I had heard Escoffier discuss her regimen. Dry toast figured in it . . .

"Call it Toast Melba," I said.

Melba is a reference to the famous opera singer from Australia, whose full name was Nellie Melba, 1859–1931.

Toast Melba
MELBA TOAST

Remove the crust from very thinly sliced good-quality white bread and cut into rectangles or rounds. Use rye bread for cheese. Brush each slice with melted unsalted butter. Bake the slices in a 200°F. oven, turning several times with a spatula until crisp and evenly browned. Keep in an airtight container.

Mousse de Foies de Volaille
CHICKEN LIVER MOUSSE

This delicious mousse can be served with hot toast triangles or Melba toast.

6 servings

1½ pounds chicken livers, trimmed
Salt
½ pound unsalted butter, at room temperature
⅓ cup minced onion
2 tablespoons minced shallot
1½ tablespoons Cognac
1½ tablespoons white wine or white vermouth
Freshly ground pepper
1 teaspoon ground allspice
¾ cup heavy cream
2 small truffles, finely chopped, plus the juice, reserving 1 slice
    for garnish (optional)
Quick Aspic (see Index)

1. Soak the chicken livers in a bowl of slightly salted cold water for 20 minutes. Drain and pat dry with a paper towel.

2. Melt 3 tablespoons of the butter in a skillet and sauté the onion and shallot over medium heat until tender but not brown. Add the livers and sauté over medium-high heat for several minutes, until cooked but not brown. Do not overcook.

3. Purée the liver mixture with the remaining butter, the Cognac, wine, salt and pepper to taste, and the allspice in a blender or food processor until smooth.

4. Whip the cream until stiff and blend thoroughly into the liver mixture. Add the truffles and juice. Chill the mousse in an earthenware dish or a china crock. Center a truffle slice on the top, then cover with a thin layer of syrupy aspic flavored with Port. Cover with plastic wrap until ready to serve. This keeps for several days.

◆   U N D E R   T H E   C O O K ' S   H A T   ◆

Mousse de foies de volaille packed in earthenware crocks, decorated with truffles or sliced stuffed olives, then sealed with aspic, makes delightful gifts.

If the mousse is part of a buffet, double the recipe. Line the bottom of a small ring mold with syrupy aspic and decorate with sliced truffles. Fill the ring mold with the mousse, using a spoon or a pastry bag fitted with a large plain tube, leaving space between the mousse and the sides of the mold. Fill the empty space with additional aspic on the point of setting, then chill. Unmold before serving and decorate the center with sprigs of parsley.

Leftover mousse can be mixed with cream cheese or sour cream for a dip.

Extra mousse can be piped from a large rosette tube over thick slices of hard-cooked eggs, then placed on toast rounds. Brush eggs with syrupy aspic to keep them from discoloring.

◆   *Foie Gras*   ◆

Foie gras (goose liver) is not a recent discovery. It goes back to the Egyptians, who, 4,000 years ago, depicted on their bas-reliefs the technique of force-feeding geese. This technique, still in use today, produces enlarged livers weighing about two pounds. Three times a day the goose's neck is held while food (a mixture of corn, fat, and water) is crammed into its gullet.

Goose liver was very much appreciated by the Egyptians and later also by the Romans, who force-fed geese with figs. Etymologically, the word *foie* derives from the Latin *ficus* (fig), preserving a record in language of the ancient method.

The Gauls, who also knew how to force-feed geese, exported their *foie gras* extensively even at that time. The *pâté de foie gras* itself, the king of all pâtés, is relatively new.

Maréchal de Contades, who was military commander of the province of Alsace (1782–1789), brought his cook, Jean-Pierre Clausse, with him to Strasbourg. There, Clausse had the ingenious idea for this pâté, consisting of an Alsatian *foie gras* surrounded by finely ground forcemeat and a crust, a recipe he kept secret for several years. As it was the fashion, the Maréchal sent several pâtés to Louis XVI, who graciously acknowledged the gift by giving land in the province of Picardy to the Maréchal, and money to Clausse— 20 pistoles.

After the French Revolution, the *pâté de foie gras* became internationally known because of the addition of truffles, an idea of Nicolas Doyen, native of the province of Périgord and chef to the President of the Parlement of Bordeaux.

Depending on the origin, *foie gras* varies in taste and appearance. The *foie gras* of Strasbourg is more orange and more pungent than the *foie gras* of Les Landes, which is pink and *au naturel;* while the *foie gras* of Périgord is more yellow and is enriched with truffles.

Serve *foie gras* either as a first course or after the main course, but never with a salad. The vinaigrette would overpower the delicate taste of *foie gras* and the great wines that should be served with it. These wines, such as Corton-Charlemagne, Meursault, or Montrachet, blend beautifully with *foie gras.*

Chill the *foie gras* and serve as is, or set it on a bed of chopped aspic flavored with Cognac or Port wine, or on unseasoned Boston lettuce leaves. Cut the *foie gras* with a stainless-steel or silver knife that has been previously heated under hot water and dried.

Serve with French bread, canapés, or Melba toast.

3. *Les Soupes et les Potages*
SOUPS

⚜ ⚜ ⚜

A gourmand, truly worthy of the name, always eats his soup boiling and takes his coffee burning.
—GRIMOD DE LA REYNIÈRE (1758–1838),
publisher of *Almanach des Gourmands*

Brillat-Savarin, the famous epicure, said: "It is generally agreed that nowhere else can be found such good potage as in France, and during my travels I have confirmed this truth. This result will not come as a surprise, for soup is the basic diet of the French nation, and centuries of experience have brought it to perfection." And Carême, who was sometimes called "the Napoleon of the kitchen," included 500 soup recipes in his repertoire.

Today, *Venez tremper la soupe!* (Come and get it! or Soup's on!) can still be heard at noontime over much of the French countryside, but it has roots deep in the past. In the Middle Ages, *soupe* was actually the word for the slice of bread one dipped into the meat and vegetables, and only gradually did it acquire the meaning it has now. The connection is strengthened by the French habit of serving fried bread or croutons in the soup occasionally.

Gilles de Retz, a close companion of Jeanne d'Arc, described her on the battlefield: "She only has wine poured in a silver cup, in which she put half water and five or six *soupes* which she ate and did not take anything else." In the farmland of Touraine where Jeanne d'Arc battled, bread crumbled in sweetened wine (called *miotte*) is still served on hot afternoons.

The importance of soup and the respect in which it is held by the French is proven time and time again by stories and quotations from numerous sources. For instance, at the turn of the century, Frédéric, owner of La Tour d'Argent, was provoked enough to criticize none other than the Grande Duchesse Wladimir of Russia, who had dared to speak while eating her *potage:* "Your Imperial High-ness, when one does not know how to eat such a *potage* with due respect to it, one does not permit oneself to ask for it."

A *soupe* was made with vegetables and water or occasionally with milk, while a *potage* had meat broth as its base. *Potage* with rice, made using either broth or milk, is one of the oldest soups, dating back to the thirteenth century, when the Crusaders returned from the Middle East with rice. It was served at every feast. The celebrated soups of that era were so popular that several soups, heavily spiced with aromatic herbs, cinnamon, saffron, and wine, were served at the same meal. This lavish display of soups so upset the Church that the Council of Compiègne issued a decree in 1304 forbidding the clergy to serve more than one soup in their homes, except when they received a king, duke, count, or baron.

President Charles de Gaulle was so fond of soup that he wanted a different one served every day. He explained, *"La soupe est un plat national!"*

◆　◆　◆

Stock is everything in cooking, at least in French cooking.
Without it, nothing can be done.
—ESCOFFIER

Bouillon de Boeuf

BEEF STOCK

Beef stock is a great asset to cooking. It is a base for numerous dishes—soups, aspics, sauces—and is used for braising meat.

2 leeks, chopped
8 cups cold water
2 pounds beef bones, cut into 2-inch pieces
2 carrots, chopped
1 celery rib, chopped
1 onion, sliced
8 to 10 parsley sprigs
2 garlic cloves
2 cloves
Coarse salt
1 teaspoon commercial meat extract

Makes about 6 cups

1. Place all ingredients except the meat extract in a pot. Bring

almost to a boil, then simmer, with the pot partially covered, for 1½ hours. Do not allow the stock to boil. Remove any scum on the surface.

2. Stir in the meat extract.

3. Let the stock cool before straining. Refrigerate and remove solidified fat from the surface. If the stock is not used the same day, do not remove the fat; it serves as a seal.

◆   ◆   ◆

It was in the early part of the eighteenth century that J. Lebas, an officer of the King's kitchen, invented bouillon cubes for the use of travelers. They had only to add hot water to his *consommé en pastille* to produce a cup of steaming broth. M. Lebas showed his originality also by writing a book called *Happy Feast, or Cooking with Music*. In it, the recipes were all written in verse and set to music!

Consommé de Boeuf
BEEF CONSOMMÉ

5 to 6 cups beef broth from the pot-au-feu, or Beef Stock
    (preceding recipe), defatted
1 pound raw lean beef, chopped
3 or 4 chicken wings
1 large leek, chopped
1 celery rib, chopped
1 onion, chopped
2 garlic cloves, chopped
½ bay leaf
¼ teaspoon thyme
2 teaspoons peppercorns
Coarse salt
2 egg whites
⅓ cup Madeira or Port wine, or Cognac (optional)
Dash of caramel coloring

1. Mix the raw beef thoroughly into the broth or stock. Add the chicken wings, vegetables, herbs, and seasonings to taste. Stir continuously until the broth comes to a boil; then barely simmer for 1 hour. Strain through triple layers of cheesecloth.

2. To clarify the consommé, add the egg whites to the cool broth. Pour the mixture into a saucepan set over low heat and beat constantly with a whisk until simmering. Simmer for 10 minutes.

3. Strain the consommé through cheesecloth. Add the wine or Cognac and caramel coloring. Taste for seasonings.

✦ *Restaurants* ✦

Restaurants came into being in 1765. The first restaurant started on the rue Bailleul in Paris when a certain Monsieur Boulanger, a bouillon vendor, placed a sign outside his establishment: *Boulanger débite des restaurants divins.* (Boulanger sells divine restaurants.) At that time *restaurant* meant restorative. The sign also had the Latin words for: "Come, come all, oh you whose stomach cries misery, come and I will restore you!"

In addition to his bouillon, Monsieur Boulanger served simple food, such as chicken and eggs, at individual tables, a great innovation in those days. Until then, there were two alternatives for a meal prepared out of one's home: taverns, which were frequented by questionable characters, and where everyone ate at a common table; or a *traiteur* (caterer), where large orders had to be placed well in advance.

Boulanger added mutton feet with *sauce poulette* to his menu. The *traiteurs*, who had the exclusive right to sell stew, feared the competition and went to court. The matter grew to such proportions that the French parliament intervened with an official decree stating that mutton feet with *sauce poulette* did not constitute a stew.

The mutton dish made Boulanger's fortune; all of Paris wanted to taste it.

Bouillon de Volaille

CHICKEN STOCK

1 pound chicken wings, necks, or backbones   *Makes about 5 cups*
1 roast chicken carcass
1 carrot, sliced
1 onion, studded with 2 cloves
1 leek, sliced
1 celery rib, chopped
2 garlic cloves, minced
Bouquet garni
Salt and freshly ground pepper
6 to 8 cups water

1. Place all ingredients in a large pot. Cover and simmer for 1½ hours.

2. Let the broth cool, then strain it.

♦ *Variation* ♦

To serve as a soup, after straining, thicken slightly with 6 tablespoons of cornstarch mixed with a few tablespoons of cold water. Remove the pan from the stove and add the well-beaten yolks of 2 eggs combined with ½ cup heavy cream. Sprinkle with minced chervil or parsley.

Consommé de Volaille

CHICKEN CONSOMMÉ

7 cups water *6 servings*
1 pound short ribs of beef, cut into small pieces
1 pound chicken wings, necks, or backbones
1 roast chicken carcass
1 pound marrowbones
2 carrots, cut into pieces
1 white turnip, cut into pieces
1 garlic clove, chopped
1 onion, cut into pieces
2 leeks, chopped
1 celery rib, chopped
Coarse salt
Peppercorns
¼ teaspoon ground cloves
2 tablespoons tapioca (if served hot)

1. Place all ingredients except the tapioca in a large pot. Simmer, covered tightly, for 2 hours.

2. Strain through a triple layer of cheesecloth. Clarify, following directions for Beef Consommé (see Index).

3. If consommé is to be served hot, add the tapioca and simmer for 15 minutes. If it is served cold, the tapioca is omitted because the consommé will gel.

♦ *Variation* ♦

Sprinkle as much uncooked vermicelli, broken into short pieces, as desired into the consommé. Boil until the vermicelli is cooked, 7 to 10 minutes.

◆   U N D E R   T H E   C O O K ' S   H A T   ◆

The flavor improves if the consommé is made the day before it is served.

When serving a cold jellied consommé, pipe a large rosette of salted sour cream from a pastry bag onto the top of each cup.

Freeze leftover consommé in ice-cube trays. Store the frozen cubes in a plastic bag. They will be useful for a *sauce velouté* or *riz pilaf.*

Consommé can be flavored with Port or Madeira wine. Simmer the wine first in a small enamelware saucepan, then stir into the consommé just before serving.

◆   ◆   ◆

For informal occasions, soup is served from a tureen placed on the table.

For formal dinners, soup is served from a nearby station and placed in front of the guests.

Soup plates should be heated and the soup should be very hot when served.

◆   *Pot-au-Feu and Petite Marmite*   ◆

In French cuisine, we often find a specific recipe named for the pot in which it is cooked. *Le pot-au-feu,* for instance, refers to an earthenware pot placed on or near the hearth, in which almost all the cooking was done. In the Middle Ages, both meat and vegetables would be added to the pot and simmered to make up the whole meal. *Pot au feu,* definitely considered a national dish, is treated with great consideration. Escoffier said, "In France, the *pot-au-feu* is the symbol of family life." There is little to equal the combination of flavors and aromas of simmering beef and vegetables in a *pot-au-feu* that permeates the house and welcomes the family home. We find the same applies to the *chaudrière*—a soup cauldron—and especially to *la petite marmite:* The name of the pot has become the name of the recipe. In 1867, Monsieur Magny, who owned a restaurant on the rue Contrescarpe in Paris, created a dish that was a variation of the *pot-au-feu* and served it in the small earthenware pots called *petites marmites.* He tied together individual portions of beef and chicken and cooked them in a big pot with other meats such as oxtail or rump and some vegetables. When partially cooked, each portion was untied and placed in the appropriate sized *marmite,* then cooked for another two hours with more raw vegetables added. The subtle difference in the flavor came from the ingredients used in the original braising and it could not be duplicated in the home kitchen without complications too time-consuming to consider. Monsieur Magny was proud of his *petite marmite* with its clear consommé, its meat and vegetables, and the croutons spread with bone marrow, and he served it with great flourish to his customers. It is a typical French restaurant dish, and a recipe that has no place here. The *pot-au-feu* which follows—as delicious in its own way—is a meal in itself.

Pot-au-Feu

BEEF AND VEGETABLE SOUP

Traditional accompaniments for *pot-au-feu* are coarse salt, pickled white onions, gherkins, and French mustard. A piece of cheese with crusty bread is all that is needed to complete this delectable meal.

2 pounds short ribs of beef, cut into pieces   *6 servings*
4 quarts water
1 roast chicken carcass
3 to 4 chicken wings, necks, and backs
1 onion, studded with 2 cloves
Coarse salt
4 pounds boneless rump roast, chuck roast, or brisket of beef,
    well tied
1 large marrowbone, cut into pieces
3 garlic cloves
3 or 4 parsley sprigs
12 peppercorns
4 onions
1 celery heart, quartered
1 small parsnip, quartered
3 small turnips
6 medium-size carrots
1 small cabbage, quartered
5 large leeks, sliced lengthwise, tied in a bundle
French bread
Swiss cheese, grated (optional)

1. Bake the short ribs of beef in a 450°F. oven until golden brown on all sides.

2. Pour the water into a large pot. Add the short ribs, the chicken carcass and raw chicken pieces, the onion, and coarse salt to taste. Bring the water to a boil, then cover and simmer for 1 hour. (Do not boil or the bouillon will become opaque.) Skim off the foam, and remove the chicken bones.

3. Add the boneless beef, marrowbones, garlic, parsley, and peppercorns, and any one vegetable from the list given, except for the cabbage or leeks, which are added 30 minutes before soup is done. (After several hours of cooking, the vegetables disintegrate, so it is better to use a few vegetables for flavoring the broth and add the rest closer to the end of the cooking time.) Simmer for 2 hours.

4. Remove the marrowbones and the short ribs and add the remaining vegetables, except for the cabbage and leeks. Check the seasonings and continue to cook, partially covered, for 2 hours longer.

5. About 30 minutes before soup is done, add the leeks. Cook the cabbage separately in some of the bouillon from the pot, along with some fat taken from the top of the broth.

6. Remove the meat and vegetables and keep warm. Skim some of the fat off the soup. (Usually a little fat, called "the eyes," is left in the broth.) Strain broth through a layer of cheesecloth lining a colander.

7. Serve the broth over thin slices of buttered French bread, toasted in the oven, and accompany with grated Swiss cheese. Serve the meat as the main dish, surrounded with the vegetables and some steamed potatoes. Or serve meat, vegetables, and broth together in deep soup plates, an excellent way to serve *pot-au-feu*.

◆   U N D E R   T H E   C O O K ' S   H A T   ◆

Leftover stock from the *pot-au-feu* makes an excellent base for sauces, aspics or onion soups.

If there is any leftover boiled beef, cube it and dress it with vinaigrette, finely minced shallots, and minced parsley. It makes a fine cold *hors-d'oeuvre* called *salade parisienne*.

◆ *Onion Soup* ◆

Onions have always been revered. In ancient times they were offered by priests to the gods. Onions were fed to the slaves during the construction of the Pyramids and were also wrapped and placed in the pharaohs' tombs.

Onion soup—this truly French soup—was created in the fourteenth century by Taillevent, the first great French chef. It is appreciated and loved by both the humble and the high-born.

One day, in the eighteenth century, King Stanislas of Poland was on his way to Versailles to visit his daughter, Marie Leczinska, the wife of Louis XV, when he stopped overnight at an inn in Châlons. The onion soup served to him was so delectable that he refused to continue his trip until he knew how to prepare it. Before leaving the next morning, he went down to the kitchen in his robe and, peeling onions, with tears streaming from his eyes, learned from the chef how to make the delicious soup.

Neighborhood bistros have served this soup to the workers of Les Halles since the Middle Ages. Although the colorful food markets recently moved to Rungis on the outskirts of Paris, the best versions of onion soup are still found near the original site.

Onion soup has the reputation of being able to restore the strength of the drunkard and the *bon vivant!*

Soupe à l'Oignon Gratinée

ONION SOUP WITH CHEESE

4 tablespoons unsalted butter
3 large Bermuda onions, thinly sliced
Salt and freshly ground pepper
1 tablespoon flour
6 cups Beef Stock (see Index)
Butter
8 to 10 thin slices of French bread
¼ pound Parmesan cheese, freshly grated
½ pound Gruyère cheese, cut into slivers

4 servings

1. Melt the butter in a large skillet and cook the onions for at least 40 minutes, or until they are evenly golden and thoroughly

cooked. If the onions stick to the skillet, add more butter. Season with salt and pepper.

2. Sprinkle flour over the onions and cook for about 2 minutes. Add a little of the stock and transfer the mixture to a large pot. Add the remaining stock, bring to a boil, and simmer for 10 minutes.

3. Generously butter the French bread slices and toast under the broiler until golden. Put 2 slices of bread in each of 4 small oven-proof tureens, or 8 to 10 slices in a large one.

4. Sprinkle the Parmesan over the bread. Add the slivers of Gruyère. Ladle the soup over the bread. Place in a 425°F. oven until the top of the soup is golden brown.

♦ UNDER THE COOK'S HAT ♦

A dash of Cognac or a cup of fine white wine gives added zest to onion soup.

The following method should be used for slicing onions: After peeling the onions, cut each one from stem to root end into halves. Place cut side down on the cutting board and slice evenly and paper-thin, starting at the stem end.

♦   ♦   ♦

Achille Ozanne, a poet-cook of the nineteenth century, who worked for the famous caterer Potel et Chabot, saluted onion soup in verse.

Elle est prête! . . . Alors, on s'y met.
O simple et délicat fumet!
Tous les parfums de l'Arabie,
Et que l'Orient distilla,
Ne valent pas une roupie
De singe, auprès de celui-là.
Et puis! . . . quel fromage énergique!
File-t-il! cré nom! file-t-il,
Il va filer jusqu'en Belgique!

The soup is ready! . . . so let's
   tackle it!
Oh what a simple and delicate
   aroma!
All the perfumes of Arabia,
Which the Orient distilled,
Are not worth a wooden
Nickel, compared with this!
And besides! . . . what active
   cheese!
See it run! by Jove, does it run!
If we don't cut the thread
It will run to Belgium!

Soupe à l'Oignon Gratinée, à la Bière

ONION SOUP WITH BEER

This version of onion soup originated in the province of Champagne. It is ideal for one person because the preparation is so simple, the stock being replaced by beer.

1½ tablespoons unsalted butter   *1 serving*
1 teaspoon olive oil
2 medium-size onions, sliced paper-thin
1 garlic clove, chopped
1 teaspoon flour
1 bottle (12 ounces) beer
Salt and freshly ground pepper
Butter
2 thin slices of French bread
½ cup grated Swiss cheese

1. Heat the butter and oil in a small skillet. Add the onions and cook over medium-low heat, stirring occasionally, until soft and evenly golden. When halfway cooked, add the garlic.

2. Sprinkle on the flour and cook for 2 minutes, stirring constantly. Add the beer and seasonings to taste. Bring almost to a boil, then lower the heat. Cover and simmer for 45 minutes.

3. Generously butter the French bread slices. Toast under the broiler until golden. Place the slices in a soup bowl, sprinkle with the cheese, and pour the soup on top. Place in a 450°F. oven until lightly browned.

• *Oxtails* •

Some French Protestants took refuge in England after the Revocation of the Edict of Nantes in 1685, which ended religious tolerance. They were happy to find that English butchers did not sell oxtails but sent them with the hides to tanners. The tanners, having no use for the tails, sold them to the poor French exiles for a few pennies. The exiles, in turn, made them into a soup that was so delicious that it soon became a favorite far and wide.

Potage aux Queues de Boeuf

OXTAIL SOUP

2 pounds oxtails, cut into 1½-inch pieces   *6 servings*

1½ tablespoons unsalted butter
1½ tablespoons peanut oil
2 onions, diced
2 carrots, diced
2 turnips, diced
2 garlic cloves, chopped
4 tablespoons flour
2 tablespoons tomato paste
6 cups Beef Stock (see Index), or boiling water
2 leeks, chopped
1 celery rib, chopped
Bouquet garni (1 bay leaf, 3 parsley sprigs, ¼ teaspoon thyme)
Salt and a few peppercorns
2 cloves
Pinch of ground sage
6 tablespoons sherry or Madeira wine

1. In a large saucepan, brown the oxtails in butter and peanut oil. When golden, add the onions, carrots, turnips, and garlic. Brown lightly for 5 to 8 minutes.

2. Sprinkle the meat and vegetables with flour, stirring until the flour is lightly browned. Add the tomato paste.

3. Pour in the beef stock or boiling water, add leeks, celery, *bouquet garni*, and seasonings to taste. Simmer, covered, for 4 hours.

4. Remove excess fat from the soup. Strain the soup, add the wine, and simmer briefly before serving in cups.

◆ UNDER THE COOK'S HAT ◆

A *brunoise*, a combination of ¼-inch diced vegetables such as carrots, turnips, and celery sautéed in butter, is traditionally added after the soup has been strained. About 1 tablespoon per cup is sufficient.

◆ ◆ ◆

Doctor Louis Lémery wrote about the importance of garlic in his *Treatise on Food* (1702):

> Garlic is of great assistance to people who go to sea. It alleviates the sea-sickness that is caused quite often by the salt air. That is why, as a rule, sailors eat garlic with their bread every morning.

Potage de Légumes

VEGETABLE SOUP

6 tablespoons unsalted butter
1 large onion, chopped
2 leeks, most of the green discarded, the rest finely chopped
4 carrots, finely diced
1 turnip, finely diced
1 celery rib, finely diced
2 garlic cloves, minced
7 cups light chicken broth made with the carcass of a roast
    chicken
Coarse salt
Freshly ground pepper
2 teaspoons sugar
1 teaspoon dried tarragon
3 medium-size potatoes, cooked and puréed with 4 tablespoons
    butter and ½ cup cream
1 head of Boston lettuce or small romaine, shredded
3 tablespoons chopped fresh parsley

6 servings

1. Melt 4 tablespoons of the butter in a deep pot and sauté the
onion until soft. Add the leeks, carrots, turnip, celery, and garlic.
Cover and simmer for 5 to 8 minutes, stirring occasionally.

2. Add the broth and season with salt, pepper, sugar, and tarragon. Simmer, partially covered, for 40 minutes.

3. About 15 minutes before the end of the cooking time, add the
potato purée.

4. In the remaining 2 tablespoons of butter cook the shredded
lettuce until wilted. Add lettuce to the soup and stir in the parsley.
Serve in a warmed tureen.

• *Bouillabaisse* •

A ce plat phocéans, accompli sans défaut,
Indispensablement, même avant tout, il faut
La rascasse, poisson, certes des plus vulgaires.
Isolé sur un gril, on ne l'estime guère,
Mais dans la bouillabaisse aussitôt il répand
De merveilleux parfums d'où le succès dépend.

To make this Phocaean dish perfectly
The rascasse, although a very common fish,
Is indispensable.
Served on a grill alone, it is not valued,
But in a bouillabaisse it does give forth
The marvelous aroma on which success depends. . . .
—JOSEPH MÉRY (1798–1865)

Bouillabaisse, this golden soup, this incomparable golden soup which em-
bodies and concentrates all the aromas of our shores and which permeates,
like an ecstasy, the stomach of astonished gastronomes.
—CURNONSKY

Marseilles, the home of bouillabaisse, was founded by the Greeks
in 600 B.C., and bouillabaisse itself goes back to the days of mythol-
ogy. It is said to be the creation of Venus, who wanted to put
Vulcan, her spouse, to sleep because she had a rendezvous with
Mars. Fish soup with saffron in it was thought to be a soporific.

Although bouillabaisse is also a great specialty of Provence, the
authentic bouillabaisse is from Marseilles, for it requires the varieties of rockfish only found in the waters of its bay. Bouillabaisse,
or *boui-abaisso* in the Provençal dialect, means boiling and lowering,
which describes the way it is cooked.

Recently seventeen restaurant keepers from Marseilles got together and established a charter defining the authentic contents of
a true *bouillabaisse marseillaise.* Under the shield of the *Chambre syn-*
dicale de la restauration and with the technical aid of the *Chambre*
régionale de commerce, they published a pamphlet that says in part:

> Originally it was made by fishermen who, when sorting fish
> intended for sale, set aside certain ones that they prepared for
> themselves and their families. It is, therefore, a simple family dish,
> which throughout the years has been perfected and which now
> includes a fish base and even some shellfish.
>
> *La bouillabaisse marseillaise* is a dish that demands a variety of
> fish from the Mediterranean. It is their particular taste that makes
> the dish so famous—and it must be made up only with ingredients
> of the highest quality.

The official recipe goes on to give the names of the fish, of which
four should be used, as well as a spiny lobster if desired, and a list
of the other ingredients to be included in the soup. The fish, being
all native to the waters of Marseilles, are not easily available in the
United States, although similar fish, under a variety of local names,

may be found in large fish markets. A true bouillabaisse includes four of the following: *rascasse, Saint-Pierre, fielas, galinette, vive, baudroie* (look for scorpionfish, John Dory, and anglerfish), as well as the shellfish and whatever fish you use for the base. Fish available locally are substituted here, but otherwise this recipe follows the dictates of the charter.

Bouillabaisse

1 onion, chopped   *6 servings*
4 garlic cloves, minced
3 tomatoes, quartered
Olive oil
2 pounds fish for soup base (whiting, cut into pieces, is
    satisfactory)
2 quarts boiling water
Fennel twigs
Parsley sprigs
Sea salt and freshly ground pepper
2 Idaho potatoes
8 pounds fish chosen from the following list (at least four
    different kinds): sea bass, haddock, cod, halibut, conger eel,
    red and gray snapper. (Sometimes anglerfish is available.)
    One lobster or 2 rock lobsters, split lengthwise, or a few
    prawns, can be used.
A generous pinch saffron in threads

PREPARATION FOR THE BASE
1. Sauté the onion, garlic, and tomatoes in olive oil over high heat.
2. Add the fish for the soup base, dressed and cut into sections. Stir together until the mixture reaches the consistency of a purée, about 15 minutes.
3. Add the boiling water and boil for at least 1 hour. Add several fennel twigs, several parsley sprigs, and salt and pepper to taste.
4. Put through a vegetable mill, then through a *chinois* (fine sieve), pressing well to extract all the juice.

THE BOUILLABAISSE
1. To the base, add the raw potatoes cut into thick slices (2 slices per person), then the firm fish according to size. Boil for 20 minutes.
2. About 5 minutes before serving, season with salt and pepper and saffron and add the soft fish and shellfish. When fish and

shellfish are cooked, remove them and the potato slices and arrange them on a serving plate.

LA ROUILLE

The usual recipe has for its base Aïoli (see Index), with the addition of ½ teaspoon saffron and fresh chili peppers or 1 teaspoon cayenne.

HOW TO SERVE

Generally bouillabaisse is served in two different plates: the fish on one and the bouillon in a chafing dish. The two can be mixed in a deep plate according to the taste of the guest, or served separately. The fundamental rule is that the fish must be sliced before the guests. The sauce (*aïoli* or *rouille*) will then be served, accompanied finally by croutons rubbed with garlic.

Serve with a chilled, dry rosé wine from Provence.

◆ UNDER THE COOK'S HAT ◆

The most important fish in a bouillabaisse is the *rascasse*, not available here. The most characteristic spice is saffron, and that, of course, is available. Buy it in threads and crumble the threads into the soup. If chili peppers are not available, use a few drops of Tabasco. Unless you are using garden-ripe tomatoes, add 1 tablespoon tomato paste.

If you use lobster, cut it into halves, saving the juice. Remove and discard the gravel sac and gut lobster before adding it to the soup. Croutons for bouillabaisse are never toasted but are dried in the oven. Make them with ¼-inch-thick slices of French bread, cut on the bias.

If any bouillabaisse is left, you can make another delicious soup. Mash leftover fish through a colander, discarding bones and skin. Cook 2 tablespoons of unconverted rice in 1 tablespoon of butter until opaque, then add to the soup. If too thick, add some clam juice and simmer until the rice is cooked.

◆ *Saffron* ◆

Saffron, the principal flavoring in a bouillabaisse, is named after the Arabic word for yellow. These golden threads, the stigmas of the saffron crocus, have provided us with an expensive but important seasoning and coloring agent from ancient times. In confirmation, we read of Pliny the Elder (A.D. 23–79) mentioning that the plaster on the wall of the Temple of Athena at Elis was mixed with saffron and milk. He wrote, "If the finger is moistened in the mouth and rubbed on the wall, it smells and tastes like saffron."

Soupe des Pêcheurs
FISHERMEN'S SOUP

While similar to bouillabaisse, this soup is much simpler to prepare and just as delectable.

¼ cup olive oil   *6 to 8 servings*

2 medium-size onions, diced

3 leeks, finely chopped

5 garlic cloves, minced

4 ripe medium-size tomatoes, peeled and chopped, or 1 can (1 pound) whole tomatoes

Bouquet garni (2 bay leaves, 1 teaspoon thyme, 6 parsley sprigs)

4 medium-size potatoes, cubed

½ cup dry white wine

7 cups water

1 teaspoon whole saffron

1 small piece of dried orange peel

Sea salt and freshly ground black pepper and cayenne

3 pounds assorted lean fish, such as halibut, sole, haddock, or striped bass, cut into large chunks

12 to 16 slices of French bread, ½ inch thick

Olive oil

1 garlic clove, split

1. Heat the olive oil in a large saucepan. Cook the onions, leeks, and garlic for 10 minutes. Do not let them color. Add the tomatoes and *bouquet garni*. Cook for 5 minutes.

2. Add the potatoes and cook for 1 or 2 minutes, stirring well. Add the wine, water, saffron, orange peel, and salt, pepper and cayenne to taste. Cover and boil for 15 minutes.

3. Add the fish, then simmer for 15 minutes longer.

4. Brush the bread slices with olive oil and toast under the broiler until golden. Rub them with a garlic clove while hot, and place 2 slices in each warmed soup plate. Ladle the hot soup over the bread.

◆ UNDER THE COOK'S HAT ◆

A few lobster tails enhance this soup immensely.

◆ ◆ ◆

Take care of your soup with the solicitude of a composer toward the overture of his opera.
—CHÂTILLON-PLESSIS, 1894

Chaudrière

BRETON FISH SOUP

The fishermen from the northern shores of France prepared this thick soup aboard their ships, using whatever fish their nets brought up. It was called *chaudrière* after the name of the cauldron in which the soup was cooked. It was probably the Bretons who introduced the soup to the new continent through Newfoundland and Cape Breton, where milk or cream was added and it became known as "chowder."

3 tablespoons unsalted butter　　　　　　　*8 servings*
4 tablespoons olive oil
4 onions, chopped
3 garlic cloves, chopped
3 large leeks, white part only, minced
½ cup diced celery
4 cups diced potatoes
3 pounds assorted fish such as halibut, haddock, and striped
　　bass, cut into chunks
2 cups dry white wine
4 cups water
Sea salt and freshly ground pepper
Bouquet garni (½ teaspoon thyme, 1 bay leaf, 3 parsley sprigs)
3 egg yolks
1 cup heavy cream
French bread, cut into ½-inch-thick slices
Olive oil
1 garlic clove, split

1. Melt the butter and olive oil in a large heavy pot. Add the onions and sauté until wilted. Add the garlic, leeks, celery, and potatoes. Cook for 5 to 8 minutes, stirring well.

2. Add the fish, wine, water, seasonings to taste, and *bouquet garni.* Bring to a boil and cook for 25 minutes.

3. Remove the soup from the heat. Discard the *bouquet garni.* Just before serving, combine the egg yolks with the cream. Blend into the soup.

4. Fry slices of French bread in olive oil. Rub them with a garlic clove while hot. Place them in deep serving plates or earthenware soup bowls and cover with the hot broth and fish pieces.

◆   UNDER THE COOK'S HAT   ◆

Add milk to any leftover soup and purée in a blender or food processor. Serve cold with a sprinkling of fresh parsley or chives.

Fishermen cook this soup using deep ocean water. If you are near an area with safe, clean seawater, substitute it for tap water but do not add salt. You will be surprised at the difference in taste.

◆ ◆ ◆

During the eighteenth century, the *soupière* (soup tureen) was created in France. These tureen masterpieces were wrought of silver or made elaborately of china.

A well-known actress of the Comédie Française, Emilie Contat, in the early nineteenth century, became annoyed by the inconvenience of passing filled soup plates from the tureen. At her dinners, she had the soup plates placed on the table just before everyone was seated, a custom that had prevailed prior to the eighteenth century, was dropped, and now once again is usual at formal meals.

This same actress also originated the idea of preheating the plates, to prevent the soup from cooling off too quickly.

Potage Crécy

CREAM OF CARROT SOUP

The origin of the name *potage Crécy* has generated some controversy over the years. It probably refers to the small village of Crécy-en-Ponthieu, where the Battle of Crécy was fought in 1346. The other contender for this honor is Crécy-en-Brie, but both areas grow exceptionally fine carrots, the soup's main ingredient.

6 tablespoons unsalted butter   *4 to 6 servings*
3 tablespoons water
1 bunch young carrots, sliced

1 medium-size onion, finely minced
1 tablespoon shallots, finely minced
2 tablespoons flour
5 cups Chicken Stock (see Index)
Salt and pepper
2 tablespoons quick-cooking tapioca
1 cup heavy cream
Fresh parsley, chopped (for cold soup)

1. Melt 2 tablespoons butter in a large skillet. Add the water and the carrots. Cover and simmer for 20 minutes, shaking the pan occasionally. Do not let carrots sizzle; add water if necessary.

2. Purée the carrots through a vegetable mill or whirl in a blender for 1 to 2 seconds. Reserve.

3. In a large pan, melt 2 more tablespoons of the butter. Sauté the onion and shallots until wilted, then sprinkle with flour.

4. Add the stock, carrot purée, and seasonings to taste. Stir constantly. Bring to a boil. Gradually stir in the tapioca. Simmer for 25 minutes.

5. Gently reheat when ready to serve. Stir in the cream and the remaining butter. If served cold, sprinkle with parsley.

Potage Crème à la Dubarry

CREAM OF CAULIFLOWER SOUP

This soup was dedicated to Madame Du Barry, a favorite of Louis XV.

1 large cauliflower, cut into flowerets   *8 to 10 servings*
Salt
3 tablespoons unsalted butter
1 onion, minced
2 tablespoons water
6 cups Beef Stock or Chicken Stock (see Index)
2 egg yolks
1 cup heavy cream
Freshly ground white pepper
Dash of grated nutmeg
Fresh parsley or chervil, finely minced
Croutons

1. Drop the cauliflower into boiling salted water. Cook for 10 minutes, then drain.

2. Melt the butter in a large skillet. Add the onion and sauté until golden. Add cauliflower and 2 tablespoons water. Cover and simmer slowly for 10 minutes. Do not let the cauliflower change color. Add an extra tablespoon of water if necessary.

3. Bring beef or chicken stock to a simmer in a large saucepan. Add the cauliflower and simmer, partially covered, for 30 minutes.

4. Purée soup, 2 cups at a time, in a blender or food processor.

5. Just before serving, bring the soup to the boil. Beat the egg yolks with the cream and stir into the soup off the heat. Correct the seasonings. Add a pinch of nutmeg and sprinkle with parsley or chervil and croutons.

♦   UNDER THE COOK'S HAT·   ♦

Turkey broth instead of beef or chicken stock is a good variation.

♦   ♦   ♦

Around the middle of the seventeenth century, the individual soup plate appeared. Until then it had been the custom to drink soup from a bowl made of wood, metal, coconut shells, or ostrich eggs shared with one's dinner partner. The soup plate with a rim was introduced around 1655 and was regarded as an extraordinary novelty.

Because of the fashionable high collars worn during the 1500s, eating was virtually impossible without spilling food. Marguerite de Valois, first wife of Henri IV, is credited with the idea of using a spoon with a long handle.

Velouté à la Reine
CHICKEN VELOUTÉ

Marguerite de Valois, known as Queen Margot, was so fond of chicken soup that it was served to her at the court every Thursday. Any French dish made with chicken is called *à la Reine* in her honor.

5 tablespoons unsalted butter   *6 servings*
1 onion, chopped
2 leeks, white part only, chopped
2 carrots, chopped
1 celery rib, chopped
7 cups water

1 large chicken breast, split
3 or 4 chicken wings, necks, or backbones
⅓ cup raw unconverted rice
1 garlic clove
1 clove
Coarse salt and freshly ground pepper
1 cup heavy cream
Croutons

1. Melt 3 tablespoons of the butter in a soup kettle and add the vegetables. Simmer for 8 to 10 minutes, stirring occasionally.

2. Add the water, chicken, rice, garlic, clove, and seasonings to taste. Cook, covered, over medium heat for 1 hour.

3. Discard the wings, necks, or backbones. Remove skin and bones from the chicken breast. Cut the meat into small pieces. Purée the soup and chicken in a blender or food processor until no trace of graininess is left.

4. Correct the seasonings. Reheat the soup before serving. Stir in the remaining butter and the cream. Add a few croutons to each serving.

◆ *Billi-Bi* ◆

The origin of this soup goes back to 1925, when Chef Louis Barthe made it at the request of William Bateman Leeds, an American who was known as the "tin-plate king."

Monsieur Louis Vaudable, onetime owner of Maxim's, is now retired but remembers the occasion. Chef Barthe presided some-times at Maxim's in Paris and sometimes at Ciro's in Deauville, and Mr. Leeds, who greatly appreciated Barthe's artistry, frequented both restaurants. Because of the abundance and superiority of mus-sels in the Deauville area, the chef had made a particularly delicious sauce to complement them, and the combination became a great favorite of Mr. Leeds. With a napkin draped around his neck, he would happily eat a plateful of these mussels, using one-half of the shell as a spoon to dig the mussel out of the other half and carry it dripping to his mouth.

When the time came, however, to entertain friends at dinner so that they might enjoy this flavorful combination, he decided that this informal way of eating was not in harmony with the dignity of his friends and so he asked that the dish be properly prepared and then the mussels removed, leaving a delectable creamy soup. The chef did as he was asked, and the resulting dish was greeted by the group with great admiration. His friends called it "Billy B.'s soup," and its fame spread far and wide.

Usually it now appears on menus as *billi-bi*—a natural evolution in spelling, but the same delicious soup. The following recipe is based on this dish but substitutes clams for the traditional mussels, which are not always available.

Crème de Palourdes
CREAM OF CLAM SOUP

Although this is a very simple soup to make, it is very elegant.

1 tablespoon chopped shallot   *4 servings*
1 small onion, minced
2 tablespoons unsalted butter
½ cup dry white wine
2 bottles (8 ounces each) clam juice
2 tablespoons cornstarch
2 tablespoons water
1 can (8 ounces) shelled whole clams
½ cup heavy cream
2 egg yolks
Freshly ground pepper
Fresh parsley, finely chopped

1. Sauté the shallot and onion in the butter until golden. Add the wine and simmer for 5 minutes.
2. Add the clam juice. Bring to a boil and simmer for 8 to 10 minutes. Strain through a fine sieve and return the broth to the pan.
3. Add the cornstarch diluted in 2 tablespoons water. When broth is thickened, add the clams and their liquor.
4. Remove from the heat. Add the cream mixed with the egg yolks. Bring the soup almost to a boil. Correct the seasonings.
5. Sprinkle the soup with parsley just before serving.

Potage de Poireaux à la Crème
CREAM OF LEEK SOUP

This is a soup for fall and winter, when leeks are at their best.

5 leeks, white part only, finely chopped   *6 servings*
6 tablespoons unsalted butter
5 tablespoons flour
6 cups Beef Stock or Chicken Stock (see Index)
4 tablespoons heavy cream
Croutons

1. In a large saucepan cook the leeks in 4 tablespoons of the butter until soft. Sprinkle the flour over the leeks and stir well.
2. Add the stock and simmer for 15 minutes.
3. Add the cream and remaining butter just before serving. Sprinkle with croutons.

♦　♦　♦

A 1955 survey asked the French to list their favorite soups. Almost 75 percent chose both vegetable and leek soups.

Velouté de Champignons

MUSHROOM VELOUTÉ

3 medium-size onions, finely chopped   *6 servings*
6 to 7 tablespoons unsalted butter
¾ pound mushrooms, finely chopped
7 tablespoons flour
5 cups Beef Stock or Chicken Stock (see Index)
2 egg yolks
¾ cup heavy cream
2 tablespoons lemon juice
Salt and freshly ground pepper

1. In a large saucepan sauté the onions in 4 to 5 tablespoons of the butter until golden. Add mushrooms, and cook briskly until soft and almost dry. Sprinkle with flour; stir well; cook until blended.
2. Add the stock and bring to a boil. Simmer for 20 minutes.
3. Combine the egg yolks and cream. Add the egg-cream mixture and the remaining butter to the soup. Do not boil. Add lemon juice and seasonings to taste.

♦　UNDER THE COOK'S HAT　♦

In a nonstick pan the mushrooms would just stew, so use a pan without a nonstick surface to bring out the flavors best.

◆　◆　◆

In 1132 the monks of Cluny were forbidden to eat curry. It was considered an aphrodisiac, which made it incompatible with monastic life.

Bisque de Crevettes

SHRIMP BISQUE

This quick soup makes an excellent preface for an elegant dinner. Curry adds a special zest.

1 tablespoon unsalted butter
2 tablespoons olive oil
1 medium-size onion, finely chopped
2 garlic cloves, minced
1 pound fresh shrimp or crayfish, shelled
1½ tablespoons flour
2 tablespoons Cognac
1½ cups dry white wine
2 tablespoons tomato paste
Coarse salt and freshly ground pepper
¼ teaspoon curry powder
¼ teaspoon thyme
2 cups water
1 cup heavy cream
Fresh parsley, finely chopped

3 or 4 servings

1. Heat the butter and olive oil in a large saucepan. Add the onion and garlic. Cook until golden.
2. Add the shrimp. Sauté for 3 minutes, then sprinkle with flour. Stir for about 1 minute.
3. Add the Cognac, white wine, tomato paste, seasonings to taste, and water. Simmer for 10 minutes, then add the cream and simmer for another 15 minutes.
4. Purée the soup in a blender or food processor until smooth. Reheat. Serve in soup cups with a sprinkling of parsley.

◆　UNDER THE COOK'S HAT　◆

To accentuate the flavor of the soup, make a Shrimp Butter with the shrimp shells. (Follow directions for Shellfish Butter; see Index.) Stir the butter into the soup just before serving.

Velouté de Soles

SOLE VELOUTÉ

This soup is an excellent start to an elegant dinner.

6 servings

Fish Fumet (see Index) Triple the recipe and add 2 extra cups
    water
½ cup raw unconverted rice
1 cup heavy cream
3 egg yolks
4 tablespoons unsalted butter
Fresh chervil or parsley, minced

1. Make a triple batch of *fumet*, and add the extra 2 cups water.
2. Strain the sole *fumet* and add the rice. Cook, covered, for about 45 minutes.
3. Purée through a blender or food processor with the cream and egg yolks until smooth.
4. Reheat the soup and stir in the butter. Serve in heated soup plates with a sprinkle of chervil or parsley on top.

◆   U N D E R   T H E   C O O K ' S   H A T   ◆

The velouté of sole may be the base of a delicious seafood velouté, with the addition of lobster or crab meat, cooked in a *mirepoix* (see Index) and reheated briefly in butter, and add Shellfish Butter (see Index) to soup.

Soupe Germiny

SORREL SOUP

Adolphe Dugléré, the celebrated chef of the Café Anglais, created this well-known elegant soup in May 1860. He named it for the Comte de Germiny, Governor of the Banque de France, in gratitude for the many kindnesses the governor had shown him. The following is based on the recipe Dugléré dictated that May evening to one of the guests, the Marquis de Saint-Georges, who had congratulated the chef and predicted that his soup would be known around the world.

½ pound sorrel leaves, cut into thin strips with scissors   *4 servings*
3 tablespoons unsalted butter
4 cups Beef Stock (see Index)
Salt and white pepper
1 thin loaf of French bread, cut into ½-inch slices
Clarified Butter (see Index)
6 egg yolks
1 cup heavy cream
Fresh chervil, minced

1. Simmer the sorrel leaves in the butter until soft. Add the beef stock and seasonings to taste, and cook for 10 minutes.
2. Fry the bread slices in the clarified butter. Place them in the bottom of a soup tureen.
3. Remove the soup from the heat. Beat the egg yolks and cream together. Add to the soup, turning gently with a wooden spoon until well blended. Pour soup over the bread slices. Sprinkle with chervil. Serve immediately.

Velouté de Courges

SQUASH VELOUTÉ

4 tablespoons unsalted butter   *4 servings*
2 pounds small yellow squash, peeled and thinly sliced
1 large onion, chopped
2 cups Chicken Stock or Beef Stock (see Index)
2 cups water
Salt and freshly ground pepper
3 tablespoons quick-cooking tapioca
2 egg yolks
½ cup heavy cream
Fresh parsley, chopped, or chives, snipped

1. Melt the butter in a large saucepan. Sauté the squash and onion for 5 minutes.
2. Add the stock, water, and seasonings to taste. Bring to a full boil, then sprinkle the tapioca into the soup. Simmer for 20 minutes.
3. Purée the soup in a blender or food processor. Just before serving, add the egg yolks mixed with the cream. Reheat but do not

boil. If served cold, omit the egg yolks. Sprinkle with parsley or chives.

Velouté de Tomates Provençale
TOMATO VELOUTÉ

4 tablespoons unsalted butter   *4 servings*
3 tablespoons olive oil
3 medium-size onions, chopped
3 garlic cloves, chopped
5 large ripe tomatoes, peeled and cut into chunks
3 cups Beef Stock or Chicken Stock (see Index)
⅓ cup white wine or dry vermouth
3 tablespoons quick-cooking tapioca
Bouquet garni (3 parsley sprigs, ½ bay leaf, ¼ teaspoon thyme)
2 teaspoons sugar
Salt and pepper
½ cup heavy cream
Fresh parsley, minced

1. Heat 2 tablespoons of the butter and the olive oil in a skillet. Sauté the onions until golden, then add the garlic and cook for 1 minute. Add the tomatoes and cook for 4 or 5 minutes.

2. Add stock and wine. When the liquid comes to a boil, sprinkle the tapioca over it. Add the *bouquet garni*, sugar, and seasonings to taste. Cover and simmer for 20 minutes.

3. Just before serving, add the heavy cream. Reheat, but do not boil. Serve hot or cold, sprinkled with parsley.

Soupe au Pistou
VEGETABLE SOUP WITH PISTOU

This hearty summer soup is a famous dish from Nice. *Pistou*, from the verb *pista* in the Provençal dialect, means "to crush." Fresh young basil leaves are pounded to a paste, which gives the soup a delicious flavor typical of Provence. As early as 25 B.C., we read that the Roman epicurean Apicius, author of ten recognized cookbooks, ground basil into his soups. The consistency of this soup is very thick, almost a meal in itself.

1 large onion, peeled and sliced   *6 servings*
3 tablespoons olive oil
4 large ripe tomatoes, peeled and sliced
2 quarts water
3 potatoes, peeled and diced
2 carrots, diced
Coarse salt and freshly ground pepper
½ pound yellow snap beans, cut into ½-inch lengths
½ pound green snap beans, cut into ½-inch lengths
2 small yellow summer squash or zucchini, sliced and cut into
    halves
¼ pound broken vermicelli or elbow macaroni
Gruyère or Parmesan cheese, grated

PISTOU
4 bunches of fresh basil leaves
4 garlic cloves, peeled and minced
Pulp of 1 tomato
3 tablespoons olive oil

1. Cook the onion in olive oil until golden. Add tomatoes and
cook for 5 minutes. Add the water, potatoes, carrots, and seasonings to taste. When the water boils, add the beans. After 10 minutes, add the squash. Add the vermicelli after the soup has cooked
for 45 minutes.

2. Make the *pistou* as follows: Purée the basil, garlic, tomato
pulp, and olive oil in a blender, food processor, or mortar.

3. Just before serving, add a little soup to the *pistou*, then add
this mixture to the soup. Do not let the soup boil. Serve grated
Gruyère or Parmesan cheese separately.

◆   UNDER THE COOK'S HAT   ◆

Pistou makes a very fine sauce for plain, buttered spaghetti.

Mayonnaise mixed with *pistou* is excellent on top of halves of
hard-cooked eggs. Add *pistou*, thinned out with a little white wine,
to potato salad.

During the summer, make *pistou* in quantity and freeze in tiny
paper cups for the winter months.

◆   ◆   ◆

I made soups marvelously well and received great compliments.
—CHATEAUBRIAND

Soupe de Cresson

WATERCRESS SOUP

Eighteenth-century Parisian street merchants sold watercress by shouting, *à la santé du corps* (for the health of the body).

2 large onions, chopped   *6 to 8 servings*
6 tablespoons unsalted butter
2 tablespoons olive oil
1 garlic clove, minced
2 bunches of watercress, thoroughly washed and picked over
5 medium-size potatoes, peeled and thinly sliced
7 cups boiling water, preferably spring water
Salt and freshly ground pepper
½ cup heavy cream (optional)

1. In a large saucepan, sauté the onions in 3 tablespoons of the butter and the olive oil until soft. Add the garlic and cook for 1 minute.

2. Reserving a few watercress leaves for garnish, add the rest to the saucepan and cook for 5 minutes. Add the potatoes and cook for 5 minutes longer.

3. Add the boiling water and seasonings to taste. Cook, uncovered, over medium heat for 30 minutes, or until the potatoes are done.

4. Purée the soup in a blender, food processor, or food mill until partially blended. (Just turn the motor on and off once or twice so that there is still some texture left in the soup.)

5. Reheat the soup before serving. Add the remaining butter and the heavy cream. Decorate with the reserved watercress leaves.

◆   *Variation*   ◆

A flavorful soup can be made by substituting 2 large bunches of chervil or Italian parsley (just the leaves, with the bitter stems removed) for the watercress.

This soup is also good served cold.

◆   ◆   ◆

I set much more value on a ray of sunshine and a soup than all the courts of the world.
—VOLTAIRE (1694–1778)

Soupe de Lentilles Basquaise

BASQUE-STYLE LENTIL SOUP

1½ cups dried lentils   *4 to 6 servings*
4 tablespoons goose fat or unsalted butter
2 tablespoons olive oil
2 medium-size onions, finely chopped
2 leeks, finely minced
3 garlic cloves, finely minced
1 can (15 ounces) tomato sauce
1 ham hock (½ pound), split by the butcher
6½ cups hot water
Salt and freshly ground pepper

1. Rinse and sort the lentils under cold water. Set aside.
2. Melt the goose fat and olive oil in a large soup pot. Sauté the onions, leeks, and garlic for 6 to 8 minutes.
3. Add the tomato sauce and cook for 5 minutes.
4. Add the lentils and ham hock pieces. Pour in the water, cover, and simmer for 1½ hours. Add seasonings to taste halfway through the cooking time.
5. When the soup is done, remove the ham hock pieces. Purée three-quarters of the soup in a food processor or blender. Combine with the remaining soup and reheat before serving.

◆   UNDER THE COOK'S HAT   ◆

This soup reheats very well. Add a little broth if the soup is too thick.

Potage Saint-Germain, Chantilly

GREEN PEA SOUP

This famous soup was named for the Comte de Saint-Germain, Minister of War during the reign of Louis XIV.

4 servings
4 cups shelled peas, or 2 boxes (10 ounces each) frozen peas
4 large Boston lettuce leaves
1½ teaspoons sugar
Salt

4 cups water
1 medium-size leek, with most of the green part removed,
    finely diced
1 carrot, finely diced
1 small onion, finely diced
3 tablespoons unsalted butter
½ cup heavy cream

1. Bring the peas, lettuce, sugar, salt to taste, and water to a boil
in a large pot.
2. Sauté the leek, carrot, and onion in butter until golden. Add
to the boiling soup. Add more salt to taste. Cook for 15 minutes.
3. Put the soup through a food mill.
4. Whip the cream until stiff and season with salt. Place a dollop
of cream in the center of each portion.

Potage Parmentier

POTATO AND LEEK SOUP

This simple soup is one of the best loved of all French soups. It is
named for Parmentier, who promoted potatoes in France during
the eighteenth century.

2 medium-size onions, chopped   *4 servings*
6 tablespoons unsalted butter
4 or 5 large leeks, with most of the green removed, finely
    chopped
2 medium-size potatoes, peeled and diced
5 cups water
Salt and freshly ground pepper
½ cup heavy cream
Croutons

1. Cook the onions in 4 tablespoons of the butter until they start
to color. Add the leeks and cook for about 5 minutes. Add the
potatoes and mix well. Add the water and seasonings to taste.
Cover and simmer for 1 hour.
2. Mash the potatoes to a fine consistency in the pan with a
meat mallet.
3. Reheat the soup just before serving. Add the cream and the
remaining butter. Garnish with croutons.

4. *Les Beurres et les Sauces*
BUTTERS AND SAUCES

✤ ✤ ✤

Les Beurres
B U T T E R S

✤ ✤ ✤

Butter, the gold of the kitchen that is so vital to French cuisine, was introduced to France when the Vikings settled in Normandy. It became such an important item of the Normans' daily fare that, in medieval times, they were willing to pay the clergy for special dispensation so that they could use it during Lent. The revenue from the dispensations built the tower Saint-Romain (nicknamed the Tower of Butter), which is part of the Cathedral of Notre-Dame in Rouen, a masterpiece of Gothic architecture.

The butter of Isigny in Normandy has been praised for centuries because of its nutty flavor. It is considered the best choice for use in classic French cuisine.

Because France has such a variety of the best butters in the world, it is rather surprising to learn that a Frenchman invented margarine.

In 1868, Napoleon III sponsored a contest to find a substitute for butter. It had to be an "edible fat product that would keep longer than butter" and would be used to supply the crews of the French fleet.

A year later, an engineer named Hippolyte Mège-Mouriès registered his product and called it margarine. It was soon widely copied in other countries. In 1880, the Academy of Sciences issued this critical report: "Margarine can be utilized exceptionally in some stews, some vegetables, but in any case, never in the preparation of potatoes."

74

The true French attitude toward butter is reflected in the opinions of its cooks.

Fernand Point, founder of the famous Pyramide in Vienne, one of the best restaurants in France, wrote this maxim in his notebook: *"Du beurre! Donnez-moi du beurre! Toujours du beurre!"* (Butter! Give me butter! Always butter!)

And Pierre Descave said in 1961, "Margarine, the butter of the poor? No, the poor butter."

There is no real substitute for butter and it continues to be essential to French cuisine.

Beurre d'Anchois

ANCHOVY BUTTER

Cream 6 tablespoons of butter with 2 tablespoons of anchovy paste, a sprinkle of lemon juice, and salt and pepper to taste. Shape it and chill well. Slice before serving.

◆　◆　◆

To shape flavored butter: Wet your hands; this will prevent the butter from sticking. Pat the butter into a frankfurter shape. Place between 2 pieces of wax paper and roll back and forth until smooth. Chill until the butter is very firm, and it is time to serve.

Before handling, chill your hands in ice water. Then, with a zester, make grooves the length of the roll of butter, spacing them ¼ inch apart. Slice off ¼- to ½-inch rounds.

◆　◆　◆

To keep butter usable under refrigeration for up to 6 months, cream 1 pound of unsalted butter with 2 tablespoons of honey.

Beurre de Homard

LOBSTER BUTTER

This butter adds distinction to and intensifies the flavor of fish sauces or soups. There are two methods.

I

1. Purée the creamy part inside the lobster, and the coral, in an electric blender or food processor with an equal amount of softened unsalted butter.

2. Strain through a fine mesh strainer. Add 1 or 2 drops of red food coloring.

II

1. Chop the shell of a cooked lobster, cut into small pieces, in an electric blender or food processor until pulverized. Weigh the shell.

2. Transfer shell to the top pan of a double boiler. Add an equal weight of unsalted butter, cut into small pieces. Simmer until the butter has absorbed all the flavor, about 15 minutes.

3. Strain butter through a fine-mesh strainer set over a bowl of cold water with a few ice cubes in it. Press hard with the back of a spoon to extract as much of the butter as possible from the pulverized shell.

4. When the butter has solidified on the ice water, skim it off and refrigerate. The cold water can be strained and used for other recipes, as a base for fish soups or sauces; it will have absorbed a certain amount of flavor.

Beurre de Crustacés

SHELLFISH BUTTER

The shells of crayfish, shrimp, or crab can be used to make this flavorful butter, which should be used within 24 hours of being made. The shells should weigh the same as the butter.

2 tablespoons plus ¼ pound unsalted butter
1 onion, finely chopped
2 shallots, finely chopped
1 small carrot, finely diced
1 small piece of bay leaf
Pinch of thyme
¼ pound crayfish or shrimp or crab shells, pulverized
1 or 2 drops of red food coloring

1. Melt 2 tablespoons butter in the top pan of a double boiler. Add the onion, shallots, carrot, bay leaf, and thyme, and cook over direct heat for a few minutes, or until tender.

2. Add the pulverized shells and ¼ pound butter. Place the pan over hot water and simmer for 15 minutes, until the butter has melted and absorbed all the flavors. Add the food coloring.

3. Strain butter through a fine-mesh strainer set over a bowl of cold water with a few ice cubes in it. Press hard with the back of a spoon to extract as much of the butter as possible from the pulverized shells.

4. When the butter has solidified on the ice water, skim off and refrigerate. Strain the water for use in fish soups or sauces.

Beurre d'Escargots

SNAIL BUTTER

This butter was created for use on snails but is also delicious on broiled mushrooms, clams, mussels, fish, and meats.

1 garlic clove, finely minced
1 shallot, finely minced
5 tablespoons unsalted butter, at room temperature
1 tablespoon finely minced fresh parsley
Salt and freshly ground pepper

1. Pound the garlic and shallot to a smooth paste. Combine with the butter, parsley, and salt and pepper to taste. Mix until well blended. Refrigerate.

◆   UNDER THE COOK'S HAT   ◆

A parsley mill or a food processor is ideal for mincing shallots.

There are two kinds of shallots in France—pink and gray. This recipe calls for the finer-flavored gray shallots. Because they are unavailable in the United States, you will have to use the pink ones, which will give a slightly rosy color to the butter.

◆   ◆   ◆

This is the recipe Alexandre Dumas wrote in 1873 for making butter.

In whichever countries I have traveled, I always have had fresh butter every day. I give my recipe to the travelers. It is quite simple and at the same time infallible.

Wherever I could get milk, either from cow or she-camel or ewe—and particularly from ewe—I would get it and would fill three-quarters of a bottle with it, cork it, hang it at the neck of my horse and let my horse do the rest. Upon arrival at night, I would break the neck of the bottle and would find inside a piece of butter as big as a fist which was made by itself.

In Africa, in Caucasus, in Sicily, in Spain, this method always has been successful for me.

Beurre Maître d'Hôtel

PARSLEY BUTTER

Broiled meat and fish are enhanced when topped by a slice of chilled *beurre maître d'hôtel*.

5 tablespoons unsalted butter, at room temperature
3 tablespoons chopped fresh parsley
3 tablespoons snipped fresh chives
4 teaspoons lemon juice
Salt and white pepper

1. Cream the butter. Add the herbs, lemon juice, and seasonings to taste. Chill until ready to use.

◆ *Variation* ◆

Beurre d'Échalotes SHALLOT BUTTER Substitute 2 tablespoons of minced shallots for the chives. This is especially fine on steak.

Beurre Clarifié

CLARIFIED BUTTER

Clarified butter is simply melted butter with the milk solids removed. Clarified butter does not burn as easily as whole butter so it is used for sautéing over high heat.

1. Melt the desired amount of butter over low heat in a small heavy pan. Do this very slowly so there is no possibility of the butter burning. When the froth rises, spoon it off. Carefully pour the liquefied clear butter into another pan or dish. Discard the milky sediment that has settled at the bottom.

Boulettes de Beurre
BUTTER BALLS

1. Chill grooved butter paddles in ice water.
2. Holding paddles at right angles to each other, place 1½ to 2 teaspoons firm butter on one paddle, then quickly rotate both paddles to form a ball. Dip the paddles into a bowl of ice water before making each one, dropping the butter balls into another bowl of ice water. Refrigerate them until ready to use.

Beurre Manié
KNEADED BUTTER

Beurre manié is used to thicken sauces and stews. With a fork mash an equal quantity of softened butter and flour, until thoroughly blended.

Just before serving, drop tiny bits of the *beurre manié* into the pan in 2 or 3 places. Swirl the pan until it is all blended in, and the sauce is thickened to the desired consistency. Do not boil the sauce after *beurre manié* is added.

Les Sauces
S A U C E S
✤ ✤ ✤

Talleyrand said, "England has three sauces and 360 religions; whereas France has three religions and 360 sauces."

A Frenchman can be more impressed by a great sauce than by a whole meal, which may be why Alexandre Dumas referred to France as a *nation saucière*—sauceboat nation!

The importance of sauces in French cooking goes back many centuries. In the thirteenth century, the *sauciers* (sauce cooks) would come hurrying into the streets of Paris at mealtimes shouting, *"Sauce au verjus! Sauce à la moutarde! Sauce à la ravigote! . . ."* Anyone who needed a sauce for his meal would go into the street and buy his favorite one. Their excellence was guaranteed by a decree, which can be read in the Paris Police treatise of year 1258 as follows:

". . . and since the lives of men depend on the inviolable accuracy in the concoction of sauce, mustards and other foods subordinated from this art, from now on, no one shall undertake their preparation unless he is an expert, skillful, and acknowledged by general approbation."

"Sauce cook" was a trade and in 1292 they numbered seven in Paris. A tremendous change in the flavor of French cooking occurred about 1670 when Pierre de Lune, a kitchen squire, thought of replacing the usual seasoning of heavy spices, typical of the Middle Ages, with a *bouquet garni*, a combination of aromatic herbs which he called *pacquet* (bundle), because the herbs were tied together.

Until then, sauces were thickened with bread soaked in milk or broth, and ground almonds. Again Pierre de Lune changed this method and replaced it by a *roux* (flour and butter cooked together), to which a liquid was added.

The basic stocks, or *fonds de cuisine*, indispensable for French cooking, were the invention of François Marin. He said in *Les Dons de Comus* in 1739: "Modern cooking is a kind of chemistry," and he originated the formulas for the basic stocks, which he termed "the soul of cooking."

The two basic sauces of France are brown sauce and white sauce, and from them are produced an infinity of variations.

The secret of a flavorful sauce is in the reduction of the liquid, whether it consists of stock, wine, cream, or meat juices. This liquid becomes thicker in consistency without the help of starch, and because of the concentrated and blended flavors, the sauce is enhanced. It will acquire more delicate flavor when 1 or 2 tablespoons of cold unsalted butter are added after the pan has been removed from the heat. Only unsalted butter is used in French sauces.

Fernand Point says: "It is by his sauce that a good cook distinguishes himself; moreover, in the orchestra of a large kitchen, the sauce cook is the soloist."

◆ *Brown Sauce and Variations* ◆

◆ ◆ ◆

Cuisine is not invariable—but one must guard against tampering with the essential bases. —FERNAND POINT

Sauce Brun (Fonds de Veau)
BASIC BROWN SAUCE

This is one of the two most important sauces in French cuisine; along with béchamel, the white sauce, it is used in innumerable ways. In place of the time-consuming preparation of the classic *sauce espagnole,* most cooks find this simplified version quite acceptable to use as a base for a variety of sauces.

2 pounds veal bones, thinly sliced
3 ounces Polish ham, diced
2 carrots, cut into 1-inch pieces
1 celery rib, cut into 1-inch pieces
2 unpeeled onions, thickly sliced
3 unpeeled garlic cloves, crushed
½ cup flour
2 quarts boiling water
1 cup dry white wine
2 tablespoons tomato paste
2 leeks, sliced
Few parsley sprigs
2 bay leaves
1 teaspoon dried thyme
¼ teaspoon dried tarragon
2 teaspoons coarse salt
1 teaspoon commercial browning agent

1. In a lightly greased large roasting pan combine the bones, ham, carrots, celery, onions, and garlic. Place in a preheated 425°F. oven and roast for 1½ hours, turning the ingredients several times, until golden brown.

2. Remove the pan from oven and sprinkle the contents with the flour. Stir thoroughly and put back in the oven for 15 minutes, mixing all ingredients once or twice and being careful they do not burn. Transfer everything to a large pot containing 2 quarts of boiling water.

3. Add the wine to the roasting pan and deglaze on top of the stove. Pour this liquid into the pot. Add the tomato paste, leeks, parsley, dried herbs, and salt. Simmer, uncovered, for about 3 hours. Remove the scum that comes to the top.

4. Add the browning agent, then strain through a sieve lined

with a double thickness of dampened cheesecloth. Cool, then refrigerate in glass jars.

5. To use, remove the layer of fat from the surface, then proceed with the directions for any recipe calling for brown sauce. In only 15 minutes, you can make a beautiful, classic French sauce.

♦ UNDER THE COOK'S HAT ♦

Check the veal bones when you buy them to be certain there is no odor, as bones tend to deteriorate quickly.

The *fonds de veau* can be frozen in 1½-cup containers, enough for a sauce.

Sauce Brune Simple

EASY BROWN SAUCE

Since good beef broth is available in cans, it can be used in this recipe to make an easy substitute for a Basic Brown Sauce.

3 tablespoons beef suet
3 tablespoons flour
2 tablespoons tomato purée
1 can (13½ oz.) beef broth
¼ cup water

Makes about 1 cup

1. Melt the fat in a small heavy saucepan. Add the flour. Cook over low heat for about 20 minutes or longer, until the *roux* is the color of a chestnut.

2. Add the tomato purée, then the beef broth and water. Barely simmer the sauce for 2 hours. Skim off the fat and foam that accumulate on the surface.

♦ UNDER THE COOK'S HAT ♦

The best fat to use for brown sauce or for browning beef is prepared as follows: Cover 1 pound of finely chopped, fresh beef suet with water. Boil until all the water has evaporated and the fat starts to sizzle. Halfway through the cooking time, add 1 chopped onion. Strain the fat through a fine sieve.

If a brown sauce is stirred, it will lose its shine and the rich, dark color will become lighter. If necessary, the pan can be lifted up and swirled occasionally.

Sauce Bordelaise

BORDELAISE SAUCE

One of the great French sauces, it is served with steak.

Makes about 1½ cups

3 to 4 pounds marrowbones, parboiled for ½ minute
2 tablespoons unsalted butter
3 tablespoons finely minced shallots
¾ cup fine Bordeaux wine
1 tablespoon Cognac
Salt
3 or 4 peppercorns, crushed
½ bay leaf
Thyme
1 cup Brown Sauce (see Index)

1. With a small knife dipped into hot water, remove the marrow from the bones. Dice the marrow; there should be about ¼ cup.

2. Melt the butter. Add the shallots and cook until wilted. Add the wine and Cognac, salt to taste, peppercorns, and herbs, and cook until reduced by half.

3. Add the brown sauce. Simmer for 10 minutes. Strain through a *chinois* or fine sieve, mashing with the back of a spoon.

4. Add the marrow and simmer the sauce for a few minutes before serving in a sauceboat or over meat.

◆   U N D E R   T H E   C O O K ' S   H A T   ◆

It is important to stir the sauce as little as possible or it will turn gray and lose its shine.

◆   ◆   ◆

Fernand Jobert, a member of the Académie des Gastronomes, had a perfect definition for sauces: "A sauce must hold the essence of the flavor of a dish, but never disguise or adulterate it."

Sauce Charcutière

CHARCUTIÈRE SAUCE

This sauce derives its name from *chaircuite* (cooked meat). During the Middle Ages it designated the sausage makers who had the exclusive right to sell cooked pork products. *Sauce charcutière* is usually served with panfried pork chops.

3 tablespoons finely chopped onion *Makes about 1½ cups*
3 tablespoons finely chopped shallots
½ cup dry white wine
¼ cup wine vinegar
1½ cups Brown Sauce (see Index)
1 teaspoon Dijon mustard
1 gherkin, cut into thin strips
2 tablespoons cold unsalted butter

1. In the same skillet used to fry the pork chops, sauté the onions and shallots for about 2 minutes, or until golden. Add the wine and vinegar. Cook until the liquid has almost evaporated.

2. Add the brown sauce and cook for about 6 minutes, or until thickened.

3. Remove saucepan from the heat. Swirl in the mustard, gherkin strips, and butter in small pieces.

Sauce Diable

DEVILED SAUCE

This sauce is served with broiled chicken, squab, Cornish game hens, and other small birds.

2 tablespoons finely minced shallots *Makes about 1 cup*
½ cup dry white wine
1½ tablespoons wine vinegar
1 cup Brown Sauce (see Index)
Pinch of cayenne pepper
1 tablespoon minced fresh parsley
1 teaspoon chopped fresh tarragon, or ½ teaspoon dried
2 tablespoons cold unsalted butter
Salt and freshly ground pepper

1. Place the shallots, wine, and vinegar in a small saucepan. Reduce by half over medium heat.

2. Add the stock and reduce for another 2 or 3 minutes.

3. Just before serving, remove saucepan from the heat. Add the cayenne pepper, parsley, tarragon, and butter in small pieces. Season to taste. Swirl the pan until blended and serve immediately.

Sauce Marchand de Vin

BORDEAUX WINE SAUCE

One of the best-known and best-liked French sauces. It is served with grilled steak.

⅓ cup shallots, finely chopped   *Makes about 2 cups*
4 tablespoons unsalted butter
¾ cup plus 2 tablespoons fine Bordeaux wine
1½ cups Brown Sauce (see Index)

1. Sauté the shallots in 2 tablespoons of the butter. When golden brown, add ¾ cup wine and boil over high heat until reduced by half.
2. Add the brown sauce and cook over medium high heat, swirling the pan occasionally, for about 8 minutes.
3. Strain through a fine sieve. Swirl in the remaining 2 tablespoons butter, cut into small pieces, then add remaining 2 tablespoons wine. Serve hot.

Coulis de Tomates

TOMATO SAUCE

Tomatoes are rarely ripe and flavorful outside their short season, but canned tomatoes combined with flavoring agents will produce a fine, easily prepared tomato sauce. Of course, this sauce can be prepared the same way with fresh tomatoes.

¼ cup good-quality olive oil   *Makes about 1½ cups*
2 tablespoons unsalted butter
1 pound canned peeled tomatoes
2 tablespoons tomato paste
Salt and freshly ground pepper
Pinch of ground cloves
Pinch of sugar
Pinch of thyme
2 garlic cloves, minced
2 tablespoons minced fresh parsley

1. Heat olive oil and butter in a heavy skillet. Add the tomatoes and juice and mash with a fork. Stir in the tomato paste and season

to taste with salt and pepper, cloves, sugar, and thyme. Add garlic and parsley.

2. Cover and cook for 10 to 15 minutes. Then cook uncovered for a few minutes, until sauce reaches the right consistency. Put the sauce through a fine sieve. If the sauce is too thin, reduce over high heat. Reheat before serving.

◆　*Variation*　◆

Add 3 tablespoons of butter and ½ cup of brown sauce and use with rice or leftover meat.

◆ *Truffles* ◆

It is said about truffles that they are born during the autumn rains, especially when the thunder is frequent, as if the storm were the principal cause of their creation.
　　　　　　　—ATHENAEUS, *Deipnosophists*,
　　　　　　　Book II, third century B.C.

What causes truffles to grow is still not understood. They have been used for thousands of years in Périgord. This prized black fungus that grows underground imparts a very French flavor to any dish worthy of its addition.

Truffles are harvested from the end of November until March. They have traditionally been hunted by specially trained pigs, but today dogs are being used more frequently.

The country people of Périgord claim that good truffles "must be as black as the soul of a damned man."

Duc Jean de Berry, known for *Les Très Riches Heures* (*Book of Hours*), introduced truffles around 1375 to the court of his brother, Charles V. Truffles were previously unknown outside Périgord.

George Sand called truffles *la pomme féerique* (fairy apple), as truffles have always been associated with feasts and elegance. Though extravagant to use, and not easily available, they cannot be omitted from any French cookbook.

Sauce Périgueux

TRUFFLE SAUCE

Makes about 1¾ cups

Trimmings of truffles, or 1 ounce canned truffles
⅓ cup Madeira wine

2 tablespoons Cognac
1½ cups Brown Sauce (see Index)
Salt and freshly ground pepper
2 tablespoons unsalted butter

1. Finely chop truffles. Pour the juice from the truffle can into a small pan with the Madeira wine and the Cognac. Cook over medium heat until reduced by half.

2. Add the brown sauce. Season with salt and pepper and cook for about 8 minutes. The sauce should have the consistency of whipping cream. Swirl butter in bits just before serving.

Sauce Madère

MADEIRA SAUCE

1. Cook 3 tablespoons chopped shallots in 1½ tablespoons butter. Add ½ cup Madeira wine and reduce by half.

2. Swirl in 1½ cups brown sauce, season and cook for about 5 minutes.

3. Strain the sauce through a fine sieve. Reheat without stirring and swirl in 2 tablespoons butter, cut into bits, until dissolved.

◆ UNDER THE COOK'S HAT ◆

If the Périgueux or Madeira sauces are too thin, swirl in 1 teaspoon arrowroot stirred into 1½ teaspoons water. Stir into the sauce just long enough to blend. Cook until you reach the right consistency, swirling the pan several times. Add 1½ tablespoons Madeira wine.

◆ *White Sauce and Variations* ◆

During the reigns of Louix XIV and Louis XV it was the fashion of the aristocracy to cook and to give one's name to a new culinary creation.

Louis de Béchameil, Marquis de Nointel, a financier who brought the post of *maître d'hôtel* to Louis XIV, created this famous sauce for a turbot dish. The spelling of his name was later altered.

Here is a 1739 recipe for béchamel sauce given by François Marin in *Les Dons de Comus:*

Put in a pan, 3 or 4 butter pats, with a little parsley, chives, chopped shallots, salt, crushed pepper, a little nutmeg, some flour to thicken the sauce. Moisten with fine cream, stir on the fire to give it flavor and consistency, and use when needed.

Today the cream of the original recipe is replaced by milk and the shallots and herbs are omitted when making a classic béchamel. I prefer the extra flavor, however, and include 1 chopped shallot or ½ medium-size onion, grated, and a *bouquet garni*. Strain the sauce before using.

Sauce à la Béchamel

WHITE SAUCE

This is the mother sauce of all the white sauces.

3 tablespoons unsalted butter   *Makes about 2 cups*
3 tablespoons flour
2 cups milk
Pinch of grated nutmeg or ground cloves
Salt and white pepper
Butter

1. Melt 3 tablespoons butter in a saucepan and add the flour. Stir with a wooden spoon until bubbling and smooth.
2. Add the milk slowly, stirring briskly with a whisk. Simmer for 10 minutes, stirring occasionally. Add the nutmeg or cloves and salt and pepper to taste. Keep warm in a double boiler. Dot with butter, which will melt and prevent a skin from forming.

◆   UNDER THE COOK'S HAT   ◆

A white sauce should cook for at least 10 minutes or it will have the taste of raw flour.

The longer a white sauce is whipped or stirred, the whiter and shinier it becomes.

◆   *Variation*   ◆

SAUCE NANTUA Nantua is a city renowned for its crayfish and for this sauce, developed there. To prepare Sauce Nantua, make a white sauce and season with a pinch of cayenne pepper. Simmer for 25 minutes. Just before serving, add 5 tablespoons of crayfish butter, made following the directions for Shellfish Butter (see Index). Lobster or Shrimp Butter can be substituted; in that case, add a dash of Port or Madeira wine. If Shrimp Butter is used, add 2 drops of red food coloring for the characteristic pink color of Sauce Nantua.

Sauce Mornay
MORNAY SAUCE

This sauce was created a century ago by Joseph Voiron, chef of Le Grand Véfour, which still exists in Paris. The sauce was probably named in honor of Philippe Mornay (1549–1623), a great gastronome and friend of Henri IV.

6 tablespoons unsalted butter *Makes about 3 cups*
½ medium-size onion, grated
3 tablespoons flour
1½ cups milk, scalded
Salt and freshly ground white pepper
Pinch of cayenne pepper
2 egg yolks
½ cup heavy cream
⅓ cup grated Swiss cheese
⅓ cup grated Parmesan cheese

1. Melt 3 tablespoons of the butter in a heavy saucepan. Add the onion and sauté until wilted. Add the flour and stir until smooth. Cook over moderate heat, stirring constantly, until bubbly.

2. Remove from the heat. Add the milk and beat vigorously with a wire whisk. Add salt and peppers to taste. Return the saucepan to the stove. Continue to cook over moderate heat, stirring constantly with a whisk, until the sauce returns to the boil. Simmer for 10 minutes. Remove from the heat and cool slightly.

3. Combine the egg yolks and cream. Add to the sauce. Beat vigorously with a whisk, adding the rest of the butter a bit at a time.

4. Just before serving, *fold* in the cheese with a spatula. Do not use a whisk and do not stir, lest the cheese become stringy.

Sauce Smitane
SOUR CREAM SAUCE

This is the sauce used to accompany a coulibiac of salmon, but it is also excellent for poached fish, fish soufflé, and poached eggs. For coulibiac of chicken, substitute chicken broth for the fumet.

3 tablespoons unsalted butter   *Makes about 6½ cups*
3 tablespoons minced shallots
1 tablespoon flour
½ cup white wine
1 cup Fish Fumet (see Index) or clam juice
5 cups sour cream
Salt and pepper

1. Melt the butter and sauté the shallots until soft. Stir in the flour, then add the wine and fish fumet. Simmer for 10 minutes.

2. Strain the sauce. When lukewarm, stir in the sour cream. Season to taste. Just before serving heat the sauce in a double boiler until warm.

Sauce Soubise

ONION SAUCE

The Maréchal de France, Prince de Soubise, was a great financier and *grand intendant* at the court of Louis XIV. His chef Bertrand created this sauce for a mutton dish.

6 tablespoons unsalted butter   *Makes about 2 cups*
1½ pounds or 4 cups yellow onions, chopped
Salt and white pepper to taste
Pinch of grated nutmeg
Pinch of sugar
2 cups chicken broth
2 tablespoons flour
1 cup heavy cream

1. Melt one-half of the butter in a large skillet and cook the onions for 5 minutes, stirring occasionally. Do not let them brown. Add the salt, pepper, nutmeg, sugar, and chicken broth. Simmer uncovered for 20 minutes.

2. Melt the remaining butter in a saucepan. Mix in the flour. When bubbling, add half of the cream, stirring constantly with a whisk until thickened. Add this sauce to the onion mixture and cook until very thick.

3. Purée in a blender or food processor and reheat before serving. Add the remaining cream, if desired, for thinning.

❖ *Duxelles* ❖

La Varenne was the kitchen squire of the Marquis d'Uxelles, Maréchal de France. He was the first great chef since Taillevent to establish modern French cuisine.

La Varenne created this sauce, called *les champignons à l'olivier* in his book *Cuisinier François*, 1651. It was later that it became known as sauce d'Uxelles.

His directions say to take some mushrooms and "cut them in quarters and wash in several waters, one after another to remove the dirt. When well cleaned, place them between two plates with [sliced] onion and salt, then upon the plate warmer, in order that they may get rid of their water. Press them between the two plates. Take very fresh butter, with parsley and shallots and fricassé them. After that, let them stew, and when they are well done, you can add cream or blanc-mange."

Sauce Duxelles

MUSHROOM SAUCE

This sauce is excellent to serve on poached eggs, fish, or chicken breasts. Without the cream, this preparation is used as an addition to stuffing or to a sauce.

3 to 4 tablespoons unsalted butter   *Makes about 2 cups*
¼ cup finely minced shallots
1 small onion, finely chopped
½ pound mushrooms, finely chopped
Salt and freshly ground pepper
1 cup Crème Fraîche (see Index)
1 tablespoon finely chopped fresh parsley

1. In a skillet, sauté the shallots and onion in the butter until golden. Add the mushrooms and cook over medium-high heat until almost dry. Season to taste.

2. Add the *crème fraîche* and parsley. Simmer for 2 to 3 minutes. Serve hot.

Sauce Velouté

VELOUTÉ SAUCE

Velouté (velvety) sauce, based on stock rather than milk, is used almost as often in French cuisine as béchamel. Richer than béchamel, it too has endless variations.

4 tablespoons unsalted butter   *Makes about 2 cups*
3 tablespoons flour
1½ cups Chicken Stock or Fish Fumet (see Index), heated
Salt and freshly ground white pepper
2 egg yolks
½ cup heavy cream

1. Melt 2 tablespoons of the butter in a small heavy pan. Add the flour, stirring constantly with a wooden spoon until smooth.
2. Add the stock slowly, mixing with a whisk until the sauce thickens. Add seasonings to taste. Simmer for 10 minutes, stirring occasionally. Set aside.
3. Combine the egg yolks and cream in a small bowl. Add a little of the sauce to this mixture, stirring until well blended. Pour the cream mixture into the sauce. Cook until sauce almost reaches the boil, stirring with a whisk.
4. Remove from the heat and stir in the remaining butter.

Sauce Cardinal

LOBSTER SAUCE

This is a delicious sauce for egg dishes, for fillet of sole, or for rice pilaf with seafood.

Makes about 2 cups

1. Make a Velouté Sauce (preceding recipe) with Fish Fumet. Add a pinch of cayenne pepper and 1 tablespoon flambéed Cognac.
2. Just before serving, stir in 5 tablespoons Lobster Butter (see Index) and ⅓ cup finely diced cooked lobster meat. Add 1 tablespoon finely chopped truffles if desired.

◆   *Variation*   ◆

Sauce Crevette (Shrimp Sauce) can be made in the same way. Simply substitute shrimp for the lobster.

Sauce Normande

Makes about 1⅔ cups

Make a Velouté Sauce (see Index) with 1 cup of Fish Fumet (see Index) or oyster liquor or clam juice. Add ¼ cup mushroom broth. Finish the sauce with ⅓ cup heavy cream.

To make mushroom broth: Chop about ¾ cup mushroom stems coarsely. Sauté in butter for 1 minute. Add ⅓ cup water, a little lemon juice, and salt and pepper. Cover and simmer for 6 to 8 minutes. Strain.

Sauce Joinville

JOINVILLE SAUCE

This fish sauce was dedicated to the Prince de Joinville, the third son of King Louis Philippe. Joinville was the commander of the ship that brought Napoleon's remains from St. Helena back to France.

Makes about 2 cups

Make a Sauce Normande (preceding recipe) with Fish Fumet (see Index). Finish the sauce with 3 tablespoons each of Crayfish Butter and Shrimp Butter, made according to directions for Shellfish Butter (see Index). Add a truffle, cut into fine julienne, to the sauce.

◆ *Béarnaise* ◆

Sauce béarnaise was created by Maître Colînet at Saint-Germain-en-Laye on the outskirts of Paris. It was served for the first time in 1861 at the hotel-restaurant Le Pavillon Henri IV.

Henri IV was born in the province of Béarn. He held the title of Viscount of Béarn and often went to the Château Neuf in Saint-Germain-en-Laye with Marie de Médicis. It was one of his favorite residences; it is now part of Le Pavillon Henri IV.

Sauce Béarnaise

BÉARNAISE SAUCE

This classic sauce is a royal accompaniment for grilled meats such as filet mignon, chicken, fish, and egg dishes.

Makes about 1½ cups

½ pound unsalted butter, cut into 16 pieces, at room
    temperature
1½ tablespoons finely chopped shallots
⅓ cup French white-wine vinegar
1 tablespoon fresh tarragon, or 2 teaspoons dried
1 tablespoon minced fresh chervil
Salt and freshly ground white pepper
2 tablespoons cold water
4 egg yolks

1. In a heavy-bottomed saucepan, melt 1 tablespoon butter. Add the shallots and cook over low heat until shallots are very soft but not colored.

2. Add the vinegar, 1½ teaspoons each of tarragon and chervil, and salt and pepper to taste. Reduce to 1 teaspoon. Off the heat, add the cold water and the egg yolks and mix quickly with a whisk.

3. Place the saucepan over very low heat and keep whisking for a few minutes, until mixture is thick enough so the bottom of the pan stays visible for a brief moment when the mixture is whisked. Do not let the egg yolks become hot or they will curdle.

4. Remove saucepan from the heat and add the rest of the butter, 1 tablespoon at a time, beating continuously with the whisk. When the sauce has the consistency of mayonnaise, add the remaining tarragon and chervil. If the sauce is too thick, add 1 teaspoon or more of water. Set the saucepan in a shallow pan of warm water until ready to use.

♦ *Variation* ♦

SAUCE CHORON, a tomato-flavored Béarnaise sauce, was created a century ago by Choron, one of the celebrated chefs of the Paris restaurant Voisin. It is used on fish, broiled meat, and vegetables.

Add thickened Tomato Sauce (see Index) equal to one-quarter the volume of the Béarnaise Sauce.

Sauce Maître d'Hôtel
LEMON AND HERB BUTTER SAUCE

Monsieur Baleine, of the famous restaurant Le Rocher de Cancale in Paris, was the first to create and serve this sauce with fish in 1906. He served it warm with grilled mackerel.

Serve with grilled or poached fish.

6 ounces unsalted butter *4 servings*
2½ tablespoons lemon juice
1½ tablespoons minced fresh parsley
Salt and finely ground white pepper

1. Slowly melt the butter in a saucepan. Remove from heat.
2. Add lemon juice, parsley, and salt and pepper to taste. Serve immediately.

♦ *Beurre Blanc* ♦

Beurre blanc was created by accident. Around 1900, Clémence, the excellent cook of the Marquis de Goulaine, asked one of her helpers to make a béarnaise sauce. The helper forgot to add the egg yolk. The Marquis tasted it, liked it, and baptized it *beurre blanc*. This regional sauce of Anjou, which often embellishes pike and shad dishes, became famous when La Mère Clémence was innkeeper at Saint-Julien-de-Concelles near Nantes.

Beurre Blanc
WHITE BUTTER SAUCE

This sauce from the Loire Valley takes only a few minutes to prepare. It is an exquisite accompaniment for freshwater fish such as bass, halibut, or salmon that have been poached in a wine court-bouillon, as in Fish in Court-Bouillon (see Index).

2 tablespoons chopped shallots   *4 servings*

¼ cup good French white-wine vinegar

¼ cup dry white wine (Muscadet or wine of the Loire)

¼ cup Court-Bouillon (see Index) or cooking juice strained from fish

1½ sticks (6 ounces) unsalted butter, cut into small pieces, at room temperature

Salt and white pepper

1. Combine the shallots, vinegar, wine, and court-bouillon in a small thick-bottomed saucepan. Bring to a boil, then reduce to 3 tablespoons of liquid.

2. When the liquid is tepid, add small pieces of the butter. Stir with a small whisk off the heat. Put the pan on and off low heat so the butter does not liquefy. Continue beating until the sauce is thick and creamy.

3. Add salt and pepper to taste. Serve the sauce separately or pour over the fish.

Sauce Hollandaise

HOLLANDAISE SAUCE

This sauce of melted butter and lemon juice was known in Holland for a very long time as a simple sauce for fish. When the Huguenots lost their freedom of worship in 1685, with the Revocation of the Edict of Nantes, some escaped to Holland. They liked this sauce and brought it back to France. The French gave it a touch of their own by adding egg yolks, but the name remained *la sauce hollandaise*.

5 egg yolks, without any trace of egg white   *Makes about 2 cups*

⅓ cup cold water

Salt

2½ sticks (10 ounces) unsalted butter, clarified (see Index)

Lemon juice

White pepper

Pinch of cayenne pepper

1. Beat the egg yolks with a whisk for 1 minute.

2. Place water and salt to taste in a small heavy pan set on a Flame-Tamer over low heat, or into the top pan of a double boiler set over hot water in the lower pan. Add the yolks and beat with

the whisk until they thicken. For safety's sake, keep a little cold water near at hand; if the sauce shows any sign of curdling from too high heat, add 1 tablespoon cold water and beat vigorously.

3. Add the clarified butter slowly, a little at a time, until all is absorbed. Immediately remove the pan from the heat and add a sprinkle of lemon juice and seasonings to taste. Hollandaise sauce is served warm, never hot.

◆   U N D E R   T H E   C O O K ' S   H A T   ◆

For a foolproof hollandaise sauce, add ¼ teaspoon cornstarch or arrowroot to the cold water. The starch prevents the eggs from curdling.

For all the sauces based on hollandaise sauce, such as mustard, anchovy, and curry sauces, reduce 3 tablespoons white wine and 2 tablespoons wine vinegar to 1 tablespoon. Add to the cold water before making the hollandaise sauce.

Sauce Mousseline

MOUSSELINE SAUCE

Especially delicious with poached fish or asparagus.

For Mousseline Sauce, make a hollandaise sauce as in the basic recipe. At the last minute, add ½ cup heavy cream that has been firmly whipped. The cream fluffs up the hollandaise sauce like a mousse. Correct seasoning.

Sauce Moutarde

MUSTARD HOLLANDAISE

Mix 2 tablespoons Dijon mustard, or to taste, with 1 tablespoon dry white wine. Stir into 2 cups of hollandaise sauce.

Sauce aux Anchois

ANCHOVY HOLLANDAISE

Stir 1 teaspoon anchovy paste, or to taste, into each cup of hollandaise sauce.

Sauce au Curry

CURRY HOLLANDAISE

To 1 cup hollandaise sauce, add ¼ teaspoon curry powder, or to taste, while adding the butter to the sauce.

This sauce may be served on poached eggs, or as an accompaniment to a soufflé, or with a chicken and rice dish.

Sauce Crevette

SHRIMP SAUCE

Make half a recipe of the Hollandaise Sauce (see Index), substituting Shrimp Butter (see Index) for the unsalted butter. Add a few finely chopped shrimp just before serving.

Sauce Bâtarde

BÂTARDE SAUCE

This is an economical approximation of a hollandaise sauce.

8 tablespoons unsalted butter *Makes about 1½ cups*
1½ tablespoons cornstarch
1 cup warm water
Salt and freshly ground white pepper
3 egg yolks
Lemon juice or vinegar

1. Melt 2 tablespoons of the butter. Stir in the cornstarch, then add the water a little at a time. Stirring constantly, cook for about 1 minute, until thickened.

2. Season with salt and pepper. Add the egg yolks and stir vigorously. Do not boil.

3. Remove from heat and add remaining 6 tablespoons of butter. Finish the sauce with a sprinkle of lemon juice or vinegar to taste.

◆ UNDER THE COOK'S HAT ◆

If preparing this sauce for asparagus, use 1 cup of the water in which the vegetable was cooked.

For fish, use 1 cup of Fish Fumet (see Index). The sauce will be similar to a sauce normande.

◆ *Mayonnaise* ◆

Mayonnaise was the creation of the cook of the Duc de Richelieu and was served for the first time in 1756.

There are many stories concerning the origin of the name "mayonnaise." According to one version, it was named by the Duc de Richelieu after the 1756 capture of Port Mahon, the capital of the island of Minorca. Originally the sauce was spelled "mahonnaise." Others feel that its name comes from *moyeu*, which meant egg yolk in medieval French.

Sauce Mayonnaise

MAYONNAISE

3 egg yolks, at room temperature   *Makes about 1½ cups*
½ teaspoon Dijon mustard
Pinch of salt
Freshly ground black pepper or cayenne
1½ cups peanut oil, or olive or vegetable oil, or a combination
     of the last two, at room temperature
2 teaspoons French wine vinegar, or lemon juice, or both
1 tablespoon boiling water

1. With a small whisk, beat together the egg yolks, mustard, and salt and pepper to taste in a bowl until thickened and firm.

2. Add the oil almost drop by drop at first, then in a very thin stream, stirring vigorously until all the oil is added. Halfway along, when the mayonnaise is very thick, add the vinegar or lemon juice.

3. To stabilize the emulsion, stir in 1 tablespoon of boiling water at the end.

◆ UNDER THE COOK'S HAT ◆

The oil and the egg yolks must be at the same temperature; the success of the mayonnaise depends on this. If the oil is too cold, place the container under hot water. If the egg yolks are too cold, put them in a bowl, set it in a pan of hot water, and stir until the yolks seem to be at the same temperature as the oil.

Mayonnaise should be creamy, never firm. Add 1 tablespoon of water if it seems too stiff.

The addition of 2 teaspoons of Cognac gives the mayonnaise zest.

◆   *Variations*   ◆

MAYONNAISE CHANTILLY Add stiffly whipped heavy cream to a well-seasoned, freshly made mayonnaise. The cream should equal one-third of the volume of the sauce. It is appropriate with cold fish, artichokes, asparagus, and cauliflower.

ANCHOVY MAYONNAISE Combine 1½ cups mayonnaise with 3 teaspoons anchovy paste and 2 teaspoons lemon juice. Mix thoroughly. Serve with hard-cooked eggs, watercress sandwiches, or potato salad.

AÏOLI is a wonderful sauce for boiled codfish; or serve it with boiled beef and vegetables as they do in Provence. Make a firm mayonnaise with French olive oil, omitting the mustard. Place 2 chopped garlic cloves in the blender. Add the mayonnaise and blend until smooth. Add an additional teaspoon of lemon juice and some chopped tarragon—not traditional but tasty.

MAYONNAISE SMITANE is used on a fruit salad. Combine equal amounts of mayonnaise and sour cream. Season to taste with Dijon mustard. Stir in 1 tablespoon of defrosted pineapple-juice concentrate.

Mayonnaise Collée
ASPIC MAYONNAISE

Mayonnaise with the addition of gelatin is known as *collée* (glued) because it retains its shape well for molded salads and decorative garnishes.

1½ tablespoons unflavored gelatin   *Makes about 2 cups*
½ cup Beef Stock (see Index)
1½ cups freshly made Mayonnaise (see Index)

1. Soften the gelatin in the beef stock. In a small saucepan, bring to the boiling point. Remove from the heat. Cool until syrupy.

2. Combine the dissolved gelatin with the mayonnaise, beating until it has the consistency of heavy cream.

Use at once for molded salads, such as Mixed Vegetable Salad (see Index), or chill for decorative purposes.

Sauce Mayonnaise Verte

GREEN MAYONNAISE

This sauce was created in 1855 by Balvay, chef to Napoleon III.

1 tablespoon minced fresh parsley   *Makes about 1 cup*
1 tablespoon minced fresh chervil
½ tablespoon minced fresh tarragon, or 1 teaspoon dried
1 tablespoon snipped fresh chives
½ tablespoon capers, steeped in vinegar
1 cup freshly made Mayonnaise (see Index)
1½ tablespoons lemon juice
1 or 2 drops of green food coloring

1. In a food processor or blender, chop all the herbs and capers into a fine purée. Add the mayonnaise, lemon juice, and food coloring, and blend well.

Sauce Mayonnaise à la Tomate

TOMATO-FLAVORED MAYONNAISE

Delicious over shrimp, hard-cooked eggs, or cold macaroni, with a sprinkle of chopped parsley. For cold poached fish, add ½ cup sour cream to the sauce.

1 medium-size onion, finely minced   *Makes about 1½ cups*
1 tablespoon unsalted butter
2 tablespoons olive oil
2 large ripe tomatoes, peeled, seeded, and cubed
1 garlic clove, minced
Salt and pepper
Pinch of cayenne pepper
Pinch of saffron (optional)
1 cup freshly made Mayonnaise (see Index)
Dash of lemon juice

1. Sauté the onion in butter and oil until lightly colored.

2. Add the tomatoes, garlic, and seasonings to taste. Cook for about 15 minutes, or until all liquid has evaporated and the mixture becomes a thick purée. Press it through a fine-mesh sieve.

3. When cooled, stir into the mayonnaise. Add lemon juice.

Sauce Rémoulade

RÉMOULADE SAUCE

Sauce rémoulade is a very old French sauce, described in *Les dons de Comus* by François Marin, 1739, among 92 other sauces. Its base then was a vinaigrette, as mayonnaise was only two years old and not yet widely used. With the mayonnaise base, it is even better. This is the perfect sauce for boiled fish or hard-cooked eggs.

1 cup freshly made Mayonnaise (see Index)   *Makes about 1¼ cups*
1 tablespoon finely snipped chives
1 teaspoon finely chopped fresh tarragon, or ½ teaspoon dried
1 tablespoon finely chopped fresh chervil or parsley, pressed in
    a towel
2 tablespoons finely chopped sour dill pickles
1 teaspoon capers, finely cut
1 teaspoon Dijon mustard
½ teaspoon anchovy paste
Lemon juice
Salt and white pepper

1. Combine first 7 ingredients. Add the anchovy paste, or more to taste, and lemon juice and seasoning to taste. Blend well. Let stand for several hours before serving.

5. *Les Oeufs, les Soufflés, et les Crêpes*
EGGS, SOUFFLÉS, AND CRÊPES

⚜ ⚜ ⚜

Since earliest times, eggs have been symbolic. The philosophers of antiquity looked upon the egg as a symbol of the world and the four elements. The shell represented the earth; the white symbolized water; the yolk stood for fire; and air was found under the shell.

One of the pagan customs was to give eggs, colored red, to parents and friends for good luck because, supposedly during the third century, a chicken in the palace laid a red egg on the day that the Roman emperor, Alexander Severus, was born.

Later, during the Middle Ages, most eggs given at Easter were tinted red in memory of the blood of the Christian martyrs. This custom of tinting eggs dates to the time of Louis IX (Saint Louis) in the thirteenth century, when both religious and mystic practices were followed.

Eggs would be brought to the churches to be blessed the day before Easter, before being given as gifts to friends and relatives.

They were especially welcome at that time because Christians were not allowed to eat eggs during Lent.

It was also during that period that they made sure that the shell was broken after eating the egg so as to prevent an evil spirit from using it as shelter.

Several centuries later, on Easter day after High Mass, Louis XV distributed engraved and decorated eggs of great value to his favorite courtesans. The tradition of distributing eggs was continued at Versailles by Louis XVI. After the King had washed the feet of twelve children, commemorating the Last Supper, he had the eggs distributed with great ceremony.

The original egg "holder" was a thick piece of bread with a hole cut out of the middle for supporting the egg. In the sixteenth century the bread was replaced by an oval-shaped, metal egg holder with small handles. A large hole was made in the center of the egg and it was eaten by dipping buttered *nouillettes*, pieces of bread shaped like fingers, into it.

Sometimes Louis XV would eat in public at the Louvre, a custom much to the liking of the Parisians. The King had such a knack of opening a boiled egg with a fork that the performance would bring admiration from onlookers. One of the King's attendants, a "gentleman usher," would always announce the event: "Attention! The King is going to eat his egg."

In France eggs are rarely served for breakfast but are most often served as a first course at luncheon or dinner, or as the main dish. Since eggs are usually eaten by themselves, they must be very carefully and beautifully prepared.

Oeufs Pochés

POACHED EGGS

1. Fill a large frying pan or a shallow pot with water. Add 2 tablespoons of vinegar.

2. When the water is barely simmering, break 1 egg at a time into a cup and slip the egg gently into the water. Gather the egg white around the yolk with a spoon. When all the eggs are in the water, bring to a simmer again and cook for 3½ to 4½ minutes, or until the egg yolks are set but not hard.

3. Transfer the eggs to a bowl of hot water to keep them warm until serving time, or place in cold water if they will be served cold.

◆ UNDER THE COOK'S HAT ◆

To prevent eggs from sticking to the pan and to facilitate the cleanup, rub the pan with butter before adding the water.

The shells of fresh eggs are tough and chalky in appearance. Old ones are smooth and shiny.

Oeufs à l'Indienne

CURRIED EGGS ON CANAPÉS

Serve for a delicious, simple luncheon.

4 commercial patty shells, defrosted   *8 servings*
8 eggs
4 tablespoons unsalted butter
1 tablespoon finely minced onion
5 tablespoons flour
2 cups Beef Stock or Chicken Stock (see Index)
2 teaspoons curry powder
Salt
4½ ounces cream cheese, or Petit-Suisse

1. On a lightly floured surface, roll each patty shell into an oval 4 by 6 inches. Bake on an ungreased cookie sheet in a preheated 400°F. oven for 15 to 20 minutes, or until golden.

2. Poach the eggs in simmering water for exactly 6 minutes. Immerse immediately in warm water to keep them from cooling off.

3. Make a curry sauce: Melt the butter and sauté the onion until golden. Add the flour and stir well before adding the stock, curry powder, and salt to taste. Simmer, stirring, until thickened. Add the cream cheese and simmer for 5 to 10 minutes.

4. Split the pastry horizontally. Place 1 egg on each piece of pastry. Spoon the curry sauce over the eggs. Serve immediately.

◆ UNDER THE COOK'S HAT ◆

For serving in quantity, place all the pastry, topped by the eggs and the curry sauce, on an ovenproof serving dish. Place it under the broiler for 1 to 2 minutes to glaze without coloring.

A thin slice of ham or prosciutto, arranged on the pastry before adding the egg, will make this dish more substantial.

Oeufs Gratinés Lapérouse

EGGS AU GRATIN LAPÉROUSE

1 recipe Mushroom Purée (see Index) *4 servings*
8 eggs
Hollandaise Sauce (see Index)
Parmesan cheese, grated

1. Make Mushroom Purée.
2. Poach the eggs in simmering water for exactly 6 minutes.
3. Spread the mushroom mixture in the bottoms of 4 ovenproof gratin dishes. Arrange 2 eggs in each dish. Cover with hollandaise sauce and sprinkle with Parmesan. Glaze briefly under the broiler.

◆　◆　◆

The eleventh century was a period of much religious fasting. When the fast was over, the first meal taken was called *déjeuner* (out of fast), the word still used for the first meal of the day.

Croûte Savoyarde

SAVOYARDE CROÛTE

6 eggs *6 servings*
6 slices of sandwich bread
Butter
1 cup grated Gruyère cheese
2 cups sour cream
1 egg, lightly beaten
Salt and freshly ground pepper
Nutmeg
2 tablespoons dry Chablis wine
6 slices of Polish ham or prosciutto

1. Poach the eggs and transfer them to a large bowl of hot water.
2. Remove the crusts from the bread, and then fry each slice in butter.
3. Mix the cheese with the sour cream. Add the beaten egg, salt and pepper and nutmeg to taste. Heat slowly, but do not boil or the sauce will disintegrate.
4. Place the fried bread slices in individual ovenproof dishes and sprinkle each slice with 1 teaspoon wine. Cover with the ham slices.

5. Pat the eggs dry with a towel and place on top of the ham. Cover with the cream sauce.

Serve with Chablis wine.

Oeufs à la Portugaise

PORTUGUESE-STYLE EGGS

8 eggs, in the shell   *6 servings*
1 onion, finely minced
1½ tablespoons unsalted butter
1½ tablespoons olive oil
4 tablespoons tomato paste with 2 or 3 tablespoons water
2 cups White Sauce (see Index)
1 cup grated Swiss Gruyère cheese
1 cup raw, unconverted rice, cooked

1. Cook the eggs in simmering water for 6 minutes. The center should be slightly runny, or as it is called in French, *mollet.*

2. Sauté the onion in the butter and olive oil until golden. Stir in the tomato paste and 2 or 3 tablespoons water, and cook for about 1 minute. Remove from the heat. Add the white sauce and fold in half of the Gruyère cheese.

3. Cover the bottom of a buttered ovenproof dish, such as a buttered fluted white porcelain quiche pan, with the rice. Spoon a little of the sauce onto the rice.

4. Shell the eggs. Cut them into halves and place them, cut side down, on the rice. Cover with the rest of the sauce and sprinkle cheese on top. Place under the broiler until golden.

Oeufs sur le Plat à la Tomate

SUNNY-SIDE-UP EGGS WITH TOMATO SAUCE

Tomato Sauce (see Index)   *3 servings*
6 eggs
Fresh parsley, minced

1. Cover the bottom of 3 shallow ramekins with tomato sauce.

2. Break 2 eggs into each dish. Bake in a preheated 350°F. oven for 6 to 7 minutes. Sprinkle with parsley.

Serve with French bread and a rosé wine.

Oeufs au Plat Façon du Belley

SUNNY-SIDE-UP EGGS AU GRATIN

8 tablespoons unsalted butter   *4 servings*
8 eggs
8 tablespoons heavy cream
Swiss cheese, freshly grated
Salt

1. Melt the butter in a heavy skillet and break the 8 eggs into it. Cook over medium-low heat until almost set. Remove from the stove.

2. Pour 1 tablespoon heavy cream over the yolk of each egg and sprinkle generously with freshly grated Swiss cheese.

3. Set the skillet in a shallow pan filled with hot water. Place under a preheated broiler and glaze the eggs until golden. Sprinkle with salt.

Muscadet wine would be excellent to serve, along with crusty French bread.

• *Scrambled Eggs* •

La Varenne listed sixteen recipes for scrambled eggs in *Le Pâtissier François* (1653), which shows that they have always been a French favorite. Variations of *oeufs brouillés* were made with cucumbers, mushrooms, and cheese. One unusual recipe was for *oeufs mignons* made with meat broth, crushed macaroons, candied lemon peel, sugar, salt, rosewater, and hypocreas wine.

The art of making scrambled eggs is reflected by the seriousness of this comment from Jean Jacques Barthélemy, the author of *Voyage du jeune Anacharsis en Grèce*, who wrote in 1771: "Madame Lauzun is going tomorrow. Do you know that no one in France possesses to a higher degree, a quality that you do not know, that of making scrambled eggs. It is a hidden talent. She does not remember the time when she received it. I believe that it was at birth."

Oeufs Brouillés

SCRAMBLED EGGS

Scrambled eggs are rarely well prepared. They are either over-cooked or too runny. The secret of creamy scrambled eggs the way the French like them is very slow cooking.

12 eggs   *4 servings*
Salt
3 tablespoons unsalted butter
2 to 3 tablespoons heavy cream

1. Break the eggs into a bowl and beat with a fork until thoroughly mixed, but not frothy. Season lightly with salt.
2. Place the eggs in the top pan of a double boiler set over 2 inches of simmering water in the bottom pan. The top pan should not touch the water. Stir constantly until the eggs begin to set. Add the butter in small pieces. Add the cream and cook until eggs are creamy and moist.
3. Serve immediately in warmed individual porcelain egg dishes, garnished with triangular toasts or with a few Puff Pastry Crescents (see Index). Or serve in a flaky pastry shell or brioche warmed.

◆ *Variations* ◆

Oeufs Brouillés au Parmesan SCRAMBLED EGGS WITH PARMESAN   Add ½ cup freshly grated Parmesan cheese to the eggs when almost set.

Oeufs Brouillés à l'Ancienne OLD-FASHIONED SCRAMBLED EGGS   Sauté 1 cup finely chopped mushrooms and 1 chopped shallot in 1 tablespoon melted butter. Add ½ cup finely diced ham, 2 tablespoons minced fresh parsley or chervil, 1 tablespoon snipped fresh chives, and 1 teaspoon minced fresh tarragon (½ teaspoon if dried). Add to the eggs when almost set.

Oeufs Brouillés Cannelons SCRAMBLED EGGS WITH TRUFFLES   For an elegant start for a meal, serve the scrambled eggs in tartlets of puff pastry. Flavor the eggs with finely chopped truffles or sprinkle the truffles on top.

◆ *Omelet* ◆

The word *omelette* is derived from the word *alemette*, an old French word for knife blade, reflecting the omelet's shape, with its curved edge and flat appearance.

The first omelet we know of was made by the Roman general Lucullus in 80 B.C. It was made with an ostrich egg and was stuffed with pheasant or some other minced meat. The Romans also liked omelets sweetened with honey.

The omelet is much loved in France and ranges from the simple *omelette paysanne* to the elegant *omelette soufflée*. Written record has it that Louis XIII invaded the kitchen of his beautiful Château d'Amboise in Touraine once when hunting to make himself an onion omelet; Henri IV's favorite dish was an omelet stuffed with garlic; and the duc d'Orléans, father of King Louis Philippe, preferred *omelettes royales*, which cost a fabulous price because the ingredients included pheasant eggs, *fumet* of rare venison, *coulis*, and truffles.

Today most Frenchmen prefer *omelette baveuse* (drooling omelet) —golden on the outside and slightly runny inside. Much practice is necessary to make an omelet properly; unfortunately, too often a mass of leathery eggs is served. If you are really serious about learning the technique, buy several dozen eggs and try until you feel the technique has been mastered.

For those unable to succeed, console yourselves with the remark of the famous chef Boulestin: "Some people are born omelet makers, some are not."

The celebrated Mère Poulard made omelets to serve as quick, hot meals for the visitors to Mont-Saint-Michel around 1875. She always made omelets on a bright oak wood fire in a long-handled omelet pan. La Mère Poulard had a well-kept secret for preparing her famous omelets. At a dinner party for her son in August 1890, she revealed it to his friends. She expertly incorporated a big spoonful of the delicious *crème fraîche* from Normandy into the eggs, just before folding the omelet.

The inscription on her tomb in a small Mont-Saint-Michel cemetery reads:

ICI REPOSENT
VICTOR POULARD ET ANNETTE POULARD
BONS ÉPOUX, BONS HÔTELIERS
DAIGNE LE SEIGNEUR LES ACCUEILLIR
COMME ILS REÇURENT LEURS HÔTES.

HERE LIE
VICTOR POULARD AND ANNETTE POULARD
GOOD SPOUSES, GOOD INNKEEPERS
MAY THE GOOD LORD WELCOME THEM
AS THEY WELCOMED THEIR GUESTS.

Omelette
OMELET

5 eggs, at room temperature   *2 servings*
1 to 2 tablespoons water or heavy cream
Salt and freshly ground pepper
3 tablespoons unsalted butter

1. *Battre les oeufs en omelette* refers to the particular technique of beating eggs with a fork underneath the surface of the liquid, which avoids making bubbles. Using this method, beat the eggs, water or cream, and salt and pepper to taste in a bowl. Do not overmix.

2. Heat the omelet pan, then add the butter. When the butter stops making tiny bubbles, add the eggs all at once in the center of the pan. Let stand for about 30 seconds, or until eggs start to set at the edges.

3. With a fork lift the edges toward the center, and tilt the pan to let the egg mixture run under. Do this step all around the edges. Shake the pan frequently to prevent the batter from sticking to it. When set but still very moist, leave the omelet on high heat for a few seconds to turn the bottom golden brown. Add desired filling.

4. Carefully slide the omelet from the pan onto a warm serving plate. Using a quick motion of the wrist, turn the pan over so the omelet is folded in half. The whole operation must be done rapidly.

◆ UNDER THE COOK'S HAT ◆

To give a shiny look to an omelet, place a very cold piece of butter on the prongs of a fork and brush all over the omelet just before serving.

◆   *Variations*   ◆

The imaginative cook can make innumerable kinds of omelets. Leftovers such as ratatouille, creamed spinach, or ham purée make excellent fillings. Omelets can be made quite elaborately by adding different fillings and using such sauces as Mousseline, Mushroom, or Tomato. All directions are based on a 5-egg omelet unless otherwise specified.

Omelette aux Champignons MUSHROOM OMELET   Sauté ½ pound sliced mushrooms with 1 tablespoon minced onion and shallots combined in 3 tablespoons butter until the mixture sizzles. Sprinkle with lemon juice, salt, pepper, and 1 tablespoon chopped parsley. Add to the omelet when ready to be folded. Garnish with a few sprigs of watercress. A colorful addition: Serve Tomatoes with Garlic and Bread Crumbs (see Index).

Omelette aux Croutons OMELET WITH CROUTONS   This recipe is from a cookbook published in 1789—*La Science du Maître d'Hôtel Cuisinier*. Trim the crusts from 2 slices of good-quality sandwich bread and cut into small cubes. Sauté in 2 tablespoons clarified butter, tossing the croutons in the pan until golden. Prepare the omelet and add the croutons when the eggs begin to set.

Omelette aux Fines Herbes HERB OMELET   Beat 2 teaspoons each of finely chopped fresh parsley, chives, chervil, and tarragon (½ teaspoon if dried) into the omelet mixture before cooking. Sprinkle the finished omelet with additional chopped parsley.

Omelette à la Tomate TOMATO OMELET   Peel, seed, and chop 3 large ripe tomatoes. Sauté in 3 tablespoons hot olive oil until soft. Add salt, pepper, a pinch of sugar, 1 minced garlic clove, and some chopped parsley. Cover and cook slowly into a thick purée, for about 20 minutes. Spoon the purée over the center of the omelet when it is ready to be folded. Garnish with watercress.

Omelette des Moissonneurs ONION OMELET   In Provence, specially at harvesttime, this onion omelet is served cold to the workers in the field at noon break. It is also perfect to take along on a picnic.

For 8 eggs, slowly sauté 1 or 2 large Bermuda onions (about 1 pound), thinly sliced, in olive oil. When golden brown, incorporate them into the omelet mixture before cooking.

Omelette aux Crevettes S H R I M P   O M E L E T   Sauté 1 cup shelled small fresh shrimps and 1 tablespoon minced shallot in 2 tablespoons butter, just until shrimps turn pink. Add seasoning to taste, ½ tablespoon Cognac or whisky, and ⅓ cup *crème fraîche* to the mixture. Add to the omelet when it is ready to be folded.

Omelette à la Paysanne C O U N T R Y - S T Y L E   O M E L E T   A great way to use leftover roasted potatoes. Sauté ⅓ cup diced bacon or ham in butter until golden. Add ¼ cup minced onion and sauté until soft. Add 1 cup diced potatoes and sauté until golden brown. Mix into the omelet batter with 1 tablespoon each of chopped parsley and snipped chives. This omelet is not folded, but turned onto a warm round serving dish.

Omelette Monselet is stuffed with diced artichoke bottoms, truffles, and cream.

Omelette diplomate is filled with diced lobster and truffles, and covered with Mornay sauce.

Omelette aux pointes d'asperges was created by the royal cook of Louis XV for Madame Du Barry. Asparagus tips are blanched in boiling water, then cooked in butter before being added to the omelet.

Pipérade Basquaise
BASQUE-STYLE OMELET

Pipérade is a specialty of the Basque region in the Southwest of France, where goose fat and olive oil are extensively used in cooking. This variety of omelet is not folded but turned over onto a serving plate.

STUFFING   *3 servings*
2 green peppers
2 tablespoons goose fat or olive oil
3 firm ripe tomatoes, peeled, seeded, and cut into wedges
1 garlic clove, minced
Salt and pepper
4 thin slices of Bayonne or other raw ham, cut into strips
   (if available)

FOR OMELET
2 tablespoons goose fat or olive oil
1 tablespoon unsalted butter
1 garlic clove, split
6 eggs, lightly beaten
Salt and pepper
Fresh parsley, chopped

1. Split the green peppers lengthwise. Remove all the stems, seeds, and thick white ribs. Place peppers under the broiler for a few minutes until the skin blisters and becomes slightly blackened. Peel off the skin and cut the peppers into very thin, long strips.

2. Heat 2 tablespoons goose fat or olive oil in a skillet until hot. Add the tomatoes, garlic, and salt and pepper to taste. Cook over high heat for 2 or 3 minutes, stirring occasionally. The tomatoes must not become a purée, only softened. Remove from the heat and set aside.

3. Melt 2 tablespoons goose fat or olive oil and butter in the omelet pan with the split garlic clove. Swirl the pan around until the fat stops bubbling and is ready for the eggs. Remove the garlic at once and pour in the eggs. Let them stand for 1 minute before adding the tomatoes, green peppers, and ham. Stir gently. Do not overcook as the eggs should remain soft. Season to taste.

4. When the eggs are ready, do not disturb for about 1 minute. If the eggs stick to the pan, loosen them with a large spatula and slip a piece of butter underneath. Turn the omelet onto a warm round plate. Garnish with parsley. Serve immediately on hot plates.

A dry white Jurançon wine is a good choice with this dish.

Omelette Chasseur

CHICKEN-LIVER AND MUSHROOM OMELET

¼ pound fresh tiny button mushrooms   *4 servings*
2½ tablespoons unsalted butter
2 shallots, finely minced
⅓ cup plus 2 tablespoons Madeira wine
1 tablespoon tomato paste
1 cup Brown Sauce (see Index)
½ teaspoon arrowroot
5 chicken livers, each cut into 3 or 4 pieces
Generous amount of fresh thyme

½ teaspoon minced fresh tarragon, or ¼ teaspoon dried
2 tablespoons chopped fresh parsley
8 eggs
Fresh parsley, chopped

1. Sauté the mushrooms in 1 tablespoon of the butter over medium-high heat for 2 or 3 minutes, or until they sizzle. Add the shallots and stir well before adding ⅓ cup Madeira. Cook over high heat until reduced to 1 tablespoon.
2. Combine the tomato paste, brown sauce, and arrowroot, mixing well. Add to the mushrooms and cook for about 5 minutes.
3. Sauté the chicken livers in remaining 1½ tablespoons of butter in a skillet for 2 to 3 minutes. Transfer to the mushroom sauce and add the herbs. Deglaze the skillet with remaining 2 tablespoons Madeira; add the deglazing to the sauce.
4. Cook the omelet. Before folding, place two-thirds of the filling along the center. Use the remainder to garnish the finished omelet. Sprinkle the top with chopped parsley.

◆　◆　◆

When Jean-Jacques Rousseau was served an omelet, he exclaimed: "Ah! If I had known that we were having an omelet, I would have made it myself, because I am an expert."

Omelette Lorraine
LORRAINE OMELET

8 thin slices of bacon, cut into ½-inch pieces   *3 or 4 servings*
8 eggs
½ cup heavy cream
1 tablespoon chopped fresh parsley
1 teaspoon chopped fresh tarragon, or ½ teaspoon dried
Salt and freshly ground pepper
1 tablespoon unsalted butter
½ cup paper-thin slivers of Gruyère cheese

1. Cook the bacon in a skillet until golden but not too crisp. Remove with a slotted spoon. Reserve the fat.
2. Mix together the eggs, cream, herbs, and seasonings to taste.
3. Melt the butter in an omelet pan and add 2 tablespoons of bacon fat. Pour in the omelet batter and cook. Halfway through the

cooking time, sprinkle cheese and bacon on top. Serve immediately.

◆   UNDER THE COOK'S HAT   ◆

If any egg remains stuck to the omelet pan, pour a little oil along with some coarse salt into pan, then rub with a paper towel.

◆　◆　◆

This excellent advice from La Varenne's cookbook, *Le Vray Pâtissier François* (1667), still holds true today:

> One must have a skillet which is used only for omelets and is not scrubbed, but only well wiped off . . . salted butter makes them liable to stick to the skillet and never makes such a beautiful omelet as fresh butter.

SOUFFLÉS
⚜ ⚜ ⚜

The art of soufflé making is only about 200 years old, since modern ranges were introduced in 1789. The first soufflé was probably served at La Grande Taverne de Londres, 26 rue de Richelieu in Paris—the first restaurant as we know them today, with individual tables, silver, linen, and menus. It was opened in 1782 by Antoine Beauvilliers, who was a great restaurateur. He wrote a remarkable cookbook, *L'Art du cuisinier* (1814), containing the first recipe for a soufflé.

The first soufflés were made with a concentrated purée of pheasant, woodcock, or poultry and were served as the main course, or entrée.

Soufflé means "blown or puffed up" in French, a very descriptive word for this dish.

To produce a perfect soufflé, well risen, light as a feather, with a golden crust quivering over a creamy center, is the ambition of every good cook.

A soufflé consists of two parts: first, the foundation sauce, with egg yolks to give the necessary consistency to the soufflé and its flavoring agents (cheese, vegetables, meat, or fish); second, the egg whites, which give the soufflé its feathery quality.

Here are a few rules to observe for a perfect soufflé:

• A good recipe will add no more than 1 or 2 extra whites in proportion to the egg yolks, or the result will be a soufflé that is tight and dry.

• Beating egg whites in a copper bowl with a large balloon whisk gives the best results. This method will produce egg whites of surprising lightness, as the copper seems to give more volume and stability to them. Or use a hand eggbeater and a china or pottery bowl. Never use an electric mixer or the egg whites will be too tight and solid, or they become *grainé* (turned), which means that there is a layer of unbeaten egg whites under the mass of beaten egg whites. Start all over again.

• The egg whites are ready as soon as small peaks stand firmly upright when the whisk is lifted up.

• If they lose their shine, you have overbeaten them and a coarser soufflé will result.

• The mixing of egg whites and foundation is crucial to make a soufflé rise.

Thoroughly mix about one-quarter of the egg whites into the foundation sauce. Add the rest of the egg whites and, with a large flat rubber spatula, fold this mixture down, up and over, turning the bowl counterclockwise. Do this step quickly. You will get a better volume because the whites have not been broken down by overfolding.

• Fill the soufflé dish to within ½ inch of the top. This will give a high, puffy soufflé.

• The base of a soufflé can be made hours before baking. Reheat to lukewarm before folding in the egg whites.

• When serving more than 6 portions, it is better to make 2 soufflés instead of a single large one. A smaller soufflé will rise higher.

• A good soufflé should be creamy in the center. If you are not sure that the soufflé is ready, insert a long metal knitting needle or a skewer to see if it is still runny or if it has become creamy. Do not let it become dry.

• If the soufflé has to wait for a few minutes, place a cake cover over it.

• The heat distribution is very important for making a soufflé. When preheating the oven, place a large cookie sheet on the middle rack. Bake the soufflé on the cookie sheet.

• To clean a copper bowl, place 1 tablespoon coarse salt and a little vinegar in it. Scrub with a paper towel, then wash with soap.

• Remember this axiom: "A soufflé can be waited for but must never wait."

Soufflé au Fromage
CHEESE SOUFFLÉ

4 tablespoons unsalted butter   *4 servings*
2 tablespoons flour
2 tablespoons potato starch
2 cups milk
Salt and white pepper
Pinch of grated nutmeg
Pinch of cayenne pepper
5 eggs, separated
2 cups Swiss cheese or 1 cup Parmesan and 1 cup Swiss cheese,
     grated

1. Preheat the oven to 375°F. Generously butter a 1½-quart soufflé dish.

2. Melt the butter in a saucepan and stir in the flour and potato starch with a wooden spoon until blended. Add the milk, stirring vigorously with a whisk until thick and smooth. Season with salt, pepper, nutmeg, and cayenne pepper. Remove from the stove and let cool slightly.

3. Add 1 egg yolk at a time, stirring well between each addition. Fold in the cheese.

4. Whip the egg whites until stiff. Fold one-quarter of the volume into the cheese base. Quickly fold the cheese base into the remaining egg whites. Spoon into the soufflé dish.

5. Place the soufflé dish on a 12-inch baking sheet on the middle rack of the oven. Bake for 25 to 30 minutes until golden brown, and serve immediately.

◆   *Variation*   ◆

Use Sauce Soubise (see Index) as a base, adding an extra tablespoon of flour, and omitting the second half cup of cream.

Soufflés d'Huîtres
OYSTER SOUFFLÉS

This soufflé is always a hit, a perfect preface to an elegant dinner. It is most attractive when baked directly in scallop shells.

24 shucked oysters, plus the oyster liquor   *6 servings*
Milk
2 tablespoons unsalted butter
3 tablespoons flour
Salt
Cayenne pepper
⅓ cup freshly grated Parmesan cheese
3 whole eggs, separated
1 extra egg white

1. Preheat oven to 375°F. Simmer the oysters in their liquor in a saucepan for exactly 2 minutes. Drain the liquor into a measuring cup. Add enough milk to make 1 cup.

2. Melt the butter in a saucepan. Add the flour, stirring well for 1 minute. Add the oyster-milk liquid, whisking until very thick. Do not boil. Season with salt and cayenne pepper.

3. Fold in the Parmesan cheese. Remove the pan from the heat and add the egg yolks, beating well after each addition.

4. Beat the egg whites until stiff. Fold one-quarter of the whites into the soufflé batter thoroughly. Pour this mixture carefully back into the remainder of the whites, folding gently and quickly.

5. Butter 6 scallop shells. Divide half the batter among the shells, leaving an inch free around the border of each shell for expansion.

6. Pat the oysters dry with a towel. Place 3 or 4 oysters on top of the batter in each shell. Cover with the remaining batter, in the shape of a dome.

7. Place shells on a baking sheet in the preheated oven for 15 to 18 minutes, or until puffed and golden. Serve with Sauce Normande or Mousseline Sauce (see Index).

Soufflé d'Epinards
SPINACH SOUFFLÉ

4 tablespoons unsalted butter   *6 servings*
1 medium-size onion, grated
1 garlic clove, minced
1 cup cooked leaf spinach (fresh or frozen), squeezed dry
Salt and pepper
White Sauce, made with 1¾ cups milk (see Index)
½ cup grated Gruyère cheese
Pinch of ground cloves
8 eggs, separated

1. Melt the butter in a skillet. Add the grated onion and garlic and cook until soft. Stir in the spinach and cook for 2 or 3 minutes or until all moisture has evaporated. Season with salt and pepper.

2. Purée spinach in a blender with the white sauce, cheese, and cloves. Transfer to a large bowl. Beat the yolks well, and add to the purée.

3. Whip the egg whites until stiff. Fold one-quarter of the volume into the spinach base. Fold in the rest of the egg whites with a large spatula. Spoon into a buttered 2-quart soufflé dish.

4. Place the soufflé dish on a 12-inch round baking sheet set on the middle rack of a preheated 375°F. oven. Bake for 35 to 40 minutes; the center should remain creamy. Serve immediately.

◆   *Variation*   ◆

Use 1½ cups of any kind of cooked, flaked fish mixed with the soufflé base. Serve with a sauce crevettes or Mousseline (see Index).

C R Ê P E S

⚜ ⚜ ⚜

Crêpes, one of the best-loved French culinary delicacies, are one of the most famous specialties of Brittany, where they originated.

In a letter to a friend, Leonardo da Vinci mentioned how he enjoyed crêpes served at the court of François I. Crêpes were probably introduced there by Yves de Kerdevot, whose father had been page to the Duchess Anne of Brittany.

Crêperies—seen all over Brittany—are small restaurants where only crêpes and cider are served. The Breton crêpes are made with buckwheat flour and served plain with butter or sometimes with a sprinkling of grated Swiss cheese. Crêpes made with wheat flour are usually spread with jam and flavored with Cognac or rum. However, their fillings can be as varied as the cook's imagination.

In France, crêpes are traditionally served for Candlemas (February 2) and Mardi Gras (Shrove Tuesday). On New Year's Day, there is an old custom of tossing a crêpe high in the air while holding a coin in your hand. If you catch the crêpe while still holding the coin, you will not lack in money for the rest of the year.

Crêpes are fun to make and are very versatile. With different fillings, crêpes can be an appetizer, a meal, or a dessert. (See also hors-d'oeuvre and dessert chapters.)

In Brittany, a *galichon* is a crêpe that is too thick or misshapen. The last crêpe, or *galichon,* often incomplete for lack of batter, is usually given to the dog.

Crêpes
CRÊPES

Crêpes should be as thin as you can possibly make them. The number of crêpes this recipe will yield depends on your skill at making them paper-thin.

3 whole eggs   *Makes 16 to 18 crêpes*
1 extra egg yolk
¾ teaspoon salt
1½ cups milk
½ cup water
5 tablespoons unsalted butter, melted until tepid
1 tablespoon oil
1¼ cups flour

1. With a hand eggbeater, lightly beat together all the ingredients except the flour. Sift the flour into a large mixing bowl. Make a well in the center. Slowly pour in the batter, and with a whisk stir the flour gradually into the liquid until all has been absorbed. Beat until smooth but do not overbeat or the crêpes will be rubbery once cooked.

2. Strain the batter through a fine sieve. Let stand at room temperature for 1 hour.

3. Heat a 7-inch crêpe pan over medium-high heat. If a few drops of water dropped on the pan sizzle and evaporate immediately, the pan is ready to use.

4. Pour about 2½ tablespoons of batter from a ladle into the pan, tilting pan quickly in a circular motion to cover the surface evenly with a thin layer. When the edges are golden brown, in about 1 minute, flip the crêpe or turn over with a round-edged metal spatula. Cook for 20 to 30 seconds, or until speckled golden brown. Turn crêpes onto a warm plate, one on top of another, and cover.

◆ UNDER THE COOK'S HAT ◆

The speckled side of the crêpe should be on the outside when the crêpes are folded.

If crêpes have a filling, cook the crêpes only on one side, unless they are coated with a sauce. When placed under the broiler, they will brown on the other side.

To toss a crêpe: Be sure the crêpe is moving freely in the pan. Raise the skillet firmly above the heat and shake the pan forward and up, then backward to catch the crêpe as it falls back into the pan.

Mark a soup ladle with a scratch to show the batter level for each crêpe. It saves time and the crêpes will be of a uniform size.

To reheat a stack of crêpes, place them on a plate and cover with another plate. Warm briefly over simmering water.

A crêpe pan should be made of cast iron, 7 to 9 inches in diameter, with a heavy bottom and a ½-inch-high rim. Treat your crêpe pan with care. When new, scrub it thoroughly with a soap pad, rinse, and dry. Place over high heat for 1 minute. When cool, rub the inside with a little oil. Always leave a film of oil in the pan to prevent rust when storing. Clean any batter stuck to the pan by rubbing with a little oil and coarse salt, with paper towels.

On hot days, leave the butter out of the batter. Refrigerate the batter for an hour, then bring it to room temperature and add the butter before proceeding with the cooking.

◆ *Variations* ◆

Crêpes are an ideal way to use leftover fish, poultry, vegetables, and sauces, such as creamed spinach, ratatouille, or Mornay sauce. The filling should not be so overpowering that it kills the delicate flavor of the crêpes.

Crêpes Fourrées aux Oeufs Brouillés au Parmesan CRÊPES STUFFED WITH PARMESAN SCRAMBLED EGGS For these crêpes, add 1 tablespoon snipped fresh chives, 1 tablespoon minced parsley, and nutmeg to taste, to give additional delicious flavors as well as color to the batter.

For 6 to 8 crêpes, lightly scramble 12 eggs with 3 tablespoons butter, 2 to 3 tablespoons heavy cream, and ¼ cup freshly grated Parmesan cheese. Place 3 tablespoons of this mixture along the center of each crêpe, roll, and arrange in a buttered baking dish. Dot with butter and sprinkle with Parmesan. Place under the broiler for 1 minute to glaze. A tomato sauce would be a fine addition.

Crêpes aux Crabes C R A B - M E A T   C R Ê P E S   These crêpes should be cooked on one side only. Combine crab meat with Hollandaise Sauce flavored with tarragon, and lemon juice or Bâtarde Sauce made with Fish Fumet or clam juice (see Index). Place 3 tablespoons filling per crêpe on the browned side, roll, and arrange side by side in a buttered baking dish. Brush the crêpes with melted butter and sprinkle with freshly grated Parmesan cheese. Pass under the broiler until lightly golden.

Crêpes à la Reine C H I C K E N   C R Ê P E S   Make a double recipe of Bâtarde Sauce (see Index). Add ½ cup sautéed mushrooms, 3 tablespoons sherry, and ½ cup heavy cream, whipped. Reserve one-quarter of the sauce, then combine the remainder with 2 cups cooked and diced chicken, turkey, or Cornish game hen. Add filling to crêpes, roll, and arrange in a buttered baking dish. Cover with the reserved sauce and ¼ cup freshly grated Parmesan cheese. Broil until lightly golden, about 1 minute.

Another variation is to use two parts Hollandaise Sauce (see Index) combined with one part whipped heavy cream before mixing with the chicken.

The poultry can be kept hot in a little chicken stock before folding it into the sauce.

Crêpes Forestière M U S H R O O M   C R Ê P E S   Make Mushroom Purée (see Index). Place about 3 tablespoons of the purée in a row down the center of each crêpe. Place side by side on a hot serving dish. Brush with melted butter. Sprinkle a little chopped fresh parsley over the crêpes.

Ficelles Picardes C R Ê P E S   P I C A R D Y   S T Y L E   This specialty of the province of Picardy is called *ficelle*, "string," because these crêpes, although quite large, are very thin once rolled.

A thin slice of ham is laid on top of each crêpe, then spread with a filling of Mushroom Purée (see Index), and rolled. Just before serving, Crème Fraîche (see Index) is spread on top with a sprinkling of freshly grated Parmesan cheese. Arrange in a buttered baking dish and glaze under the broiler.

6. *Les Poissons* FISH

⚜ ⚜ ⚜

In the hands of an able cook, fish can become
an inexhaustible source of delight.
—BRILLAT-SAVARIN

France is bounded by water on three sides and has numerous rivers crossing its landscape. Therefore, a great variety of fresh fish is available and the French have as many exciting ways to prepare it as they have for preparing meat.

Fish became important in France largely because of the strict observance of fasting during the early Middle Ages. Charlemagne sentenced to death those who ate meat during Lent or on fast days (then Wednesdays and Fridays).

In the year 1000, after many years of debilitating wars, France was at last prosperous and at peace. In thanksgiving, a council added Saturdays to the list of fast days. In 1549 a decree from Henri II prohibited the sale of meat during Lent to anyone who could not produce a doctor's certificate.

Many books have been written about fish cookery. Even Apicius, the celebrated Roman epicure, wrote two books on the subject: *The Sea* and *The Fisherman*.

The Romans brought fish from the sea, some distance away, by relay teams. Some fish were snow-packed in silos and others were mounted on sticks and preserved by a special drying process. Fish dried by this method are still eaten today, especially in Nice and the South of France.

Under the Directoire (1795–1799), an edict gave women the exclusive right to sell fish at Les Halles in Paris. These women were ironically named "Les Dames de Les Halles" and were famous for their crude and colorful language. There was a formal obligation for a fishwife to pass on to her daughter the privilege of a place at Les Halles. This custom was strictly observed until World War I, but today as many men as women are in evidence there.

◆ *How to Select Fresh Fish* ◆

• Absolute freshness and best quality are essential.
• The eyes should be clear and sparkling, protrude slightly, and fill the sockets.
• The flesh should be elastic and firm to the touch.
• The gills should be bright red.
• The aroma should be fresh and reminiscent of an ocean tide, with no ammonia or fishy odor.

Use sea salt, pulverized in a blender, for seasoning fish.

Usually a dry white wine is served with fish, but a fruity, medium-dry white wine should be served when fish is accompanied by a sauce.

Fumet de Poisson

FISH FUMET

This rich *fumet* serves as a liquid for poaching fish, and as a base for fish sauces and soups.

3 tablespoons unsalted butter   *Makes about 1½ cups*
1 medium-size onion, finely chopped
3 shallots, finely chopped
4 parsley sprigs
½ bay leaf
1½ pounds fresh lemon sole or flounder bones and trimmings,
    cut into pieces (without the gills)
6 ounces excellent dry white wine
1½ cups water
Salt
6 white peppercorns, crushed

1. Melt the butter in an enamelware or stainless-steel saucepan. Add the onion, shallots, parsley, and bay leaf. Cook for 5 minutes, then add the fish bones and trimmings. Cover and barely simmer for 5 minutes.

2. Add the white wine. (Use only 3 ounces of wine if the *fumet* is for soup.) Cover and simmer for 3 minutes, then add the water. Add salt to taste and the peppercorns. Bring to a boil and simmer gently, partially covered, for 20 minutes.

3. Strain through a *chinois* or a colander lined with cheesecloth. Store in a glass jar under refrigeration.

◆   U N D E R   T H E   C O O K ' S   H A T   ◆

Although it is preferable to make it fresh, you can freeze the *fumet* in an ice-cube tray. Place the cubes in a plastic bag to have available for any fish sauce.

Poissons au Court-Bouillon

FISH IN COURT-BOUILLON

This is the classic French recipe for the preparation of any freshly caught large fish: salmon, trout, sea bass. The fish is completely submerged in a flavored court-bouillon.

2 to 3 quarts water, or enough to cover the fish
2 onions, sliced
2 carrots, sliced
3 parsley sprigs
Coarse salt or sea salt
Coarsely ground peppercorns
2 to 3 cups dry white wine
½ bay leaf
Freshly caught fish
2 sprigs of fresh or dry thyme (not ground)

1. Combine the first 8 ingredients and boil gently for 40 minutes. Strain and cool until liquid is tepid. Correct seasoning.

2. Add the fish and bring to a boil, then barely simmer for 8 to 10 minutes for 1½ to 2 pounds fish, 15 minutes for a 4-pound fish, and 20 minutes for a 6-pound fish.

3. Remove the skin from the cooked fish while it is warm. Garnish with sprigs of parsley and thin slices of grooved lemon. Serve a sauceboat of Hollandaise, Mousseline, or Bâtarde Sauce made with the court-bouillon.

If the fish is to be served cold, shorten the cooking time and cool the fish in the court-bouillon. Chill thoroughly and serve with a sauceboat of Mayonnaise Chantilly (see Index for sauces).

Filets de Poisson en Papillote

FISH FILLETS EN PAPILLOTE

Softened unsalted butter   *4 servings*
2 pounds fish fillets
Melted butter
1 lemon, thinly sliced
Anchovy Butter (see Index)

1. Cut 4 large pieces of parchment or aluminum foil. Coat generously with butter.

2. Brush the fillets with melted butter. Place each portion on a piece of the parchment or foil. Top with 2 thin slices of lemon. Carefully fold the parchment or foil together, then double-fold the edges, making a sealed envelope, or *papillote*.

3. Bake in a preheated 450°F. oven until well puffed, about 15 minutes. To serve, place each *papillote* on a plate and let each diner

open his individual portion. Cut around 3 sides of the *papillote* within the folded edge and turn the top layer over. Serve with anchovy butter.

• *Quenelles* •

The well-known Roman epicure Apicius, born around 25 B.C., in one of his ten books on food mentioned quenelles made with crustaceans: lobsters, oysters, and shrimps. Quenelles became fashionable in France when Catherine de Médicis introduced them; these were made with poultry.

Later, the famous pike quenelles were invented by Bontemps, chef to Maréchel Jeannot de Moncey (1754–1842), whose statue stands on Place Clichy in Paris. Bontemps's quenelles became a specialty in Franche-Comté and are now also a great specialty of Lyon and Nantua. The old saying, "The sauce makes the fish," is especially appropriate for quenelles, as otherwise they would be quite bland.

Quenelles de Poisson
FISH QUENELLES

Delicate and light, quenelles are poached and usually served with Nantua sauce. For an elegant dinner, serve them in a pie shell of Puff Pastry, coated with a sauce (Nantua, Lobster, or a Velouté with tiny shrimps and sliced mushrooms), and then glazed under the broiler.

¾ cup milk   *4 servings*
7 tablespoons unsalted butter
¾ cup flour
2 eggs
1 pound pike, sole, haddock, cod, salmon, or shellfish, dressed
    and boned
2 egg whites
1 tablespoon Cognac
Salt and white pepper
Nutmeg
1 cup heavy cream

1. Start with the *panade* or flour mixture. Bring the milk and 3 tablespoons of the butter to a boil. Off the heat, add the flour all at

once, stirring well. Cook, stirring vigorously, until the mixture leaves the sides of the pan. Beat in the eggs, one at a time, and the other 4 tablespoons butter. Chill thoroughly.

2. Cut the fish into small pieces. Purée the fish in small quantities in a blender or food processor until smooth. Combine with the *panade*.

3. Add the egg whites, one at a time, beating well with a spoon after each addition. Add the Cognac, seasonings to taste, and half of the cream. Purée the mixture through a food mill or food processor. Add remaining cream, stirring until smooth. The mixture should hold its shape. Cover and chill until ready to be used.

4. Test the mixture for texture and seasoning by dropping a walnut-size ball into boiling water to poach for a few minutes. If too soft, and the ball disintegrates, add another egg white. If the mixture is too firm, add more cream.

5. Mold the quenelles, using 2 large deep soup or serving spoons. Dip one spoon into hot water, fill with the mixture, and mold it into an egg shape. Dip the second spoon into hot water and remove the mixture from the first spoon. Place the quenelle in the bottom of a buttered deep skillet. Make a single uncrowded layer of the quenelles.

6. Gently pour enough boiling salted water into the skillet, around the quenelles, to cover them. Bring the water almost to the boiling point and gently boil; in 10 to 12 minutes the quenelles will puff and rise to the surface. Remove carefully with a slotted spoon and drain on a towel.

7. Arrange quenelles while still hot in a warm serving dish. Pour the Sauce Nantua (see Index) or other appropriate sauce over them.

If quenelles are not used immediately, chill them. Reheat in hot water until just warmed, drain, and serve.

◆   *Variation*   ◆

For *quenelles gratinées* (made preferably with salmon or shellfish), place the quenelles in a buttered gratin dish. Cover with Mornay Sauce (see Index). Sprinkle with equal quantities of grated Swiss and Parmesan cheeses. Bake in a preheated 400°F. oven for 20 minutes. Serve immediately, while still puffed.

◆   ◆   ◆

There is a well-known but sad fish story related by Madame de Sévigné in one of her famous letters. In 1671 Vatel, the *maître d'hôtel* of the Prince de Condé, was in charge of a feast held in honor of Louis XIV. There were almost 3,000 guests invited. When an insufficient amount of fish was delivered, Vatel felt his honor was tarnished and fell on his sword.

Shortly afterward, the rest of the fish arrived.

Coquilles de Poisson
FISH IN SCALLOP SHELLS

4 servings

1. Season a large halibut steak, or a similar firm-fleshed fish, with salt and pepper and a little lemon juice. Simmer the fish in butter without browning.

2. When fish flakes with a fork, remove and cool to room temperature. Cut into bite-size pieces.

3. Mix fish with a Green Mayonnaise, Mayonnaise Chantilly, or Tomato-Flavored Mayonnaise (see Index). Divide among 4 scallop shells, each lined with a Boston lettuce leaf. Serve chilled, with a little minced fresh parsley or snipped chives on top.

◆ *Brandade of Salt Cod* ◆

One of the famous dishes of Provence and Languedoc is a purée of salt cod, seasoned with olive oil, garlic, and truffles. Nîmes is as famous for this codfish purée as Marseilles is for bouillabaisse. Charles Durand, a great chef of the eighteenth century and author of an outstanding cookbook, *Le Cuisinier Durand* (1830), created this specialty for his restaurant in Nîmes. He called it *Morue à la Branlade*. *Brandade* comes from an old French word, *brandir*, "to shake," because the pan was almost continuously shaken.

He advised that after two days of soaking the salt cod in four or five changes of water, the fish should be placed in a pan of fresh water and brought almost to a simmer. The cod should be removed immediately, the bones discarded, then the fish placed in a pan with the juice of a lemon.

> Crush the flesh with a wooden spoon held in your right hand while with the left, you turn the pan vigorously. During this step, another person will pour the oil drop by drop onto the cod, which will bind and thicken it. Then you will pour on a little boiling milk or water, and continue to work it until reduced to a paste. This result obtained, mix in the slices of truffles and serve hot.

Durand advised that the preparation must never boil and the wooden spoon should be used only to scrape the mixture off the sides of the pan. If the cod is too oily, 2 or 3 potatoes mashed with milk could be added.

Durand added an interesting variation which is called *Morue à la Brandade en pierres à fusil*. Besides the sliced truffles, he added anchovy, orange peel, parsley, and a little garlic, all finely chopped and sautéed in oil for 2 minutes.

Brandade de Morue
PURÉE OF SALT COD

Brandade can be served hot or cold as an *hors-d'oeuvre*.

1 pound salt cod   *3 servings*
1 large potato
1 garlic clove, finely minced
1 cup olive oil
1 cup warm heavy cream
Salt (if necessary)
Generous amount of white pepper
Small triangular croutons, fried in olive oil

1. Soak the cod in several changes of cold water for 24 hours to remove salt. Cut into large pieces.
2. Boil the potato and peel off the skin.
3. Poach the cod in simmering water for 10 minutes after the water starts to simmer. Drain and remove all bones and skin.
4. Mash the cod in a mortar or bowl with the potato and garlic. Add the olive oil little by little, alternately with heavy cream, until the mixture develops the consistency of mashed potatoes. Season.
5. Reheat over low heat. Arrange on a serving dish in the shape of a dome. Tuck the fried croutons all around the rim.

◆   ◆   ◆

During the Middle Ages, Basque fishermen found their cod supply along the Atlantic coast dwindling. Their search for new fishing grounds took them as far as Iceland and Nova Scotia, and salting preserved their catch until they returned home.

Salting evidently became a well-established habit, because today, even with an abundance of fresh fish, the taste for salted fish remains strong, and it is found in many of the favorite recipes of Provence.

Fresh cod is called *cabillaud* and salt cod is called *morue*.

Maquereaux Grillés Maître d'Hôtel

GRILLED MACKEREL WITH LEMON AND HERB BUTTER SAUCE

The savory mackerel is available year round but is at its best from April to June.

1. Ask the fish market to cut off the heads, remove the scales, gut and dress the mackerel. Make an incision along the backbone of each fish. If the mackerel is large, have it split and boned.

2. Season with salt and pepper. Brush all over with melted butter. Rub the grill with oil and preheat under the broiler for 5 minutes.

3. Broil the fish on the oiled grill for about 5 minutes on each side, or until done. Decorate with lemon slices and serve with a Lemon and Herb Butter Sauce (see Index) and parsley potatoes.

◆ *Variation* ◆

Halibut and salmon steaks are excellent prepared in the same way.

◆ ◆ ◆

Talleyrand, the famous diplomat whose full name was Charles-Maurice de Talleyrand-Périgord, was equally well known as an epicure. His table was the best in France during the Directoire period because he gave the great Carême every chance to display his culinary genius.

Talleyrand asked Louis XVIII for more "pots and pans than written instructions" because he believed that gastronomy was the best possible weapon in diplomacy.

One day Talleyrand, who had a predilection for showing off his magnificence, received two superb salmon of unusual size as a present from Chevet, the purveyor of the Palais-Royal. Talleyrand decided to have them served at a dinner party.

When the *maître d'hôtel* opened the door and two waiters entered bearing one enormous salmon on a silver tray, all the guests were very impressed and full of compliments. Unfortunately, one of the

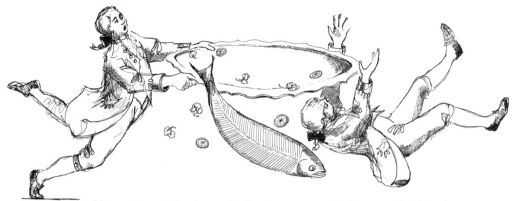

waiters slipped and the beautiful salmon went along with him down to the floor.

The guests gasped but Talleyrand calmly said, "Bring in another one." And the second giant salmon was brought in—to the amazement of the guests.

The scene had been carefully prearranged by Talleyrand.

Coulibiac de Saumon
SALMON PÂTÉ

Coulibiac is a Russian pâté served in France at festive and elegant parties. It has become part of the classic French cuisine and is an ideal entrée for summer evenings.

It is made with brioche or puff pastry filled with salmon, kasha, or bulgur wheat, replaced here with rice, mushrooms, hard-cooked eggs, and herbs. Sour Cream Sauce or Mousseline Sauce is the usual accompaniment.

2 pounds fresh salmon, sliced   *Serves 8 to 10*
10 tablespoons unsalted butter
1¼ cups Fish Fumet (see Index) or clam juice
2 large onions, finely chopped
¾ pound mushrooms, thinly sliced
1 tablespoon shallots, minced
2 tablespoons flour
½ cup heavy cream
Salt and pepper
⅔ cup raw unconverted rice, cooked in chicken broth
3 hard-cooked eggs, coarsely chopped
¼ cup fresh parsley, chopped
½ cup scallions, finely cut
1 recipe of Puff Pastry (see Index)
Glaze: 2 egg yolks beaten with 1 tablespoon of water

1. Cook the slices of salmon in a large skillet in 4 tablespoons of butter and half of the *fumet* until almost done. Reserve the *fumet* for the sauce.

2. Cook the onions in 4 tablespoons of butter and when wilted, add the mushrooms. Cook briefly and then cool.

3. Make a binding sauce as follows: Melt 2 tablespoons of butter and add the shallots. When wilted, stir in the flour, then add the rest of the *fumet* and the heavy cream. Season and cook until thickened. Let it cool.

4. Combine the salmon, cut into chunks, rice, hard-cooked eggs, mushrooms, parsley, scallions, and binding sauce.

5. Roll the puff pastry into two large thin rectangles, one slightly larger than the other. Let the dough rest for 30 minutes. Transfer the smaller rectangle onto a large baking sheet.

6. Pile the salmon mixture in the shape of a loaf about 5½ inches wide by 2½ inches high, in the center of the dough, leaving a 2-inch border all around. Place the second rectangle of dough on top, smoothing it over the filling. With a sharp knife, trim the edges, leaving 1½ or 2 inches of dough all around. Roll the two layers of dough-edging tightly together toward the pâté. With the blunt edge of a knife, make regular indentations in this roll of crust.

7. Brush the pâté covering with the glaze. Be careful not to let it drip onto the baking sheet. Then make an attractive crisscross design on the dough with the blunt edge of a knife blade, being careful not to break through the dough; or place moistened cutouts of pastry on the surface. Glaze. Puncture the dough with a fork in 4 or 5 places to let the steam escape while baking.

8. Bake the pâté in a preheated 425°F. oven for about 40 minutes, or until golden brown. Place a piece of foil loosely on top if it browns too fast.

9. Transfer to a large silver plate or tray. Garnish the corners with watercress or parsley. Serve with 2 sauceboats of Sauce Smitane (see Index).

◆ UNDER THE COOK'S HAT ◆

The salmon mixture and puff pastry can be prepared a day ahead.
   Slice the pâté using a knife with a serrated edge.
   Alsatian wine or rosé wine is perfect with this dish.

◆ *Variation* ◆

COULIBIAC OF CHICKEN Coulibiac of chicken is prepared

the same way as coulibiac of salmon. Poach the chicken in chicken broth flavored with tarragon. Use the broth for cooking the rice.

Saumon à la Gelée

SALMON IN ASPIC

4½ pounds whole fresh salmon, scaled and dressed *8 servings*
Court-bouillon (see Index for Fish in Court-Bouillon)
1 tablespoon unflavored gelatin
Few saffron threads for color
Truffles or fresh tarragon leaves (optional)
Parsley
Mayonnaise Chantilly (see Index)

1. Wrap the salmon in a double thickness of cheesecloth, then place in a fish poacher or a large roasting pan.
2. Add the court-bouillon and bring almost to a boil, using two burners for even cooking. Reduce the heat and simmer for 35 to 40 minutes, about 8 minutes per pound. Let the salmon cool in the court-bouillon. Reserve and strain the court-bouillon.
3. Place the fish on a rack over a tray. Discard the cheesecloth. Remove the skin and scrape off any dark gray flesh. Keep the head and tail intact.
4. Soften the gelatin in ½ cup court-bouillon. In a saucepan heat 1 cup court-bouillon and the saffron to boiling, then add to the gelatin mixture. Stir until gelatin is dissolved. Cool over a bowl filled with ice.
5. When the aspic is syrupy, brush over the salmon. Chill. Decorate with truffles or blanched tarragon leaves. When the first coat of aspic is firm, brush on a second coat, then chill the fish. If the aspic sets before the second coat has been added, set the pan in a bowl of hot water for a few seconds. Add a final coat of aspic.
6. Transfer the salmon to a large serving dish or silver tray. Serve with Mayonnaise Chantilly. A Mixed Vegetable Salad (see Index) is a perfect accompaniment.

◆   UNDER THE COOK'S HAT   ◆

For additional garnish, make aspic with the rest of the court-bouillon. Finely chop the aspic and pipe it out from a pastry bag fitted with a large round nozzle, around the salmon. Garnish with parsley and tomatoes stuffed with Mixed Vegetable Salad (see Index).

Mousse de Saumon

SALMON MOUSSE

This perfect summer dish can be made a day ahead.

10 tablespoons unsalted butter, softened   *4 or 5 servings*
2 tablespoons minced shallot or onion
⅓ cup dry white wine or vermouth
1 cup clam juice
1¼ pounds fresh salmon
Salt and white pepper
1 tablespoon unflavored gelatin
2 tablespoons flour
2 drops of red food coloring
1 tablespoon lemon juice
¾ cup heavy cream

1. In an enamelware pot, melt 2 tablespoons of the butter and sauté the shallot for 1 minute. Add the wine, clam juice, salmon, and salt and pepper to taste. Simmer for 10 to 12 minutes. Let the salmon cool in the court-bouillon.

2. Reserve the court-bouillon. Remove the skin and bones from the fish. Mash the fish with a fork. With your hands, blend 6 tablespoons butter with the fish to make a smooth purée.

3. Prepare the sauce: Soften the gelatin in the court-bouillon. In a saucepan, melt 2 tablespoons butter. Add the flour, mixing well. Add the gelatin mixture. Whisk until it almost reaches a boil. Remove from the heat and add the food coloring and lemon juice. Set the saucepan in a larger pan filled with ice cubes and whisk until the sauce thickens.

4. Add the salmon purée to the sauce. Whip the cream until stiff and blend into the purée.

5. Spoon the mixture into a lightly oiled 6-cup mold and chill for at least 12 hours. For serving, unmold on a chilled plate.

♦   UNDER THE COOK'S HAT   ♦

Some serving suggestions: Combine Mousseline Sauce (see Index) with 1 tablespoon Cognac and 1 tablespoon minced parsley. Garnish with lettuce or watercress sprinkled with lemon juice. Arrange mounds of Mixed Vegetable Salad (see Index) around the mousse.

Alternate asparagus tips with tomato wedges. Serve in individual ramekins, garnished with cutouts of truffles and covered with aspic.

Remember that cold dishes need more seasoning than hot dishes.

Sole à la Meunière

FRIED SOLE

A *meunière* is a woman who tends the windmills that grind flour. The use of the word for this recipe developed because the fish is dipped into flour before being cooked. This is one of the finest ways of cooking sole because it seals in the delicate flavor. It is suited for small fish or for slices of larger ones.

2 pounds sole fillets   *4 servings*
Salt and pepper
½ cup flour
Clarified butter for sautéing fish
3 tablespoons unsalted butter
Lemon juice
Chopped parsley
Lemon wedges or thin slices of grooved lemons

1. Season the fillets on both sides. Sift salt and pepper and flour onto a sheet of wax paper. Coat both sides of the fillets, shaking off excess flour.

2. Sauté fillets in clarified butter until golden on both sides. Shake the pan often to make sure the fish does not stick. Transfer to a warm serving dish.

3. Add the 3 tablespoons unsalted butter to the same pan and cook until it becomes light brown or the *noisette* stage, smelling of nuts. Pour over the fish. Sprinkle lightly with lemon juice and chopped parsley. Serve immediately with lemon wedges or surround with grooved lemon slices.

Sole Bercy

SOLE WITH WINE SAUCE

Sole Bercy takes its name from a district of Paris known for its wine trade.

9 tablespoons unsalted butter   *2 servings*
1½ tablespoons finely chopped shallots
1 pound sole fillets
Salt and white pepper
½ cup dry white wine
Lemon juice
2 teaspoons flour
Parsley sprigs

1. Generously butter a shallow ovenproof dish that is just large enough for the fillets. Sprinkle the shallots on the bottom of the pan. Season both sides of the sole fillets with salt and white pepper, and arrange fish on the shallots.

2. Pour wine over the fish and sprinkle with lemon juice. Dot with about 3 tablespoons butter, then cover the dish with foil. Bake in a preheated 400°F. oven for 15 to 20 minutes, or until done to your taste.

3. Strain the cooking liquid into a small pan. Cover the sole and keep warm in a low oven. Mash 2 teaspoons flour with 1 tablespoon butter. Reduce the cooking liquid over medium-high heat to ¾ cup. Add any other liquid the sole may have rendered in the baking dish. Beat in the butter-flour mixture (*beurre manié*). When sauce is thickened, remove from the heat. Whisk in the remaining 4 tablespoons butter, cut into small pieces. Correct the seasonings if necessary.

4. Pour the sauce over the sole and glaze briefly under the broiler without browning. Decorate with parsley.

◆   *Variation*   ◆

Add ½ cup Hollandaise Sauce (see Index) to the sauce before glazing. A few sliced mushrooms cooked in butter are a fine addition.

◆ *Sole Marguery* ◆

Filets de Sole Marguery is an outstanding recipe for fish from the classic French repertoire.

Nicholas Marguery was born in Dijon in 1834. He was an illustrious chef and owner of the famous restaurant Marguery, 34 boulevard Bonne-Nouvelle, in Paris. More than 6,000 people attended his funeral in April 1910.

This is the original recipe from Monsieur Mangin, head chef at Marguery for more than 30 years.

Our sole owes its popularity as much to the logic of its creation as to the use of the choicest ingredients.

Fillet 2 beautiful soles of the most absolute freshness. With the bones, make a *fumet* of fish. Garnish with a soupçon of minced onion, a sprig of thyme, half a bay leaf, and a sprig of parsley.

Season with salt and pepper, then moisten with dry white wine, chosen from the best.

Let this *fumet* reduce and add it to the cooking liquor of a quart of mussels prepared according to the customary formula. Meanwhile, place the fillets of sole ready and flattened on a buttered baking sheet. Season and sprinkle them with the aforementioned *fumet*. Cover them with a greased sheet of paper and poach them in the usual way. Drain and lay them in an oval dish. Surround them with a double string of mussels and shrimp. Cover and keep warm while you prepare the sauce.

With a fine strainer, strain the *fumet* together with the cooking juice of the fillets of sole. Reduce by two-thirds over high heat. Remove from the stove, add 6 egg yolks and work it up on the corner of the stove, like a hollandaise sauce, by incorporating about 1 pound of melted butter into it. Correct the seasoning, strain the sauce and coat the fillets and their garnish with this sauce.

Glaze 2 minutes in a blazing oven and serve immediately.

Filets de Sole Marguery
SOLE WITH MUSSELS AND SHRIMPS

2½ pounds large mussels   *4 servings*
10 tablespoons unsalted butter
1 small onion, minced
3 shallots, minced
Small bouquet garni (⅓ bay leaf, 1 sprig of thyme, 3 sprigs of parsley)
1 cup white wine
2½ pounds large fillets of sole
Salt and white pepper
Lemon juice
½ pound fresh shrimps
½ cup heavy cream
3 egg yolks
Puff Pastry Crescents (see Index)

1. Scrub the mussels thoroughly under running cold water with a stiff bristle brush.
2. Melt 2 tablespoons of the butter in a deep pot (not aluminum). Add the onion and shallots, stirring well until wilted. Add the *bouquet garni*, mussels, and wine. Cover and cook over high heat for 5 to 6 minutes, shaking the pan 2 or 3 times. When the shells are wide open, remove mussels from their shells over the pan, and reserve.
3. Reduce the cooking broth to 1 cup and strain through a sieve lined with cheesecloth; reserve the mussel broth.
4. Place the fillets of sole flat in a generously buttered ovenproof dish. Season with salt and pepper and add a sprinkle of lemon juice to keep the fish white. Add the reserved mussel broth. Cover the dish with foil and poach in a preheated 400°F. oven for 15 minutes or until done.
5. Shell the shrimps. Cook them in 2 tablespoons of butter until they turn pink. Season with salt and pepper.
6. Remove the sole fillets and arrange the fish on an oval serving dish. Scatter the mussels around the fish and the shrimps in the center. Cover and keep warm.
7. In a saucepan reduce the liquid to 1¼ cups. Add the cream beaten with the egg yolks. Stir until the sauce is slightly thickened but do not let it boil. Add the remaining butter bit by bit, whisking the sauce like a hollandaise. Taste for seasoning. Pour the sauce over the fish and glaze briefly under the broiler. Garnish the border with puff pastry crescents.

◆   UNDER THE COOK'S HAT   ◆

For additional flavor, use the same pan in which the shrimps have cooked to make a shrimp butter with their shells (follow directions for Shellfish Butter, see Index).

◆   ◆   ◆

In the limitless preparations which fish may undergo, the works of a skillful cook appear in all their stunning effects. Fish is the glory of the master inspired by the fire of genius; it is the stumbling block of ordinary cooks. —GRIMOD DE LA REYNIÈRE

Sole Dugléré

Adolph Dugléré created this dish in 1867 for a dinner for Czar Alexander II, Bismarck, and William I, King of Prussia, at the Café Anglais in Paris.

1 medium-size onion, finely chopped   *4 servings*
1 garlic clove, finely chopped
3 tablespoons unsalted butter
4 ripe tomatoes, peeled and diced
1 tablespoon tomato paste
2 tablespoons chopped parsley
½ cup white wine
1½ to 2 pounds fillets of sole
Salt and freshly ground pepper
½ cup Velouté Sauce (see Index) made with Fish Fumet (or 1½
     tablespoons Kneaded Butter mashed with 1½ tablespoons
     flour)
⅓ cup heavy cream
Fresh parsley, chopped

1. In a large skillet, sauté the onion and garlic in butter until golden. Add the tomatoes, tomato paste, and parsley, and cook over medium heat until reduced to a thick purée. Add the wine.

2. Season the fillets with salt and pepper, then fold in half. Place fish in the skillet and bring almost to a boil. Lower the heat, cover the skillet, and cook for 12 to 15 minutes. Remove the fish to a serving dish and keep warm in a low oven.

3. Reduce the liquid by half over high heat. Stir in the velouté sauce, or the kneaded butter and the cream, and cook until thickened. Correct the seasonings and pour the sauce over the fillets. Sprinkle with parsley.

For an attractive finish, surround the dish with Duchess Potatoes (see Index).

♦   UNDER THE COOK'S HAT   ♦

Halibut and bass can be substituted for sole.
     This dish is best when made with tomatoes fresh from the garden, when you may omit the tomato paste.

♦   *Variation*   ♦

Add a pinch of curry powder to the tomato mixture and ¾ cup of hollandaise to the sauce.

Filets de Sole aux Fines Herbes

SOLE WITH HERBS

This preparation can be used for any fish fillets.

Butter   *3 servings*
1½ pounds fillets of sole
Salt and freshly ground pepper
4 shallots, finely minced
4 tablespoons finely chopped parsley
3 tablespoons finely snipped chives
⅓ cup bread crumbs, freshly made
⅓ cup white wine
Lemon wedges

1. Generously butter a shallow baking dish. Season the fillets with salt and pepper. Spread half of the shallots, parsley, and chives in the bottom of the dish. Mix remaining herbs with bread crumbs.

2. Pour wine into the baking dish, then add the fillets. Sprinkle with the bread-crumb mixture and dot with butter. Bake in a pre-heated 400°F. oven for 20 to 25 minutes. Glaze briefly under the broiler until golden. Garnish with lemon wedges.

Filets de Sole à la Florentine

SOLE WITH SPINACH AND CHEESE SAUCE

4 servings

2 pounds fresh spinach, or 3 packages (10 ounces each) frozen
   spinach
10 tablespoons unsalted butter
1½ to 2 pounds fillets of sole
Salt and white pepper
2 tablespoons lemon juice
1¼ cups milk
2 tablespoons flour
Pinch of grated nutmeg
½ cup heavy cream
½ cup freshly grated Gruyère cheese

1. Trim spinach and cook in boiling salted water for 10 minutes. Drain and squeeze out all the water. Chop coarsely. Reheat slowly in 3 tablespoons of the butter.

2. Butter a baking dish and spread the spinach evenly on the bottom. Keep warm in a low oven.

3. Melt 3 tablespoons butter in a large skillet. Season the sole fillets with salt and pepper and brush with lemon juice so they remain white. Simmer until opaque on one side, then turn to the other side with a spatula. The fish should remain white.

4. Arrange the fillets on the spinach and keep warm. Pour the liquid from the skillet into a measuring cup and add enough milk to have 1½ cups liquid.

5. Prepare the sauce: Melt 2 tablespoons butter in a saucepan. Add the flour and cook until smooth. Add the 1½ cups liquid and stir constantly over low heat until thickened. Season with salt and pepper and nutmeg to taste. Add the cream and simmer for 5 minutes.

6. When ready to serve, fold the Gruyère into the sauce and pour all over the fillets. Dot with more butter and glaze under the broiler until golden.

◆   *Variation*   ◆

Leeks can be substituted for the spinach.

Filets de Sole de Marande
SOLE DE MARANDE

5 tablespoons unsalted butter   *4 servings*
2 pounds fillet of sole
½ cup dry white wine
½ cup Fish Fumet (see Index) made with sole trimmings, or ½
    cup clam juice
2 shallots, finely chopped
Salt and freshly ground pepper
3 egg yolks
½ cup heavy cream
½ teaspoon arrowroot
¼ pound fresh mushrooms, finely minced
1 teaspoon minced fresh tarragon
1 teaspoon snipped fresh chives
1 tablespoon minced fresh chervil or parsley
4 large mushroom caps, fluted
1 tablespoon lemon juice

1. Butter a large skillet. Arrange the fillets on it and add wine, *fumet* or clam juice, shallots, and salt and pepper to taste. Simmer until the fish flakes easily with a fork, 7 to 8 minutes. Remove fillets with a slotted spatula to a serving dish. Cover with foil and keep warm in a low oven.

2. Prepare the sauce: Reduce the poaching liquid to ¾ cup over high heat. In a heavy-bottomed saucepan, combine the egg yolks, cream, arrowroot, mushrooms, and herbs. Whisk until the sauce has the consistency of a light custard. Add the poaching liquid and 3 tablespoons butter. Correct the seasonings.

3. Sauté the mushroom caps in 1 tablespoon butter and 1 tablespoon lemon juice. Pour off any juices that have accumulated in the serving dish. Cover fish with the sauce and place the mushroom caps on top.

◆ UNDER THE COOK'S HAT ◆

Two skillets are better than one large skillet for this recipe.

◆ ◆ ◆

Fish, that marvelous food, without which no meal would be complete.
—CURNONSKY

◆ *Sole à la Normande* ◆

Contrary to popular belief, this famous dish did not originate in Normandy as the name would indicate, but in Paris. It was the creation of Chef Langlais in 1838 at the restaurant Rocher de Cancale, rue Montorgueil, one of the finest restaurants in Paris at that time.

This authentic recipe for sole Normande was given by its creator to de Gouffé, a well-known chef of the nineteenth century. It has changed slightly over the years. The onions are omitted today and the modern garnish of crawfish and shrimp is not mentioned in the original recipe.

Clean and prepare a large sole. Remove the fillets from the bone. Butter a dish and sprinkle all over it finely minced onions which you have blanched. Season the sole with salt and pepper. Add white wine and cook.

You will have prepared in a pan lean velouté to which you will add the liquor of the mussels and liquid from the cooking of the sole. Reduce it and bind with eggs.

Prepare a garnish of oysters, mussels, mushrooms, croutons of bread, and smelts. Arrange the oysters, mussels and mushrooms on the sole. Add the sauce around and on top. Place for five minutes in the oven, avoiding coloring of the sauce.

Sole à la Normande

This is a simplified version of the classic recipe, an elegant and delicious dish well worth the time involved in its preparation.

8 tablespoons unsalted butter   *8 servings*
3 tablespoons finely chopped onions
8 fillets of sole, about 4 pounds
Salt and white pepper
1½ cups dry white wine
1 quart mussels, well cleaned
12 button mushrooms
⅓ cup boiling water
1 tablespoon lemon juice, plus a few drops
5 tablespoons flour
2 egg yolks
½ cup heavy cream

1. Butter a large, shallow ovenproof dish. Sprinkle the onion on the bottom. Season the fillets with salt and pepper, then fold in half for easier handling. Place fillets in the dish, cover with wine, and dot with 3 tablespoons of the butter. Cover the dish with foil and oven-poach in a preheated 400°F. oven until fish is opaque, about 20 minutes. Carefully remove the fillets and place on a serving platter in a warm oven.

2. Steam the mussels in a large pot for 5 minutes, or until opened. Remove the mussels from the shells over the pot. Strain the liquid through a colander lined with cheesecloth and reserve liquid.

3. Cut off mushroom stems ¼ inch below the caps. Place caps in a small pan with ⅓ cup boiling water. Add 1 tablespoon lemon juice, 1 tablespoon butter, and salt to taste. Cover and boil for 4 or 5 minutes. Strain off the mushroom liquid and add it to the mussel liquid.

4. Pour off any liquid that has accumulated in the serving dish and add it to the mussel and mushroom liquid. The liquid should measure 2½ cups. Add clam juice if necessary, or reduce liquid to that amount.

5. To prepare the sauce: Melt remaining butter, stir in the flour, and cook for a few minutes. Add the 2½ cups liquid and stir until thickened. Simmer for 5 minutes. Combine the egg yolks and cream, then stir into the sauce. Simmer for 1 minute. Remove from the stove and add a few drops of lemon juice to taste.

6. Arrange the mussels and mushrooms on the fillets. Pour the sauce over all.

◆   ◆   ◆

Véronique, a comic opera by André Méssager, was performed by a French company in 1903 at the Coronet Theatre in London. For a theatrical party in the company's honor, August Escoffier, who presided over the kitchen at the Carlton Hotel from 1898 to 1919, created the Filets de Sole Véronique. This recipe is given in Escoffier's book *A Guide to Modern Cookery*, published in London in 1907.

Lift out the fillets of a fine sole; beat them slightly; fold and season them, and put them in a special earthenware, buttered dish.

With the bones, some of the trimmings of the fish, a little minced onion, some parsley stalks, a few drops of lemon juice, and white wine and water, prepare two spoonfuls of *fumet*.

This done, strain it over the fillets, and *poach* them gently.

Drain them carefully; reduce the *fumet* to the consistency of syrup, and finish it with one and one-half oz. of butter. Arrange the fillets in an oval on the dish where they have been *poached*; cover them with the buttered *fumet*, and set to *glaze* quickly. When about to serve, set a pyramid of skinned and very cold Muscatel grapes in the middle of the dish.

Put a cover on the dish, and serve immediately.

Filets de Sole Véronique
SOLE VÉRONIQUE

2 pounds fillets of sole   *4 servings*
Salt and pepper
4 tablespoons unsalted butter

FISH STOCK
Fish trimmings, heads, and bones
1 small onion, minced
½ cup water
½ cup dry white wine

1 tablespoon lemon juice

1 cup cold Muscatel grapes, skinned

1. Fold the fillets in two. Season lightly with salt and
pepper. Arrange them in one layer on a well-buttered baking
dish, either glass or pottery, that can double as a serving dish.
2. Briskly simmer the fish trimmings, heads, bones, and onion
in ½ cup water, ½ cup wine, and lemon juice for 15 minutes, or
until reduced to ½ cup.
3. Strain the stock over the fillets. Cover the dish, and oven-
poach the fish in a 400°F. oven for 15 to 20 minutes, or until done.
With a basting syringe remove the liquid from the dish to a saucepan. Keep the fish warm.
4. Boil the juices down to about ¼ cup. Add 3 tablespoons butter. Pour over the fish, and place under the broiler to glaze.
5. Heap cold grapes in the center of dish. Serve immediately.

Truite au Bleu

BLUE TROUT

Au bleu refers to the bluish color that the trout develops after being
prepared by this method. This recipe is for fishermen, as the trout
must be just out of the water and still living.

¾ cup French wine vinegar   *4 servings*
2 quarts salted water
1 large onion, sliced
10 black peppercorns
4 fresh trout
Hot vinegar, enough to cover fish

1. Make a court-bouillon: Combine the vinegar, water, onion,
and peppercorns in a large pot and simmer for 20 minutes.
2. Knock the trout unconscious by hitting on a hard surface. Do
not scale. Gut them and dip briefly into hot vinegar.
3. Place the trout in the court-bouillon. Cook for 5 or 6 minutes
for a 1-pound trout. Drain thoroughly. Serve melted butter separately, along with parsleyed potatoes.

◆   UNDER THE COOK'S HAT   ◆

Handle trout as little as possible to protect the blue viscous coating.

7. Les Crustacés, les Coquillages, et les Mollusques SHELLFISH AND FROGS' LEGS

✣ ✣ ✣

Ecrevisses à la Diable

CRAYFISH À LA DIABLE

3 tablespoons unsalted butter
2 tablespoons minced onion
2 tablespoons grated carrot
1 tablespoon minced shallot
1 garlic clove, minced
Bouquet garni (parsley sprigs, ½ bay leaf, thyme)
3 tablespoons Cognac
⅓ cup dry white wine or white vermouth
Salt and white pepper
Cayenne pepper
1 pound fresh crayfish, shelled, or shrimp
1 teaspoon Dijon mustard
Lemon juice
⅓ cup freshly made Mayonnaise (see Index)
Fresh parsley, chopped

2 servings

1. Melt the butter in a skillet and sauté the onion, carrot, shallot, garlic, and *bouquet garni* until golden. Add the Cognac, wine, salt and pepper and cayenne to taste. Simmer for 2 to 3 minutes.

2. Add the crayfish and simmer for 8 to 10 minutes. Remove the crayfish and chill.

3. Cook the sauce remaining in the skillet over high heat until reduced to ⅓ cup. Chill.

4. Combine the mustard and lemon juice to taste with the mayonnaise. Mix with the chilled sauce.

5. Fold the crayfish into the sauce and arrange on lettuce leaves, or mix with cold rice for a heartier dish. Sprinkle with parsley.

♦   ♦   ♦

In the 1800s there were vats of court-bouillon constantly boiling in Les Halles in Paris. Live lobsters were chosen by the customers, then attached to a numbered tag and lowered into the court-bouillon. Every Sunday over 800 lobsters were sold for 20 centimes each.

STEAMED LOBSTER

The way to keep the flavor of lobsters intact is to steam them, not drown them in too much highly seasoned water.

Place the lobsters in a large pot with about 2 inches of boiling seawater or water seasoned with sea salt. Cover and steam for exactly 20 minutes. Split lengthwise into halves with a heavy knife. Serve with melted butter and lemon wedges.

If you are going to serve the lobster lukewarm or cold, put it on a bed of lettuce leaves and pass a bowl of freshly made mayonnaise. The mayonnaise should be mixed in a blender with the lobster coral and additional lemon juice.

♦ *On Killing a Lobster* ♦

Prenez un beau homard, puis sur la carapace
Posez une main ferme, et, quelques sauts qu'il fasse,
Sans plus vous attendrir à des regrets amers
Découpez tout vivant ce Cardinal des mers.

Take a beautiful lobster, and upon its shell
Place a firm hand. Then, no matter how it struggles,
Without further compassion or grievous regrets,
Cut it up alive, this Cardinal of the seas.

GRILLED LOBSTER

1. Place the lobsters (1 per person) in a large pot of boiling salted water for 2 to 3 minutes. Remove and let cool.

2. Split lengthwise into halves with a heavy knife. Crack the shells with a hammer or cleaver. Season with salt and pepper. Brush the flesh with melted butter.

3. Place the lobsters in a shallow roasting pan with ½ inch of water covering the bottom of the pan. Broil 6 inches from the source of the heat at 425°F. for 10 to 12 minutes. Brush frequently with melted butter. When lobsters are golden, sprinkle with paprika. Garnish with lemon wedges and parsley.

Serve with Lemon and Herb Butter Sauce or with Sauce Nantua, or brush the lobster flesh with Snail Butter while broiling (see Index for recipes).

Serve a Pouilly-Fuissé or Montrachet wine.

◆   UNDER THE COOK'S HAT   ◆

To remove flesh from a lobster, proceed as follows:

With the back up, break off the tail section. Cut the flippers off the end of the tail and slide the tail meat out in one piece. Crack the shell of the claws in several places with a hammer or cleaver and pull out the claw meat. Then snap the knuckle and remove the rest of the meat with a lobster pick.

◆ *Homard à l'Américaine* ◆

This famous French lobster dish originated in Nice and was known as *Homard à la Niçoise.* Then, in 1853, Constant Guillots, chef of the restaurant Bonnefoy in Paris, created a new version, which became a specialty of this restaurant, and called it *Homard à la Bonnefoy.*

It was rebaptized around 1860, when Pierre Fraise became the owner of a well-known restaurant, Peter's, at the Passage des Princes in Paris.

The story goes that late one evening, some Americans came into the restaurant to dine. Although it was closing time, they insisted so strongly on being served that Pierre himself prepared a lobster similar to lobster *à la Bonnefoy* with whatever ingredients he had on hand. The Americans asked the name of this delectable dish and he replied charmingly, *"Lobster à l'Américaine."* This lobster dish made his fortune.

Homard à l'Américaine

LOBSTER AMÉRICAINE

2 live lobsters, each 2½ pounds   *4 servings*

4 tablespoons olive oil
7 tablespoons unsalted butter
8 shallots, finely chopped
6 tablespoons Cognac or Armagnac
2 garlic cloves, chopped
2 ripe tomatoes, peeled and diced
4 tablespoons tomato paste
1 cup fine dry white wine
½ cup Fish Fumet (see Index) or clam juice
Salt and freshly ground black pepper
Cayenne pepper
½ cup heavy cream
1 teaspoon minced fresh tarragon, or ½ teaspoon dried
Fresh parsley, chopped

1. Plunge a large knife into the spinal cord of the lobsters where the body and tail sections meet. This will kill the lobsters instantly. Remove and crack the claws. Remove tails by twisting them off while holding lobsters over a large skillet to catch any juices. Split the body section lengthwise into halves. Discard sand sac near the head. Remove the creamy tomalley (green is male and gray is female), and any coral, and reserve. Cut the tail section into 3 or 4 crosswise slices, following the joints.

2. Heat the oil and 2 tablespoons of the butter in a large skillet. Add the lobster pieces and claws and sauté over medium heat until shells are red, 4 to 5 minutes. Add the shallots and cook briefly.

3. Remove the pan from the heat. Add the Cognac and ignite. When the flame subsides, add the garlic, tomatoes, and tomato paste. Stir well before adding the wine and fish *fumet*. Season with salt, black pepper, and cayenne pepper to taste. Cover the pan and simmer for 15 to 20 minutes.

4. Remove the lobster pieces to a plate. Add the cream to the sauce and reduce it by half. Remove the shells from the slices of lobster as well as from the claws.

5. Cream remaining 5 tablespoons butter and the tarragon with the tomalley and coral if any. Add this mixture to the cream sauce. Correct the seasonings and simmer over low heat, stirring, until slightly thickened.

6. Slowly reheat the lobster pieces in the sauce. Sprinkle with parsley and serve with buttered steamed rice.

Serve a rosé wine, Tavel, or a white Châteauneuf-du-Pape, or Champagne.

◆ UNDER THE COOK'S HAT ◆

Cream is not traditional in this classic lobster dish but it is a delicious addition.

◆ ◆ ◆

A recipe is an idea, plus whatever personality one can make shine through it.
—ANDRÉ DAGUIN,
chef of the Hôtel de France
in Auch, in the Pyrenees

◆ *Homard Thermidor* ◆

Lobster Thermidor owes its name to a play by Victorien Sardou, called *Thermidor*. The premiere took place at the Comédie-Française on January 24, 1894, and because of its viewpoint it created a great political scandal.

Maire, the owner of the once-famous restaurant Maire of the Grand Boulevards in Paris, had the ingenious idea of naming his new lobster recipe after the play and introducing it on opening night. The lobster was an immediate culinary success and the recipe was adopted by well-known restaurants all over the world.

Homard Thermidor

LOBSTER THERMIDOR

3 tablespoons unsalted butter   *4 servings*
3 tablespoons flour
1½ cups light cream
Salt and white pepper
1 tablespoon Dijon mustard
Coral from lobster
2 steamed lobsters, each 1½ to 2 pounds
Grated Swiss Gruyère
Butter for top

1. Melt 3 tablespoons butter, add the flour, and stir until smooth. Add the cream, season to taste, and let simmer for 10 minutes.
2. Stir in the mustard and lobster coral.

3. Cut the lobsters lengthwise into halves. Remove the flesh and cut it into thick slanted slices.

4. Cover the bottom of each half-shell with some of the sauce. Arrange the slices overlapping on top. Spread the remaining sauce on top. Sprinkle with grated cheese. Dot with butter and place under the broiler for a few minutes until golden. Serve immediately.

Mouclade

MUSSELS WITH CURRY AND CREAM

This specialty of La Rochelle and the coast of Aunis goes back many centuries.

Curry might seem to be an unusual flavoring for a French dish, but La Rochelle was the first French port where the spice boats from India docked.

6 tablespoons unsalted butter   *4 servings*
3 tablespoons minced shallots
1 sprig of fresh or dry thyme (not ground)
½ bay leaf
4 pounds mussels, well scrubbed
½ cup white wine
1 garlic clove, minced
2 tablespoons flour
Pinch of curry powder
Salt and white pepper
⅓ cup heavy cream
1 egg yolk
Lemon juice
2 tablespoons chopped parsley

1. Melt 2 tablespoons of the butter in a large enamelware pot. Sauté 2 tablespoons of the shallots, the thyme, and bay leaf for 1 minute.

2. Add the mussels and wine. Cover and cook over high heat for 5 or 6 minutes, shaking the pan occasionally. When the shells are open, separate the mussels over the pot. Discard one shell from each mussel, leaving the shellfish in the remaining shell.

3. Place the shells containing the mussels on a heated large serving plate and keep warm in a low oven. Strain the liquid in the pan through cheesecloth.

4. Prepare the sauce: Melt 2 tablespoons butter in a saucepan. Sauté the garlic and remaining 1 tablespoon shallot until golden. Add the flour and stir until smooth. Add curry powder, then the reserved mussel liquid. Stir until thickened. Season sparingly with salt, as the mussel liquor is salty; add pepper to taste. Combine the heavy cream with the egg yolk. Add to the sauce, then stir in a few drops of lemon juice, to taste. Add the remaining 2 tablespoons of butter, bit by bit.

5. Spoon the sauce over the mussels and sprinkle with parsley. Serve with buttered slices of French bread (for mopping up the sauce), and a fine Muscadet wine.

◆　*Variation*　◆

Reduce the liquid from cooking the mussels over high heat to 3 tablespoons. Strain and stir into 2 cups Hollandaise Sauce (see Index). Add the juice of ½ lemon. Pour this sauce over the mussels.

◆　UNDER THE COOK'S HAT　◆

Discard any mussels that are not shut tightly or those that feel extra heavy, as they are full of sand or mud.

For extra mellowness, soak the mussels in 1 cup milk and 3 quarts water for 30 minutes. This will also help the mussels to rid themselves of sand.

Mussels are good all year long except in the spring, when they reproduce; at that time the flesh is tasteless.

Moules à la Marinière

MUSSELS WITH WINE AND CREAM

This is a specialty of Normandy. Serve with a fine hard cider or a Muscadet wine, crusty French bread, and unsalted butter.

5 pounds large mussels   *4 servings*
5 tablespoons unsalted butter
1 medium-size onion, minced
3 tablespoons minced shallots
1 cup Calvados or dry white wine
Bouquet garni (piece of bay leaf, sprig of thyme, 6 parsley
　　sprigs)
½ cup heavy cream

Salt and freshly ground pepper
Fresh parsley, chopped

1. Scrub the mussels thoroughly under running cold water with a stiff-bristle brush. With a knife, scrape off the beard protruding from the shells.

2. Melt 2 tablespoons of the butter in a deep pot (not aluminum). Add the onion and shallots, stirring well. Add the mussels, Calvados or wine, and *bouquet garni.* Cover and cook over high heat for 5 or 6 minutes, shaking the pan 2 or 3 times.

3. When the shells are wide open, transfer the mussels with a slotted spoon to a warm serving dish. Discard one shell from each mussel, leaving the shellfish in remaining shells.

4. Strain the liquid in the saucepan through cheesecloth. Add the cream and pepper to taste. Taste before adding salt. Boil rapidly to reduce the liquid. Remove from the heat and stir in remaining 3 tablespoons butter.

5. Pour the sauce over the mussels and sprinkle with parsley. Serve in warmed deep soup plates.

◆　　*Variation*　　◆

Make the basic recipe. Reduce the cooking liquor until syrupy. Cool and mix with an unsalted mayonnaise. Add sliced mushrooms simmered in butter and cooled, then the mussels. Serve in tartlet shells made of puff pastry. Sprinkle the top with snipped chives.

Coquilles Saint-Jacques à la Parisienne

PARISIAN SCALLOPS

The apostle James came to Spain just before he was beheaded in A.D. 44 by King Herod Agrippa. His head miraculously intact, it was returned to Galicia to be buried by converted Spaniards. Saint James was seen by Christian soldiers in 844 riding a white horse, during the victorious battle of Clavijo against the Moors. He became known as Santiago Matamoros (Moor-Slayer). This miracle was commemorated in the building of the Cathedral of the town Compostela in the twelfth century. The scallop shell became the symbol of Saint James after he rescued a man and his horse from the sea; they emerged covered with *vieira,* a scallop shell abundant on the coastline. It became the symbol of the pilgrims who upon returning brought a scallop shell to prove they had been to Santiago de Compostela.

1 pound fresh bay scallops, or sea scallops,   *5 or 6 servings*
    cut into 2 or 3 pieces each
¾ cup dry white wine
3 tablespoons finely minced onion
Sea salt and white pepper
6 tablespoons unsalted butter
1 tablespoon minced shallot
2 tablespoons flour
1 egg yolk
½ cup heavy cream
1 tablespoon lemon juice
½ pound finely minced mushrooms
Fresh bread crumbs
Parmesan cheese, freshly grated
Butter for top

1. Simmer the scallops in the wine with 2 tablespoons onion and salt and pepper to taste for about 5 minutes. Do not overcook or they toughen. Remove scallops with a slotted spoon to a plate. Reduce the poaching liquid to approximately ¾ cup, strain, and reserve.

2. Melt 3 tablespoons of the butter in a skillet, then sauté the mushrooms and remaining 1 tablespoon onion over high heat, stirring until the juice has evaporated. Season with salt and pepper.

3. Prepare the sauce: In a large saucepan, sauté the shallot in remaining 3 tablespoons butter until golden. Stir in the flour and cook until smooth. Add the reduced poaching liquid, whisking vigorously. When thickened, add the egg yolk combined with the cream and the lemon juice. Stir the sauce until hot but do not let it boil.

4. Combine the mushrooms, scallops, and sauce. Correct the seasonings. Spoon the mixture into 5 large or 6 small scallop shells.

5. Place the scallop shells on a baking sheet covered with a layer of coarse salt to hold the shells level. Sprinkle the scallop mixture with bread crumbs and Parmesan. Dot with butter and glaze briefly under the broiler.

♦   *Variation*   ♦

Once filled, cover the scallop shell with a very thin layer of puff pastry. Brush the underneath rim with water and press pastry to the moistened rim to prevent it from shrinking while baking. Brush the dough with an egg yolk. Make a few lines in the dough with the back of a knife to look like a shell. Bake in a preheated 425°F. oven until pastry is golden brown.

Coquilles Saint-Jacques à la Mayonnaise
BAY SCALLOPS WITH MAYONNAISE

½ cup dry white wine *4 servings*
2 tablespoons minced shallots
1 garlic clove, minced
Salt and white pepper
1½ pounds bay scallops, or sea scallops, cut into 2 or 3 pieces
  each
¾ cup freshly made Mayonnaise (see Index)
1 tablespoon snipped fresh chives
1 teaspoon minced fresh tarragon, or ½ teaspoon dried
1 tablespoon minced fresh chervil or parsley
1 tablespoon lemon juice

1. Combine the wine, shallots, garlic, and salt and pepper to taste in a saucepan. Bring almost to a boil, add the scallops, and simmer for 5 minutes.

2. Remove scallops with a slotted spoon to a plate. Reduce the liquid to approximately 3 tablespoons. Incorporate the liquid into the mayonnaise. Correct the seasonings.

3. Add the herbs and lemon juice to the sauce. Mix the sauce with the scallops. Chill. Serve on a scallop shell lined with lettuce.

Coquilles Saint-Jacques au Beurre d'Escargots
SCALLOPS WITH SNAIL BUTTER

4 servings
1½ pounds bay scallops, or sea scallops, cut into 2 or 3 pieces
  each
2 tablespoons unsalted butter
Salt and white pepper
Snail Butter (see Index), with extra lemon juice

1. Sauté the scallops in butter for 5 minutes. Season with salt and pepper. Remove the scallops with a slotted spoon to a plate.

2. Reduce the liquid in the pan to about 2 tablespoons. Return

scallops to the pan. Remove from the heat and stir in the snail butter.

3. Divide among 4 scallop shells, lined with rice.

Serve a Muscadet or Chablis wine.

Crevettes à la Bordelaise

SHRIMP WITH WINE AND TOMATOES

This delicious dish can be made in a chafing dish with crayfish or shrimp.

6 tablespoons unsalted butter *3 or 4 servings*
5 tablespoons finely minced shallots
1 garlic clove, minced
1 medium-size carrot, grated
3 tablespoons finely chopped celery
Bouquet garni (parsley sprigs, bay leaf, and thyme)
1½ pounds shrimp or crayfish, shelled
3 tablespoons Cognac, heated
¼ cup dry white wine
½ cup heavy cream
2 teaspoons tomato purée
Cayenne pepper
Salt and freshly ground black pepper
Fresh parsley, chopped

1. Melt 4 tablespoons of the butter in a skillet or chafing dish. Sauté shallots, garlic, carrot, celery, and *bouquet garni* until golden.

2. Add the shrimp and cook over high heat, stirring, until pink, 2 to 3 minutes.

3. Warm a large metal spoon. Pour in the Cognac, heat it, ignite it, and pour over the shrimp. Add the wine and cook for 1 minute before stirring in the cream, tomato purée, and cayenne pepper, salt and black pepper to taste. Simmer for a few minutes, but do not overcook the shrimp, or they will toughen.

4. Remove shrimp with a slotted spoon to a warm serving dish. Discard the *bouquet garni*. Reduce the sauce over high heat until slightly thickened. Remove from the heat and swirl in remaining 2 tablespoons butter.

5. Pour the sauce over the shrimp and sprinkle with parsley. Serve with buttered steamed rice, or in a rice ring or heated patty shells.

Vol-au-Vent à la Marinière

PATTY SHELLS FILLED WITH SEAFOOD

These small entrées can be an elegant start to a formal dinner.

1½ cups dry white wine *4 servings*
1 yellow onion, minced
4 pounds mussels, well scrubbed
3 parsley sprigs
½ pound small shrimp, shelled
5 tablespoons unsalted butter
½ pound mushrooms
Lemon juice
½ pound fillets of gray sole or flounder
Salt and freshly ground white pepper
2 tablespoons flour
2 egg yolks
½ cup heavy cream
8 Patty Shells (see Index), baked

1. In a pot, bring 1 cup wine and the minced onion to a fast boil. Add the mussels and the parsley, cover, and cook over high heat. When the mussels are open, remove them from the shells over the pot. Place the mussels in a bowl, cover, and keep warm. Discard shells.
2. Cook the shrimp in the mussel broth for a few minutes, until bright pink. With a slotted spoon, transfer the shrimp to the bowl of mussels. Strain the broth through cheesecloth into a saucepan.
3. Melt 2 tablespoons of the butter in a skillet and add the mushrooms with a sprinkling of lemon juice to keep them white. Cook over medium heat for 3 minutes. Add to the mussels and shrimp.
4. Add 1 tablespoon butter to the skillet and pour in the remaining ½ cup wine. Season the fish fillets and simmer in the skillet until opaque, for 7 to 8 minutes. Break the fish into bite-size pieces and transfer with a slotted spatula to the seafood mixture. Add the poaching liquid to the strained mussel broth.
5. Prepare the sauce: Reduce the broth over high heat for 3 or 4 minutes. Combine remaining 2 tablespoons butter with the flour and stir the mixture, a little at a time, into the broth. Simmer until broth is thickened. Add the egg yolks mixed with cream. Whisk the sauce until smooth. Correct the seasonings.
6. Combine the sauce with the seafood and keep warm until

serving time in the top pan of a double boiler, set over hot water in the lower pan, or set the pan in a skillet filled with hot water.

7. Warm the patty shells in the oven. Fill with the seafood mixture and serve without delay.

◆   *Variation*   ◆

Serve in a prebaked pastry pie shell made of Puff Pastry (see Index). Reheat in a preheated 400°F. oven for 5 minutes before filling.

Grenouilles à la Mode de Boulay

FROGS' LEGS BOULAY STYLE

Frogs are a specialty of Lorraine. A monk stated in the *Annals of the Dominicans* of Colmar, in Lorraine, that "in 1280, one started to eat frogs, a food considered abominable until now."

On November 16, 1821, the door of the fish market in Metz was inadvertently opened and 6,000 frogs jumped up and down in the streets of the town. Housewives gathered the frogs in their aprons and took them home to create the delicious recipe given below.

1 dozen pairs of frogs' legs   *4 servings*
¾ cup fresh bread crumbs
4 tablespoons finely minced shallots
4 tablespoons finely chopped parsley
Salt and freshly ground pepper
¼ pound unsalted butter, melted

1. Soak the frogs' legs in cold water for 2 hours. This whitens and swells the flesh. Drain and pat dry.

2. Combine the bread crumbs, shallots, parsley, and salt and pepper to taste.

3. Dip the frogs' legs into the melted butter, then into the bread-crumb mixture. Arrange in one layer in a buttered baking dish. Sprinkle with remaining bread-crumb mixture. Add any remaining butter.

4. Bake in a preheated 450°F. oven for 25 to 30 minutes, or until golden brown.

Serve with a chilled Riesling wine.

8. *La Volaille et le Gibier à Plume*
POULTRY AND FEATHERED GAME

✤ ✤ ✤

In Gaul, it was at the royal court and in the abbeys that the best food was found. Poultry was rare and expensive and was served only on festive occasions. Charlemagne decreed at the council of Aix-la-Chapelle in 817 that monks could eat poultry only at Easter and Christmas, but the monks gave themselves special dispensations, saying that since bird and fish were created on the same day eating them on the same day would not break fast.

A rigorous police ordinance ruled the poultry merchants; shops were inspected daily and any day-old roast poultry was burned or thrown in the river.

The proud peacock was the bird held in highest esteem throughout the Middle Ages, not so much for its dry flesh but because it was considered a noble bird. It was the "king" of every feast for more than 400 years.

The peacock was prepared by skinning the bird and keeping all the feathers intact. The head was wrapped in a wet cloth and sprayed with water during the roasting to prevent the crest from burning. When cooked, the feathered skin was replaced and the beak and feet were painted gold. Then, with great pomp, the peacock was presented to the guest of honor. Before carving, the guest made the traditional "vow of the peacock," which solemn formula begins: "I pledge to the Virgin Mary, to the ladies and to the peacock . . ." to accomplish a specific thing, for instance, to be the first to set up his banner in front of a certain city to be besieged.

From the sixteenth century on, there were many *rôtisseries*, places where one could have poultry roasted, all over France, because homes did not have ovens then.

An extremely popular place existed in Paris for

more than a century and a half called La Marmite Perpétuelle (the perpetual pot). It opened for business in 1730 on rue des Grands-Augustins and closed in the middle of the nineteenth century. During that period, over 300,000 capons were cooked in an enormous pot set over a fire that burned continuously.

There are numerous ways to prepare poultry and they differ according to the bird's size and age. Baby broilers are grilled or roasted; young chickens are roasted or baked in a casserole; older ones or fowl are poached or fricasseed.

One of the great epicures of his time, Brillat-Savarin, said, "Chicken is a canvas on which the cook paints."

✦ *How to Truss Poultry* ✦

This method for trussing a chicken will enable you to remove the string in one piece, with one cut, when it is done.

Spread the wings. Twist wing tips back and turn them under.

Place the chicken on its back, the neck facing you. Take a yard of string and place it under the ends of the legs and the tail. Cross the string, making a figure eight around the legs; make sure the ends are the same length and then pull them to tighten. Turn the bird onto its breast, with the legs facing you, and slide the string under the wings and pull to tighten. Fold the loose skin of the neck over the opening. Pull the strings as tight as you can and make a knot in the middle of the neck skin.

✦ ✦ ✦

You become a cook but are born a rôtisseur. [A *rôtisseur is one who knows how to roast.*]—old French saying

Poulet Rôti au Beurre

ROAST CHICKEN

1 roasting chicken, 4½ to 5½ pounds *4 servings*
7 tablespoons unsalted butter, softened
1 teaspoon dried tarragon

Salt and freshly ground pepper
2 to 4 tablespoons hot water
Lemon juice

1. Season the cavity of the bird with 2 tablespoons butter, mashed with the tarragon and the salt and pepper.

2. Rub 3 tablespoons butter into the skin. Truss and place in a shallow roasting pan. Roast in a preheated 400°F. oven for 1¼ hours. Baste every 8 to 10 minutes. Add 1 to 2 tablespoons hot water to the juices halfway through the cooking time.

3. Transfer the chicken to a serving platter and keep warm. Add 2 tablespoons butter, 1 to 2 tablespoons hot water, and a few drops of lemon juice to the roasting pan. Reduce the juices over high heat. Spoon around the chicken.

Serve with shoestring potatoes or French fried potatoes. Tomatoes with Garlic and Bread Crumbs (see Index) also makes an excellent accompaniment.

◆   U N D E R   T H E   C O O K ' S   H A T   ◆

Half an onion inserted in the chicken, before roasting, adds flavor and juice.

◆   *Variations*   ◆

C H I C K E N   W I T H   M U S H R O O M S   Ten minutes after placing the chicken in the oven, surround with 1 cup of very small white onions. Ten minutes before the chicken is done, add ½ pound of thinly sliced mushrooms and 2 tablespoons of minced shallots. Season to taste with salt and pepper. Stir this mixture occasionally so that it cooks evenly. When chicken is done, remove to a heated serving plate. Add 1 tablespoon of cornstarch dissolved in about ¼ cup of fine Port wine to the pan juices. Thicken to the desired consistency over very low heat. Serve with thin buttered noodles, tossed with freshly grated Parmesan cheese.

C H I C K E N   W I T H   T A R R A G O N   S A U C E   Tarragon seems to have a special affinity for chicken; the herb gives chicken a very French flavor.

Mash 2 to 3 tablespoons butter with 1 tablespoon minced fresh tarragon leaves or ½ tablespoon dried. Insert in the cavity of the chicken after you have seasoned it with salt and pepper. Add 2 or 3 shallots. Proceed to roast the chicken as in the basic recipe.

Halfway through roasting time, add 2 to 3 tablespoons dry white wine or white vermouth to the roasting pan. When the chicken is done, deglaze the pan with 2 to 3 additional tablespoons of wine. To enrich the sauce, add ½ cup Brown Sauce (see Index). Serve the sauce separately.

CHICKEN WITH TRUFFLES   For the most elegant variation, you will need 4 ounces of truffles. (Less than this amount will not give enough flavor and will be a waste of the truffles.) Peel them carefully and cut into very thin slices; reserve the trimmings. Twelve hours before roasting the chicken, insert slices of the truffles between the skin and the flesh of the bird on each side of the breast and thighs. Use the trimmings for Sauce Périgueux (see Index), which is to be served with the bird.

◆   ◆   ◆

Henri IV was born on December 14, 1553, in Béarn. It was said that his mother rubbed his lips with garlic and wine from Jurançon before he knew the taste of milk.

Henri became a great monarch, a kind man, and a *bon vivant*. He pledged, "If God wills, I will make sure that there will not be a husbandman in my kingdom who will not have a chicken in his pot." He not only accomplished his aim, he also give us a world-famous phrase still used to denote the idea of prosperity.

Poulet Rôti Farci

STUFFED ROAST CHICKEN

1 roasting chicken, 4½ to 5½ pounds	*4 servings*

1 roasting chicken, 4½ to 5½ pounds
Salt and freshly ground pepper
1 slice of bacon, ½ inch thick, blanched and diced
1 large onion, minced
11 tablespoons unsalted butter
1 chicken liver, chopped
½ pound mushrooms, finely chopped
¼ cup minced celery
3 shallots, minced
1 garlic clove, minced
3 slices of French bread
⅓ cup water
1 egg, lightly beaten

2 to 3 tablespoons chopped fresh parsley
1 teaspoon dried tarragon, or a few sprigs of fresh
Lemon juice, about 1 tablespoon
2 tablespoons hot water

1. Season the cavity of the chicken with salt and pepper and set aside.

2. Sauté the bacon and onion in 3 tablespoons of the butter until golden. Add the chicken liver, mushrooms, celery, shallots, and garlic. Cook until soft.

3. Soak the bread in the water. Add to the mushroom mixture, along with the egg. Mix in the parsley, tarragon, and salt and pepper to taste.

4. Fill the bird with this stuffing. Secure the opening with thread or skewers and truss the chicken (see Index for method).

5. Rub the chicken with 6 tablespoons butter and place it in a roasting pan. Roast in a preheated 400°F. oven for 1 hour and 40 minutes. Baste every 8 to 10 minutes.

6. Place the chicken on a serving platter and keep warm. Add lemon juice, remaining 2 tablespoons butter and the hot water to the juice in the roasting pan. Reduce over high heat. Serve this sauce around the chicken or in a sauceboat.

Serve a red Bordeaux such as a Pomerol.

◆　◆　◆

During the Middle Ages, the city of Villedieu, in Normandy, produced so many frying pans (*poêles*) that the word was added to its name and it became Villedieu-les-Poêles. Today *poêler* is the verb for the cooking procedure called for in this recipe—the slow braising of meat or poultry in a tightly covered *cocotte*, flavored by the vegetables that are cooked in butter under and around it.

◆ *Carving* ◆

Until the beginning of the nineteenth century, the carving of meat and poultry was considered a noble art, and an essential part of a good education, performed only by aristocrats bearing the special title *Écuyers tranchants.* They wore feathered hats and swords while they carved.

"The carver should be very scrupulous in his deportment, his attitude grave and dignified, his eye serene," wrote Vatel, *maître d'hôtel* of the Prince de Condé, in his seventeenth-century essay on carving.

"An *amphitryon* [gastronome] who does not know how to carve or serve can be compared to the owner of a beautiful library who does not know how to read. One is as shameful as the other," wrote Monsieur Burnet in *Dictionnaire de Cuisine et d'économie ménagère* in 1836.

Many French kings, including Louis-Philippe, were also great experts in the art of carving.

Poulet Poêlé

CHICKEN IN COCOTTE

1 roasting chicken, 4½ to 5½ pounds	*4 servings*
Salt and freshly ground pepper	
5 tablespoons unsalted butter	
1 medium-size onion, diced	
1 medium-size carrot, diced	
1 celery rib, diced	
1 garlic clove (optional)	
Bouquet garni (parsley sprigs, bay leaf, thyme)	
⅓ cup chicken broth, wine, or hot water	

1. Remove fat from the opening of the chicken and dice the fat. Season the chicken with salt and pepper. Truss (see Index).

2. Melt the butter in a flameproof casserole and brown the chicken on all sides. Remove chicken.

3. Add onion, carrot, celery, garlic, diced chicken fat, and *bouquet garni* to the casserole and place the chicken on top. Cover and cook in a preheated 425°F. oven for 1 hour, basting often. Add 1 tablespoon water halfway through the cooking time if necessary. Uncover for the final 20 minutes to brown the chicken.

4. Deglaze the casserole with a little broth, wine, or water. Skim off the fat and strain the pan juices before serving.

◆   *Variation*   ◆

Add ⅓ cup Port or sherry wine to the pan juices. Reduce on top of the stove, then add ¾ cup Brown Sauce. Strain the sauce and correct seasoning before serving with Glazed Onions and Potato Balls in Butter (see Index for recipes).

Poulet à la Bourgeoise

CHICKEN WITH CARROTS AND ONIONS

Escoffier believed that simplicity was the key to the most flavorful and successful recipes. This chicken dish is a good example of his philosophy.

1 chicken, 4 to 5 pounds   *4 servings*
Salt and freshly ground pepper
1 medium-size onion, halved
6 tablespoons unsalted butter, softened
1 teaspoon dried tarragon
½ pound pearl onions, peeled
½ pound baby carrots, washed and trimmed
Bouquet garni

1. Season the inside of the chicken with salt and pepper, and stuff the onion halves with 2 tablespoons of the butter kneaded with the tarragon into the body cavity. Spread the rest of the butter over the outside of the chicken. Truss the bird and place it in a *cocotte* or Dutch oven.

2. Surround the chicken with the pearl onions and baby carrots and add the *bouquet garni*. Season with salt and pepper.

3. Place the bird in a preheated 400°F. oven and let it cook, uncovered, 45 minutes, or until the chicken and vegetables are lightly browned. Cover and continue cooking for another 30 minutes, or until done to your taste.

4. Remove the bird from the pan and deglaze the pan with 2 or 3 tablespoons of hot water, if necessary.

Serve with plain buttered spaghetti and a separate dish of grated Parmesan cheese.

Poule à l'Ivoire

POACHED CHICKEN WITH CREAM SAUCE

1 roasting chicken, 4 to 5 pounds   *4 servings*
3 carrots, chopped
2 large onions, sliced
2 leeks, 1 inch in diameter
1 celery rib, chopped
2 garlic cloves
Bouquet garni (parsley sprigs, thyme, bay leaf)
2 cloves
Salt and freshly ground pepper
1¼ cups uncooked rice
6 tablespoons unsalted butter
4 tablespoons flour
2 egg yolks
½ cup heavy cream
Lemon juice

1. Truss the chicken.
2. In a large pot, bring to a boil enough water almost to cover the chicken. Add the carrots, onions, leeks, celery, garlic, *bouquet garni*, cloves, and salt and pepper to taste. Simmer for 30 minutes.
3. Add the chicken to the broth, cover, and simmer for 1½ hours.
4. About 30 minutes before the chicken is done, parboil the rice in boiling salted water for 10 minutes. Drain and rinse under cold water. Finish cooking the rice in some chicken broth taken from the simmering chicken. Drain rice, add 3 tablespoons butter, and fluff with a fork. Transfer rice to a warmed large serving plate and keep warm in a 350°F. oven.
5. Melt remaining 3 tablespoons butter and add the flour, stirring over low heat until bubbly. Add 2 cups of the chicken broth and stir with a whisk until thickened. Simmer for 5 minutes. Remove pan from the heat and stir in the egg yolks mixed with the cream. Simmer until hot, but do not let the sauce boil. Add a few drops of lemon juice.
6. Remove the chicken from the broth and carve into serving pieces. Arrange on the bed of rice and pour the sauce over.

A red Beaujolais, or a Loire wine, such as Chinon or Bourgeuil, is suggested.

Poulet Sauté Chasseur

HUNTER'S CHICKEN

4 servings

1 frying chicken, 3½ pounds, plus 1 breast, cut into serving
    pieces
3 to 4 tablespoons unsalted butter
4 shallots, minced
1 small onion, finely chopped
1 tablespoon flour
1 cup dry white wine
1 cup Brown Sauce (see Index)
½ pound mushrooms, thinly sliced
Salt and white pepper
Bread triangles, fried in butter

1. Discard the tips of the chicken wings. Melt the butter in a
large heavy skillet and sauté the chicken over medium heat until
golden. Remove the chicken.

2. Add the shallots and onion to the skillet and sauté until
golden. Sprinkle flour into the skillet and stir. Add the wine and
reduce for 1 to 2 minutes.

3. Add the brown sauce, stirring well. Pour the sauce into a
casserole and add the mushrooms.

4. Place the chicken in the casserole, spooning the sauce over all
the pieces until well coated. Season with salt and pepper. Cover
and bake in a 350°F. oven for about 25 minutes.

5. Transfer the chicken to a warm serving platter. Reduce the
sauce over high heat until slightly thickened. Pour sauce over the
chicken.

6. Fry small triangles of bread in butter and arrange them as a
border around the serving plate.

◆   UNDER THE COOK'S HAT   ◆

A heavy metal skillet is essential for browning chicken to prevent
burning.

◆   ◆   ◆

Oil here, which is taken out of the most beautiful olives in the world,
replaces butter and I much feared the change. But I have tasted it in sauces
and, truthfully, there is nothing better.
    —JEAN RACINE, during a visit to Provence

Poulet à la Crème

SAUTÉED CHICKEN IN CREAM SAUCE

6 servings

2 broiling chickens, 3½ pounds each, cut into serving pieces
10 tablespoons unsalted butter
6 tablespoons olive oil
1 tablespoon dried tarragon
Salt and white pepper
Pinch of cayenne pepper
1 pound small mushroom caps
6 shallots, chopped
Lemon juice
2 cups dry Chablis wine
1½ cups heavy cream
4 tablespoons flour
Puff Pastry Crescents (see Index)

1. Pat the chicken dry. In a large skillet, melt 4 tablespoons of the butter and add the oil. When hot add the chicken and tarragon and sauté over medium-high heat until golden. Season with salt and peppers. Transfer to a casserole.

2. Add 4 tablespoons butter to the skillet and sauté the mushrooms briefly before adding the shallots. Sauté for 1 to 2 minutes, shaking the pan often. Season with salt and pepper, and add lemon juice to taste; stir well. Arrange mushrooms around the chicken.

3. Pour the wine into the skillet and deglaze over medium-high heat for 3 minutes. Add the cream, then pour this sauce over the chicken.

4. Bake in a preheated 350°F. oven for about 30 minutes. Remove chicken to a serving platter.

5. Combine remaining 2 tablespoons butter and the flour to make a *beurre manié*. Add in 3 or 4 parts to the sauce. Cook the sauce on top of the stove over medium heat until thickened. Do not boil. Spoon sauce over chicken and decorate platter with pastry crescents.

An excellent accompaniment would be buttered asparagus tips.

◆ *Variation* ◆

Substitute domestic apple wine for the Chablis or use 1 cup Chablis and 1 cup white Port.

Poulet à la Basquaise

BASQUE-STYLE CHICKEN

Goose fat is extensively used in the Basque country, and it gives this dish its individuality.

3 to 4 pounds chicken, cut into serving pieces   *4 servings*
4 tablespoons goose fat, or 3 tablespoons olive oil and 2
    tablespoons butter
4 medium-size onions, coarsely chopped
4 large garlic cloves, minced
4 ripe tomatoes, peeled, seeded, and chopped, or 1 pound
    canned Italian plum tomatoes, drained
2 tablespoons tomato paste
1 large green pepper, cut into julienne
1 large red pepper, cut into julienne
¼ cup diced Bayonne or Polish ham
Bouquet garni (parsley, thyme, bay leaf)
Salt and freshly ground pepper
½ cup dry white wine
¼ cup Armagnac
Fresh parsley, chopped

1. In a large skillet, sauté the chicken pieces in the goose fat, or oil and butter, until golden on both sides. Transfer to a Dutch oven or a casserole.

2. Sauté the onions and garlic in the same skillet. Add 2 to 3 tablespoons olive oil if necessary. When golden, add the tomatoes, tomato paste, green and red peppers, ham, *bouquet garni*, and seasonings to taste. Cook for 5 minutes, then add the wine and Armagnac.

3. Transfer the mixture to the Dutch oven or casserole. Cover and simmer for 30 to 35 minutes. Taste and correct seasonings. Remove the chicken to a hot serving platter.

4. Boil the sauce for a few minutes until reduced to the right consistency. Pour the sauce over the chicken and sprinkle with chopped parsley.

♦   *Variation*   ♦

Saffron can be added when cooking the onions. Serve with a rice pilaf flavored with saffron, molded in individual baba tins or glass cups and unmolded around the chicken. Top each one with a tiny round of red pimiento.

◆ *Chicken Marengo* ◆

Poulet Sauté à la Marengo gets its name from the Italian village in the Piedmont where Napoleon Bonaparte defeated the Austrians on June 14, 1800.

To stay clearheaded, Napoleon did not eat while on the battlefield. During this battle, the army advanced so rapidly that the chef, Dunand, was separated from his supplies and so sent his helpers into the countryside to find food. They returned with chicken, onions, tomatoes, garlic, olive oil, eggs, and crayfish.

Dunand cut the chicken up with a saber and used brandy from Napoleon's canteen to create this dish, which was such a success that Napoleon ordered that it be served after each major battle.

Poulet Sauté à la Marengo

CHICKEN MARENGO

1 roasting chicken, 4 pounds, cut into serving pieces   *4 servings*
Salt and freshly ground pepper
Sifted flour for coating
6 tablespoons olive oil
2 medium-size onions, minced
3 garlic cloves
4 tablespoons tomato paste
1 cup dry white wine
Bouquet garni (parsley sprigs, bay leaf, thyme)
½ pound button mushrooms
2 slices of good-quality bread
Butter and oil for frying bread
20 Italian black olives, pitted
1 cup pearl onions, glazed (optional)
Fresh parsley, chopped

1. Pat the chicken pieces dry. Season with salt and pepper, then dip into the flour.

2. Heat the olive oil in a large skillet and sauté the chicken over high heat until golden on both sides. Remove the chicken.

3. Sauté the onions in the same skillet until golden, adding a

little more oil if necessary. Add the garlic and sauté for 1 minute. Add the tomato paste and stir well for a few seconds.

4. Return the chicken to the skillet and add the wine and *bouquet garni*. Cover and simmer. If the sauce is too thick, add a little more wine. After 15 minutes, correct the seasonings and add the mushrooms. Simmer for 10 minutes.

5. Remove the crusts from the bread and cut each piece into 4 triangles. Sauté in a combination of butter and olive oil. Drain on paper towels.

6. Add the olives and glazed onions to the chicken and warm through. Sprinkle with parsley and garnish with the fried bread triangles.

◆　UNDER THE COOK'S HAT　◆

The traditional dish is served with eggs fried in olive oil and crayfish. The chicken is trussed and cooked in a court-bouillon.

◆ *Coq au Vin* ◆

Coq au vin was the creation of Master Bertrand, owner of a hostelry in the Puy de Dôme in Auvergne, during the time of Henri IV. This inn, with a signpost Mercure Gaulois, was still in existence until about a hundred years ago. This is his original recipe, which has never been improved upon.

> When you want to make a *coq au vin*, take a young chicken from Limaigne, and after having it killed, cut it into 6 parts. Then in a kettle or earthenware pot, half cook 3 ounces of lean, firm lard cut in the shape of playing dice, and 1½ ounces of fresh butter; then add small onions.
>
> As soon as the ingredients are sautéed, throw into your kettle the said chicken and a garlic clove, finely chopped; add a bouquet of parsley and other highly fragrant plants, such as thyme and bay leaf, without forgetting morels or mushrooms. Keep covered on a brisk fire, so that the whole will be a beautiful roast color on all sides, then take off the cover and gently remove the excess fat.
>
> If then, you have a tumbler of fine old brandy, even Armagnac, pour this over the chicken, then ignite and over the whole, quickly pour a pint of good old wine, preferably from the country-place of Chanturgne. When afterward everything is perfectly cooked —chicken, spices, wine sauce—serve hot with melted butter kneaded with fine white wheat flour (*beurre manié*).

Coq au Vin

CHICKEN WITH WINE SAUCE

1 roasting chicken, 4½ pounds, cut into serving pieces   *4 servings*
5 ounces lean salt pork, diced
4 tablespoons unsalted butter
18 small white onions, peeled
2 garlic cloves, finely chopped
Bouquet garni (parsley sprigs, ½ teaspoon thyme, 1 large bay leaf)
Salt and freshly ground pepper
¾ pound morels or small mushrooms
⅓ cup Cognac or Armagnac
2 cups hearty Burgundy wine
2 tablespoons butter kneaded with 2 tablespoons flour
Croutons
Fresh parsley, chopped

Cook according to Master Bertrand's directions. Thicken the sauce with the butter and flour and garnish the dish with bread triangles fried in butter. Dip one point of each triangle into the sauce, then into chopped parsley. Tuck the triangles around the serving plate.

Serve with parsleyed steamed potatoes and the same wine used in preparing the sauce.

Poulet Grillé, Sauce Diable

GRILLED CHICKEN WITH DEVILED SAUCE

2 servings
5 potatoes, peeled, quartered, and trimmed in oval shapes
1 frying chicken, 2½ pounds, split
Paprika
Salt and freshly ground pepper
Juice of 1 lemon
5 tablespoons unsalted butter, melted
Deviled Sauce (see Index)

1. Place the potatoes in cold water and boil uncovered for 10 minutes. Drain and reserve.
2. Place the chicken between 2 sheets of wax paper and flatten it with a cleaver. Remove the wing tips. Pat chicken dry with a

towel. Season generously with paprika, salt and pepper, and sprinkle with lemon juice. Brush both sides of chicken with melted butter.

3. Place the chicken, skin side up, in a roasting pan. Arrange the potatoes around the chicken and pour any remaining butter over them. Season potatoes with salt and pepper.

4. Place the pan in the broiler 8 inches below the source of heat. Broil at 450°F. for 45 minutes to 1 hour, turning the chicken and potatoes several times. Place on a warm serving dish.

5. Remove the fat from the roasting pan and prepare the sauce in it. Serve in a heated sauceboat.

◆ *Boning a Chicken Breast* ◆

Slip two fingers under the skin to loosen it, then pull off the skin and discard. With a small sharp knife, cut along the breastbone. Scrape the meat from the bones with the knife while at the same time pulling the meat away with your fingers. Remove the white tendon from each cutlet. Shape the uneven edges with heavy shears. Cover immediately with plastic wrap to keep meat from drying out. Save the bones for chicken stock.

Suprèmes de Volaille Épicure
BREAST OF CHICKEN ÉPICURE

⅓ pound mushrooms, thinly sliced　　　　　　*6 servings*
2 to 3 tablespoons unsalted butter
3 whole chicken breasts, halved, boned, and skinned
1 medium-size carrot, finely diced
3 shallots, finely chopped
1 tablespoon finely chopped celery
1 garlic clove, chopped
Pinch of thyme
6 tablespoons Clarified Butter (see Index)
¼ cup Cognac
⅓ cup Madeira or sherry wine
2 cups heavy cream
2 egg yolks
¼ teaspoon cornstarch
Salt and freshly ground pepper
Paprika
Puff Pastry Crescents (see Index)

1. Sauté the mushrooms in unsalted butter until just cooked. Set aside.

2. Place the chicken pieces between 2 sheets of wax paper and flatten slightly with the flat side of a cleaver or mallet.

3. In a large skillet, sauté the carrot, shallots, celery, garlic, and thyme in the clarified butter. Add chicken pieces and sauté, partially covered, over medium-high heat for a few minutes on each side, or until just tender and springy to the touch. Transfer to a serving platter and top with the sautéed mushrooms. Cover with foil to keep warm.

4. Quickly prepare the sauce: Add the Cognac, wine, and half of the cream to the skillet. Reduce by half over high heat. Mix the remaining cream with the egg yolks, cornstarch, and seasonings to taste. Add to the reduced liquid and simmer without boiling, stirring constantly, until thickened. Taste for seasoning. Strain sauce through a fine sieve over the chicken. Arrange the pastry crescents around the dish and serve immediately.

Serve a light red wine—a Graves, Pomerol, or Beaune.

◆   U N D E R   T H E   C O O K ' S   H A T   ◆

Have everything ready so that you can prepare the sauce as fast as possible, no longer than 3 minutes, as the chicken pieces will toughen and harden very quickly, preventing them from absorbing the sauce.

◆ *Chaud-Froid* ◆

The Maréchal de Luxembourg was entertaining dinner guests at his Château de Montmorency in 1759 when a messenger arrived, requesting that the Maréchal come to the King at once.

The dismayed guests ate very little dinner. Two dishes were returned to the larder untouched—a fricassee of chicken and a salmis of partridge.

On his return that evening the Maréchal ordered the leftovers to be served without reheating.

Remembering how much he enjoyed those two dishes, the Maréchal later asked his chef to serve them again. The chef thought they should be called *refroidis* (chilled), but the Maréchal baptized them *chaud-froid* (hot-cold), and that term is still in use today to describe a dish that has been cooked and chilled before serving.

Chaud-Froid de Volaille

BREAST OF CHICKEN, CHAUD-FROID

Perfect for a formal summer luncheon or part of a buffet; prepare this dish a day ahead.

8 servings

4 large whole chicken breasts, halved, skinned, and boned
6 tablespoons Clarified Butter (see Index)
2½ tablespoons unsalted butter
2½ tablespoons flour
2¾ cups Chicken Stock (see Index)
⅓ cup dry white wine
¾ cup heavy cream
Salt and white pepper
1 tablespoon unflavored gelatin
Truffle slices or tarragon or chervil leaves, blanched for ½
    minute, then dipped in cold water
3 cups Aspic (see Index), plus ½ cup white wine
Watercress

1. Cook the chicken breasts in clarified butter over medium-high heat for a few minutes on each side or until just tender. Chicken should be cooked but remain springy to the touch. Wrap in foil and chill immediately.

2. Prepare the *chaud-froid* sauce: Melt the unsalted butter in a saucepan and blend in the flour. Stir in 2½ cups of the chicken stock, the wine, heavy cream, and seasonings to taste. Bring to a boil, lower the heat, and cook until reduced to 2½ cups.

3. Soften gelatin in remaining ¼ cup chicken stock. Stir gelatin into the hot sauce until it is dissolved. Set the pan of sauce in a bowl half-filled with cracked ice and stir until aspic is almost set.

4. Trim the chicken with shears into oval shapes. Dip into the *chaud-froid* sauce until evenly coated. Place on a rack over a shallow pan. Chill. If a second coating is necessary, warm the sauce until liquefied, then chill again on ice. The sauce should not run off the chicken (which would mean it is not chilled enough), nor should it form thick patches on the chicken.

5. Decorate the chicken with slices of truffle or blanched tarragon or chervil leaves.

6. Prepare the aspic, adding the ½ cup white wine, and stir it with a metal spoon over ice to cool it more quickly. When the aspic reaches the consistency of oil, spoon over the chicken. Chill. Pour

remaining aspic into a flat dish to make a ½-inch-deep layer and chill until firm. Chop it finely.

7. Arrange the coated chicken pieces on a serving plate. Garnish with the chopped aspic and watercress.

Serve with Mixed Vegetable Salad (see Index), garnished with asparagus tips.

◆   UNDER THE COOK'S HAT   ◆

If canned chicken broth is used in place of stock, add 1 small leek and ½ celery rib, chopped; 1 small garlic clove, minced; and a little thyme. Cook covered for 25 minutes, then strain.

Poulet en Gelée

CHICKEN IN ASPIC

This is an ideal summer dish, excellent for picnics. Prepare this a day in advance.

3 chicken breasts, split   *6 servings*
3 tablespoons unsalted butter
Salt and freshly ground pepper
1 medium-size onion, minced
1 sprig of fresh tarragon, or ½ teaspoon dried
1 tablespoon unflavored gelatin
3½ cups Chicken Stock (see Index)
¼ cup dry white vermouth or white wine
2 tablespoons Cognac
2 teaspoons lemon juice
½ pound boiled ham, ¼ inch thick, cut into julienne

1. Pat the chicken breasts dry. Melt the butter in a large heavy skillet and cook the chicken, skin side up, over medium heat until golden. Turn the chicken, reduce the heat, and season with salt and pepper.

2. Add the onion and tarragon. After 10 minutes, turn the chicken, and cook until done.

3. Remove the chicken. Chill.

4. Soften the gelatin in ½ cup of the chicken stock.

5. Deglaze the bottom of the skillet with the vermouth. Add the remaining chicken stock and cook for 5 minutes. Add the gelatin

mixture, stirring until gelatin is dissolved. Add the Cognac and lemon juice. Strain through a fine sieve.

6. Remove and discard the skin and bones from the breasts. Cut the meat into 2 or 3 pieces and arrange in a shallow serving dish or a mold.

7. Arrange the ham strips around the chicken. Cover with the aspic. Chill for several hours, or overnight, until firm.

8. Unmold on a chilled serving plate dipped into cold water to center the aspic.

Serve with cooked and chilled cauliflower covered with Mayonnaise Chantilly, or with Mixed Vegetable Salad (see Index).

◆   U N D E R   T H E   C O O K ' S   H A T   ◆

An attractive way of decorating this dish is as follows: Chill the aspic and remove the solidified fat on the top, then proceed to clarify it, following the directions for Quick Aspic (see Index). Add 2 tablespoons Cognac. Pour one-eighth of the aspic into a glass dish. When almost set, arrange 1 dozen slices, or more, of stuffed green olives on top. Pour over another thin layer of aspic. Let almost set, then add the chicken, ham, and the rest of the aspic. When you unmold it, the olive decoration will be on top.

◆ *Turkey* ◆

Victor Hugo was reputed to have one of the most extraordinary appetites that ever existed. He ate oranges with their skins and lobsters in their shells, claiming with an Olympian serenity that it helped pass their flesh.

Hugo said of the turkey, "This is a ridiculous animal. There is maybe a little too much for one, but certainly not enough for two!"

One of the first written reports of turkey comes from Hernando Cortés, who reported sighting turkeys in Mexico in 1519. Because America was known then as the West Indies, turkey was first known to the French as *poule d'Indes* (hen of the Indies), later shortened to *dinde*. Until the nineteenth century, it was also called *jésuite* because the Jesuits of Bourges raised many turkeys on their land.

Tradition has it that the first cooked turkey to be served in Europe was at the wedding of Charles IX of France to Elizabeth of Austria on November 26, 1570, in Mézières. It was served with all its feathers, its feet and beak painted gold, and it was filled with chestnut stuffing.

Vincent La Chapelle was head chef in the kitchen of Madame de Pompadour and later of Louis XV. French cuisine had become quite ostentatious by that time and he did much to simplify it. As a result, his recipes are still held in high esteem.

For a traditional stuffed turkey, this recipe from his book *Le Cuisinier Moderne* (1733) is as good today as it was when it was written.

Dinde aux Marrons
et Petites Saucisses à la Broche

Take a turkey, clean and empty it. Chop the liver, add parsley, chives, salt, grated pork, butter, salt, pepper, herbs, and spices.

Peel the chestnuts and place them in live charcoal to remove the thin skin, then mix with the stuffing and with little sausages sautéed in butter. Place in the body cavity of the turkey, which has been wrapped with bards of lard, and season with pepper. Put on the spit.

Take more peeled chestnuts. Place in a baking tin with fire on top and bottom and remove their thin skins. Place in a pan with bouillon and finish cooking. When cooked, drain the pan and replace the juices with half a spoon of meat glaze, a little cullis and juice. Once cooked, remove the turkey from the spit and remove the lard. Place the bird on a plate with the chestnuts around it. Sprinkle with lemon juice and serve very hot as an entrée.

Grimod de la Reynière, famous gastronome and writer, wrote in 1803, "Until now, no one knew any other way to serve a whole turkey but stuffed with truffles and on a spit; if the turkey had in the least passed the age of maturity . . . it was tough."

When Grimod de la Reynière first suggested to Chef le Gacque that he might braise a turkey, the chef stepped back three paces and vehemently listed all the principles of French cookery that could not be changed, stating that such a dish would be a failure and that to protect his honor he could not serve it.

But Grimod was determined and insisted that he would assume all the risk in addition to taking under his special protection the honor of Monsieur le Gacque, whatever the outcome.

"And the turkey was eaten November 16, in great silence which is characteristic of true gastronomes. It was unanimously voted to be excellent and superior to all those roast turkeys whose spirit had evaporated on the spit."

Dindonneau Braisé

BRAISED TURKEY

6 servings

1 freshly killed turkey, 6 to 8 pounds, cut up with wing tips
    removed
4 tablespoons Clarified Butter (see Index)
3 medium-size carrots, diced
3 medium-size onions, coarsely chopped
1 celery rib, diced
Salt and pepper
Bouquet garni (several sprigs of parsley, 1 bay leaf, 1 teaspoon
    thyme)
1 tablespoon minced fresh tarragon, or 1 teaspoon dried
1 cup Chicken Stock (see Index)
¼ cup sherry or Port wine (optional)
2 teaspoons cornstarch, diluted in ¼ cup stock for each cup of
    sauce
Watercress or parsley

1. Pat the turkey pieces dry. Heat clarified butter in a large braising pan or roaster with a tight-fitting cover. Brown the turkey pieces on all sides, using 2 spoons to turn pieces over, being careful not to burn the juices on the bottom of the pan. Transfer turkey to a platter.

2. Add the vegetables and sauté until they begin to brown. Place the turkey pieces on top. Add the *bouquet garni* and tarragon. Season with salt and pepper.

3. Set the pan in a preheated 325°F. oven. Cover tightly. After 30 minutes, add ½ cup stock. Turn the turkey pieces a few times, adding the rest of the stock toward the end of the cooking time (about 2 to 2½ hours).

4. When the turkey is done, remove the pieces to a platter and keep warm. Discard the *bouquet garni.* Add to the juice and vegetables in the pan the cornstarch mixture and simmer the sauce until thickened to the desired consistency.

5. Arrange the turkey pieces on a hot serving plate. Garnish with watercress or parsley. Serve the sauce separately.

Braised lettuce or chestnuts and puréed potatoes would be fine accompanying vegetables. A light Beaujolais is suggested with this dish.

◆ *Variations* ◆

1 pound thinly sliced mushrooms can be added 15 minutes before the turkey is done.

You may add 1 cup Brown Sauce (see Index) and Port wine to the chicken stock.

◆ UNDER THE COOK'S HAT ◆

If a smaller number of servings is desirable, buy turkey parts (now universally available) and treat in the same way.

◆   ◆   ◆

Honoré de Balzac had a prodigious appetite. One night at Véry, a renowned Paris restaurant, he ate 100 oysters, 12 lamb chops, a duck with turnips, 2 roast partridges, a sole Normande, and 12 pears, accompanied by fine wine, coffee, and liqueur. Werdet, his editor, commented that only the bones were left.

Faisan à la Sauvagine du Poitou

PHEASANT WITH APPLES, MUSHROOMS, AND CREAM

1 large pheasant   *2 servings*
Salt and freshly ground pepper
1 small onion, halved
5 tablespoons unsalted butter
3 tablespoons finely chopped shallots
½ pound mushrooms, thinly sliced
2 large flavorful apples, peeled, cored, and quartered
2 commercial patty shells
2 tablespoons Cognac or Armagnac
½ cup heavy cream

1. Season the cavity of the pheasant with salt and pepper. Insert the onion. Truss the bird (see Index) and rub with butter.

2. Heat the butter in a Dutch oven or casserole. Add the shallots and cook for 1 minute. Add the mushrooms and cook for 2 minutes, stirring constantly. Add the apples, stirring well.

3. Place the pheasant on top of the mushrooms and apples. Bake in a preheated 375°F. oven for 25 minutes, basting the pheasant 2 or 3 times. Cover and cook for another 20 minutes, or until done.

4. Roll the patty shells into 2 ovals 4 by 6 inches. Bake in a preheated 400°F. oven until golden, about 20 minutes.

5. Remove the pheasant from the casserole and discard the trussing string. Split the pheasant with a large knife and place each half on top of an oval pastry.

6. Add the Cognac and cream to the mushroom-apple mixture. Taste for seasonings. Cook sauce over medium-high heat until it is slightly thickened; spoon over the pheasant.

Serve a medium-dry Champagne.

◆   U N D E R   T H E   C O O K ' S   H A T   ◆

Two small Cornish hens can also be prepared this way.

◆ *Pigeons* ◆

Young pigeons, which have always been prized as food by the French, played an important role in nutrition in the early days and were also a source of profit because *colombin* (pigeon manure) was sought after as fertilizer. Cow manure was not readily available in early times because cattle were not numerous and pigeon manure was the main fertilizer for all agricultural purposes.

Pigeons are raised in a *colombier* (a dove or pigeon cote), often a round structure built in the same style as the main dwelling. One can see many fascinating types of architecture represented in the *colombiers* of the French countryside, some dating back to the fourteenth century.

At the time of the Revolution of 1789, there were 42,000 dove and pigeon cotes owned by noblemen. Any peasants caught killing the birds were severely punished. Olivier de Serres (1539–1619), an agronomist, referred to the *colombiers* as "these perpetual larders . . . which help to . . . nourish noblemen's families without their having to put a hand in the purse." Several hundred pigeons were consumed daily at the royal table.

Pigeon flesh was thought to create cheerfulness.

Pintadeaux en Casserole à la Mâconnaise

CORNISH GAME HENS WITH MUSHROOMS
AND GLAZED ONIONS

This recipe can be applied to any small game birds such as baby guinea hens, small pheasants, pigeon, or partridge.

1 medium-size onion, halved   *4 servings*
2 Cornish game hens, 1½ to 2 pounds each
Salt and freshly ground pepper
5½ tablespoons unsalted butter
4 tablespoons Clarified Butter (see Index)
¼ cup shallots
3 tablespoons Cognac
¾ cup light red Burgundy wine
Bouquet garni
18 to 24 small white Glazed Onions (see Index)
½ pound fresh mushrooms, sliced
1 loaf of good-quality bread, unsliced
Clarified Butter for frying bread
Watercress
2 teaspoons cornstarch dissolved in 2 tablespoons red wine
    (optional)

1. Place half of the medium-size onion in the cavity of each bird. Season with salt and pepper. Truss the birds and rub with 4 tablespoons of the unsalted butter.

2. Heat 3 tablespoons clarified butter in a large casserole. Brown the birds over medium-high heat. Drain off the fat.

3. Stir in the shallots, then add the Cognac and wine and boil for a few seconds before adding the *bouquet garni*. Cover casserole tightly and place in a preheated 350°F. oven for about 30 minutes, or until the birds are tender.

4. About 10 minutes before the birds are done, sauté the mushrooms in 1½ tablespoons unsalted butter for 2 to 3 minutes. Add to the casserole with the glazed onions.

5. Trim the bread and cut 4 lengthwise slices ¾ inch thick so they will fit under the game hens. Sauté in clarified butter until golden.

6. Remove and discard the strings on the birds. Split each bird with a large knife and place each half on a slice of sautéed bread. Arrange the onions and mushrooms around the birds and garnish with watercress.

7. Boil the sauce for 4 to 5 minutes, until slightly syrupy, or reduce for 2 to 3 minutes and add the cornstarch-wine mixture. Spoon the sauce over the birds.

Serve a Mâcon wine.

Pintadeaux Braisés à l'Orange
BRAISED CORNISH GAME HENS WITH ORANGE

To prepare enough duck for 6 people would require facilities not usually available in the home kitchen. Game hens are just as appropriate with the classic sauce and much easier to prepare.

3 Cornish game hens, 1½ to 2 pounds each   *6 servings*
6 tablespoons unsalted butter
Salt and pepper
4 oranges
8 tablespoons clarified butter
2 onions, coarsely chopped
2 carrots, finely diced
4 shallots, chopped
¾ cup Port wine
1½ cups Brown Sauce (see Index)
¼ cup Cointreau liqueur
6 Canapé Bases (see Index), each large enough for ½ bird
Watercress

1. Pat the birds dry and put 1 tablespoon unsalted butter into each one. Season the cavities and insert several orange sections from 1 orange. Sew up the openings and truss. Rub the birds all over with the remaining butter.

2. Brown one bird at a time in clarified butter in a large casserole over medium heat. Be careful that the skin does not adhere to the pan. Remove the birds and put the vegetables in the casserole. When vegetables are golden, place the birds on top. Cover and braise in a preheated 325°F. oven for 40 minutes to 1 hour, or until done.

3. Prepare the sauce: Peel the rind from 2 oranges without including any of the white inside peel. Cut rind into matchstick or julienne strips ¹⁄₁₆ inch wide and about 1½ inches long. Drop into boiling water and boil for 5 minutes, then drain.

4. Prepare the oranges for garnishing the border of the serving

plate: After removing the white inner peel of the 2 peeled oranges, slice the pulp thinly and arrange around the border of a serving platter. Warm the platter over simmering water.

5. When the birds are done, tilt them to let the juices run out. Cut each one into halves with a large knife and place them on the heated serving platter. Discard the baked orange segments from the cavities. Cover birds with foil to keep warm while preparing the sauce.

6. Discard the vegetables and fat from the pan. Deglaze the pan with Port wine and the juice of 1 orange. Reduce to half of the original volume. Strain through a fine sieve into a saucepan. Add the brown sauce and half of the orange julienne. Reduce again by one-third and correct seasoning if necessary. Remove from heat and swirl in the Cointreau.

7. Place each half bird on a canapé base. Spoon some of the orange sauce over them and serve the remainder separately. Scatter remaining orange strips on top of the bird. Garnish with watercress at both ends of the serving dish.

Serve French-Style Peas on the side, or molded Rice Pilaf (see Index for pages).

Suggested wine: a Bordeaux such as Pomerol

◆   UNDER THE COOK'S HAT   ◆

A miniature Cointreau liqueur bottle holds just the right amount for the *sauce à l'orange*.

◆   ◆   ◆

Denis Papin invented the pressure cooker in 1681. He called it a *digester*. Its purpose, then as now, was to cook meat, vegetables, and fruits quickly.

François-Nicolas Appert, founder of the canning industry, said in 1831, "This terrible machine caused an astonishment mixed with fright." Because of the many accidents with pressure cookers, it took more than a century for them to be generally accepted.

Appert greatly simplified the pressure cooker and it became essential in canning food. He also made juice of duck meat into tablets "after one was assured of delivery of three thousand ducks a month . . ." wrote Appert.

Papin's original *digester* is on display at the Conservatoire National des Arts et Métiers in Paris.

Canard à l'Orange

ROAST DUCK WITH ORANGE SAUCE

Canard à l'orange dates back to the time of the Crusaders, who introduced oranges into France.

2 ducklings, 4½ to 5 pounds each	*4 servings*

2 ducklings, 4½ to 5 pounds each   *4 servings*
Salt and freshly ground pepper
4 oranges
½ cup excellent Port wine
1½ cups Brown Sauce (see Index)
¼ cup Cointreau
Watercress

1. Wash the ducklings, then pat dry with a towel. Sprinkle the cavities with salt and pepper. Place ½ orange in each duckling. Cut the wing tips off and truss the birds.

2. Roast the ducks, breast up, in a large pan in a preheated 400°F. oven for 20 minutes. Lower the temperature to 375°F. and roast for 1 hour longer, basting frequently with the drippings.

3. Using a vegetable peeler, and being careful not to include any of the white portion, peel the rind from 2 oranges. Cut rind into thin julienne strips. Place in a pan of boiling water, boil for 5 minutes, then drain.

4. Remove the white portion of the orange peel. Thinly slice the pulp and arrange slices around the border of a serving platter. Warm the platter over a pan of simmering water.

5. Tilt the ducks to let the juices run out of them. Remove them from the oven, and place on a carving board. Cover with foil.

6. Spoon off all the fat from the roasting pan. Add the Port and the juice of 1 orange to the roasting juices. Reduce by half over medium heat. Strain into a saucepan. Add the brown sauce and julienne strips of rind. Reduce again by one-third and correct the seasonings. Add the Cointreau off the heat.

7. Carve the duck and garnish with watercress. Spoon some of the sauce over the ducks and serve remaining sauce separately.

Shoestring potatoes and French-Style Peas (see Index) are good accompaniments for duck.
    Suggested wine: a Saint-Émilion

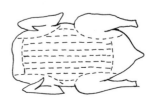

Foies de Volaille, Sauce Madère

CHICKEN LIVERS WITH MADEIRA SAUCE

4 slices of good-quality bread   *4 servings*
9 tablespoons Clarified Butter (see Index)
½ pound mushrooms, thinly sliced
1 pound fresh chicken livers, cleaned
2 tablespoons finely chopped shallots
1 tablespoon flour
⅔ cup dry white wine
½ teaspoon thyme
Salt and freshly ground pepper
1 teaspoon meat glaze
¼ cup Madeira wine
3 tablespoons chopped parsley

1. Remove crusts from the bread and cut the slices diagonally into 2 triangles each. Sauté in 4 tablespoons butter until golden. Reserve.

2. In a skillet, quickly sauté the mushrooms in 2 tablespoons butter. Transfer to a warm plate and cover.

3. Sauté the livers in 2 tablespoons butter until golden brown and add to the mushrooms.

4. Add remaining butter to the skillet and add the shallots; sauté, stirring, until wilted. Sprinkle with the flour and whisk until golden. Add the white wine, thyme, seasonings to taste, and meat glaze. Simmer for a few minutes until slightly thickened and syrupy.

5. Add the Madeira and mix well. Stir in the livers and mushrooms and cook for another minute.

6. Place 2 bread triangles on each plate, filling the center with livers, mushrooms, and the sauce, and sprinkle with parsley.

Foies de Volaille aux Fines Herbes

CHICKEN LIVERS WITH HERBS

1 pound fresh chicken livers   *4 servings*
Coarse salt
3 tablespoons Clarified Butter (see Index)
½ teaspoon thyme

1 tablespoon chopped fresh parsley
1 tablespoon finely snipped fresh chives
Sprinkle of lemon juice
Salt and pepper
Canapé Bases (see Index)
Watercress

1. Soak chicken livers in a bowl of cold water, salted with coarse salt, for 30 minutes.

2. Pat the livers dry, then sauté in clarified butter. When almost done, sprinkle on a generous amount of thyme, the parsley, chives, and lemon juice. Season with salt and pepper.

3. Serve on canapé bases. Garnish with watercress.

9. *Les Viandes* MEATS

• *Le Boeuf* •
B E E F

The ancients regarded it as a crime to eat the flesh of cattle—indeed, the Egyptians consulted the bull Apis as an oracle.

Beef was so scarce in France that in the year 1122, only one butcher could be found in Paris. The butcher's trade was passed from father to son or nephew. Only the King of France could appoint a new butcher and that only once in his lifetime.

In 1387, the butchers of Paris established a corporation which, by its great wealth and power, played a part in the political life of the Middle Ages.

Animals were slaughtered on the banks of the Seine, on a street then called rue de la Tuerie (street of the butchery), before slaughterhouses were built on the borders of the Bièvre river.

The *Parlement* in 1589 passed laws governing the butchers and formed them into a community.

Until the eighteenth century, no cattle could be killed during Lent. Butchers were authorized by the king to sell only to people who had a dispensation from the clergy or the Hôtel-Dieu (the oldest hospital of Paris, dating back to the year 656).

The butchers cooked in water the pieces of meat too small to be sold. The rendered fat served to feed the wicks which lighted the streets of Paris.

It was Napoleon who created public slaughterhouses, and they, in turn, gave birth to the wholesale and retail meat trades. The number of butcher shops in Paris, under Napoleon, was fixed at 400.

Held in high regard, the butchers "hardly deign to count the receipts in the chops, which they left in the lily-white hands of some *dame de compagnie*. They spent the evening dressed in their brown suits and wearing kid gloves in the most comfortable drawing-rooms."

From the 1300s to the 1800s, the parade of *le boeuf gras* (fat steer) was celebrated by Parisians on Shrove Tuesday. *Le boeuf gras* was crowned with flowers and led through the streets of Paris. The most memorable parade was held in 1739. *Le boeuf gras* was led through the Sainte Chapelle and up the stairs, into the *Parlement*, where he bowed his head to the Président.

Under the reign of Napoleon III, the selected animal was named for a famous battle or a well-known personality.

Greater consumption of beef in France started only after World War I.

During the Seven Years' War (1756–1763), the Maréchal, Duc de Richelieu, decided to release the prisoners—princes and princesses and their attendants who had been captured during the war of Hanover. Before freeing them, the Maréchal wished to offer them a meal.

When the *officier de bouche* learned this, he despairingly said, "My Lord, the countryside is devastated for more than 84 kilometers and there is nothing left in the kitchen but a beef and a few roots [vegetables]." The Maréchal then composed a menu of twenty-two dishes using beef in every dish, from *hors-d'oeuvre* to desserts.

A note was added at the end of the menu which read:

> If by misfortune, this meal turns out not to be very good, I shall withhold from the wages of Maret and Rouquelère [probably his maître d'hôtel and master chef] a fine of 100 pistoles. Go, and entertain no more doubt!
>
> —RICHELIEU

Fine quality beef should be a true red, veined with ivory-white fat. The fat around the meat should be very white and firm to the touch. Inferior quality beef varies from pale red to dark brownish red with dark yellow fat.

Meat should be at room temperature before cooking. Except for steaks, add salt toward the end of the cooking time of the meat. Salt draws out juices and toughens the meat.

Turn the meat and transfer it to the serving plate using 2 wooden spoons. Forks pierce the meat, causing the juice to escape.

Let a roast rest for 15 minutes before carving. As it rests, the meat juices become evenly distributed; if you carve a roast immediately after removing it from the oven, most of the juice will run out, leaving the meat dry.

Filet de Boeuf

BEEF FILLET

1 fillet of beef, 4 pounds, trimmed and tied   *6 servings*
Melted butter
Salt and freshly ground pepper

1. Brush the fillet with butter. Roast in a preheated 400°F. oven for about 35 minutes, or until a meat thermometer inserted into the thickest part of the meat registers 125°F. Season with salt and pepper halfway through the cooking time. The fillet should be crusty brown on the outside and pink-to-rare inside.

2. Let the roast rest for 10 to 15 minutes. Skim and discard the fat from the pan. Boil the pan juices and strain.

3. Slice the meat into 1-inch-thick slices and cover with the juices.

Serve a great Burgundy wine such as a Chambertin.

♦ *Variation* ♦

A more refined sauce can be made by adding 1 cup Brown Sauce (see Index) to the roasting pan and boiling over medium-high heat until reduced. Add 2 tablespoons sherry and swirl in 2 tablespoons cold butter, in small pieces. Coat the meat with the sauce.

Chateaubriand

CHATEAUBRIAND

This steak recipe was invented by chef Montmireil in 1822 when the great writer and statesman Chateaubriand was France's Ambassador to England.

The Chateaubriand is a grilled, thick slice of the beef fillet, weighing ¾ pound to 1½ pounds, cut from the large end.

Flatten the meat slightly with the side of a cleaver, then brush the steak with Clarified Butter (see Index). Broil to the rare stage without charring the surface. Season with salt and pepper.

Serve with a Béarnaise Sauce (see Index). Garnish with a few sprigs of watercress. Carve the meat in diagonal slices at the table.

• *Tournedos* •

The name *tournedos*, for a thin slice of beef fillet, comes from a spelling mistake. During the nineteenth century, all the stands in the famous Parisian market, Les Halles, faced the main alleys. A few stands with their backs to the alleys (*tourne le dos*) sold fish that were less than fresh. Pieces of beef fillet which were not of the freshest quality, sold at Les Halles, were also called *tourne le dos,* comparing the old beef to the stale fish.

Around 1860, a restaurant near Les Halles put *tournedos* for fillet of beef on its menu by mistake. The clients, not knowing the meaning, liked it and the new name was kept.

Tournedos, also called medallions of beef, are tender, lean morsels about 1 inch thick, cut from the section of fillet between the filet mignon and the Chateaubriand.

Tournedos Rossini was the creation of chef Joseph Voiron when he was managing the Bonvalet restaurant in Paris, in the last century. He named the dish after Rossini, the Italian opera composer, who arrived in Paris in 1824 to direct the Theâtre des Italiens.

Rossini was excessively fond of truffles. He himself invented an extraordinary dish of macaroni—each piece of pasta was stuffed with a mixture of foie gras and truffles. The ivory syringe that was specially made for this task was sold at an auction after Rossini's death for a considerable amount of money.

Tournedos Rossini

TOURNEDOS WITH FOIE GRAS AND TRUFFLES

1 small truffle   *4 servings*
⅓ cup Madeira wine
4 tournedos (1-inch slices of beet fillet, about 6 ounces each)
4 slices of fine-quality sandwich bread
Clarified Butter (see Index)
6 tablespoons unsalted butter
¼ teaspoon oil
Salt and freshly ground pepper
4 ½-inch slices from a small *bloc de foie gras* (5-ounce)
1 cup Brown Sauce (see Index)

1. Slice 4 thin slices from the center of the truffle. Chop the rest and reserve. Add the truffle juice to the Madeira.

2. Slightly flatten the tournedos. Tie each with a string so it will retain its round shape when cooked.

3. With a glass or cookie cutter, trim the bread to rounds to fit the tournedos. Fry bread rounds on both sides in clarified butter. Place on a hot serving plate and keep warm in a low oven.

4. Sauté the tournedos very quickly in 3 tablespoons of the butter and the oil for 1 or 2 minutes on one side. Turn over and season with salt and pepper. When small drops of blood appear on the surface, the meat is done to the medium-rare stage. Discard the strings and place the tournedos on the bread rounds.

5. Warm the 4 slices of truffle with the slices of *foie gras* in 1 tablespoon butter in a pan.

6. Pour off excess fat from the pan used for the tournedos, and deglaze with the Madeira. Boil until reduced by half. Blend in the brown sauce, and simmer for a few minutes with the chopped truffles. Off the heat, swirl in remaining 2 tablespoons butter, cut into small pieces. Pour the sauce over the tournedos. Top each with a slice of *foie gras* and a slice of truffle. Serve immediately.

Suggested wine: red Bordeaux, Saint Julien; or red Burgundy, Pommard

◆　　◆　　◆

Telle, quand vient la nuit, après le crépuscule
Brille l'étoile d'or qu'on voit au firmament.
Sur nos tables tu luis, précieux tubercule,
Et semble des festins être le diamant.

Just as, when night arrives, after the twilight,
We see a golden star shine in the sky,
So does the precious truffle shine on our table
And seem to be the diamond of the feast.
—ACHILLE OZANNE

Tournedos aux Champignons
TOURNEDOS WITH MUSHROOMS AND MADEIRA SAUCE

Prepare the tournedos as in the preceding recipe, omitting the truffles and *foie gras*. Sauté in butter ½ pound button mushrooms, stems removed. Top the tournedos with the mushrooms and spoon Madeira sauce over all.

Tournedos à la Béarnaise
TOURNEDOS WITH BÉARNAISE SAUCE

Prepare the tournedos as in the preceding recipe, without the Madeira sauce. Garnish each tournedos with a large sautéed mushroom cap filled with Béarnaise Sauce (see Index). Serve additional Béarnaise sauce separately.

Entrecôte Grillée à la Bordelaise
BROILED STEAK WITH BORDELAISE SAUCE

This classic grilled steak recipe from Bordeaux is served immediately after being grilled, with the bordelaise sauce over it.

The French cuts of meat are very different from those in the United States. *Entrecôte* means, literally, meat from between the ribs and is the equivalent of a boned rib steak. Club and sirloin steaks make fine substitutes.

Bordelaise Sauce (see Index)   *4 servings*
1 pound entrecôte or rib (without the bone), club or sirloin
    steak, 1¼ inches thick
2 tablespoons oil
2 tablespoons unsalted butter, melted
Salt and freshly ground pepper
Fresh parsley, chopped

1. Prepare the bordelaise sauce. Reserve.
2. Preheat the grill or broiler.
3. Brush the meat with the oil and butter. Place the meat as close as possible to the source of heat. After 5 or 6 minutes, turn the meat with tongs. Season with salt and pepper. Broil for 4 or 5 minutes on the other side for medium rare meat.
4. Place the meat on a warm serving plate. Cover with the sauce and sprinkle with parsley.

Suggested wine: a Bordeaux, Médoc, or red Graves

◆   *Variation*   ◆

For a simpler way, but just as delicious, grill the meat as in the basic recipe. Prepare Snail Butter (see Index). Spread the butter generously all over the top of the meat and serve immediately.

Boeuf à la Bourguignonne
BEEF BOURGUIGNONNE

This stew is one of the favorite French beef recipes.

1 cup cubed lean salt pork, rinsed   *6 servings*
1 to 2 tablespoons rendered beef fat or unsalted butter
18 to 20 small white pearl onions, peeled
3½ pounds chuck pot roast or bottom round, cut into 2-inch cubes
2 large onions, quartered
3 tablespoons flour
2 garlic cloves, minced
2 cups hearty red Burgundy wine
1 cup broth or water
Bouquet garni (parsley sprigs, 2 bay leaves, thyme)
Salt and freshly ground pepper
¾ pound tiny mushroom caps
3 tablespoons butter
Fresh parsley, chopped

1. Parboil the salt pork for 5 minutes. Pat dry with paper towels.
2. Melt fat or butter in a Dutch oven and sauté the salt pork until golden. In the same fat sauté the pearl onions slowly until golden, stirring occasionally, adding more fat as necessary. Remove with a slotted spoon, cover, and reserve.

3. Sauté beef and quartered onions in the same fat over medium-high heat. Do this step in 2 or 3 batches as the meat must be in one layer and not too crowded. Be careful not to burn the meat on the bottom of the pan.

4. Lower the heat. Sprinkle meat with the flour and stir until golden brown. Add the garlic, wine, broth or water, and *bouquet garni.* Season with salt and pepper. Cover and place in a preheated 325°F. oven for about 3 hours. Correct seasoning if necessary. If the sauce gets too thick, add more broth.

5. About 10 minutes before the meat is done, sauté the mushrooms in butter.

6. Add mushrooms, salt pork, and onions to the beef. Sprinkle with parsley.

Serve with parsleyed potatoes, mashed potatoes, or noodles.

◆ *Boeuf à la Mode* ◆

Beat it well, lard it with big pieces of lard, sear in a frying pan, and place it in an earthenware bowl with a glass of dry white wine, 2 glasses of water, a pacquet [bouquet garni], salt, pepper, bay leaf, lime, half a dozen mushrooms; cover well with another bowl sealed with dough, and cook it on a slow fire. When it is cooked, strain and add the juice of a lemon.

—PIERRE DE LUNE,
Le Cuisinier, 1656

One of France's best loved meat dishes, this became popular when, about 1792, two brothers from Marseilles opened a restaurant in Paris, 8 rue de Valois, called Restaurant du Boeuf à la Mode, which lasted until World War II.

Over the restaurant entrance was a swinging sign depicting a steer dressed as a *Merveilleuse* (term for the latest style of fashion during the Directoire), or *à la mode.* The steer wore a large, blue fringed scarf draped around its shoulders, and on its head was a bonnet trimmed with an ostrich feather.

The restaurant specialty was, of course, the *boeuf à la mode.* The original recipe has long since changed but carrots and onions, not mentioned by Pierre de Lune, are today an essential part of this superb dish.

Boeuf à la Mode

BRAISED BEEF IN WINE WITH CARROTS AND ONIONS

Ask the butcher to lard the meat in 4 or 5 places with pencil-thin strips of pork fat taken from a roast.

MARINADE   *6 servings*
1 tablespoon coarse salt
1 teaspoon pepper
2 or 3 garlic cloves, chopped
1½ tablespoons chopped parsley
½ cup Cognac

5 pounds of rump roast, cut from the midsection of the rump,
    in a rectangular piece
Clarified Butter (see Index)
1 medium-size onion, finely chopped
6 shallots, finely chopped
1½ cups dry white wine
1½ cups Brown Sauce (see Index)
1 large bay leaf
½ teaspoon thyme
1 pound young carrots, peeled and cut into 1½- to 2-inch pieces
Glazed Onions (see Index)

1. Rub the coarse salt and the pepper into the surface of the meat, then the garlic and parsley. Place the meat in a nonmetallic bowl that is as deep as the roast. Add the Cognac, cover, and let the beef stand at room temperature for 2 to 3 hours, turning the meat occasionally with 2 wooden spoons.

2. Dry the meat. Heat clarified butter in a heavy casserole or Dutch oven. Brown the meat on all sides, turning it with the wooden spoons to brown evenly.

3. Add the chopped onions and shallots and stir until golden. Add the wine, brown sauce, remaining marinade, bay leaf, and thyme. Bring almost to a boil, cover tightly, and braise in a pre-heated 325°F. oven for 4 to 4½ hours.

4. Add the carrots 2 hours before the meat is done, and the glazed onions 5 minutes before the meat is ready.

5. Place the meat, on an ovenproof serving plate, in an oven heated to 500°F. and then turn it off. Glaze the meat by repeatedly spooning the sauce over it until a layer is set. Surround the meat

with the onions and carrots and some of the sauce. Serve the rest of the sauce separately.

Parsleyed potatoes or noodles make a good accompaniment.

◆ *Mustard* ◆

Greeks and Romans used mustard seeds or a mustard flour called *sinapis* to flavor stews. Pythagoras believed that mustard increased the memory.

Dijon was, until the fourth century, the only city in France that had the privilege of making mustard. Palladius, son of the prefect of the Gauls, at that time gave a recipe for mustard that is similar to the mustard of Dijon today.

"Pulverize a seventh and a half measure of mustard seeds to make mustard flour, add a pound of honey, a pound of Spanish oil, a seventh measure of strong white vinegar, and when all is mixed well, you can use it."

When Louis XI was a guest for a meal, he always carried with him a pot of Dijon mustard. Louis XIV honored this mustard with a coat of arms featuring a silver funnel superimposed on sky blue.

In the eighteenth century, a vinegar-maker named Maille became well known when he became the purveyor to the Marquise de Pompadour and created eighty-four varieties of mustard, some flavored with garlic, tarragon, and truffles.

◆ ◆ ◆

There is no city but Dijon. There is no mustard but Dijon.
—JEAN MILLOT, *Proverbes*

Carbonnade de Boeuf à la Flamande

BRAISED BEEF WITH ONIONS AND BEER

Extraordinary as it may seem, the first alcoholic drink of the Gauls was beer, which was called *cervoise*. Sometimes honey was added.

During the Roman occupation, the Gauls were taught how to make wine. The wooden barrels used for their beer by the Gauls were perfect for wine; until then the Romans had kept wine in terracotta jugs.

Carbonnade de boeuf, dating back to the Middle Ages, is a very old dish from the province of Flandre, with a typical sweet-and-sour taste. Beer is the principal flavoring agent.

This dish is traditionally served with French fried potatoes, but steamed potatoes seem more appropriate with the flavorful sauce.

Rendered beef fat or Clarified Butter (see Index)   *6 servings*
3½ to 4 pounds beef rump or boneless chuck roast, cut into ½-inch slices
5 large yellow onions, coarsely chopped
1 tablespoon light brown sugar
1 tablespoon vinegar
1 tablespoon flour
1 bottle (16 ounces) beer
Salt and freshly ground pepper
½ teaspoon thyme
1 large bay leaf
2 tablespoons Dijon mustard
2 slices of stale French bread
Fresh parsley, chopped

1. Melt the fat or butter in a large heavy skillet. Brown 2 slices of beef at a time on both sides, over medium-high heat. Repeat until all the slices are done, being careful not to burn the meat on the bottom of the skillet.

2. Add more fat to the pan and sauté the onions until golden. Sprinkle with brown sugar, stirring well. Add the vinegar and sprinkle the flour over, stirring until the flour is golden. Add 1 cup of the beer, stirring quickly.

3. Alternate a layer of onion with a layer of meat and seasonings in a heavy casserole or Dutch oven, just large enough to hold the meat. Add the thyme, bay leaf, and mustard, and shred the bread over the top. Pour in remaining beer.

4. Cover and bake in a preheated 325°F. oven for about 3 hours. Sprinkle with parsley before serving directly from the casserole.

Serve cold beer with this.

♦   UNDER THE COOK'S HAT   ♦

The stale bread lessens the bitterness of the beer.

♦   ♦   ♦

Président Émile Loubet gave a memorable banquet in 1900 for more than 22,000 French mayors to commemorate the declaration of the first Republic.

Enormous tents were set up in the gardens at the Tuileries. There were 4 miles of tables, 250,000 plates, 700 pots of mustard, and 50,000 bottles of wine.

Potel et Chabot, the Parisian caterers, supplied food and wine for the occasion. The waiters performed their duties on bicycles and roller skates!

The menu was as follows:

Darnes de saumon glacées
Filet de boeuf en Bellevue
Pains de canetons de Rouen
Poulardes de Bresses rôties
Ballotines de faisan Saint-Hubert
Camemberts
Glaces à la vanille
Fruits

A few more interesting statistics show that 2,500 liters of mayonnaise were used for the salmon; it took 500 whole beef for the fillets, and 700,000 pheasants for the *ballotines de faisans*.

Estouffade de Boeuf à la Niçoise

BRAISED BEEF WITH WHITE WINE, TOMATOES, AND OLIVES

Estouffade is a Provençal word for braised stew. It is a very flavorful meat dish that cooks slowly in a closed casserole. It is served traditionally with noodles, sprinkled with freshly grated Parmesan cheese.

2½ pounds stewing beef, cut into 2-inch cubes   *4 servings*
2 marrowbones, each 2 inches long
3 tablespoons olive oil
3 or 4 onions, quartered
2 tablespoons flour
4 garlic cloves, minced
2 cups white wine
Bouquet garni (2 bay leaves, ½ teaspoon thyme, 2 sprigs of celery tops)
Salt and freshly ground pepper
Pinch of ground cloves

Pinch of cayenne pepper
4 tomatoes, peeled and chopped, or 1 pound canned tomatoes
2 tablespoons tomato paste
¾ pound button mushrooms, sautéed in butter with a minced
    garlic clove and fresh parsley
½ cup black olives, pitted
Lemon juice
Fresh parsley, chopped

1. In an ovenproof casserole, brown the meat and marrow-bones in hot olive oil on all sides, being careful not to burn them on the bottom of the pan. Remove the meat and bones and set aside.

2. Brown the quartered onions lightly. Return the meat and bones and sprinkle with the flour. Stir well and add the garlic. Pour in the wine and add the *bouquet garni* and seasonings to taste. Bring almost to a boil, then seal the casserole hermetically, and place in a preheated 325°F. oven.

3. After 1½ hours, add the tomatoes and the tomato paste. An hour later, add the sautéed mushrooms. Cook for 30 minutes longer.

4. Remove the *bouquet garni* and the bones. Add the olives, which should not cook but be thoroughly heated, and lemon juice to taste. Serve from the casserole with a sprinkle of chopped fresh parsley on top.

◆   UNDER THE COOK'S HAT   ◆

Chicken or guinea hen can be prepared the same way but with a shorter cooking time.

◆ *Daube* ◆

Meat cooked *en daube* is virtually synonymous with *braiser*. Both methods of cooking meat are named after the pans, *daubière* and *braisière*, in which the meat is cooked.

Before the oven, as we know it today, was invented, meat was cooked in a *braisière*. The lid was indented to hold live coals (*braises*) on top. This cooked the dish on top as well as on the bottom. This method of very slow cooking in tightly covered pots for several hours makes the meat very tender and flavorful.

Jean-Jacques Rousseau gives the following recipe for Daube à la Montigny-en-Vexin.

Take a two-pound piece of beef, plus a beautiful slice of ham, fat and lean. Add a knuckle of veal and a calf's foot for the jelly.

Chop the ham with a large carrot and a big onion. All this very, very fine.

Cover the bottom of the *cocotte* with this and place over it the beef and the veal.

Moisten with two-thirds of white wine and one-third of water so that the beef bathes well in it.

Let it cook in the *cocotte* for six hours.

Let it cool, skim the fat and put in a cool place, for this daube must be served cold in its jelly, the next day.

Let me know how you like it!

◆ UNDER THE COOK'S HAT ◆

Because a calf's foot is not readily available, once the meat has cooked, soften 1 tablespoon unflavored gelatin in 3 tablespoons white wine and add to the hot juice.

This *daube* is best braised in an earthenware *cocotte* just large enough to hold the meat.

Leftover *daube* can be put through a meat grinder, then mixed with a thick mushroom purée. Flavor generously with onion, garlic, and parsley, and season with salt and pepper to taste. Use as a filling for turnovers.

Boeuf Miroton

Very simple to prepare, boeuf Miroton is a classic and delicious way to use leftover boiled meat from a *pot-au-feu*.

¾ pound cold boiled beef — *2 or 3 servings*
3 onions, minced
Butter
2 tablespoons flour
2 cups broth from the pot-au-feu
Sprinkle of wine vinegar
Fresh bread crumbs

1. Cut the cold meat into very thin slices and place slices overlapping in a gratin dish.

2. Sauté onions in melted butter until golden. Sprinkle the flour over them and stir well before adding the broth and vinegar.

3. Pour sauce over meat. Sprinkle with bread crumbs and bake in a preheated 400°F. oven for 30 minutes, or until golden brown.

Boulettes de Boeuf, Sauce Moutarde
HAMBURGERS WITH MUSTARD SAUCE

1½ pounds beef chuck, ground
1 tablespoon minced shallot
1 tablespoon chopped fresh parsley
Salt and freshly ground pepper
2 tablespoons unsalted butter
1 tablespoon tarragon vinegar
2 tablespoons Dijon mustard
1 teaspoon fresh tarragon, snipped with scissors
¾ cup heavy cream

4 servings

1. Lightly mix the meat, shallot, parsley, and salt and pepper to taste. Shape four 1-inch-thick hamburgers from the meat, without pressing the meat too firmly when forming them.

2. Melt the butter in a heavy skillet. When sizzling, add the meat and brown on both sides but keep it juicy and red on the inside. Transfer hamburgers to a warm serving plate.

3. Discard only the fat from the pan. Add the vinegar, then stir in the mustard, tarragon, and cream. Add any juices from the serving plate. When sauce is thickened, pour it over the hamburgers and serve very hot.

Boulettes de Boeuf Grillées, Beurre d'Anchois
GRILLED HAMBURGERS WITH ANCHOVY BUTTER

Mash 1 part butter with 1 part anchovy paste. Prepare the hamburgers with the same flavoring as in the basic recipe. Grill or panfry the hamburgers. Immediately, while very hot, generously spread the anchovy butter all over. Serve hot buttered toast on the side.

Boulettes de Boeuf, Sauce aux Champignons
HAMBURGERS WITH MUSHROOM SAUCE

Prepare the hamburgers with the same flavoring as in the preceding recipe. Discard the fat from the pan and add 1 tablespoon butter and 2 tablespoons finely chopped shallots; stir well. Sprinkle 1 tablespoon flour into the skillet and stir until golden. Add ⅓ cup sherry or Madeira wine, ⅔ cup white wine, ½ pound sliced mushrooms, salt, pepper, a pinch of ground cloves, and 1 teaspoon meat glaze. Simmer for a few minutes. Warm the hamburgers in the sauce. Transfer to a hot serving plate and pour the mushroom sauce over.

◆ *On Refrigeration* ◆

Since ancient days, ice and snow have been useful in preserving food. The Romans used ice to keep their fish and shellfish from spoiling.

Ferdinand Carré, a Frenchman, invented artificial icemaking. He introduced his ice-cube machine at the Universal Exhibition of London in 1857.

Ten years later, a new method of food preservation was made possible when Charles A. Tellier (1828–1913), inspired by Carré's machine, invented mechanical refrigeration. Until then, most of the ice for Europe had been shipped from the lakes of Norway and this unpurified ice was held to be the cause of many ailments.

Tellier's first commercial icebox was installed in the shop of the famous chocolate dealer, Menier, in Paris, and shortly afterward (1876), he presented his process for freezing foods to the Académie des Sciences.

The same year, Tellier equipped a ship named *Le Frigorifique* with his invention. Ten sides of beef, 12 lambs, 2 calves, and 50 chickens were frozen at 2°C. and transported to Argentina. The trip lasted 105 days. The controllers who sailed with the ship, after eating some of the three-month-old meat, declared it to be superior to fresh.

Tellier's idea started the refrigerated shipping and frozen-food industry.

◆ *Le Veau* ◆
V E A L
✤ ✤ ✤

Veal lends itself to so many metamorphoses that one can, without offense, call it the chameleon of cuisine.
—GRIMOD DE LA REYNIÈRE

Fine veal is a pale gray-pink. It does not keep well and should be cooked as soon as possible.

• Cook a veal roast surrounded by veal bones; they improve the quality of the gravy.

• A thin slice of bacon across the top of a veal roast adds a delicious flavor.

• When sautéing veal, the meat must not be crowded in the pan or it will stew. Turn the meat *only* when well browned on one side, being careful not to burn the bits on the bottom of the pan, on which the quality of the sauce depends.

• Because veal does not contain much fat, spread butter on 1-inch-thick veal loin cutlets before broiling. Top each one with Parsley Butter (see Index).

Côtelettes de Veau aux Fines Herbes

VEAL CHOPS WITH MIXED HERBS

4 veal chops, each 1 inch thick   *4 servings*
3 tablespoons Clarified Butter (see Index)
Salt and pepper
⅓ cup white wine
2 tablespoons hot water
2 tablespoons chopped fresh parsley
1 teaspoon chopped fresh tarragon
¼ cup finely minced shallots
2 to 3 tablespoons unsalted butter
Lemon juice

1. Sauté the veal chops in very hot clarified butter in a heavy skillet (not cast iron). When golden on one side, season with salt and pepper, and then cook on the other side until golden.

2. Add the wine and hot water. Cover the skillet and simmer for 5 minutes. Sprinkle with the parsley, tarragon, and shallots. Cover and simmer for another 10 minutes.

3. Transfer to a heated serving plate. Add the butter to the pan juices and reduce until slightly thickened and syrupy. Add a sprinkle of lemon juice and spoon the sauce over the chops. Serve with rice.

Côtelettes de Veau Sauté à la Crème
VEAL CHOPS WITH CREAM

4 slices of fine white sandwich bread *4 servings*
6½ tablespoons unsalted butter
4 large veal chops, each 1½ inches thick
1½ tablespoons oil
Salt
1 small onion, or 3 shallots, minced
½ cup white wine
1½ cups heavy cream
Paprika

1. Remove the crusts of the bread and slice diagonally both ways, making 4 small triangles. Sauté on both sides in 3 tablespoons of the butter or more, until golden.

2. In a heavy skillet, sauté the veal chops in very hot oil and 1½ tablespoons of the butter for about 4 minutes on each side, or until golden brown, being careful not to burn them on the bottom of the pan. When almost done, season with salt. Arrange chops on a warm serving dish, surround with the bread triangles, and keep warm in a low oven.

3. Prepare the sauce: Sauté the onions or shallots in the same skillet until soft. Add the wine and boil until syrupy, or until just 1 tablespoon remains. Stir in the cream and cook over high heat until thickened. Sprinkle with paprika and remove from the heat. Add the remaining butter in bits and pour the sauce over the chops. Serve immediately.

Braised Endive (see Index) would be the perfect accompaniment. Drink a Chinon, Vouvray, or Saumur wine.

◆   UNDER THE COOK'S HAT   ◆

A large veal steak can be substituted for the chops.

Rôti de Veau à la Parisienne
PARISIAN VEAL ROAST

This veal roast, surrounded by Stuffed Artichoke Bottoms, makes an elegant dinner.

4 pounds boneless veal roast   *6 servings*
7 tablespoons unsalted butter
3 onions, quartered
Salt and freshly ground pepper
1 tablespoon water
Stuffed Artichoke Bottoms (see Index)
Watercress

1. Place the veal in a roasting pan and pour on 5 tablespoons of melted butter. Add the onions and season with salt and pepper. Roast in a preheated 350°F. oven for about 2 hours, or for 30 minutes per pound.

2. Remove the string from the roast and slice the meat. Place on a heated serving platter. Deglaze the roasting pan with 2 tablespoons butter and the water. Bring the sauce almost to a boil. Season with salt and pepper and strain into a sauceboat.

3. Surround the roast veal with the artichokes and a few sprigs of watercress at both ends of the serving dish.

Serve Potato Balls in Butter (see Index) to accompany the veal. Serve a red Bordeaux such as a Médoc.

Sauté de Veau Printanier

SAUTÉED VEAL WITH SPRING VEGETABLES

An elegant and colorful dish with its garnish of fresh peas, tiny carrots, and sautéed little potatoes.

3 tablespoons oil   *4 servings*
3 tablespoons unsalted butter
2½ pounds veal, cut into 2-inch cubes
1 onion, finely chopped
4 shallots, chopped
1 garlic clove, chopped
2 tablespoons flour
1½ cups dry white wine
⅓ cup Madeira wine
½ cup Beef Stock (see Index)
3 tablespoons tomato paste
5 tablespoons chopped parsley
2 teaspoons chopped tarragon
Salt and freshly ground pepper

1½ pounds fresh green peas, shelled
1 pound small new potatoes, peeled
1 pound tiny fresh carrots, peeled
Unsalted butter for sautéing vegetables

1. Heat the oil and butter in a casserole or Dutch oven, and sauté the veal in 2 batches until golden brown. Add the onion, shallots, and garlic and stir until vegetables are wilted.

2. Sprinkle with flour and stir until flour is cooked. Add the white wine and cook for 2 minutes.

3. Add the Madeira, beef stock, tomato paste, 3 tablespoons of the parsley, the tarragon, and salt and pepper to taste. Cover and braise in a preheated 325°F. oven for 2 to 2½ hours.

4. Cook each of the spring vegetables separately in salted water, then drain. Sauté the potatoes and carrots separately in unsalted butter until they begin to color.

5. Place the meat in the center of a warm large serving plate. Arrange the vegetables in alternating mounds around the meat. Pour some of the sauce over the meat and serve the remainder separately. Sprinkle the meat with remaining parsley.

Sauté de Veau à la Provençale en Gelée

VEAL PROVENÇALE IN ASPIC

1½ tablespoons unsalted butter   *6 servings*
1½ tablespoons olive oil
2 pounds shoulder of veal, cut into 2-inch cubes
1½ cups coarsely chopped onions
3 thin slices of bacon
4 carrots, peeled and diced
1 veal knuckle, cut into several pieces
2 garlic cloves, minced
2 tablespoons tomato paste
2 tablespoons Cognac
1½ cups dry white wine
¾ cup hot water
Bouquet garni (parsley sprigs, bay leaf, thyme)
1 whole clove
Salt and freshly ground pepper
Pinch of cayenne pepper

1. Melt the butter and oil in a casserole or Dutch oven until very hot. Sauté the meat in 2 batches over high heat until golden. Remove meat to a plate.

2. In the same casserole sauté the onions, bacon, carrots, and veal knuckle until golden. Add the garlic and cook for 1 minute, then stir in the tomato paste. Add the Cognac, wine, water, *bouquet garni*, clove, and seasonings to taste. Bring to a simmer.

3. Cover and braise in a preheated 325°F. oven for 2 hours.

4. Discard the *bouquet garni*, bacon, and veal knuckle. Place the meat in a 6-cup ring mold and surround with the cooking liquid. Refrigerate for at least 6 hours, or overnight.

5. Discard the fat that accumulates on the top. Unmold the jellied veal on a chilled serving plate lined with Boston lettuce or watercress.

Serve a chilled rosé of Provence.

◆ *Variety Meats* ◆

Variety meats have always played an important part in the history of French cooking. Certain cities acquired worldwide reputations because of the special recipes they developed, such as the black pudding from Nancy, the pigs' feet from Sainte-Menehould, and the tripe from Caen.

The tripe was made famous in the fourteenth century by a Caen chef named Benoît, who added special seasonings. A Norman gastronomic society in Caen known as La Tripière d'Or annually judges the best tripe recipes from around the world.

Tongue was so highly prized during the reign of Louis XII that in certain parts of France it was understood that all the tongues of slaughtered cattle belonged to the feudal lords.

Rognons de Veau en Croûstade

VEAL KIDNEYS IN PASTRY SHELLS

6 Patty Shells (see Index)   *2 or 3 servings*
2 or 3 small veal kidneys, about 1 pound altogether
Freshly ground pepper
3 tablespoons unsalted butter
⅓ pound mushrooms, quartered
1 tablespoon finely minced shallots
3 tablespoons Cognac

2 tablespoons cornstarch
1 cup Beef Stock (see Index)
Salt
Watercress
Lemon juice

1. Bake the patty shells and keep them warm while preparing
the filling.

2. Split the kidneys. Remove the fatty core and tubes. Peel the
membrane and cut the meat into 1-inch dice. Sprinkle with pepper.

3. Melt 2 tablespoons of the butter in a skillet and sauté the
kidneys over high heat for about 4 minutes. Transfer to a plate. Add
the mushrooms, shallots, and remaining 1 tablespoon butter to the
skillet and sauté until sizzling. Return the kidneys to the skillet and
remove from the heat.

4. Pour the Cognac into a warmed soup ladle, ignite, and pour
over the kidneys and mushrooms.

5. Dilute the cornstarch in the beef stock and add to the sauce.
Cook until sauce is thick and clear; do not boil. Add salt and pepper
to taste.

6. Fill the patty shells with the mixture, garnish with watercress,
and sprinkle with lemon juice.

◆　　UNDER THE COOK'S HAT　　◆

Never salt kidneys while cooking as it will harden them.

◆　◆　◆

*Veal sweetbreads may be looked upon as one of the greatest delicacies in
meats, and may be served at any dinner, however sumptuous.*
　　　　　　　　　　　—ESCOFFIER

Ris de Veau Fréville

VEAL SWEETBREADS FRÉVILLE

Édouard Nignon (1865–1934), one of the great names of French
cuisine, practiced his art in the best restaurants of the time, Café
Anglais, Voisin, and Lapérouse. He was chef to the Czar and to the
Emperor of Austria. This recipe is taken from one of his three au-
thoritative cookbooks.

1 pound veal sweetbreads *2 servings*
Salt
Juice of 1 lemon
4 tablespoons Clarified Butter (see Index)
½ cup excellent Port wine
½ cup Crème Fraîche (see Index) or heavy cream
3 tablespoons Brown Sauce (see Index)
1 truffle, sliced
¼ pound fresh button mushrooms, sautéed in butter
Lemon juice
Cayenne pepper

1. Soak the sweetbreads in ice water for 1 hour, changing the water until no trace of blood remains. Parboil them in salted water with the juice of 1 lemon for 10 minutes. Plunge into cold water. Discard the tubes and gristle, then carefully remove the membranes or rubbery skin. Press sweetbreads to remove excess water.

2. Lightly brown the sweetbreads in the clarified butter over medium-high heat. Add the Port, cover, and reduce liquid by half.

3. Add the *crème fraîche*, brown sauce, truffle, sautéed mushrooms, a little lemon juice, salt to taste and a pinch of cayenne pepper. Cook briefly until the flavors are blended.

Serve very hot, along with buttered asparagus tips.

◆ UNDER THE COOK'S HAT ◆

This recipe will fill 4 patty shells.

Sweetbreads are very perishable and should be prepared as soon as purchased.

Foie de Veau Sauté Maître d'Hôtel

CALF'S LIVER WITH PARSLEY BUTTER

This is a very simple but extremely good way to serve calf's liver. The liver should be pale pink and fresh. Cook it the same day it is purchased.

1 pound calf's liver, thinly sliced *4 servings*
¼ cup Clarified Butter (see Index)
Salt and freshly ground pepper
Parsley Butter (see Index)

1. Season the liver with salt and pepper. Sauté in clarified butter over medium-high heat for 2 minutes on each side or until it is pink inside. Do not overcook.

2. Serve with a piece of parsley butter on each slice.

♦ *Agneau* ♦
L A M B
⚜ ⚜ ⚜

Gigot is an old French word meaning to gambol, the way young lambs do.

The lamb most renowned for outstanding flavor and tenderness comes from the area bordering the bay of Mont-Saint-Michel or from Pauillac. The pastures and the lambs from these areas are both called *prés-salés* (salt marshes).

Lamb on Easter Sunday is an honored French tradition, particularly in the province of Île-de-France. A *gigot d'agneau* (leg of spring lamb), which is pink inside with crusty skin outside and flavored with garlic, is a truly great French preparation. "A leg of lamb without garlic is like a kiss without a mustache" is an old French saying.

The stronger-flavored older lamb, or mutton, is excellent for *navarin* (lamb stew). According to des Essarts, an actor of the Comédie Française about 1770, these are the requisites for a perfect roast: "Let the leg of mutton be awaited as the first lovers' meeting, mortified as a liar caught in the act, golden as a young German, and bloody as a Carib."

Gigot d'Agneau Rôti

ROAST LEG OF LAMB

In France lamb is preferred medium rare. When it is cooked this way, it is delicious and juicy.

5 pounds leg of lamb   *6 to 8 servings*
2 garlic cloves, split
Butter
Salt and freshly ground pepper

1. Make 4 slits in the meat and insert the garlic slivers. Spread the meat with butter. Season with salt and pepper.

2. Place the lamb in a roasting pan. Roast in a preheated 375°F. oven until a meat thermometer indicates an internal temperature of 135°F. Baste often while roasting.

3. Carve the lamb in long thin slices, slanting the knife to the bone on one side and parallel to the bone on the other. Serve the juice separately. Garnish with watercress.

Suggested wine: Bourgeuil or Beaujolais

♦   UNDER THE COOK'S HAT   ♦

Because lamb fat congeals very rapidly, the meat should be served on very hot plates as soon as it is cooked.

Cold roast lamb is delicious served with a freshly made mayonnaise, French fried potatoes, and a mixed green salad.

Gigot à la Bretonne
LEG OF LAMB BRETON STYLE

Gigot à la Bretonne is one of the most delectable ways of serving a leg of lamb as well as one of the most classic of French cooking.

Roast the leg of lamb as indicated in the preceding recipe. When half done, season the roast with salt and pepper. When lamb is done, deglaze the roasting pan with ½ cup of white wine or preferably a Muscadet wine that is to be served with the leg of lamb. Serve Breton-Style White Beans (see Index) separately.

♦   ♦   ♦

Henry III of England, a great lover of food, was enchanted by the appetizing appearance of a beef loin and dubbed it "Sir Loin."

The French bestowed the royal appellation "baron" on the saddle and two legs of spring lamb. This became known as *baron d'agneau*. This large piece of meat is usually roasted on a spit.

Gigot d'Agneau à la Boulangère
LEG OF LAMB WITH POTATOES AND ONIONS

5 pounds leg of lamb   *6 to 8 servings*
2 garlic cloves, split
½ cup hot water
5 potatoes, thinly sliced
5 onions, thinly sliced
Salt and freshly ground pepper
Fresh parsley, chopped

1. Make 4 incisions in the meat and insert the garlic slivers.
2. Roast in a large roasting pan in a preheated 375°F. oven for 30 minutes. Add the hot water to the juices. Place the potatoes and onions around the meat. Season with salt and pepper. Turn the vegetables 2 or 3 times during the cooking. Roast for about 15 minutes per pound for rare meat.
3. Remove the roast and place on a serving platter. Surround with the potatoes and onions and sprinkle with parsley. Serve hot.

◆　◆　◆

Many kings of France were expert cooks, from Henri IV, who loved to make garlic omelets, to Louis XVIII, a great gastronome, who invented the *côtelettes à la martyre* (martyr chops).

This dish consists of a lamb chop placed between two other lamb chops. Both sides are grilled, but the only chop eaten is the one in the middle—juicy and cooked to perfection.

Noisettes d'Agneau Béarnaise
NOISETTES OF LAMB WITH BÉARNAISE SAUCE

Noisettes are the equivalent of the filet mignon of beef; they are the finest part of lamb or mutton, taken from the first ribs. Ask the butcher to bone and trim 6 loin lamb chops, each 1⅓ inches thick.

Béarnaise Sauce (see Index)   *6 servings*
6 Canapé Bases (see Index)
6 large mushroom caps
Oil and butter
6 noisettes of lamb
Salt and freshly ground pepper
Watercress

1. Prepare the sauce, the canapés, and then the mushrooms in that order. Brush the mushroom caps with oil or melted butter, and broil under moderate heat. Remove a little of the flesh to deepen the caps so they can be filled more generously with Béarnaise sauce.

2. Sauté the *noisettes* in butter over medium heat. Season with salt and pepper before turning over with tongs. Cook until some drops of blood appear on the surface.

3. Place each *noisette* on a canapé. Top with a grilled mushroom filled with Béarnaise sauce. Garnish with watercress. Serve with shoestring potatoes.

◆   *Variation*   ◆

For an elegant dinner, make this sauce to be served separately with the *noisettes d'agneau:* Deglaze the pan with ½ cup excellent dry white wine. Boil until reduced to ¼ cup. Add 1½ cups Brown Sauce (see Index) and boil for 2 minutes. Swirl in 2 tablespoons butter. Serve immediately.

Veal *noisettes* are prepared the same way.

◆   ◆   ◆

Louis Pasteur ate a lamb chop every day of the week except Thursdays, when he was served hot sausage with red beans.

◆   ◆   ◆

Le Gigot

J'aime mieux un tendre gigot
Qui sans pompe et sans étalage
Se montre avec un entourage
De laitue ou de haricots.
Gigot recevez mon hommage;
Souvent j'ai dédaigné pour vous
Chez la Baronne ou la Marquise
La poularde la plus exquise
Et même la perdix au choux.

Leg of Lamb

I prefer a tender leg of lamb
That, without pomp and without display,
Appears with a garnish
Of lettuce or beans.

Oh Lamb, accept my homage;
For many times at the Baroness's or at the Marquise's
I have chosen you rather than
The most exquisite fat pullet
Or garnished partridge.
　　　　—JOSEPH DE BERCHOUX (1762–1838),
　　　　　La Gastronomie

Navarin d'Agneau à la Printanière

SPRING LAMB STEW

Navarin d'agneau à la printanière is a springtime dish and one of the best loved stews in France. It was named after the city of Navarino, today called Pylos. It was there, in 1827, that the Ionian sea battle was fought between the French, English, and Russian allies and the Turkish-Egyptian navy.

3 pounds lamb shoulder, cut into 1½-inch cubes　　*6 servings*
Clarified Butter (see Index)
2 medium-size yellow onions, quartered
2 garlic cloves, minced
2 tablespoons flour
1 tablespoon tomato paste
Beef Stock (see Index) or 3 cups water
Salt and pepper
¼ teaspoon rosemary
Bouquet garni (thyme, few parsley sprigs, 1 bay leaf)
10 small new potatoes or potato balls
4 small white turnips, quartered
12 tiny new carrots, whole, about 2 inches long
18 tiny white onions
Butter
1 tablespoon sugar
1½ cups fresh or frozen green peas
Beurre manié (optional)
Fresh parsley, minced

1. Dry the meat with paper towels.
2. In a Dutch oven, brown the lamb in several batches in very hot clarified butter over moderately high heat. Halfway through, add the yellow onions and continue cooking until onions are golden brown.

3. Stir in the garlic, then sprinkle the flour over the meat. Stir well until flour sizzles. Stir in the tomato paste. Add the stock, which should barely cover the meat. Season with salt and pepper and rosemary and add the *bouquet garni.* Cover and place in a pre-heated 325°F. oven.

4. About 45 minutes later, add the potatoes.

5. Place the turnips, carrots, and white onions in a large frying pan with butter. Sprinkle vegetables with the sugar, cover, and cook slowly until vegetables are evenly glazed. Shake the pan often. Set aside.

6. Cook the peas in boiling salted water for 5 minutes, strain, and set aside.

7. After the meat has cooked altogether for 1¾ hours, add the vegetables. Correct the seasoning and cook for 10 more minutes.

8. Remove excess fat from the juices. If the consistency is too thin, add 2 tablespoons *beurre manié.* Arrange meat on a hot serving plate surrounded by vegetables. Sprinkle with minced fresh parsley and serve very hot on warm plates.

◆ *Le Porc* ◆
P O R K
⚜ ⚜ ⚜

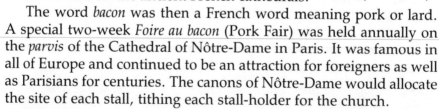

For many centuries, pigs and wild boars roamed the abundant forests of Gaul, fattening themselves on acorns. They were the main source of meat in France at the time, as is evident by the prevalence of statues depicting these animals on the ancient French cathedrals.

The word *bacon* was then a French word meaning pork or lard. A special two-week *Foire au bacon* (Pork Fair) was held annually on the *parvis* of the Cathedral of Nôtre-Dame in Paris. It was famous in all of Europe and continued to be an attraction for foreigners as well as Parisians for centuries. The canons of Nôtre-Dame would allocate the site of each stall, tithing each stall-holder for the church.

Pigs also roamed freely in the streets of Paris during the Middle Ages, serving as an efficient garbage disposal system for the city. Unfortunately, a fatal accident occurred when the son of Louis VI was riding a horse that became entangled with these pigs. After that tragedy, only the pigs belonging to the Abbey of Saint-Antoine were allowed on the streets, and they had to wear a small bell to warn pedestrians of their presence.

Today pork does not hold the high place it once had in France. Still, many provinces have their own ways of preparing it—usually by combining it with some of the products predominant in the area, for instance, *choucroute garnie* (pork, sausage, and sauerkraut) from Alsace, *cassoulet* (pork, beans, and sausage) from Languedoc, and *noisettes de porc à la Tourangelle* (pork with prunes and cream) from Touraine.

The various pork dishes started as country fare, but an exception is roasted milk-fed suckling pig. This is one of the best-known and least plebeian of pork dishes, and, indeed, is considered a delicacy.

Noisettes de Porc à la Tourangelle
NOISETTES OF PORK WITH PRUNES AND CREAM

This specialty originated in the province of Touraine, an area famous for its prunes.

24 prunes   *4 servings*
1½ cups dry white wine
4 to 5 tablespoons Clarified Butter (see Index)
8 pork noisettes, 1½ inches thick, cut from the loin
Salt and freshly ground pepper
1 tablespoon currant jelly
1 cup heavy cream
1 teaspoon cornstarch
Fresh parsley, chopped

1. Soak the prunes in the wine overnight.
2. Simmer the prunes for 30 minutes; pour off and reserve wine.
3. Melt the butter in a large skillet and cook one side of the *noisettes* over medium-high heat until lightly colored. Season with salt and pepper. Cook the other side until done. Remove *noisettes* and keep them warm in a slow oven while preparing the sauce.
4. Add 1 cup of the reserved wine to the skillet and reduce over high heat to ⅓ cup. Add the jelly and the cream mixed with the cornstarch. Stir and cook until thickened to the right consistency.
5. Gently reheat the prunes in the sauce, then arrange them around the meat. Spoon the sauce over the pork and prunes and sprinkle the center of each *noisette* with parsley.

Serve a fine Vouvray wine.

Côtelettes de Porc à la Dijonnaise

PORK CHOPS WITH MUSTARD AND CREAM

4 loin pork chops, each 1 inch thick   *2 servings*
1 tablespoon unsalted butter
1 tablespoon oil
Salt and freshly ground pepper
2 tablespoons minced shallots
1 tablespoon wine vinegar
2 tablespoons Dijon mustard
¾ cup heavy cream

1. Sauté the pork chops in the butter and oil in a large skillet over medium heat for about 10 minutes on each side, or until golden brown. Season with salt and pepper. Cover and cook for 5 to 8 minutes, or until done. Transfer to a heated serving plate and keep warm.

2. Remove excess fat from the skillet and sauté the shallots, stirring, until wilted. Add the vinegar, mustard, and cream. Season with salt and cook over medium-high heat until the sauce is slightly thickened.

3. Return the chops to the pan to heat through on both sides. Serve immediately.

Côtelettes de Porc du Morvan

MORVAN PORK CHOPS

6 loin pork chops, each 1 inch thick   *3 or 4 servings*
2 to 3 tablespoons unsalted butter
1 teaspoon oil
Salt and freshly ground pepper
6 shallots, chopped
2 garlic cloves, chopped
1½ cups full-bodied red wine
1 tablespoon cornstarch

1. Trim excess fat from the chops and slash the edges in a few places to prevent curling. Sauté the chops in butter and oil until thoroughly cooked. Season with salt and pepper. Place on a heated serving plate and keep warm.

2. Add the shallots and garlic to the skillet and cook over medium heat until wilted. Add the wine mixed with cornstarch, stirring constantly. Reduce the sauce to 1 cup, season, and pour over the chops.

Serve with French fried potatoes.

◆   U N D E R   T H E   C O O K ' S   H A T   ◆

Do not use a cast-iron or aluminum pan, as it would alter the taste of the wine sauce.

Côtes de Porc à la Charcutière

CHARCUTIÈRE PORK CHOPS

6 loin pork chops, each ¾ inch thick
1 tablespoon unsalted butter
1 tablespoon oil
Salt and freshly ground pepper
1 small onion, chopped
3 shallots, chopped
½ cup dry white wine
1½ cups Brown Sauce (see Index)
1 teaspoon meat glaze
1 tablespoon Dijon mustard
5 to 6 tablespoons minced gherkins

3 to 4 servings

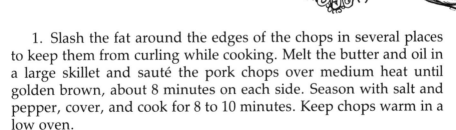

1. Slash the fat around the edges of the chops in several places to keep them from curling while cooking. Melt the butter and oil in a large skillet and sauté the pork chops over medium heat until golden brown, about 8 minutes on each side. Season with salt and pepper, cover, and cook for 8 to 10 minutes. Keep chops warm in a low oven.
2. Sauté the onion and shallots in the same skillet for 2 minutes. Add the wine and reduce to 3 or 4 tablespoons. Add the brown sauce and meat glaze and cook for 3 to 5 minutes. Remove from the heat.
3. Add the mustard and stir well. Add the gherkins. Spoon some of the sauce over the pork chops and serve the rest in a sauceboat.

Côtes de Porc à la Provençale

PORK CHOPS WITH TOMATOES AND OLIVES

3 tablespoons olive oil
4 loin pork chops, each 1 inch thick
3 medium-size onions, chopped
3 garlic cloves, chopped
1 tablespoon chopped shallots
5 tablespoons tomato paste
½ cup dry white wine or vermouth
½ cup water
½ teaspoon sugar
½ bay leaf
Fresh basil, minced, to taste
Thyme, to taste
Salt and freshly ground pepper
24 black olives, pitted
Chopped parsley

4 servings

1. Heat the olive oil in a large heavy skillet (not cast iron or aluminum). Sauté the pork chops over high heat until golden brown on both sides and partially cooked.

2. Add the onions, garlic, and shallots and stir until golden. Add the tomato paste to the pan and stir for about 1 minute.

3. Add the wine, water, sugar, bay leaf, basil, thyme, and salt and pepper to taste. Stir and bring to a boil. Cover, reduce the heat, and simmer for 15 minutes.

4. Add the olives and cook for 5 minutes longer. Pour the sauce over the pork chops and sprinkle with parsley.

Serve with rice and a rosé wine.

• *Cassoulet* •

Of very ancient origin, cassoulet is one of the most famous dishes of French regional cooking. It originated in Castelnaudary in Languedoc province.

Cassoulet consists of a combination of white beans, pork, fresh sausage, and *confit d'oie* (goose preserved in its own fat). Lamb, bacon, and smoked sausage are never used in the traditional cassoulet, but towns within the region add different ingredients to their versions of the dish. Toulouse adds its famous garlic sausage and Carcassonne features a small leg of lamb and a partridge.

Cassoulet is baked in an earthenware pot made with the clay from Issel in the region of Castlenaudary. The pot is called *la cassolo*, which gave the name to this dish. Castelnaudary claims that their water has a unique quality for cooking the beans.

Prosper Montagné recalled in one of his cookbooks that he had once gone to the shoemaker in his hometown of Carcassonne and saw a notice on the door that read, "Closed on account of cassoulet."

Cassoulet

BEANS WITH PORK, SAUSAGE, AND GOOSE

1½ pounds white pea beans or navy beans   *6 servings*
½ pound fresh pork rind, cut into squares
¼ pound lean salt pork, finely chopped
9 garlic cloves
1 bay leaf
1 teaspoon dried thyme
Coarse salt
2 or 3 pieces of *confit d'oie* (preserved goose), if available
2½ pounds country-style pork, in 1-inch slices
2 medium-size onions, coarsely chopped
Freshly ground pepper
1 pound garlic sausage from Toulouse, or kielbasy
Goose fat, rendered pork fat, or butter

1. Place the beans in a large pot with 3 quarts cold water. Bring slowly almost to a boil. Remove the pot from the heat. After 30 minutes, drain beans and return them to the pot.

2. Add 3 fresh quarts of boiling water, the pork rind and salt pork, 6 garlic cloves, chopped, the bay leaf, and thyme. Simmer slowly for 1½ to 2 hours, or until the beans are tender but remain intact. Add salt to taste 10 minutes before the end of cooking time. Drain the beans and reserve the liquid.

3. While the beans are cooking, sauté the preserved goose in its own fat in a large Dutch oven. Remove goose pieces. Brown the pork slices in the same pan and fat. When almost done, add the onions and brown lightly. Add remaining garlic cloves. Season with salt and pepper.

4. Cover the casserole and bake in a preheated 325°F. for 1½

hours. After 20 minutes, add 1 cup of the reserved bean liquid.

5. Meanwhile, prick the sausage with a fork. In a frying pan, sauté the sausages in a little goose fat until lightly browned.

6. Remove the pork from the Dutch oven and discard the bones. Deglaze the Dutch oven with 1 cup of bean liquid. In a large deep earthenware casserole, put a layer of beans, then a layer of pork, and the preserved goose, if available. Add another layer of beans. Place the sausage, cut into 6 pieces, on top, pushing it slightly into the beans. Pour in the juice from the casserole and ½ cup of the reserved bean liquid. Season generously with pepper.

7. Cover and bake in a preheated 325°F. oven for 2 hours. The beans should be very moist and creamy. If they look dry during the baking, add a little reserved bean liquid.

Serve from the casserole with a fine light red wine.

Choucroute Garnie

SAUERKRAUT WITH PORK AND SAUSAGES

Sauerkraut (see Index)   *6 servings*
6 smoked pork chops
2 knockwurst
6 frankfurters
3 tablespoons kirsch
Steamed potatoes

1. Prepare the sauerkraut.

2. One hour before the sauerkraut is done, bury the smoked loin of pork in it.

3. Thirty minutes later add the knockwurst, frankfurters, and the Kirsch.

4. To serve: Slice the knockwurst in ½-inch slices. Place the sauerkraut in a deep, round serving dish. Arrange the pork chops and the knockwurst and frankfurters on top. Serve the potatoes separately. French mustard should accompany this dish.

◆ *Ham* ◆

The process of making ham was invented by the Gauls, who regarded ham so highly that the head of a pig was on their coins.

Ham was sold to the Romans, who ate it as an *hors-d'oeuvre*, then again at the end of the meal to create thirst and stimulate drinking.

In the French countryside, salted or smoked hams were, and still are, stored by being hung over chimneys, to be taken down and eaten as needed.

France produces remarkable hams, notably the country hams of Morvan, Alsace, Auvergne, Bayonne, and Ardennes.

One of the most outstanding hams, the *jambon de Bayonne*, is referred to in the following excerpt, which appeared in the *Almanach des gourmands* in 1806:

> Our readers will learn with pleasure that the cat, faithful "guardian" of Monsieur Le Blanc's 1800 Bayonne hams, still feels marvelously well and does not let any gnawing animal approach this beautiful store, so interesting to the real gastronome.

Jambon Braisé

BRAISED HAM

6 to 8 servings

1 mild-cured ham, 4 to 5 pounds, trimmed of excess fat
2 medium-size onions, quartered
2 medium-size carrots, cut into pieces
1 cup dry white wine
½ cup Beef Stock (see Index)
1 tablespoon tomato paste

1. Place the ham, fat side down, in a roasting pan. Surround with onions and carrots.

2. Roast in a preheated 350°F. oven for a total of 1 hour. Stir the vegetables 2 or 3 times during the first 15 minutes. When the vegetables are golden, pour the wine over the ham. Bake for 10 minutes, then add the stock combined with the tomato paste. Baste often.

3. Remove the ham, place on a warm serving plate, and keep warm. Skim off the fat from the roasting pan and discard it.

4. Purée the vegetables and meat juices in a food processor or blender. Add stock to thin the mixture if necessary.

5. Carve the ham. Serve the sauce separately, along with buttered spinach.

◆ *Variation* ◆

Add 2 to 3 tablespoons of Madeira, Port, or sherry wine to the sauce.

Jambon au Madère

HAM WITH MADEIRA SAUCE

1½ pounds ham steak, ½ inch thick

3 tablespoons unsalted butter

2 tablespoons minced shallots

10 to 12 mushrooms, thinly sliced

1 tablespoon chopped parsley

½ cup dry white wine

¼ teaspoon thyme

Freshly ground pepper

½ cup heavy cream

1 teaspoon arrowroot

5 tablespoons Madeira wine

Salt, if necessary

2 to 3 servings

1. Trim the fat from the ham and chop enough of the fat to measure about 3 tablespoons.

2. In a skillet melt the butter and the ham fat. Add the shallots and sauté for about 2 minutes without browning. Add the mushrooms and parsley. Cook over medium-high heat for 2 to 3 minutes.

3. Push the mushrooms and shallots to one side and place the ham steak in the center of the pan. Sauté for 2 to 3 minutes on each side, until golden. Add the wine, thyme, and pepper to taste, and simmer on each side. Remove the ham and keep warm.

4. Combine the cream with the arrowroot and 4 tablespoons of the Madeira. Deglaze the skillet with the cream mixture and simmer until the sauce is thickened, 1 to 2 minutes. Taste for seasonings. Remove from the heat and add the remaining tablespoon of Madeira. Pour the sauce over the ham.

Tourte Feuilletée au Jambon

HAM PIE

A tourte is similar to a pie with a crust on top and can be filled with fish, meat, or fruit. Much appreciated from earliest times, tourtes were mentioned in a charter from Louis le Débonnaire in 822. As for La Varenne, 75 tourtes appeared in his book *Le Vray Cuisinier François* (1667). They were replaced by Carême's creation, the vol-au-vent, but have regained popularity in recent years.

1 recipe Puff Pastry (see Index)   *6 servings*
3 tablespoons unsalted butter
1 tablespoon minced shallots
3 tablespoons flour
2 cups half-and-half
Salt and pepper
Pinch of nutmeg
Rice, raw
1 egg white, slightly beaten
1 pound Polish ham, cut into ½-inch cubes
1½ cups imported Swiss Gruyère, cut into ½-inch cubes
1 egg yolk, beaten with 2 teaspoons water

1. Roll out the dough ⅛ inch thick on a floured surface and cut out 2 circles to fit into a 9-inch fluted pie tin: one approximately 10½ inches in diameter and the other 1 inch smaller.

2. Make a béchamel sauce: Melt the butter; add the shallots. When wilted, stir in the flour. Cook for 1 minute, then stir in the cream. Cook, stirring constantly with a whisk, until thickened. Season sparingly with salt (the ham is salty), pepper, and nutmeg. Cool to room temperature.

3. Fit the larger circle of dough into the pie tin. Ease it into the pan without stretching. Cut the dough all around, leaving ½ inch of the dough hanging over the rim.

4. Line the shell with foil and fill with raw rice. Bake on a baking sheet in a preheated 400°F. oven for 10 minutes. Remove the foil and rice and bake for 10 minutes more or until golden.

5. While the dough is still hot, brush it with the egg white. Cool for 15 minutes and then spread the ham and cheese on the dough. Spoon over the sauce.

6. Cover the pie with the other circle of dough, pressing slightly down to prevent air pockets. Press the two edges firmly together. With the prongs of a fork, press down to make an attractive ¾-inch border all around.

7. Brush the whole surface, except the edges, with the egg yolk and water. With the back of a 3-prong fork or a knife, make a crisscross design over the surface. Prick the dough with the tines of a fork in 4 or 5 places to release steam while baking. Bake in a preheated 450°F. oven for 25 minutes or until golden brown. Remove from the pie tin before serving.

10. *Les Légumes* VEGETABLES

❧ ❧ ❧

The first real interest in vegetables dates back only to the seventeenth century, when the brilliant agriculturalist La Quintinie was placed in charge of the *jardin potager* (vegetable garden) of Louis XIV at Versailles.

The unusual and beautiful garden was often visited with great interest by the King and the court and earned a royal title for La Quintinie. Under his care, strawberries ripened in April and asparagus appeared in December. Louis XIV had La Quintinie make similar gardens for several noblemen of the court and the practice spread throughout the rest of Europe.

Before that time vegetables had been largely neglected as a food. They were called roots and were used primarily as a seasoning for soups or *potages,* from which came the name *jardin potager.*

During the same period, Nicolas de Bonnefons, the King's valet, contributed to this new awareness of vegetables in his book, *Les Délices de la campagne*, published in 1662. In the section entitled "About Roots," he gave recipes for preparing vegetables such as carrots, beets, and turnips. He recommended boiling the vegetables in water in their skins, then peeling and seasoning with butter or preparing them as fritters.

De Bonnefons's wish "that roots would be cultivated and loved in France" has certainly been granted; today the French have great love for fresh vegetables and take great care and imagination in their preparation.

French menus can be deciphered quickly if you remember that the following words indicate the particular ingredient used in the preparation of a dish, or that serves as the significant garnish.

Argenteuil	Asparagus	*Marie-Louise*	Artichokes
Caroline	Rice	*Maltaise*	Oranges
Châtelaine	Chestnuts	*Montmorency*	Cherries
Clamart	Green Peas	*Mornay*	Cheese Sauce
Condé	Red Beans	*Parmentier*	Potatoes
Conti	Lentils	*Lyonnaise*	Onions
Crécy	Carrots	*Saint-Germain*	Purée of Peas
Dubarry	Cauliflower	*Soubise*	Purée of Onion
Forestière	Mushrooms	*Portugaise*	Tomatoes
Florentine	Spinach	*Rossini*	Foie Gras and Truffles
Fréneuse	Turnips		

◆ *Artichokes* ◆

I will always associate artichokes with my youth in Geneva, when my father was at the League of Nations, serving as Consul General of France. Colette, the French writer, would invite herself to our home for a meal and bring a little package of artichokes which, to our great amusement, had to be prepared for her immediately.

Colette liked her artichokes boiled in salted water and served with a *sauce béchamel,* lightly salted and generously buttered. In her collection of recipes published in 1923, Colette advised that if you prick your fingers on the tips of the leaves when choosing artichokes, you should not buy them because this means they are old and hard.

To serve artichokes ''à la Colette,'' prepare them as described in the recipe that follows and serve with White Sauce (see Index).

Artichauts

ARTICHOKES

Artichokes originated in Ethiopia. Although known to be growing in the wild earlier, their cultivation as food started only in the fifteenth century.

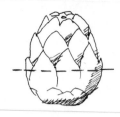

1 serving

1. Place the artichoke on the edge of a table. Holding it with your left hand, bear down and break off the stem, thus also pulling out the fibrous portion from the bottom.

2. With a sharp knife, remove all the big leaves around the bottom of the artichoke.

3. With a large knife, cut right through the artichoke at a level with the top of the young leaves rising from the center.

4. Rub the artichoke bottom and all cut edges with lemon juice to prevent them from darkening.

5. Add the juice of 1 lemon to enough salted water to cover the artichoke. Bring to a boil and simmer 20 to 40 minutes, depending on size. It will be tender when one of the leaves is easily pulled off.

Serve with a vinaigrette or hollandaise sauce.

Fonds d'Artichauts

ARTICHOKE BOTTOMS

Choose the largest artichokes available so as to have the right size for stuffing. Prepare whole artichokes as in the preceding recipe. Remove the leaves and carefully remove the choke with a pointed teaspoon. The bottom is then ready to be used as each recipe requires.

Fonds d'Artichauts à la Barigoule

STUFFED ARTICHOKE BOTTOMS

Artichoke bottoms, or *fonds d'artichauts,* are often used as a garnish around a meat dish for formal occasions, but also as an *hors-d'oeuvre.* The barigoule is a Provençal mushroom that grows on thistle roots. Because of its scarcity, it is replaced by cultivated mushrooms. There are many versions of this dish. Allow 2 artichokes per person if they are small.

6 tablespoons unsalted butter   *8 servings*
2 shallots, chopped
½ pound mushrooms

¼ pound Virginia ham, finely chopped
1 tablespoon chopped parsley
¼ teaspoon arrowroot
⅓ cup heavy cream
8 artichoke bottoms, freshly cooked or canned

1. Melt 3 tablespoons of the butter in a skillet, add the shallots, and cook until soft. Add the mushrooms and cook until the mushrooms are dry.

2. Add the ham and parsley and stir well. Mix the arrowroot with heavy cream and stir into the mixture. Cook until thickened.

3. Reheat the artichoke bottoms in the remaining butter.

4. Spoon the filling into the artichoke bottoms and serve.

Asperges

ASPARAGUS

Asparagus began to be cultivated in France in 1608. It is so much relished for its own flavor that it is often served plain, but it is delicious in a variety of ways. Serve it as a salad with a Vinaigrette or a Mayonnaise Chantilly, or as a vegetable, *à la flamande*—sprinkled with finely chopped hard-cooked egg and hot melted butter and lemon juice. For more festive occasions, serve asparagus warm with Hollandaise Sauce or Mousseline Sauce. (See Index for all sauce recipes.) To appreciate the flavor of asparagus at its best, one should always eat it warm—never cold or hot. Avoid serving wine with asparagus. Traces of sulfur in the asparagus would ruin a fine wine.

Preparing asparagus: Allow ½ pound per serving. Line up the asparagus spears and cut them all the same length, cutting off the butt ends. Peel off the outer skin, which is tough, with a vegetable peeler. Tie the stalks together in 2 or 3 bundles, so that the spears can be removed from the pan more easily. In a shallow pan bring enough salted water to a boil to cover the asparagus generously. Place the bundles in the boiling water and cook over medium-high heat for about 12 minutes, or longer, depending on size and age, or until the stalks are tender when pierced with a knife. Do not overcook. Remove and drain thoroughly before placing stalks on a warm serving plate, lined with a folded white napkin to absorb excess moisture. Remove the strings.

♦ UNDER THE COOK'S HAT ♦

Place a towel, dipped into the cooking water and wrung out, over the asparagus to keep it warm.

Avoid buying asparagus that has open, spreading tips. It is past its prime.

If the asparagus has flattened stalks, it is likely to be tough.

Haricots Verts au Beurre

GREEN BEANS WITH BUTTER

Most green vegetables will keep their bright color when prepared with this method. So as to appreciate and savor their flavor fully, they are served as a separate course. Be sure to use only the freshest beans.

4 servings

1. Snap off the ends of 1½ pounds of young green beans. Wash, then place in cold water with a few ice cubes.

2. Bring a large amount of water, lightly seasoned with coarse salt, to a boil in a pot. Throw the beans into the water, a few handfuls at a time, and cook over high heat for 10 to 15 minutes, until tender but still a little crunchy. Drain and immediately plunge the strainer full of beans into a bowl of ice water to set the color. Drain again.

3. When ready to serve, place the beans in boiling salted water just long enough to heat through. Drain. Melt a large piece of unsalted butter in a skillet. Add the beans and heat for 5 minutes, shaking the pan often. Serve immediately.

♦ UNDER THE COOK'S HAT ♦

Beans may be prepared as far as step 3 several hours ahead of time.

Haricots Blancs Frais à la Maître d'Hôtel

FRESH WAX BEANS WITH PARSLEY BUTTER

This excellent recipe is based on one taken from *La Cuisinière de la campagne,* a classic French cookbook by Audot, published in 1818.

4 servings

1. Snap off the ends of 1 pound of yellow wax beans. Drop into a large kettle filled with boiling water. Boil uncovered until tender

but not limp, for 10 to 15 minutes. Add salt toward the end of the cooking time.

2. Drain beans and return them to the same pan. Toss over high heat for about 1 minute, just long enough to evaporate excess moisture. Remove from heat.

3. Toss the beans with 4 tablespoons Parsley Butter (see Index) until thoroughly coated.

◆   U N D E R   T H E   C O O K ' S   H A T   ◆

Green beans are also delicious prepared *à la maître d'hôtel.*

Haricots Blancs à la Bretonne

BRETON-STYLE WHITE BEANS

These white beans are the traditional accompaniment for leg of lamb à la Bretonne. They are also good with roast pork.

1 pound dried white pea beans or marrow beans   *6 servings*
1 large onion, stuck with 2 cloves
5 garlic cloves, minced
Bouquet garni (3 parsley sprigs, thyme, 1 bay leaf)
Freshly ground pepper
Salt
2 medium-size onions, chopped
5 tablespoons unsalted butter
1½ tablespoons tomato paste
Fresh parsley, chopped

1. Place beans in a large pan filled with cold water. Bring to a boil and cook for 5 minutes, then drain. Return the beans to the same pot and add warm water to reach 4 inches above the level of the beans.

2. Add the onion stuck with cloves, 3 garlic cloves, the *bouquet garni,* and pepper to taste. Simmer beans until cooked but still firm, about 1½ hours. Add salt 30 minutes before the beans are done.

3. Drain the beans; discard the large onion and the *bouquet garni.* Reserve 1½ cups of the cooking liquid.

4. If the beans are to accompany a roast leg of lamb or pork, use some of the fat taken from the roasting pan. About 20 minutes before serving, sauté the chopped onions in 3 tablespoons of the butter and the fat. Add remaining garlic and cook for 1 to 2 minutes.

5. Add the tomato paste and mix well for 1 minute. Add the reserved bean liquid and cook uncovered over medium heat for 5 minutes. Add the drained beans and season with salt and pepper. Cover and simmer for 20 minutes, stirring occasionally. The liquid will be absorbed by the beans, but they must remain very moist.

6. Before serving, add remaining 2 tablespoons butter or 3 to 4 tablespoons of the juice from the roast meat. Sprinkle with parsley. Serve immediately on hot plates.

Choux de Bruxelles

BRUSSELS SPROUTS

2 pounds small, firm Brussels sprouts
2 slices of bacon, cut into ¼-inch pieces
5 tablespoons unsalted butter
1 large onion, finely minced
1½ tablespoons tarragon vinegar
Fresh parsley, chopped

6 servings

1. Trim the bases and outside leaves from the Brussels sprouts.
2. Cook sprouts in boiling salted water for 10 to 15 minutes.
3. Sauté the bacon in 2 tablespoons of the butter until golden but not dry. Remove and reserve bacon. Sauté the onion in the same pan until golden. Deglaze the pan with the vinegar.
4. Return the bacon and Brussels sprouts to the pan and add remaining butter. Cover and simmer for 5 to 8 minutes, shaking the pan occasionally. Sprinkle with parsley.

Choux à la Lilloise

CABBAGE IN THE STYLE OF LILLE

A perfect vegetable to serve with roast pork.

1 large cabbage, 2 pounds, quartered
3 tablespoons unsalted butter
2 tablespoons olive oil
2 medium-size onions, chopped
2 garlic cloves, chopped
Salt and freshly ground pepper
½ cup white wine (optional)
1 tablespoon wine vinegar

4 servings

1. Remove the core and outer leaves of the cabbage. Wash under running water, then cut into ½-inch slices.

2. Heat the butter and olive oil in a skillet and sauté the onions and garlic until soft. Add the cabbage, season with salt and pepper, add white wine if desired, and pour in the vinegar.

3. Cook uncovered, stirring often, for 15 to 20 minutes. The cabbage should be slightly crunchy.

◆   *Variations*   ◆

Before serving, mix in 1 recipe of Mornay Sauce (see Index).

Leftover cabbage makes a delicious *potage*. Purée in a blender with beef broth, cream, and butter.

◆ *Choucroute Alsacienne* ◆

One of the oldest known vegetables to be preserved is cabbage. When the Great Wall of China was being built 2,000 years ago, the workmen were fed cabbage mixed with rice wine, which acted as a preservative. Then when the Tatars invaded China in the ninth century, they used salt on the cabbage instead of rice wine and, in time, the cabbage became sour. It also became one of their main food supplies, easy to carry and to keep, so that when they invaded Europe in the thirteenth century, the European countries crossed by the Tatars learned about this food and liked it. The Germans called it *sauerkraut* (sour cabbage) and that is the name we know it by. The French word is *choucroute*. *Choucroute alsacienne* is one of France's most famous regional dishes.

Choucroute Alsacienne

ALSATIAN SAUERKRAUT

Sauerkraut is served as part of *choucroute garnie* or as an accompaniment to a roast of pork, surrounded with small white onions and potatoes in their jackets. Boiled potatoes served this way sometimes are poetically called *robes des champs* or field robes.

4 pounds fresh sauerkraut
½ cup goose or bacon fat, or pork fat from a roast
2 medium-size onions, finely chopped
1 garlic clove, minced
1 pound slab bacon, rind removed
1 cup Beef Stock (see Index), or as needed
2 cups Riesling or other dry white wine
10 juniper berries tied in a small muslin bag
1 bay leaf
½ teaspoon ground cloves
Coarse salt and pepper

6 servings

1. Place the sauerkraut in a colander and wash lightly under running water for a few seconds. (If imported, taste first, for it may not need washing.) Thoroughly drain, then untangle sauerkraut.

2. Melt the fat in a casserole or Dutch oven (not aluminum) and add the onions and garlic and sauté. Cut slab bacon into 2 slices, then cut each slice into 3 pieces and add to pan. Cook for 2 or 3 minutes. Add the beef stock, wine, and seasonings.

3. Add the sauerkraut, and cover. Bake in a 325°F. oven for 2 to 3 hours, watching the sauerkraut does not stick to the pan. Add a little additional stock if necessary. When done, almost all the liquid should have been absorbed. Remove the juniper berries and bay leaf. Serve *choucroute* very hot.

Petits Choux Farcis à la Crème

CABBAGE LEAVES STUFFED WITH HAM, CHESTNUTS, AND CREAM

1 large cabbage, 2 pounds
2 slices of bread
½ cup milk
1 large onion, finely chopped
1 garlic clove, finely chopped
8 tablespoons unsalted butter
1 cup finely chopped Polish ham
2½ cups Braised Chestnuts (see Index), chopped coarsely
Salt and freshly ground pepper
1 egg, beaten
1½ tablespoons flour
½ cup white wine
1 cup heavy cream

4 servings

1. Pull off the outermost cabbage leaves and discard. With a sharp knife, remove the entire core. Plunge the cabbage into a large pot of boiling salted water, and cook for about 15 minutes. Drain, cool slightly, and remove all the sizable leaves. Chop the cabbage heart.

2. Soak the bread in the milk.

3. Sauté the onion and garlic in 3 tablespoons of the butter until soft. Add the ham and chopped cabbage heart and cook for 5 minutes.

4. Add the soaked bread and the chestnuts. Season with salt and pepper. Add the egg, mixing well.

5. Trim off the tough stems of the cabbage leaves before stuffing. Spoon some of the mixture onto each leaf, and roll and fold the sides under to hold the filling, making neat bundles. Use 2 or 3 smaller leaves together if necessary. Place the bundles side by side in a generously buttered baking dish.

6. Melt 2 tablespoons of the butter. Stir in the flour until smooth, then add the wine and heavy cream. Bring to a boil, and season lightly with salt and pepper.

7. Pour this sauce over the cabbage and dot with remaining butter. Bake in a preheated 350°F. oven for about 1 hour, until golden.

Carottes à la Vichy
VICHY-STYLE CARROTS

Madame de Sévigné, famous for her letters to her daughter, said in the summer of 1676, "As for the Vichy waters, I praise them, my Dear Daughter, they have given me strength."

This is probably the best-known French way of preparing carrots. The real flavor comes from cooking the carrots in Vichy water.

2 pounds fresh carrots, peeled and thinly sliced   *4 servings*
5 tablespoons unsalted butter
2 tablespoons sugar
1 teaspoon salt
Vichy water or spring water
2 tablespoons finely chopped fresh parsley

1. Place the carrots in a saucepan and barely cover with Vichy water. Bring to a simmer.

2. When halfway cooked, add the butter, sugar, and salt. Boil

quickly until the water has evaporated. Shake the pan to glaze the carrots. Sprinkle with parsley, and give another toss. Serve immediately.

Chou-Fleur à la Polonaise

CAULIFLOWER POLONAISE

1 large very white cauliflower
Salt
¼ pound unsalted butter
2 tablespoons fresh bread crumbs, made in a blender or food processor
Lemon juice
3 hard-cooked egg yolks, chopped
1½ tablespoons chopped fresh parsley

4 servings

1. Make a deep incision around the hard center stem of the cauliflower and remove it. Break the cauliflower into florets, and shorten the stems. Rinse under cold water. Drop into a large pot of salted boiling water. After the water has returned to a boil, cook for about 20 minutes. Drain thoroughly.

2. Arrange the florets in a bowl in their original shape, pressing down gently. Unmold on a warm serving plate.

3. Melt the butter until deep golden and mix in the bread crumbs. Pour over the cauliflower. Sprinkle with lemon juice, chopped egg yolks and parsley combined.

♦ UNDER THE COOK'S HAT ♦

Wear rubber gloves while arranging the hot florets in the bowl because this must be done quickly so that the cauliflower can be served hot.

Chou-Fleur Royale

CAULIFLOWER ROYALE

This delicious recipe dates back to the time of Louis XIV, when cauliflower was introduced into France.

1 cauliflower, 2 pounds, cored and trimmed
2 cups Chicken Stock or Beef Stock (see Index)

4 servings

Pinch of grated mace
4 tablespoons butter

1. Parboil the cauliflower for 10 minutes. Drain.
2. Place the cauliflower in a large pan with the broth and the mace. Cook until just done. Pour off the broth, but keep it for soup, except for 4 tablespoons.
3. Melt the butter with the 4 tablespoons cooking broth. Pour over the cauliflower.

Chou-Fleur, Sauce Mousseline

CAULIFLOWER WITH MOUSSELINE SAUCE

This vegetable is an excellent accompaniment for cold meat or as part of a cold buffet.

Simmer a nicely shaped cauliflower in salted water with 1 tablespoon lemon juice, until tender but not overcooked. Drain and place upside down in a bowl just large enough to hold it, to retain its shape. Chill. Remove the hard center stem and unmold on a serving plate. Coat with Mousseline Sauce or Mayonnaise Chantilly (see Index for pages). Sprinkle with paprika. Serve the rest of the sauce separately.

◆ UNDER THE COOK'S HAT ◆

If you add 2 tablespoons of flour to the water when cooking cauliflower, the vegetable will remain snowy white. You must watch carefully because this addition will make the water boil over easily.

Céleris en Branches Braisés

BRAISED CELERY

3 large bunches of celery   *4 servings*
6 tablespoons unsalted butter
1 carrot, thinly sliced
1 onion, thinly sliced
2 thin slices of bacon, cut in pieces
1 bay leaf
½ teaspoon thyme
½ teaspoon peppercorns
Beef Stock (see Index)
3 tablespoons freshly grated Parmesan cheese

1. Cut off the leafy ends and the tough, outside ribs from the celery, leaving bunches about 6 inches long. Parboil the celery in salted water for 8 minutes. Drain and rinse under cold water. Drain again and cut each bunch lengthwise into halves.

2. Melt 3 tablespoons of the butter in a large skillet. Add the carrot, onion, bacon, bay leaf, thyme, and peppercorns. Cover and sauté the mixture over medium heat until soft.

3. Place the celery on top of the vegetable mixture. Add 2 tablespoons butter and enough stock to cover. Bring to a boil, cover, and simmer for about 30 minutes. Let celery cool in the broth.

4. Drain celery and place in a buttered baking dish. Sprinkle with Parmesan cheese and dot with remaining butter. Place in a preheated 400°F. oven until heated through, then glaze briefly under the broiler.

◆　　*Variation*　　◆

If serving this recipe at a formal dinner, reduce the braising stock by half. Strain and add 1 cup Brown Sauce (see Index) and 1 tablespoon cornstarch diluted in 1 tablespoon cold stock, and thicken the sauce. Simmer the celery in this sauce for 5 minutes. Add 2 tablespoons cold butter to the sauce. Transfer to a hot serving plate. Sprinkle a little freshly minced parsley over all.

Céleris à la Crème

CREAMED CELERY

2 large, very white bunches of celery　　　　　*6 servings*
Salt
6 tablespoons unsalted butter
1 tablespoon minced shallot or onion
3 tablespoons flour
1 cup milk
1 cup heavy cream
½ cup freshly grated Parmesan cheese
Salt and white pepper

1. Trim the roots and remove the outer ribs of the celery. If the ribs are very wide, cut into 2 or 3 lengthwise sections. Remove the leaves and cut the ribs into ¾-inch pieces. Drop into boiling salted water and simmer for 10 minutes, or until just tender. Do not overcook. Drain thoroughly.

2. Sauté the celery in 2 tablespoons of the butter in a skillet until all the moisture has evaporated.

3. Prepare the sauce: Melt 2 tablespoons of butter and sauté the shallot or onion until golden. Blend in the flour. Stirring with a whisk, slowly add the milk, cream, cheese, pepper to taste, and the rest of the butter. Taste, and add salt if needed. Simmer for 5 minutes. Add the celery and serve hot.

Especially good with chicken or veal.

◆   UNDER THE COOK'S HAT   ◆

Leeks or Swiss chard can be prepared in the same way.

◆ *Chestnuts* ◆

Chestnuts are a delicious and elegant "vegetable," and since time immemorial they have been a staple food in France. Chaplain Fortunat, who served Queen Radegonde, was the best gastronomic chronicler of the sixth century. When he wanted to make a gift, he would weave a basket with his own hands and fill it with chestnuts he had picked in the forest.

There are numerous ways of peeling chestnuts, and all call for first cooking or sautéing them. My own method of peeling them uncooked has many advantages. The chestnuts can be quickly and easily peeled without burning or discoloring fingers. Before they have been dropped into the boiling water they can be frozen without losing texture and flavor.

Cover the chestnuts with cold water in a large bowl. Add ⅓ cup sugar for each quart of water and soak for 2 hours. With a sharp little knife, and starting at the pointed top, remove the brown outer shell. Drop them into boiling water and cook for a moment, then skin the chestnuts while hot.

A *marron* has a shiny, tight shell that is convex on both sides. If convex on only one side and flat on the other, it is a *châtaigne*. A *châtaigne* is inferior, smaller, and harder to peel than a *marron*.

Never use canned unflavored chestnuts; they are tasteless and limp. However, the sweetened purée is fine for dessert.

Marrons Braisés

BRAISED CHESTNUTS

This is an excellent garnish for duck and game. It can be added to the roasting pan 5 minutes before a chicken is done, along with sautéed mushrooms.

2 pounds chestnuts, peeled (preceding page)   *6 servings*
Hot Beef Stock (see Index)
4 tablespoons unsalted butter
1 teaspoon sugar
Salt

1. Place the chestnuts in one layer in a baking dish just large enough to hold them. Barely cover with hot stock. Add 2 tablespoons butter, the sugar, and salt to taste.
2. Braise in a preheated 325°F. oven until tender, about 1 hour. Do not stir while braising.
3. Place the chestnuts on a hot serving plate. Reduce any stock that is left in the baking dish until syrupy. Swirl in the remaining butter, then pour sauce over the chestnuts. Serve immediately.

◆ *Endive* ◆

Endive, a relative newcomer among vegetables, was discovered accidentally in 1850 by Monsieur Brézier, the head gardener of the Belgian Society of Horticulturists.

To obtain whiter chicory for salad, he kept it covered with soil in a dark underground area reserved for the cultivation of mushrooms. The young shoots formed leaves overlapping each other, due to the weight of the soil. For several years this new vegetable was consumed locally and was called in Flemish *chicorée witloof*. In 1878, when the first cargo arrived in Paris, for some unknown reason it was announced as *endives de Bruxelles* and this became its name.

Endives Braisées

BRAISED ENDIVE

6 servings

2 pounds firm endives with tightly closed leaves, or 2 endives
   per serving

2 tablespoons unsalted butter
½ cup boiling water
Salt
Juice of ½ lemon
2 to 3 tablespoons Clarified Butter (see Index)

1. Remove the core at the root of each endive.

2. Melt the butter in a large skillet. Add the endives in one layer, then pour in the boiling water. Season with salt and add the lemon juice. Cover with a piece of buttered wax paper cut to fit the pan. Cover tightly and simmer over low heat until tender, about 25 minutes. Remove endives with a slotted spoon to a plate.

3. Discard the bitter cooking liquid. Heat the clarified butter and sauté the endives for a few minutes, until golden on all sides.

◆ *Variations* ◆

For an elegant dish, add ½ cup of Brown Sauce (see Index) and 2 to 3 tablespoons butter to the endive juices in the pan in step 3.

Endives Gratinées E N D I V E S A U G R A T I N   Place the braised endives side by side in a generously buttered gratin dish. Dot with butter and sprinkle with a combination of freshly grated Gruyère and Parmesan cheeses. Place under the broiler until golden.

Lentilles

LENTILS

Lentils go back to biblical times. They were cultivated extensively, especially in Egypt.

The obelisk that stands in Saint-Peter's Square in Rome was brought to Rome during the reign of Caligula (A.D. 37–41) in a boat from Egypt; the obelisk was packed in lentils.

Lentils were the favorite vegetable of Napoleon Bonaparte. They are very nourishing, full of protein, and especially delicious with pork or sausages.

2 medium-size onions, chopped

1 large leek, chopped

6 tablespoons unsalted butter

2 garlic cloves, minced

1½ cups dried lentils

1 tablespoon tomato paste

2 cups water

Salt and freshly ground pepper

Fresh parsley, chopped

4 servings

1. In a large *sauteuse* or skillet, sauté the onions and leek in 4 tablespoons of the butter until soft. Add the garlic and cook for 2 minutes.

2. Add the lentils, tomato paste, 2 cups water, and seasoning to taste. Cover and cook over medium-low heat for about 40 minutes. It might be necessary to add ½ cup water during the cooking.

3. The lentils are done when tender but still intact and all the liquid is absorbed. During the final 10 minutes of cooking, uncover. Before serving, gently mix in the remaining 2 tablespoons of butter and sprinkle with parsley.

Laitues Braisées

BRAISED LETTUCE

6 servings

1 large slice of fresh pork fat, from an uncooked pork roast

6 large firm heads of Boston lettuce

2 to 3 tablespoons butter

1 onion, diced

1 carrot, finely diced

½ teaspoon thyme

½ teaspoon ground bay leaf

1½ to 2 cups Beef Stock (see Index)

Salt and freshly ground pepper

½ cup Brown Sauce (see Index)

1. Freeze and then grate the pork fat. (It should make about ¼ cup.)

2. Discard the outer leaves of the lettuce. Plunge the heads into cold water, then drop them into a large kettle of boiling water and let them cook for 3 minutes. Transfer heads with a perforated spoon to a basin of cold water and let them stand for 3 minutes. Drain and press out as much water as possible.

3. Melt the grated pork fat and the butter in a large *sautoire* or skillet. Add the onion, carrot, thyme, and bay leaf and sauté over medium heat until golden.

4. Split the lettuce heads lengthwise into halves. Fold the leaves under to shape into round bundles. Arrange tightly together in the skillet and cook until all the moisture has evaporated.

5. Add enough beef stock to reach halfway up the sides of the lettuce. Season with salt and pepper. Simmer, uncovered, for about 30 minutes, basting often. Transfer the lettuce to a hot serving dish.

6. Add the brown sauce to the cooking juices and cook over high heat until reduced slightly. Discard any liquid that has collected on the serving dish, then cover the lettuce with the reduced sauce. Serve immediately.

◆   U N D E R   T H E   C O O K ' S   H A T   ◆

Whenever it is necessary to grate fat, freeze it first and you will find it much easier to grate than if it were soft.

◆ *Mushrooms* ◆

Abandoned quarries and caves near Paris were converted to mushroom cultivation during the reign of Louis XIV, and the little button mushrooms became known as *champignons de Paris.* They make especially attractive garnishes, either fluted and boiled, or sautéed.

If mushrooms need to be cleaned, rinse quickly under running water in a colander. Pat them dry with a towel. Do not peel or soak fresh mushrooms.

Fresh mushrooms should be very white, with their caps completely closed on their stems.

Do not use an aluminum saucepan; it darkens the mushrooms.

Champignons Sautés
SAUTÉED MUSHROOM CAPS

1. Remove the stems of large mushrooms. Sauté the caps in hot butter and oil over high heat for 3 to 4 minutes. Keep shaking the pan so they will not stick. They should be lightly brown.

2. Add 1 minced garlic clove and stir it in briefly before removing from the heat. Sprinkle with parsley and lemon juice. These mushrooms and watercress make a good garnish for steak.

Champignons Tournés

FLUTED MUSHROOMS

1. Slice off the stems of 8 mushrooms so that they are even with the caps. Wipe them off.

2. Hold the mushroom cap in your left hand, stem side down; lightly pressing with the tip of a zester or citrus peeler, make an arch-shaped groove running from the center to the rim of the mushroom while turning the cap in the other direction. Repeat in the same manner all around the cap.

3. Place the caps in ½ cup water and add 1 tablespoon butter, 1 teaspoon lemon juice, and salt to taste. Bring to a boil, cover, and boil for about 5 minutes. Drain immediately. Use as a garnish with fish, omelets, and meat.

◆   U N D E R   T H E   C O O K ' S   H A T   ◆

Use the mushroom liquor for a velouté sauce, or freeze it for later.

Purée de Champignons

MUSHROOM PURÉE

3 tablespoons unsalted butter   *2 to 3 servings*
1 tablespoon oil
2 tablespoons finely chopped onion
1 pound mushrooms, finely chopped
1 teaspoon cornstarch
½ cup heavy cream
Lemon juice
1½ tablespoons chopped parsley
Salt and freshly ground pepper

1. Melt the butter and oil in a large skillet and sauté the onion until wilted. Add the mushrooms and cook on medium high heat until all the liquid has evaporated.

2. Add the cornstarch mixed with the cream and cook until thickened.

3. Add a dash of lemon juice and the parsley, and season with salt and pepper.

◆   *Variation*   ◆

Mix this mushroom purée with cooked noodles for a delicious and substantial dish.

◆ U N D E R   T H E   C O O K ' S   H A T   ◆

Bake little tartlets with Tart Pastry (see Index), made without sugar, and fill with this mushroom purée. They make an attractive border for fish or meat dishes. When topped with hollandaise sauce and a sprinkle of paprika, then glazed, they can be served as a hot *hors-d'oeuvre*.

Oignons Glacés

GLAZED ONIONS

2 cups tiny white onions, about ½ pound
3 tablespoons unsalted butter
Stock or water
Salt and freshly ground pepper
1 teaspoon sugar

4 servings

1. Parboil the onions in boiling water for 1 minute, then drain and peel.
2. Melt the butter in a heavy-bottomed pan and add the onions in one layer. Shake the pan often over low heat and cook until onions are golden. Barely cover with stock or water. Season with salt and pepper and sugar. Simmer uncovered until all the liquid has evaporated and the onions are light golden brown and glazed.

◆   *Variations*   ◆

Carrots and turnips can be glazed in the same way.

◆ *Green Peas* ◆

No other vegetable throughout the centuries created such excitement as did fresh green peas when they were introduced in France. Audiger brought them back from Genoa in January 1660. He wrote in his book *La Maison reglée* that the King and several lords of the court all said, "Nothing is more beautiful or unusual! Never in France have we seen anything like it for the time of the year.

"His Majesty, having the kindness to show his satisfaction, ordered me to bring them to Sieur Baudoin, Contrôleur de la Bouche, and to tell him to have a small dish prepared for the Queen, one for

the Cardinal, and to keep what was left so the King could eat them with the Queen."

Green peas became the craze and everyone ate them, spoke about them, and wrote about them. The Marquise de Sévigné wrote in one of her famous letters, "There are ladies who, well supped, after eating with the King, risk indigestion by eating peas at home before retiring!"

Petits Pois à la Française
FRENCH-STYLE PEAS

18 tiny white onions   *4 to 6 servings*
3 tablespoons unsalted butter
1 firm head of Boston lettuce, cut into 8 wedges
2 pounds fresh peas, or 3 packages (10 ounces each) frozen tiny
    peas
2 parsley sprigs
2 teaspoons sugar
Salt
Butter

1. Parboil the white onions for 1 minute, then peel.
2. Melt the butter in a heavy pan. Add the white onions and lettuce. Cover and simmer for a few minutes. Add the peas, parsley, sugar, and salt to taste. Cook until the peas are done.
3. Remove the parsley sprigs and add a large piece of butter.

◆   U N D E R   T H E   C O O K ' S   H A T   ◆

Rinse frozen peas quickly under cold water before cooking. You will find they taste fresher.

Petits Pois à la Nivernaise

NIVERNAISE-STYLE PEAS

1 pound baby carrots   *4 to 5 servings*
1½ cups tiny white onions
7 tablespoons unsalted butter
½ cup water
3 hearts of Bibb lettuce, or 1 heart from a large Boston lettuce,
    washed and cored

3 cups tiny fresh peas
¾ cup heavy cream
Salt
1 teaspoon sugar
1½ tablespoons flour

1. Sauté the carrots and onions in 5 tablespoons of the butter over medium heat, shaking the pan often. When the vegetables begin to color, add the water and cook for another 10 minutes, until the water has evaporated and the mixture is syrupy.

2. Add the lettuce, peas, cream, salt to taste, and sugar. Cover and simmer until the vegetables are done.

3. Combine remaining 2 tablespoons butter with the flour to make *beurre manié*. Add the *beurre manié* to the vegetables and cook without boiling until sauce is thickened. Serve very hot.

Ratatouille Niçoise

RATATOUILLE FROM NICE

The word *ratatouille* comes from the Provençal dialect *ratatoulho*, or vegetable stew. It is one of the most popular Provençal summer dishes, containing ingredients typical of the region. Green peppers are often omitted, as in this recipe, as being too overpowering. Ratatouille can be served hot as a hearty dish, or cold, garnished with a few black olives, as an *hors-d'oeuvre*.

Fine olive oil   *6 servings*
2 medium-size eggplants, peeled and cut into ¼-inch-thick
    slices
2 yellow summer squash, cut into ½-inch-thick slices
2 large onions, minced
4 or 5 large garlic cloves, minced
4 or 5 large ripe tomatoes, coarsely chopped
2 tablespoons tomato paste
Thyme
Basil
Salt and freshly ground pepper
1 tablespoon lemon juice

1. Pour enough olive oil into a large skillet to reach ¼-inch depth. Heat oil. Sauté the eggplant slices, a few at a time, over

medium heat until golden brown on both sides. Add more oil if necessary. Set eggplant aside.

2. Sauté the squash in the same skillet until golden, and add to the eggplant slices.

3. Sauté the onions and garlic in the same olive oil left by the vegetables until golden, adding more oil as needed.

4. Add tomatoes and tomato paste and cook for 5 minutes. Combine with eggplant and squash. Season with herbs and salt and pepper to taste. Simmer for about 30 minutes, stirring occasionally. Add the lemon juice just before serving.

◆   U N D E R   T H E   C O O K ' S   H A T   ◆

Leftover ratatouille is a delicious filling for omelets or crêpes.

A poached egg on ratatouille makes a delicious combination for a light lunch.

Do not use an iron skillet for this dish, as the chemical reaction of the acid in the tomato with the iron produces an unpalatable taste.

Épinards à la Crème

CREAMED SPINACH

Spinach was introduced in the South of France by the Arabs in the twelfth century.

3 pounds fresh spinach   *6 servings*
Salt
¼ pound unsalted butter
1 garlic clove
Freshly ground pepper
1 teaspoon sugar
1 cup heavy cream
Puff Pastry Crescents (see Index) (optional)

1. Wash the spinach in 2 changes of water. Drain well. Place in a pan of ice water for 5 minutes, then drain again.

2. Drop the spinach, one handful at a time, into a large pot of boiling salted water, dropping it in slowly enough to keep the water boiling. Cook for about 5 minutes, then drain and spray with cold

water to keep the bright green color. Press as much water as possible from the spinach, then chop finely.

3. When ready to serve, melt half of the butter with the garlic clove in a skillet. When the butter foams, remove the garlic and add the spinach. Stir until the spinach is dry and begins to stick to the skillet.

4. Add salt and pepper to taste, the sugar, cream, and remaining butter. Serve in a hot round serving plate, garnished with 6 to 8 puff pastry crescents around the edge of the plate.

Tomates à la Provençale

TOMATOES WITH GARLIC AND BREAD CRUMBS

The tomato was introduced into France from Spain around 1816 through the provinces of Languedoc and Provence. In 1836, Burnet wrote in his cookbook that it is "a harmful custom to eat the tomatoes alone," which points out the cautious concern with which they were received. Although today they are widely used, it took a long time for their acceptance to grow, for they were first considered poisonous.

5 medium-large tomatoes   *5 servings*
Olive oil
Salt and freshly ground pepper
⅓ cup fresh bread crumbs, made from French bread
2 tablespoons finely minced fresh parsley
1 tablespoon finely minced garlic

1. Halve the tomatoes through the stems. Spread a baking dish with a little olive oil. Add the tomatoes, skin side down and in one layer; do not overcrowd. Season with salt and pepper.

2. Sprinkle the tomatoes with a mixture of the bread crumbs, parsley, and garlic. Generously moisten with olive oil.

3. Bake in a 350°F. oven for 1 hour and 20 minutes. Do not baste.

◆ UNDER THE COOK'S HAT ◆

These are also delicious cold.

A white fluted quiche dish is an attractive container for baking and serving the tomatoes.

Tomates à la Hussard

STUFFED TOMATOES

The Provençals love tomatoes so much that they believe it could only have been a tomato that Eve used to tempt Adam, and therefore they call tomatoes *pommes d'amour,* or apples of love. This is one of the earliest recipes for stuffed tomatoes and is described in the *Dictionnaire de cuisine et d'économie ménagère,* written by Burnet in 1836.

10 medium-sized tomatoes   *5 servings*
Salt and freshly ground pepper
3 to 4 tablespoons olive oil, approximately
4 tablespoons unsalted butter
3 tablespoons minced shallots, or 1 medium-size onion, finely
    minced
2 garlic cloves, minced
¼ pound mushrooms, finely minced
¼ pound ham, finely minced
1 cup fresh bread crumbs, made from French bread
2 tablespoons chopped parsley
2 tablespoons anchovy paste
1 egg, beaten

1. Cut a shallow slice off the stem end of each tomato and scoop out the upper half of the pulp. Reserve the pulp for later. Sprinkle the cavities with salt and pepper and invert over a plate to drain for 30 minutes.

2. Heat 1 tablespoon of the olive oil and 2 tablespoons of the butter in a skillet and sauté the shallots and garlic until translucent. Add the mushrooms and sauté until almost done, stirring constantly. Add the ham when the mixture begins to sizzle, sprinkle in the bread crumbs (reserving enough to sprinkle the tops), parsley, and salt and pepper to taste. Stir well and remove from the heat.

3. Mash together the anchovy paste with remaining 2 tablespoons butter. Mix into the filling along with the beaten egg. If the mixture is too dry, add some of the reserved tomato pulp, mashed.

4. Fill the tomatoes with the mixture and sprinkle the tops with remaining bread crumbs and a little olive oil. Place in a buttered baking dish, such as a porcelain quiche dish, and bake in a preheated 375°F. oven for about 40 minutes. If there is a lot of juice in the baking dish, remove the tomatoes and reduce the juice over high heat until syrupy, then pour it over the tomatoes.

Purée Fréneuse Gratinée
TURNIP PURÉE AU GRATIN

This is especially appropriate with turkey, duck, pork, or sausage.

6 to 7 tablespoons unsalted butter *4 servings*
8 medium-size (1½ pounds) white or yellow turnips, peeled
    and thinly sliced
2 to 3 tablespoons water
1 teaspoon sugar
Salt and freshly ground pepper
3 potatoes (1 pound), peeled
¾ cup heavy cream, or as needed
⅓ cup grated Parmesan cheese

1. Melt 3 tablespoons of the butter in a large skillet. Add the turnips and water and season with sugar and salt and pepper. Cover and simmer until the turnips are soft. Add a little more water if necessary, as they must not color. Reserve.

2. Cook the potatoes in water until done. (There should be one part potatoes to three parts turnips.)

3. Purée the potatoes and turnips through a food mill. Add 3 more tablespoons of the butter and the cream. Mix well.

4. Spoon the purée into a buttered baking dish. Sprinkle with Parmesan cheese and dot with remaining butter. Bake in a preheated 350°F. oven until golden.

◆ ◆ ◆

While working at the Austrian embassy in 1823, the illustrious chef Carême was approached one day by an eight-year-old girl wearing a toque "bonnet," which was the fashion for women. "How about exchanging our ugly cotton caps, which make us look like sick patients, for these light, pretty toques?" said Carême to the little girl, "I believe neatness and taste would be gained by it." The next day Carême wore a white toque. Soon all the famous chefs in France and the rest of the world were wearing them.

Jardinière de Légumes
GARDEN VEGETABLES

This is a delicious way to serve vegetables just picked from the garden.

5 medium-size potatoes   *6 servings*
8 new carrots
4 medium-size white turnips
2 slices of slab bacon, ½ inch thick
4 to 5 tablespoons unsalted butter
12 to 18 small white onions
1 pound fresh green peas, shelled
Salt and pepper
1 firm head of Boston lettuce, shredded
1 tablespoon sugar

1. Peel the potatoes, carrots, and turnips and cut them into small cubes.
2. Cut the bacon into *lardons,* or 1-inch-long sticks. Place in a saucepan of cold water and bring to a boil for 4 minutes. Drain.
3. Melt 2 tablespoons of the butter in a *sautoire* or large skillet. Sauté the *lardons* until they begin to color. Add the onions, continue to cook, shaking the pan often, until the *lardons* are golden.
4. Add the rest of the butter and all the other vegetables except the lettuce. Shake the *sautoire* until the vegetables are coated with the butter. Season with salt and pepper. Cover tightly and simmer for 15 minutes, continuing to shake the pan frequently.
5. Add the shredded lettuce and the sugar. Cook for another 10 minutes, until just done. Be careful not to overcook.

◆ *Potatoes* ◆

A wonderful plant called *papa* (potato) was cultivated by the Incas in Peru in ancient times, and Francisco Pizarro, who led the conquistadores into Peru in 1531, sent a few of the plants to Pope Clement VII.

A French scholar, Charles de Lécluse, decided that the plant was related to truffles and gave it the name of *taratoufli* (little truffle). It was cultivated in botanical gardens as a simple curiosity.

In 1573, the monks of a hospital in Seville, Spain, experimented using potatoes as food for the first time in Europe, to feed the poor. But two centuries passed before potatoes were accepted as a vegetable in France. Antoine-Augustin Parmentier, a military chemist, worked for years to prove that the potato was a valuable food— easy to grow, inexpensive, and versatile, hoping that eventually potato flour would be used in bread making. He sent a bouquet of potato flowers to Louis XVI for his birthday. The Queen placed a few in her hair and it soon became the fashion to wear a potato flower in the lapel. The blossoms cost up to ten golden louis apiece!

Louis XVI gave Parmentier an acre of land in the Sablons Plains on the outskirts of Paris for his experiments. The field was planted with potatoes and protected during the day by the *Garde Française* as a plot to pique the curiosity of the Parisians. As a result, those who at first were very suspicious of the potatoes decided they must be extremely valuable vegetables, and they began to steal the potatoes at night and cook them. By the time of the French Revolution five years later, potatoes had become so indispensable that the flower beds of the Tuileries were replanted with potatoes.

Pommes de Terre Noisette

POTATO BALLS IN BUTTER

These potatoes are called *noisette* (hazelnut) because of the color the butter gives them while cooking. For each serving, allow a potato large enough to yield 6 or 7 balls, made with a potato-ball cutter or melon-ball scoop.

4 extra-large potatoes, cut into balls   *4 servings*
Salt
4 tablespoons unsalted butter
1 tablespoon finely chopped parsley

1. Parboil the potato balls in salted water for 2 to 3 minutes, just long enough to tenderize. Drain thoroughly and cool.

2. Melt the butter in an ovenproof dish on top of the stove. Add the potato balls and shake the dish so they are well coated with butter. Finish cooking in a preheated 350°F. oven until potato balls are tender and golden. Shake the pan occasionally, so that they will brown evenly.

3. Just before serving, sprinkle with finely chopped parsley.

◆   U N D E R   T H E   C O O K ' S   H A T   ◆

Use the leftover potato trimmings for soup.

Pommes de Terre à la Maître d'Hôtel
PARSLEYED POTATOES

Perfect for any fish or meat dishes made with a fine sauce.

Scrape small new potatoes, or shape small balls from large potatoes with a potato-ball cutter. Steam until just done. Toss with Parsley Butter (see Index) and serve immediately.

Pommes de Terre Anna
POTATOES ANNA

This well-known potato dish was created by chef Adolphe Dugléré of the famous restaurant Le Café Anglais, a temple of gastronomy in the nineteenth century. It was dedicated to Anna Deslions, an actress. Rounded, thin slices of potato are arranged to form a pattern in a special utensil with a cover, designed for this dish, but an 8-inch layer-cake pan can be substituted.

6 to 8 medium-size potatoes   *4 servings*
Unsalted butter
Salt and freshly ground pepper
Pinch of grated nutmeg

1. Peel the potatoes and trim to form cylinders matching in shape and size. Slice the cylinders into thin, round slices with a *mandoline,* a special utensil for slicing potatoes.

2. First sauté the potatoes in butter in a skillet just long enough to soften them. Generously butter a round, shallow glass dish or a tin layer-cake pan.

3. Overlap a layer of potatoes around the edge to form a design before filling. Line the bottom of the pan with slices of potatoes in circles, overlapping first in one direction and then in the other to make an attractive pattern. Continue to fill the dish in this fashion, seasoning each layer with salt and pepper and nutmeg. Pile the potatoes higher in the center as they will settle once cooked.

4. Place the pan in a preheated 500°F. oven and bake for 30 to 40 minutes. The potatoes will be golden on top as well as underneath. Let them stand for 10 minutes before unmolding on a serving plate.

Pommes de Terre Voisin
POTATOES VOISIN

This recipe is from Voisin, the great nineteenth-century French restaurant, which contributed much to the glory of French cuisine.

Prepare the potatoes in the same way as for *pommes de terre Anna,* covering each layer of potatoes with very thin slices of Swiss cheese.

Le Gratin Dauphinois
SCALLOPED POTATOES

The Dauphiné province is famous for its many kinds of gratin dishes but the most famous of all is this gratin of thinly sliced potatoes with cream, cheese, and garlic.

5 Idaho potatoes, peeled and thinly sliced   *4 servings*
·1 large garlic clove
5 tablespoons unsalted butter
1 cup freshly grated Gruyère cheese
Salt and freshly ground pepper
1 cup heavy cream
1 cup milk
Pinch of grated nutmeg

1. Dry the potatoes. Cut the garlic clove and rub it around a gratin or earthenware baking dish. Butter the dish. Finely mince the garlic and spread it in the bottom of the dish.

2. Arrange the potatoes in 3 layers in the dish, sprinkling a little cheese and some salt and pepper on each layer. Combine the cream and milk and pour over the potatoes. Dot the top with remaining butter and sprinkle with nutmeg.

3. Bake in a preheated 375°F. oven until a golden crust forms, about 1 hour and 10 minutes. Let the dish stand for 10 minutes before serving.

◆ *Variation* ◆

For Gratin Savoyard, substitute bouillon for the cream.

◆ *Pommes de Terre Soufflées* ◆

This is a charming, authentic account of the creation of the intriguing *pommes de terre soufflées*. On August 24, 1837, the train track that previously ended at Pecq was extended to Saint-Germain-en-Laye, near Paris. Typical of all French inaugurations, a big banquet with a band and flags awaited the officials of the train at the end of the line. The train carried Queen Marie Amélie and two of her sons—the duc d'Orléans and duc de Montpensier—replacing King Louis Philippe who could not expose his invaluable person in the "perilous" adventure of the train ride.

French fried potatoes were on the menu and were put in deep fat to be ready for the officials' arrival. At that time, potatoes for frying were still cut into thin slices instead of small sticks. When they had been cooking for a few minutes, a messenger came rushing into the kitchen of the restaurant Le Pavillon Henri IV to warn: "Hold everything! The train is having difficulty climbing the hill!" Immediately Maître Colînet, the chef, removed the potatoes, but left the fat on the heat. Shortly thereafter, they told the chef the officials had suddenly appeared, and he put the potatoes back in the fat. It had become even hotter by then and he was amazed when he saw how the slices puffed up. They were the hit of the meal and he was congratulated by all.

Thus were created the deliciously crisp *pommes soufflées*.

Pommes de terre soufflées are usually eaten in a restaurant—the fat has to be so hot that it is rather risky to try making them at home.

Pommes de Terre Frites, or Pont-Neuf
FRENCH FRIED POTATOES

On restaurant menus, these fried potatoes are called *pommes de terre Pont-Neuf* (new bridge) after what is, ironically, the oldest bridge in Paris. In early times, merchants selling these fried potatoes congregated at the corners of this bridge; then, too, the shape of the slices was round, reminiscent of the 12 arches under the bridge. About a century ago, French fries began to be cut into sticks, the same form as we know them today.

1. Choose large, hard-pulp potatoes such as Idahos.

2. Peel the potatoes and trim on all four sides to make them rectangular. Cut them lengthwise into ½-inch-thick slices, then into ½-inch-wide sticks. Dry the potatoes thoroughly in a towel and keep wrapped until ready to fry, so they won't discolor.

3. Fill a deep, heavy cast-iron pan half full of peanut oil. Heat oil to 350°F., or test by putting in a potato stick. If bubbles form around it immediately, the fat is ready. Fry the potatoes in small batches so they can move freely in the oil. When they are a uniform light beige, remove.

4. When ready to serve, but no longer than an hour later, place the potatoes back in oil heated to 375°F. and let them cook until they are golden brown. Transfer immediately to a hot serving plate. Sprinkle lightly with fine salt and serve immediately.

◆ UNDER THE COOK'S HAT ◆

The oil can be reused 2 or 3 times. Filter it after each use through a fine sieve lined with cheesecloth.

Buy the freshest beef suet (from around the kidney) from your butcher and render it to use for frying these potatoes. This gives a specially fine flavor.

Bordure de Pommes de Terre Duchesse

DUCHESS POTATOES FOR GARNISHING

This is an excellent accompaniment for any meat or fish dish and will enhance its appearance.

6 medium-size Idaho potatoes, peeled and quartered   *6 servings*
Salt
5 tablespoons unsalted butter
2 whole eggs plus 2 extra egg yolks, well beaten
White pepper
Freshly grated nutmeg
2 tablespoons freshly grated Parmesan cheese
Butter

1. Cook the potatoes in a pan of salted water until just done. Drain potatoes and force through a mill or potato ricer.
2. Mix in the butter, beaten eggs, salt, pepper and nutmeg to taste, and Parmesan cheese. Beat until smooth. If not to be used immediately, place a sheet of buttered wax paper directly on the purée.
3. Put the potato purée into a pastry bag fitted with a 1½-inch star tube. Pipe in an attractive pattern (slightly overlapping or in zigzag or make large individual rosettes) around the edge of a buttered serving plate.
4. Just before serving, drizzle or brush melted butter on the border and place under the broiler until the potatoes are golden. Place the meat or fish inside the border.

Purée de Pommes de Terre

MASHED POTATOES

It is best to prepare mashed potatoes just before serving.

1. Choose large, mealy potatoes, counting 1 potato per serving. Peel them and cook in salted water for about 30 minutes, or until done. Drain.
2. Force the potatoes through a potato ricer into a bowl set over a large pot of hot water. This should be done quickly so the potatoes do not cool off.
3. Add simmering milk and small pieces of unsalted butter until

the right consistency is reached, while mixing them in an electric blender at the *lowest* setting. (This will keep the purée from becoming rubbery.) Season lightly with salt and white pepper. If the purée is to stand for a short while, cover it directly with a sheet of buttered wax paper, and set the bowl in a larger bowl of hot water. Serve very hot.

◆   *Variations*   ◆

Purée de pommes de terre mousseline is made as in the preceding recipe with the addition of ½ cup heavy cream, whipped and folded into the purée. A little nutmeg may also be added to flavor the purée.

Add Sauce Soubise (see Index) to the purée.

◆   UNDER THE COOK'S HAT   ◆

Do not use new potatoes for mashed potatoes.

L'Aligot

POTATO PURÉE WITH CHEESE AND GARLIC

This regional dish from Auvergne is a variation on potato purée. It consists of a purée of potatoes blended with fresh, unfermented Tomme de Cantal cheese and flavored with garlic. It is beaten over heat until it becomes very stringy. A mild Muenster cheese is substituted for the Tomme de Cantal, which is not readily available.

2 pounds Idaho potatoes   *4 servings*
Salt and white pepper
4 to 5 tablespoons unsalted butter
1 garlic clove, minced
¾ cup light cream, or as much as needed
¾ pound soft Muenster cheese, cut into very small cubes

1. Peel the potatoes and cook in water seasoned with salt and pepper. Drain and purée through a potato ricer or a vegetable mill. Return the purée to the pan.

2. Melt the butter with the minced garlic until barely tepid. Add it to the potatoes along with the cream and mix with an electric beater.

3. Put the pan over low heat and stir in the cheese cubes until melted and thoroughly blended. Serve immediately.

Inasmuch as this is heavy fare, you may prefer to decrease the cheese to ¼ pound for a lighter result. This purée is especially good with liver.

Riz au Gras

RICE AU GRAS

A very old French way of cooking rice, which makes it flavorful and fluffy.

1½ cups raw unconverted rice   *6 servings*
4 tablespoons unsalted butter
2½ cups broth, preferably from a *pot-au-feu* or *poule-au-pot*
1 small onion
1 small bouquet garni (¼ bay leaf, thyme, 3 parsley sprigs)
Pepper

1. Pour the rice into a saucepan of cold water. Bring to a boil and boil for 3 minutes. Drain; rinse the rice under warm water; drain thoroughly.

2. Melt the butter and stir in the rice to coat the grains. Add the broth, onion, and *bouquet garni*. Bring to a boil, then simmer covered, without stirring, for 15 minutes, or until the broth is completely absorbed and the grains are separate.

3. Discard the *bouquet garni* and onion. Fluff the rice with a fork, season with pepper, and serve immediately.

◆   UNDER THE COOK'S HAT   ◆

Once the rice is cooked do not cover to keep warm or it will become mushy. The pan may be set over a larger pan of hot water.

◆   *Variations*   ◆

An attractive way to serve rice pilaf is to fill baba molds or small buttered glasses with rice, pressing down with the back of a spoon. Unmold the rice on a warm serving plate, or arrange as a garnish around meat or fish. Garnish the top of each portion with a tiny round piece of pimiento or a slice of stuffed olive, or cover partially with Brown Sauce (see Index).

Cook rinsed rice in salted water. Sauté 6 to 8 shallots in butter until softened and add to rice with 3 tablespoons chopped fresh parsley, a sprinkle of lemon juice and lots of white pepper.

Mix leftover rice with a highly seasoned mayonnaise, herbs, chopped black olives, and tuna. Stuff ripe tomatoes with mixture.

Riz Pilaf en Couronne
CROWN OF RICE PILAF

1 medium-size onion, finely minced   *6 servings*
5 tablespoons unsalted butter
2 tablespoons olive oil
2 cups raw unconverted rice, well rinsed
4 cups Chicken Stock (see Index), fish stock, or clam juice
1 bouquet garni
Salt and freshly ground pepper

1. In a heavy saucepan, sauté the onion in 2 tablespoons of the butter and the oil over medium heat, stirring constantly, until golden. Add the rice and cook for 2 minutes, or until rice is opaque.

2. Add the stock, *bouquet garni,* and salt and pepper to taste. Bring to a boil, then cover tightly. Lower the heat and simmer until the rice has absorbed all the liquid, about 20 minutes. Do not stir while cooking or the rice will stick.

3. Remove the *bouquet garni.* Add pieces of the remaining butter and pepper to taste. Mix gently with a fork.

4. When ready to serve, generously butter a 5-cup ring mold. Fill the mold with the rice, pressing lightly with the back of a spoon.

5. Place the mold on a baking sheet in a preheated 325°F. oven for 10 minutes, or until thoroughly heated. Unmold on a warm serving plate. Fill the inside of the ring with meat, fish, or chicken, or serve as is.

Riz à la Tomate
RICE WITH TOMATOES

1 medium-size onion, finely chopped   *4 servings*
1 garlic clove, minced
4 tablespoons unsalted butter
2 tablespoons olive oil
3 ripe tomatoes, peeled and coarsely chopped
1½ cups raw unconverted rice

¼ cup dry white wine
2½ cups Chicken or Beef Stock (see Index for pages) or water
1 small bay leaf
Salt and freshly ground pepper
½ cup freshly grated Parmesan or Gruyère cheese
Fresh parsley, chopped

1. Cook the onion and garlic in 2 tablespoons of the butter and the olive oil until golden. Add the tomatoes and cook for 5 minutes.

2. Add the rice and stir until opaque. Add the wine, stock or water, bay leaf, and seasonings to taste. Bring to a boil, lower the heat, cover, and simmer for 20 to 25 minutes, until rice has absorbed all the liquid. Do not stir.

3. Fluff the rice with a fork. Add remaining butter and the cheese. Press into individual buttered baba molds or glasses and unmold immediately onto a warm serving plate. Sprinkle the top with parsley.

Spaghetti au Roquefort
SPAGHETTI WITH ROQUEFORT CHEESE

1 pound spaghetti   *4 servings*
Coarse salt
1 tablespoon olive oil
2 garlic cloves
Unsalted butter
White pepper
½ pound Roquefort cheese or other blue cheese
½ cup heavy cream
1 tablespoon Cognac

1. Cook spaghetti in boiling salted water with the olive oil. When cooked but still firm, rinse under cold water for a few seconds. Drain thoroughly and place in a serving dish rubbed with a split garlic clove. Add a generous piece of butter and a sprinkle of white pepper.

2. Prepare the sauce: Mash the Roquefort with the cream in a pan set over boiling water. When smooth, add the Cognac and the second garlic clove, finely minced.

3. Combine the sauce with the spaghetti and serve immediately.

◆ UNDER THE COOK'S HAT ◆

If the strong flavor of the Roquefort is too much for your taste, use less Roquefort or a Blue cheese.

Gnocchi à la Parisienne

GNOCCHI PARISIENNE

The etymology of *gnocchi* proves that it originated in Nice in Provence.

¾ cup milk
5 tablespoons unsalted butter
Generous pinch of grated nutmeg
Salt and pepper
¾ cup flour
5 eggs
¼ cup finely grated Swiss Gruyère cheese
Mornay Sauce (see Index) with ⅓ cup additional grated cheese
    and a good pinch of grated nutmeg, but omitting the eggs
Butter for top

4 to 6 servings

1. Bring the milk, butter, and seasoning to taste to a fast boil.
2. Remove from heat and add the flour all at once. Stir vigorously with a wooden spoon. Place back on the heat and stir until the batter forms a shiny ball, about ½ minute.
3. Transfer to a mixing bowl and add eggs, one at a time, beating well after each addition. Stir in the cheese.
4. Pipe the batter, in 1½-inch-long pieces, from a pastry bag with a large plain tube (No. 8) into 1 or 2 large skillets of gently boiling salted water. Or drop the batter in by the tablespoon.
5. Gently boil the *gnocchi* until done; they will turn over by themselves. Remove with a skimmer from the water onto a towel, to drain and cool.
6. Arrange the *gnocchi* in one layer in a buttered shallow baking dish lined with some of the Mornay sauce. Pour the rest of the sauce over and dot with butter. Bake in a preheated 375°F. oven for about 40 minutes without opening the oven door, or until the *gnocchi* are well puffed and golden. Serve immediately before they flatten.

◆   *Variations*   ◆

Make half the amount of Mornay sauce and mix with an equal quantity of Tomato Sauce (see Index).

Place the *gnocchi* in a baked pastry case made of Puff Pastry (see Index), and bake as indicated in the recipe.

◆   ◆   ◆

Contrary to what is widely believed today, aside from introducing in France poultry quenelles and haricot beans, native of the new world, Catherine de Médicis did not contribute anything to French cuisine, which at the time was already well established. In fact, according to the contemporary chronicler Brantôme, during the reign of Henri II, "It was by whim that one could fare well at the court." He also speaks of "the abuse of simplicity of the fare at the table of the king," while in Catherine's native city of Florence, where severe restrictions were the rule. The famous Dominican preacher Savonarola complains bitterly of the "extravagance" of the Florentines eating their spaghettis with garlic and even with Parmesan!

It was indeed to make up for this lack of good fare at the court that Anne de Poitiers, mistress of Henri II, entertained lavishly at her Château d'Amboise.

11. *Les Salades* SALADS

⚜ ⚜ ⚜

Perhaps the first indication we have of salad making and salad dressing is in reading that Apicius, the eccentric Roman gastronome, had all the lettuce in his garden sprinkled every night with a sweet wine.

The French have been fond of salad since the early days of Gaul. It was eaten then at the beginning of the meal, as it was in the Middle Ages during Lent, because it "represented the Word of God, which gives us appetite and courage," according to *Les Salades de Carême*, published in Paris about 1580.

"A good salad must pass through the hands of four persons to be as it should be; namely, a mad man for the choice and great variety of good herbs, a wise man for the salt, a miser for the vinegar, and a spendthrift to pour unsparingly the oil," asserts *La Civilité nouvelle*, a cookbook published in 1667.

Many aristocrats who lost all they owned during the French Revolution crossed the English Channel to escape and were forced to work for the first time in their lives. The Marquis d'Albignac made a fortune in London giving consultations on the art of salad preparation, because using seasonings in salad was a new concept for the British. He would rush to different parties in a specially designed fast carriage, accompanied by a servant who carried a mahogany box with all the necessary ingredients. The finishing touch to his famous salads was a sprinkling of nasturtium blossoms.

La Salade

Lave ta main, qu'elle soit belle et nette,
Marche après moi, apporte une serviette.
Une salade amassons, et faisons
Part à nos ans des fruits de la saison.

. . . .

Je m'en irai solitaire à l'écart.
Tu t'en iras, Jamyn, d'une autre part,
Chercher soigneux la bourcette touffue,
La pâquerette à la feuille menue,
La pimprenelle heureuse pour le sang.
Et pour la rate, et pour le mal de flanc,

. . . .

Puis, en lisant l'ingénieux Ovide,
En ces beaux vers où l'amour est le guide,
Regagnerons le logis pas à pas.
Là, retroussant jusqu'au coude nos bras,
Nous laverons nos herbes à main pleine
Au cours sacré de ma belle fontaine:
Là blanchirons de sel en mainte part,
L'arroserons de vinaigre rosart,
L'engraisserons d'huile de la Provence: . . .

The Salad

Wash your hands until they are beautifully clean
And walk behind me with your towel.
Let us gather the makings of a salad,
Being mindful of our years and the fruits of the season.

I shall go by myself in one direction.
You go, Jamyn, another way.
Look carefully for the tufted corn-salad,
For the tiny, small-leaved daisy,
And for the pimpernel, so soothing to the blood and all internal
   ailments.

Then, by reading the clever Ovid,
Whose beautiful verses use love as a guide,
We shall slowly find our way back home.
There, with sleeves rolled up to the elbow
We shall wash our herbs
In the sacred stream of my beautiful fountain;

We shall whiten the leaves with salt, sprinkle with rose vinegar,
And we shall enrich it all with oil from Provence.
—PIERRE DE RONSARD (1524–1585)

◆　◆　◆

S A L T :   The word *salad* is derived from the Latin *sal* (salt), because
originally salt was the only seasoning used. It was the "condiment
of condiments," according to Plutarch, and has been indispensable
since biblical times. In addition to its use as a seasoning, salt was
essential as a preservative.

In 1343 Philippe VI of Valois instituted *La Gabelle*, an unpopular
tax on salt. It was still in effect 200 years later when Henri III decreed
that salt could be purchased only from the King, thereby financing
the constant wars. This law was sternly enforced with prison terms
and death sentences, and its unfairness caused many insurrections.

P E P P E R :   Because of the slow transportation and lack of refrigeration until comparatively recent times, seafood and meat often
developed unpleasant odors that could be hidden by pepper and
other spices, and pepper, known for more than 3,000 years, became
the most important of all of these. It was one of the earliest articles
of trade between the Orient and Europe; ships sailed from the ports
of Venice and Genoa for the Orient and returned laden with spices.
Pepper, especially, has always been costly and these cities, capitals
of the spice trade, became fabulously wealthy. It was in search of a
more direct route to India (and the indispensable spices) that Chris-
topher Columbus sailed to the Americas.

During the Middle Ages, pepper was also used as currency.
Taxes, judges, and even rent were frequently paid with peppercorns. In addition, pepper was used as a medicine, aiding digestion
and treating cholera.

In France today, the milder flavor of white pepper (peppercorns
with the outer husk removed) is preferred to the stronger black
pepper.

O I L :   The word *oil* is derived from the old French word for olive,
which remains the oil *par excellence* for salads.

The quality of the oil is very important when seasoning a salad.
The olive oil of Provence is held in great esteem because of its fruity
but not overpowering flavor.

Virgin oil (from the first pressing) is the most desirable. This oil
is light-colored and has a pleasant flavor. Peanut oil is also excellent
for salads.

The oldest olive tree on record grows near Nice. It is believed to be 2,000 years old and has a circumference of 10 meters (about 24 feet).

VINEGAR: The corporation of vinegar makers received their statutes from King Charles VI in Orléans in 1394. Their coat of arms depicts a small cask lying on a wheelbarrow, reflecting the way vinegar was sold in the streets by itinerant merchants. Until the end of the Renaissance, vinegar was spelled as two words: *vin aigre* (sour wine).

For centuries, wine was mixed with water for drinking, and vinegar was substituted when the wine was lacking. It is said that Louis XIV never drank pure wine until he was forty years old. The Romans drank vinegar and water, to which they attributed their strength and endurance. Hippocrates said, "Pure water cannot go down the stomach . . . *vin aigre* makes it go through anywhere."

Until the middle of the eighteenth century, vinegar was flavored with carnations, roses, strawberries, and fruit juices. Maille, vinegar purveyor to the Marquise de Pompadour, is still in business. At one time they made 92 differently flavored vinegars.

Vinegar was used to treat melancholy moods, to lose weight, to cleanse the liver, and to fight bubonic plague.

The city of Orléans, still the vinegar capital of the world, produces such excellent vinegar because of the fine wines of the Loire. Orléans vinegar is not acidic or bitter. Most of the vinegar made in the United States is distilled and rather acid. Therefore, when using domestic vinegar, the classic proportions for a vinaigrette (3 tablespoons of oil to 1 tablespoon of vinegar) should be changed to 4 tablespoons of oil to 1 of vinegar.

Sauce Vinaigrette
VINAIGRETTE

The French way is to make the dressing fresh for each salad. It is not made up in quantity and bottled as it is in America. However, if you keep to these proportions, you can make up any amount in a blender and bottle it. Remember to shake well before using. The quantity given below is enough for a large head of Boston lettuce.

3 to 4 tablespoons good-quality olive or peanut oil
1 tablespoon French wine vinegar
Coarse salt and freshly ground pepper

1. Pour oil and vinegar in a bowl and add seasoning to taste. Mix thoroughly.

◆　　*Variation*　　◆

Add chopped fresh herbs such as parsley, tarragon, or chives; shallots; anchovies and chopped hard-cooked eggs; garlic; or mustard to taste.

◆　◆　◆

Lettuce comes from the Latin Lactuca *(milk) because it is filled with a milky sap. This plant encourages sleep, stimulates the milk of wet nurses, and calms the temperament, preventing fits of temper.*
—DR. NICOLAS LÉMERY, 1707

Vinaigre Aromatisé

AROMATIC VINEGAR

This delicious aromatic vinegar is a great seasoning agent for flavoring *salades composées* or cold *hors-d'oeuvre* such as leeks, rice salad, and lentils.

2 cups excellent wine vinegar
2 garlic cloves
4 shallots, peeled
1 small bay leaf
3 parsley sprigs
¼ teaspoon dried thyme
Pinch of salt
½ teaspoon dried tarragon
3 or 4 peppercorns, crushed
3 whole cloves

1. Boil all the ingredients together for 5 minutes. Transfer to a bowl, cover, and let stand for 12 hours.
2. Strain the vinegar before putting it into a bottle for future use.

Assaisonnement à la Crème

CREAMY SALAD DRESSING

½ cup Crème Fraîche (see Index) *Makes ¾ cup*
1 large shallot, finely minced
1 tablespoon wine vinegar, or 2 teaspoons lemon juice
3 tablespoons oil
1 tablespoon snipped fresh chives
1 tablespoon minced fresh parsley
1 teaspoon minced fresh tarragon
Salt and freshly ground pepper

1. Mix all the ingredients together, with seasoning to taste. Place in the bottom of a salad bowl.
2. When ready to serve, add the prepared salad greens and toss lightly.

Assaisonnement au Roquefort

ROQUEFORT DRESSING

2 ounces Roquefort cheese *Makes ½ cup*
⅓ cup heavy cream
Lemon juice
Salt and pepper

1. Mash the cheese in a mixing bowl and add enough cream to make a smooth dressing.
2. Add lemon juice, salt, and pepper to taste; mix well.

◆ *Les Salades Simples* ◆

Salades simples are composed of greens, such as Boston lettuce, watercress, escarole, chicory, and lamb's-lettuce, dressed with a vinaigrette, and usually served as a separate course between the main course and cheese or dessert. Vinaigrette is the classic dressing for these salads, and its name comes from the early French word for vinegar—*vin aigre*. Made up of 3 to 4 parts salad oil, 1 part vinegar, and coarse salt and pepper from the mill, the sole additions permitted are herbs such as tarragon, parsley, chives, and chervil.

There are two ways of dressing a salad—by adding the greens to the vinaigrette or by adding the vinaigrette to the greens. In the first case, the dressing is made in the bottom of the salad bowl; the greens are added and tossed just before serving. In the second case, the greens are placed in the bowl and the dressing ingredients are added one at a time. First, add the salt and pepper, then the vinegar. Toss the salad to impregnate the leaves with flavoring ingredients. Add the oil and toss again to coat the leaves.

The dressing should be added just before serving so that the salt and vinegar will not have a chance to wilt the leaves, but if herbs are to be used they should be added to the greens an hour or two before serving, so as to let the flavors permeate.

The secret of a good salad is in the way the lettuce is washed and dried, thoroughly and carefully. First, discard the outside leaves and remove the hard core by twisting it hard. Tear the leaves into bite-size pieces and wash quickly in a large quantity of water (never let the lettuce soak). Dry the leaves with great care but be sure that they remain uncrushed. Form a little cage with your hands —palms touching at the wrists and fingertips touching. Take a few leaves at a time and shake them vigorously until almost dry.

◆　◆　◆

Lettuce, this pleasant intermission of regal repasts.
—VIRGIL, 70–19 B.C.

Salade Verte

MIXED GREEN SALAD

The most popular salad in France is this classic green salad, used as a refreshing interlude. It can be the basis of endless variations.

4 servings

2 heads of Boston lettuce, washed, with outer leaves removed
4 endives, cut lengthwise, then into 1-inch pieces
1 large bunch of watercress, stems removed
1 chicory heart
Vinaigrette (see Index)

1. Prepare the greens and tear them into bite-size pieces.
2. Mix the vinaigrette and pour into the bottom of a salad bowl.
3. Add the greens and toss.

◆ *Variations* ◆

Salade d'Endive et Cresson ENDIVE AND WATERCRESS SALAD *Salade d'Endive et Bettèraves* ENDIVE AND BEET SALAD   This salad is also tasty with just the endive and watercress seasoned with olive oil, lemon vinaigrette, and Dijon mustard or with the endive and 4 small cooked beets. Add a little garlic to the dressing as well as a little extra vinegar and salt, and use walnut oil, if available.

Another attractive variation of this salad is Salade Mimosa. With the regular vinaigrette, use only Boston lettuce in a crystal bowl. Just before serving, sprinkle 2 sieved hard-cooked egg yolks over the top. The finished salad should remind one of the yellow mimosa flower nestled in its green leaves.

Salade Fontaine

FONTAINE SALAD

This salad is colorful and refreshing.

2 large heads of Boston lettuce	*6 servings*

2 large heads of Boston lettuce
1 large bunch of watercress
2 hard-cooked egg yolks
½ teaspoon Dijon mustard
Salt and freshly ground pepper
2 tablespoons chopped fresh chervil or parsley
2 tablespoons wine vinegar
7 tablespoons oil
Lemon juice
4 ripe tomatoes, peeled and thinly sliced

1. Tear the lettuce into bite-size pieces. Wash and dry thoroughly. Cut off the stems of the watercress, wash, and dry the leafy sprigs.

2. Mash the egg yolks with a fork. Add the mustard, salt and pepper to taste, chervil, vinegar, and oil.

3. Toss the lettuce leaves with the dressing. Arrange the watercress on top, forming a crown, and sprinkle with a little lemon juice. Arrange the tomatoes overlapping in a circle on the center of the salad.

◆ UNDER THE COOK'S HAT ◆

A piece of bread or a crouton rubbed with garlic is often added to tossed green salads for flavoring. It is called a *chapon*. This will give only a faint garlic flavor. If a stronger taste is preferred, chop a garlic clove and put it in the bottom of the salad bowl with salt and pepper. Crush it with the back of a spoon until completely mashed, then add vinegar, oil, and seasoning.

It is interesting to note that this custom originated in Gascony, and it is said that this piece of garlic bread was called a *chapon* (capon) so that those who could not afford the real thing could still boast that they had dined on a meal of salad and capon.

◆　◆　◆

The watercress of Normandy was so popular in the fourteenth century that it was mentioned in a poem of the time:

> *Pour gens dégoûtez non malades,*
> *J'ai du bon cresson de Caillier,*
> *Pour un peu vos coeurs escaillier*
> *Il n'est rien de meilleur pour salades.*

> For people who are finicky but not sick
> I have good watercress from Caillier.
> It should cheer your heart a bit
> For nothing makes a better salad.

Salade au Lard

SALAD WITH BACON

This salad is a specialty of the province of Champagne.

4 or 5 slices of bacon, cut into small pieces   *4 servings*
1 large head of curly chicory or very young spinach leaves
2 tablespoons tarragon vinegar
3 to 4 tablespoons oil
1 teaspoon finely minced shallot
Salt and freshly ground pepper
1 hard-cooked egg, sieved

1. Sauté the bacon in a large skillet until cooked but not too crisp. Remove the skillet from the fire and pour off all but 2 tablespoons fat.

2. Add the chicory or spinach leaves to the skillet. Pour in the vinegar and oil, and add the shallot and salt and pepper to taste. Toss quickly and transfer to a salad bowl. Sprinkle with sieved egg.

◆　◆　◆

When Rabelais, creator of Gargantua and Pantagruel, returned from a trip to Italy in 1534 he brought back the seeds of a new type of lettuce. They had been given to him by Pope Paul III from lettuce that had been cultivated in the Papal garden.

Rabelais gave the seeds to Bishop d'Estissac and he christened them *laitue romaine* because they had originated in Rome.

Romaine à la Crème

ROMAINE WITH CREAM

This simple way of dressing romaine is delicious. A combination of cream cheese and heavy cream is here substituted for the traditional French double cream.

1 large head of romaine lettuce, in bite-size pieces   *4 servings*
⅓ cup heavy cream
2½ tablespoons cream cheese
1½ tablespoons lemon juice
Salt and white pepper

1. Wash the romaine lettuce and dry thoroughly.
2. Combine cream, cheese, and lemon juice with a fork or mixer until smooth. Season to taste. Toss with the lettuce.

◆　*Variation*　◆

This dressing is equally delicious on Bibb or Boston lettuce.

◆　◆　◆

Meats are cut with a knife and herbs with scissors.
—**ALEXANDRE DUMAINE**

◆　*Variations*　◆

S U M M E R   S A L A D S   Combine thinly sliced tomatoes and thinly sliced cucumbers, peeled and seeds removed, with a vinaigrette flavored with *fines herbes* and some finely chopped onion.

Toss cold cooked green beans with Aïoli Sauce (see Index), flavored with lemon juice, chopped fresh tarragon, and parsley. Chill.

F A L L   S A L A D S   Combine 1 cup cooked cauliflowerets, 2 tomatoes, peeled and coarsely chopped, and 1 head of escarole cut into bite-size pieces. Add a tarragon vinaigrette and 2 minced shallots.

Combine cooked, sliced carrots with sour cream, snipped chives, 1 tablespoon soy sauce, and lemon juice to taste.

WINTER SALADS Fold a vinaigrette into a combination of salad greens, thin wedges of hard-cooked eggs, small pieces of sautéed bacon, herring fillets, chopped parsley, and minced shallots.

Salade de Carentan: Combine Bibb lettuce leaves with sliced endives, coarsely chopped walnuts, and thinly sliced, peeled apples. Dress with a vinaigrette made with cider vinegar and either *crème fraîche* or heavy cream.

SPRING SALAD Mix hearts of Bibb lettuce with peeled grapefruit and orange sections and sliced avocado. Dress with a vinaigrette, *fines herbes*, minced shallots, and chopped hard-cooked egg.

◆ ◆ ◆

Louis XIV was often served a salad of lettuce leaves mixed with rose or violet petals.

To prepare this colorful salad, use flowers that have not been sprayed or chemically treated. Toss with Bibb lettuce and dress with a vinaigrette made with unflavored oil, lemon juice, salt, and herbs.

◆ *Les Salades Composées* ◆

These salads are composed of cooked vegetables, meat or fish, dressed with a vinaigrette sauce or mayonnaise, garnished with hearts of lettuce, hard-cooked eggs, wedges of tomatoes, black olives or any variation to your taste.

Macédoine de légumes is the best example of this type of salad, and it is extensively served in Paris.

Macédoine de Légumes
MIXED VEGETABLE SALAD

Macédoine implies a mixture of ingredients. The word is traced back to the time of Alexander, King of Macedon, whose empire included a great variety of people from different countries. This salad is perfect for a summer buffet, combining a salad and vegetable dish in one.

4 cups finely cubed cooked potatoes   *12 servings*
2 cups finely diced cooked carrots
2 cups, ¼-inch pieces of cooked green beans
2 cups cooked peas
2 or 3 shallots, minced, or 2 tablespoons minced onion
½ cup finely chopped celery heart (optional)
2 tablespoons chopped fresh parsley
1 teaspoon chopped fresh basil
4 teaspoons chopped fresh tarragon, or 2 teaspoons dried
2 tablespoons lemon juice
2 tablespoons vinegar
1½ cups freshly made Mayonnaise (see Index)
1 tablespoon soy sauce
1 tablespoon Dijon mustard
Salt and freshly ground pepper
1 large head of Boston lettuce

1. Combine the first 6 ingredients in a mixing bowl.
2. Mix the next 8 ingredients together, beating well. Season with salt and pepper to taste.
3. Toss the vegetables with the dressing 1 hour before serving.
4. Wash lettuce and separate leaves. Line a large salad bowl with the leaves and turn the salad into the center.

◆ UNDER THE COOK'S HAT ◆

Make an attractive border with wedges or slices of hard-cooked eggs, tomatoes, or asparagus tips.

La Salade Parisienne

PARISIAN SALAD

This elegant salad, consisting of *macédoine de légumes*, molded and garnished with lobster, is usually served as part of a buffet. Ask your fish dealer to pick out the female lobsters, because they have the delicately flavored red coral.

Mixed Vegetable Salad (preceding recipe) *12 servings*
3 live lobsters, 1½ pounds each
Cream (optional)
1 recipe Aspic Mayonnaise (see Index)
2 hard-cooked eggs, sliced

1 can (1 ounce) truffles (optional)
Clear aspic (optional)

1. Prepare the mixed vegetable salad, omitting the mayonnaise.
2. Place the lobsters in 2 inches of boiling salted water. Cover and steam for exactly 20 minutes. Remove at once and let cool. Crack the lobster claws to remove the claw meat and add it to the vegetables.
3. Split the lobsters lengthwise, remove the meat from the tails in one piece, and chill. Reserve coral and tomalley.
4. If there is coral, mix it in a blender with a small amount of cream and then blend it with the lobster tomalley, the aspic mayonnaise, and the vegetable mixture. Fill a 3-quart mold with the mixture, and chill until set.
5. To serve, unmold on a chilled serving plate. Place the cold lobster tails vertically against the molded salad. Garnish with thin slices of hard-cooked eggs and, if you like, with thin slices of black truffles, both brushed with clear aspic.

Céleri à la Sauce Moutarde

CELERY WITH MUSTARD SAUCE

The mustard sauce must be made just before serving.

2 celery hearts, cut into julienne *4 servings*
2 large green apples, peeled and thinly sliced
1 tablespoon Dijon mustard
Salt and freshly ground pepper
Paprika
⅓ cup heavy cream
1 teaspoon prepared horseradish
1 teaspoon lemon juice
Fresh parsley, chopped

1. Soak the celery julienne in ice water for 30 minutes. Dry with a towel. Combine with the apple slices.
2. Combine the mustard with salt and pepper and paprika to taste. Add the cream drop by drop, whisking as for a mayonnaise until dressing is thickened. Add the horseradish and lemon juice.
3. Mix the celery and apples with the mustard sauce. Sprinkle with parsley.

Salade Niçoise

This famous salad from Provence was created in the eighteenth century by a peasant woman from Nice known as Tanta Mietta. The true salade niçoise does not include green beans or potatoes; the only cooked vegetables are the artichokes.

4 tomatoes, quartered   *4 servings*
1 cucumber, peeled, seeded, and thinly sliced
6 small cooked artichokes, quartered
2 green peppers, seeded and cut into thin strips
4 hard-cooked eggs, cut into wedges
4 small white onions, thinly sliced
8 to 10 anchovy fillets, rinsed and cut into pieces, or 8 ounces
    canned tuna, shredded
12 oil-cured black olives
1 garlic clove, split
3 to 4 tablespoons olive oil
1 tablespoon vinegar
1 teaspoon Dijon mustard
1 garlic clove, minced
Basil leaves, chopped

1. Arrange the first 8 ingredients on a large serving plate that has been rubbed with a garlic clove.

2. Combine the oil, vinegar, mustard, and minced garlic. Sprinkle over the salad just before serving. Garnish with basil.

◆ ◆ ◆

A teaspoon of soy sauce enhances the taste of salad just as it did this famous salad invented by Alexandre Dumas.

It was a salad of high fantasy formed by five principal ingredients. Sliced beets, sliced celery, minced truffles, rampion, and boiled potatoes.

I place in a salad bowl the yolk of one hard-boiled egg for each two people. I crush it with oil, making a paste. To this paste, I add chervil, some crushed tuna, some ground anchovies, some mustard of Maille, a big spoon of soya [soy sauce], some chopped gherkins, and the chopped white of the hard-boiled eggs.

I mix everything with the best vinegar I can find. Lastly, I put the salad in the salad bowl. I have it tossed by my servant and on the tossed salad, I drop from a height a pinch of paprika.

This salad of mine gave so much pleasure to my guests that when Ronconi, one of my most assiduous dinner guests, could not come, he would send for his portion of salad. When it rained, this was sent to him under a huge umbrella so that no foreign particles would become mixed in with it.

—ALEXANDRE DUMAS, PÈRE

Tomates Mano

TOMATOES MANO

1 large celeriac (celery root), cut into julienne
1 cup freshly made Mayonnaise (see Index)
1 tablespoon Dijon mustard
Lemon juice
1 cup julienne strips of ham
4 to 6 large tomatoes
Salt
1 large bunch of watercress
Fresh parsley, chopped

4 servings

1. Parboil the julienne of celeriac in boiling water for 1 minute. Drain and pat dry.

2. Flavor the mayonnaise with the mustard and lemon juice to taste.

3. Combine the celeriac with the ham and mayonnaise. Chill.

4. Drop the tomatoes into boiling water for a few seconds, then peel. Cut each tomato into 8 wedges from the top to the stem, but do not slice all the way through. Open out like a daisy, and season with salt. Invert and drain for 30 minutes.

5. Sprinkle the tomatoes with lemon juice, then place them on individual plates lined with watercress. Spoon the ham mixture into the center of each tomato. Sprinkle with parsley.

Salades de Pommes de Terre

FRENCH POTATO SALAD

The secret of a good potato salad lies both in the cooking process and in the dressing. Be sure to cook the potatoes in their skins at a slow boil, and add the dressing to the peeled, sliced potatoes while they are still hot. Serve at room temperature.

5 medium-large potatoes   *4 servings*
¼ cup dry white wine
5 tablespoons peanut or olive oil
3 tablespoons lemon juice or tarragon vinegar
1 tablespoon finely minced shallots
1 tablespoon finely minced fresh parsley
1 tablespoon finely snipped chives
Salt and white pepper

1. Cook the potatoes in a saucepan of water, keeping the water temperature just below boiling until just done. Drain potatoes, peel while hot, and slice into a bowl.

2. Combine all the other ingredients, with seasoning to taste, and pour over the hot potatoes. Let stand for 1 hour before serving.

◆   *Variation*   ◆

Add watercress, diced cooked beets, and 2 hard-cooked eggs. A little anchovy paste can be added to the dressing.

Salade Lapérouse

LAPÉROUSE SALAD

4 large tomatoes   *4 servings*
Salt
2 cups thinly sliced cooked artichoke hearts
1½ cups diced boiled ham
1½ cups sour cream
2 tablespoons snipped fresh chives
Lemon juice
Freshly ground pepper
Watercress

1. Drop the tomatoes into boiling water for a few seconds. Peel. Cut into 8 sections through the stem end but do not slice all the way through. Open like a daisy and season with salt.

2. Combine the artichokes, ham, sour cream, chives, and lemon juice, and salt and pepper to taste. Fill the tomatoes with the mixture. Chill and serve on individual beds of watercress.

◆   *Variation*   ◆

Substitute tiny cooked shrimps for the ham.

• *Salade Francillon* •

It was Rossini, the famous composer of operas, who created this salad. He was so fond of truffles that several dishes with truffles bear his name.

But it was Alexandre Dumas, fils, author of *La Dame aux Camélias* (*Camille*), who immortalized this salad in the following dialogue from his play *Françillon*, which was first produced at the Comédie-Française.

ANNETTE: Cook some potatoes in bouillon, cut them in slices as for an ordinary salad, and while they are still warm, season them with salt, pepper, and a very good fruity olive oil, vinegar . . .

HENRI: Tarragon?

ANNETTE: Orléans is better, but that is not of great importance. What is important is a half glass of white wine: Château-Yquem if possible. A great deal of *fines herbes* finely chopped. At the same time, cook some very large mussels in a *court-bouillon* with a stalk of celery; drain them well and add them to the potatoes.

HENRI: Less mussels than potatoes?

ANNETTE: A third less. So you can taste the mussels little by little. One should not foretaste them, nor should they obtrude. When the salad is made, gently toss it; then cover it with round slices of truffles to look like the cap of a scholar.

HENRI: And cooked in Champagne?

ANNETTE: That goes without saying. All this, two hours before dinner so that this salad is very cold when it is served.

HENRI: The salad bowl could be surrounded with ice.

ANNETTE: No! No! No! It must not be hurried. It is very delicate and all its flavors need to be blended slowly. The one you ate today, was it good?

HENRI: Marvelous!

ANNETTE: Ah! Good! Follow these directions and you will have the same pleasure.

Salade Francillon

Alexandre Dumas would have been delighted to know his salad was served at the Palais de l'Elysée in 1896 to honor Nicholas II of Russia. This is a more economical version of the recipe.

6 medium-size potatoes   *6 servings*
5 cups Beef Stock (see Index)
1½ cups shelled mussels, cooked in white wine for 1 minute
2 teaspoons minced fresh tarragon, or 1 teaspoon dried
1 tablespoon finely chopped parsley
1 tablespoon finely snipped chives
⅓ cup olive oil
2 tablespoons vinegar
½ cup white wine
Salt and freshly ground pepper
1 can (2 ounces) truffles, finely chopped

1. Cook the potatoes in the stock in a large saucepan. Peel and slice the potatoes while warm. Mix with the mussels.

2. Combine the tarragon, parsley, chives, olive oil, vinegar (add more or less if you prefer), wine, and salt and pepper to taste. Toss with the potatoes and mussels. Garnish with the truffles.

Salade Orientale

ORIENTAL SALAD

A summer salad for a buffet or to take on a picnic.

6 cups cooked rice   *6 servings*
3 large ripe tomatoes, cubed
1 celery heart, chopped, including leaves
¾ cup oil-cured black olives
2 cups diced Polish ham, about ½ pound
Vinaigrette (see Index)
1 small red onion, chopped
Fresh parsley, chopped
1 large head of Boston lettuce, leaves separated
Watercress (optional)

1. Combine the rice, tomatoes, celery, olives, and ham.

2. Mix the vinaigrette, onion, and parsley together in a small mixing bowl. Pour over the salad ingredients and chill.

3. Line a large salad bowl with the lettuce leaves and fill with the rice salad. Or fill a ring mold and invert on a serving plate. For a garnish, place a few sprigs of watercress in the center, if you wish.

◆   *Variations*   ◆

Replace the ham and olives with 2 cups grapefruit sections, 1 cup sliced avocado, and 1 cup crab meat.

A little mayonnaise can be added to the vinaigrette for a better binding of the ingredients.

◆   UNDER THE COOK'S HAT   ◆

In a rice salad, you use twice as much rice as other ingredients.

◆ ◆ ◆

Qui vin ne boit après salade
Est en danger d'être malade.

Who fails to drink wine after salad
Is in danger of becoming sick.
                    — an old saying

12. *Les Entremets* DESSERTS AND CONFECTIONS

⚜ ⚜ ⚜

Entremet (in-between courses) originally meant any dish served between the fish and meat courses. Later it was applied to entertainments during the meals as well as to vegetables and desserts. Today *entremet* means dessert and includes crêpes, mousses, puddings, and fruit concoctions, but does not include cakes, which are served at teatime.

Grimod de la Reynière wrote, "True gourmands have always finished their dinner before the dessert. What they eat after dinner is merely politeness, but in general they are very polite."

Serve Monbazillac or Sauternes with desserts. Or offer the world's greatest white wine, Château d'Yquem—a dessert by itself.

Champagne is a good accompaniment for any French dessert. Madame de Pompadour said, "Champagne is the only wine that leaves a woman beautiful after she drinks it!"

The importance of desserts in a French meal, expressed by Louis Outhier:
"One must never neglect the exit. It must be in grand style."

• *Champagne* •

Champagne has been the wine of French royalty since Clovis became the first King of France in A.D. 481. Some of the wine of Champagne was red and slightly sparkling in those days.

In 1668 Dom Pérignon became cellarmaster and purveyor of the Benedictine Abbey in Hautvillers. He noticed that the wine of Champagne, mostly the white, had a tendency to bubble after a second fermentation had begun, which was considered a fault. Dom Pérignon turned this fault into an asset. By adding peaches, sugar, cinnamon, nutmeg, and brandy to the wine, he developed a method to make the wine sparkle, and on his deathbed divulged his secret formula to Canon Jean Godinot. (Today, the formula has changed and only sugar and brandy are added.) When Dom Pérignon had the first sip of his Champagne, he exclaimed, "I am drinking stars!"

He was also the one who had the ingenious idea of substituting cork and strings for the traditional wax seal so that the bubbles could not escape. But it was the Duc de Vendôme, fifty years later, who set the fashion of drinking Champagne and he was the one who made it known.

The venerable Abbey of Hautvillers is owned today by Moët & Chandon, the firm which dates back to 1743. They own sixteen miles of underground cellars that were Roman quarries when Caesar occupied Gaul.

De ce vin frais l'écume pétillante
De nos Français est l'image brillante.

The sparkling froth of this cool wine
Reflects the spirit of our people.
—VOLTAIRE

◆ *Kir* ◆

A dry sherry, a dry Champagne, or a very fine French apéritif called Kir will not spoil the palate for the ensuing courses. Kir is a combination of crème de cassis, chilled white Burgundy wine, and seltzer. It was created in Dijon, Burgundy, to replace Champagne as the official welcoming drink for guests when Champagne became too costly. Although the municipality of Dijon stopped serving Champagne in 1804, the apéritif that replaced it was not named until 1945, when Canon Félix Kir became mayor. Kir served this drink so lavishly to guests of the city that it became known far and wide by his name. The classic version is one part cassis to three or four parts ice-cold wine.

Fruits Rafraîchis au Champagne
FRUITS IN CHAMPAGNE

In a large crystal bowl, arrange layers, of equal proportion and depth, of well-ripened, peeled, and seeded fruits, thinly sliced.

Use 1 layer each of these fruits: apples, peaches, strawberries, seedless grapes, pears, red currants, pineapple, apricots (unpeeled and cut into 4 sections), and bananas thinly sliced on the bias.

Sprinkle sugar on each layer, and pour Champagne over them, just to cover the fruits. Kirsch can be added. Chill for 1 to 2 hours before serving with a bowl of sweetened whipped cream.

Pommes Viviane

APPLES VIVIANE

8 large baking apples, peeled and cored   *8 servings*
1 lemon
Butter for baking dish
8 tablespoons unsalted butter
1 cup apricot jam
⅓ cup sugar
2 tablespoons rum
⅓ cup almonds, thinly sliced and slightly crushed
½ cup heavy cream, whipped, sweetened, and flavored with
     rum
4 candied red cherries, halved

1. Brush the apples with lemon juice to prevent discoloration. Arrange the apples in a buttered baking dish. Place 1 tablespoon of butter in each apple cavity. Bake in a preheated 375°F. oven until the apples are done and hold their shape, about 25 minutes.

2. Cook the jam and sugar in a small saucepan for 4 to 5 minutes, or until it is of a thick spreading consistency. Stir in the rum. Brush the apples with the mixture and spoon the remainder into the centers. Sprinkle with the almonds.

3. Bake apples in a hot oven until almonds are lightly toasted. Watch this process carefully.

4. Pipe whipped cream into the cavity of the apples and top each with a large rosette of cream and ½ candied cherry.

◆ *Cherries Jubilee* ◆

Cerises Jubilée was created by Auguste Escoffier in honor of Queen Victoria's golden jubilee in 1887.

Here is the original recipe:

Pit some fine cherries; *poach* them in syrup and set them in small silver *timbales*. Reduce the syrup and thicken it with a little arrowroot or cornstarch diluted with cold water; allowing one tablespoon of thickening per half-pint of syrup. Cover the cherries with the thickened syrup; pour a teaspoonful of heated Kirsch into each *timbale*, and set a light to each when serving.

Cerises Jubilée

CHERRIES JUBILEE

This simple but festive dessert is especially delicious when served over very hard vanilla ice cream, or even on yogurt.

¾ cup sugar   *6 servings*
½ cup water
1½ pounds fresh black cherries, pitted
1 tablespoon arrowroot and 1 tablespoon water, mixed
3 tablespoons kirsch

1. Combine the sugar and the ½ cup water. Bring to a boil and simmer for 3 minutes. Add the cherries. Cook for 3 to 5 minutes. Remove the cherries with a slotted spoon and place in individual serving dishes.
2. Add the arrowroot diluted with cold water to the syrup and cook until syrup is clear. Pour over the cherries.
3. Add a little of the warmed kirsch to each serving and flambé.

◆ UNDER THE COOK'S HAT ◆

There is a special gadget for stoning cherries.

Salade de Pamplemousses et d'Oranges

GRAPEFRUIT AND ORANGE FRUIT BOWL

4 large grapefruits   *4 to 6 servings*
2 large eating oranges
1 cup sugar
3 tablespoons water
¼ cup Grand Marnier liqueur

1. Peel and section the fruits over a bowl to save all the juices.

2. Cook the sugar with 3 tablespoons water until sugar is completely dissolved and no trace remains visible. Add to the juices of the fruits and chill.

3. Just before serving, stir in the liqueur. Serve in a crystal bowl along with Almond Wafers (see Index).

◆   UNDER THE COOK'S HAT   ◆

A few slices of fresh strawberries may be added for color.

◆ *To Section Citrus Fruits* ◆

Set a fruit on a cutting board and cut off both ends of the fruit with a sharp serrated knife. Set the fruit on one end. With a firm, even, but curving stroke, cut off a thick slice of rind from top to bottom, removing in this way the rind and white inner membrane. Repeat all around the fruit until the pulp is free of all white membrane on the outside.

Hold the fruit over a bowl. Cut along the side of each dividing membrane, moving the knife from outer edge to core, then turn and cut up to the outer edge again, dropping the whole section into the bowl. Repeat until all sections have been removed. Squeeze the remaining fruit juice from the pulp into the bowl.

 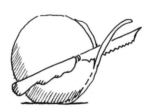

◆ *Melon* ◆

Melons are indigenous to southern Asia and were brought from there to the Mediterranean regions.

While many species of melon were known in earlier centuries, the first cantaloupe seeds to grow in Western Europe were brought to Rome from Armenia in the sixteenth century, at a time when there was a great interest in new vegetables and fruits. This melon took its name from Cantalupo, the papal villa near Rome where it was first cultivated.

In France, melon was eaten at the beginning of a meal as early as the time of Henri IV, who was very fond of the fruit. Doctors recommended it as being good for one's health.

Melon became such a success that a book written in 1583 by Jacques Pons gave fifty different ways to eat it, among them, in soup and fritters.

Alexandre Dumas, fils, was so fond of Cavaillon's melon that he gave the small city in the Vaucluse a complete edition of his works in exchange for an annual supply of twelve melons.

◆ *Cointreau* ◆

Two brothers, Édouard-Jean and Adolphe Cointreau, created the great liqueur named after them, in their confectionery-distillery on the rue Saint-Laud in Angers in 1849. Here, in the heart of France, the distillery is still owned by the Cointreau family, although they have moved it to a larger location on the quai des Luisettes.

Melon aux Fraises

MELON WITH STRAWBERRIES

For each serving, use half of a very small ripe and fragrant canta-loupe. Remove the seeds and scoop out the flesh with the small end of a potato-ball cutter or melon baller.

Mix the melon balls with the same amount of wild strawberries (*fraises des bois*) or very small cultivated ones, which have been sprinkled with a little lemon juice and sugar 1 hour beforehand.

Just before serving, place the fruits in the melon shells and sprin-kle with Cointreau liqueur. Place each melon half on a plate lined with a large fresh leaf.

◆ UNDER THE COOK'S HAT ◆

When a cantaloupe in France is very sweet and fragrant, it is eaten with just a sprinkle of salt (and even pepper), which brings out all its flavor.

Beside being fragrant, a fine melon must feel heavy and yield lightly under the pressure of the thumb at the opposite side of the stem.

◆ *Peach Melba* ◆

Pêches Melba was created by Auguste Escoffier for Nellie Melba, the Australian diva. Madame Melba came to the opening of the London Ritz Hotel in 1905 and asked Escoffier for a recipe that she especially liked, *pêches Cardinal*. While Escoffier was writing the recipe he decided to add vanilla ice cream and renamed it *pêches Melba*.

Here is the original recipe:

> Pick peaches with tender flesh that does not cling to their pits. Plunge 1 minute in boiling water, then in iced water. Remove their skins. Place on a plate; powder with sugar and keep under refrigeration. Meanwhile, prepare a very creamy vanilla ice cream and a purée of sweetened raspberries as fresh as possible.

> Dish the vanilla ice cream into a timbale or crystal bowl; arrange the peaches on the ice; then coat with raspberry purée.

This recipe is simple and needs no adapting for present-day use. It would be well, however, to brush the flesh of the peaches with lemon juice if they are to be put aside for any length of time. The raspberries should be mashed with a fork and sweetened with a little sugar to taste.

◆　◆　◆

When Escoffier was working at the London Ritz, Madame Duchêne, the manager's wife, asked him, "What do you consider to be the secret of your art?"

Escoffier replied, "Madame, the secret is that most of my best dishes are created for ladies."

"God in creating women, created the flower. Both are captivating and graceful and have not lost their charm." These lines are from the preface of a charming and little-known book, *The Wax Flowers*, written by Escoffier in 1910. It details the art of making wax flowers and contains poems on a variety of flowers.

Poires Hélène

PEARS HÉLÈNE

Created by Escoffier, this dessert was dedicated to Hélène, the Duchess d'Aosta, sister of the Duc d'Orléans.

1. Place a scoop of vanilla ice cream on individual dessert plates. Top with 1 or 2 pear halves that have been poached in vanilla syrup, then drained. (Canned pears can be used. Add vanilla to the syrup and let them stand in it for a few hours.)

2. Sprinkle with crystallized violets and serve with hot Chocolate Sauce (next recipe).

Sauce au Chocolat

CHOCOLATE SAUCE

6 ounces semisweet chocolate   *Makes approximately 1 cup*
4 tablespoons cold water
2 tablespoons unsalted butter
1 teaspoon vanilla extract

Combine all the ingredients in the top pan of a double boiler set over simmering water in the bottom pan; the top pan should not touch the water. Stir until just smooth and immediately remove the top pan from the heat. If the sauce is too thick, add a little boiling water. Do not refrigerate or the sauce will harden.

◆   UNDER THE COOK'S HAT   ◆

This sauce is also delicious over vanilla, coffee, or chocolate ice cream.

◆   ◆   ◆

Guillaume Tirel, nicknamed Taillevent, was the first great French chef. He wrote the first cookbook in French (Latin had been used prior to that time), and the manuscript remained unprinted for more than a century—awaiting the invention of the printing press. The book, published in 1490, was entitled *Le Viandier*.

In 1326, when Taillevent was about 15 years old, he became an apprentice cook in the kitchen of Queen Jeanne d'Évreux. In 1330 he was the kitchen valet of Queen Jeanne de Bourgogne. For his services he was rewarded with a piece of land and seven oak trees in Saint-Germain-en-Laye. He was ennobled, became a squire and sergeant-at-arms to Charles V, and was in charge of the royal kitchen in 1373. He was also in charge of the kitchen of Charles VI.

Taillevent's tombstone is in the crypt of the Saint-Léger church in Saint-Germain-en-Laye. His richly carved tombstone is flanked by the graves of his two wives (he had been a widow and remarried). He is represented in his coat of mail with a dagger and sword at his side. On his shield are three kettles framed by six roses.

Poires au Vin

PEARS IN RED WINE

Taillevent created this dessert, which was known as *poires à l'hypocras* and was flavored with an apéritif wine inspired by a formula of Hippocrates. It was the ancestor of apéritifs such as Dubonnet and Byrrh.

2 cups excellent red wine, Bordeaux or Beaujolais   *8 servings*
¾ cup sugar
8 large pears, peeled, halved, and cored
3-inch piece of lemon peel, without the white portion
1 small cinnamon stick
3 to 4 tablespoons kirsch

1. Cook the wine and sugar in a saucepan until the sugar is completely dissolved.
2. Add the pears, lemon peel, and cinnamon. Simmer covered until the pears are tender, about 15 minutes.
3. Remove the pears with a slotted spoon. Discard the lemon peel and cinnamon stick. Reduce the syrup over high heat for about 10 minutes, then add the kirsch. Pour over the pears. Serve cold.

Fraises au Fromage Blanc

STRAWBERRIES WITH FRESH WHITE CHEESE

1 quart strawberries, hulled   *4 servings*
Sugar
1 pound cottage cheese
1 cup Crème Fraîche (see Index)

1. About 1 hour before serving, sprinkle the strawberries with sugar (the amount depends on the sweetness of the berries).
2. Blend the cottage cheese with the *crème fraîche* and ½ cup sugar, or sugar to taste. Chill. Serve with the strawberries.

◆ *Variation* ◆

Combine 1 pound cottage cheese with 1 cup sour cream, sugar to taste, ¼ teaspoon grated lemon rind, and 1 teaspoon vanilla extract. The flavor improves if prepared several hours ahead.

Fraises, Sauce Glacée

STRAWBERRIES WITH ICE-CREAM SAUCE

1 pint vanilla ice cream
1 cup heavy cream, whipped
3 tablespoons kirsch
1 quart strawberries, hulled
2 to 3 tablespoons sugar

6 servings

1. Soften the vanilla ice cream in the refrigerator for several hours. Add the whipped cream and kirsch just before serving; mix well.
2. Combine the strawberries with sugar 1 hour before serving. Serve berries with the ice-cream sauce.

Fraises Melba

STRAWBERRIES MELBA

1 quart strawberries, hulled
Sugar
1 quart vanilla ice cream
Sauce Melba (see Index)
3 teaspoons slivered almonds, toasted
1 cup sweetened heavy cream, whipped, flavored with vanilla

4 servings

1. Sprinkle the strawberries with sugar to taste 1 hour before serving. In a large bowl or individual cups put a layer of ice cream and arrange the strawberries on top.
2. Prepare the Sauce Melba. Pour it over the strawberries and garnish with the almonds and rosettes of the whipped cream.

Mousse aux Fraises

STRAWBERRY MOUSSE

4 cups strawberries, hulled, or 1 pound frozen whole   *6 servings*
    strawberries, thawed
1 cup confectioners' sugar, plus 1 cup sugar for fresh
    strawberries
1 tablespoon unflavored gelatin
4 tablespoons kirsch
2 cups heavy cream
2 egg whites
10 ladyfingers, split
Sauce Melba (optional)
Sugar

1. Reserve a few strawberries for decorating the mousse, then slice remaining berries. Mix with confectioners' sugar and let stand for 1 hour.

2. Mash the strawberries with a fork. Place them in a saucepan and sprinkle with gelatin. Heat almost to the boiling point, stirring constantly. Cool, then stir in the kirsch.

3. Whip cream until firm. Fold half of the cream into the strawberries, reserving the remainder for garnish.

4. Beat the egg whites until stiff and fold into the strawberry mixture.

5. Arrange the ladyfingers on the bottom and around the sides of a low crystal bowl. Spread the strawberry mousse over the ladyfingers, making a flat surface.

6. Add sugar to taste to the remaining whipped cream. Spoon cream into a pastry bag fitted with a large star tube. Make a border with 2-inch-wide rosettes of whipped cream, and place one large one in the center. Place 1 fresh strawberry in the center of each rosette. Chill for several hours or overnight.

Sauce Melba can be served separately.

♦   *Variations*   ♦

For raspberry mousse, substitute 2 packages (10 ounces each) frozen raspberries for the strawberries. Heat only the juice of the berries when adding the gelatin.

Other fruits such as apricots, peaches, or rhubarb also make delicious mousses.

Parfait au Café

COFFEE PARFAIT

3 egg yolks

6 servings

1¼ cups plus 6 tablespoons sugar

¼ cup water

1½ tablespoons instant coffee dissolved in 2 tablespoons hot
water

1 tablespoon plus 1 teaspoon pure vanilla extract

½ teaspoon salt

2½ cups heavy cream

Chocolate shavings or cocoa powder

1. Beat the egg yolks in a large bowl with an electric beater until they are thick and lemon-colored.

2. Combine 1¼ cups sugar and ¼ cup water in a small saucepan. Boil for about 3 minutes, or until large bubbles begin to form. Cool until tepid.

3. Beating constantly, pour the syrup into the egg yolks in a slow thin stream. Continue beating for about 5 minutes, until the mixture thickens and cools.

4. Stir in the coffee extract, 1 tablespoon vanilla, and the salt.

5. Whip 1½ cups heavy cream with a rotary eggbeater until cream is stiff enough to form soft peaks. With a large rubber spatula, fold thoroughly into the egg-yolk mixture. Spoon mousse into a plastic container, cover, and freeze for at least 6 hours, or until firm to the touch.

6. Take the coffee parfait out of the freezer 1 hour before serving and keep under refrigeration. Before serving, whip remaining 1 cup heavy cream. Add 6 tablespoons sugar and 1 teaspoon vanilla. Spoon the whipped cream into a pastry bag fitted with a star tube.

7. Pipe layers of cream alternating with layers of coffee ice cream in parfait glasses. Decorate the top with a swirl of whipped cream and top with a sprinkling of chocolate shavings or cocoa powder.

♦ *Variations* ♦

Add Praline Powder (see Index) to the coffee mixture just before freezing.

For a delicious vanilla ice cream, omit the coffee extract and add an additional ½ tablespoon vanilla extract.

◆ *Omelette Norvégienne* ◆

Omelette norvégienne originated in China. The recipe was given to Chef Balzaac by the Chinese chef of the mission of the Celestial Empire while he was in Paris for the opening of the Grand Hotel in 1862. It was named *omelette norvégienne* because it was reminiscent of the snows of Norway and because most of the ice used in Europe before the invention of the refrigerator came from Norwegian lakes.

The dessert did not become popular at that time but Jean Giroix began serving it again at the end of the nineteenth century, when he was in charge of the kitchen at the Grand Hôtel in Monte Carlo. Then, at the turn of the twentieth century, a French chef at Delmonico's in New York served an *omelette norvégienne*, renaming it Baked Alaska because of the interest in the Alaskan gold rush. It is a spectacular and very impressive dessert and yet is simple to make.

Omelette Norvégienne à l'Orange
BAKED ALASKA

1 quart vanilla ice cream
1 pint orange sherbet
18 ladyfingers
2 to 3 tablespoons kirsch
6 egg whites
2 tablespoons granulated sugar
¼ teaspoon salt
1½ cups confectioners' sugar
1 tablespoon vanilla extract

6 to 8 servings

1. Place the ice cream and sherbet in the refrigerator for several hours until soft.

2. Mix the orange sherbet into the ice cream with a long-pronged fork, swirling thin ribbons of the sherbet into the ice cream. The colors should remain distinct from one another. Transfer to a slightly oiled loaf pan, 9 by 5 by 3 inches. Cover with foil and freeze for several hours. Unmold and wrap in foil. Refreeze.

3. Just before serving, place the ladyfingers in two rows to form a compact rectangle on a long metal dish. Sprinkle with kirsch.

4. Beat the egg whites until stiff. Add the granulated sugar and salt, then the confectioners' sugar and vanilla, beating after each

addition to keep the mixture stiff. Spoon about 3 cups of the meringue into a pastry bag fitted with a large decorative tube.

5. Place the block of ice cream on the ladyfingers. Quickly and carefully spread the meringue over the ice cream. Pipe decorative designs from the pastry tube on top and around the base and sides.

6. Bake in a preheated 400°F. oven for 5 minutes, or until the meringue is golden brown. Cut into ½-inch slices to serve.

◆ *Variations* ◆

Combine raspberry sherbet with vanilla ice cream.

Flavor ladyfingers with 2 or 3 tablespoons rum and use 1½ quarts of coffee ice cream. Reduce the confectioners' sugar to ¾ cup and add ¾ cup Praline Powder (see Index) to the egg whites. Swirl the meringue with the back of a spoon to make a design.

◆ *On Ice Cream* ◆

Ice cream originated in China and came to the Occident through India, Iran, and the Arab countries. Then it was actually *sorbet*, so called after the Turkish word for drink. *Sorbet* was made with water, fruit juices, or liqueur and sugar, and it became very much the fashion. It became known as *délicieuse et parfaites*, the probable origin of our word "parfait," although with a slightly different meaning.

When the procedure for mixing and freezing had been perfected, these iced liqueurs became known as *glaces rares*, or rare ices. They were frozen with snow or crushed ice and sea salt in boxes made of tin or lead. *Plomb* (lead) was the name that was later given to a famous ice cream, *crème plombière*, containing preserved fruits.

These sorbets were served only at the most sumptuous meals and were looked upon as something "supernatural." Guests were astonished. This was due, in part, to a lack of understanding of the freezing process. In his *Traité de la glace* in 1680, Monsieur de la Hire attributed the formation of ice to a volatile salt, which spread in the air and condensed everything it touched. It was thought that the molecules of water clinging around this salt became small threads of ice which in turn would congeal liquid. The chemists declared that air, being filled with these numerous salts, produced a vitriolic acid, and that the salt employed for freezing had a volatile penetrating particle, which inserted itself through the pores of metals.

Therefore, ice cream was, at the time, thought by many people to be unhealthy.

The first ice creams were publicly consumed when the coffee shop Procope opened in Paris in 1686 on the rue de l'Ancienne-Comédie. At first many unusual flavors were used such as truffles, Parmesan cheese, cinnamon, Muscat wine, and all kinds of fruits. But then it became more fashionable to serve various fruit sherbets in the shapes of the fruits whose juice was used. After they had been removed from their molds, they were painted with a brush dipped into various colored syrups to make them look like real fruits. Their natural stems and leaves were stuck in place on the sherbet fruits for a realistic effect.

Ice cream became such a success that in 1750 the number of the *limonadiers*, who sold not only ice cream but liqueur and coffee, in Paris was 250. The Frescatti ice-cream parlor was very much in fashion around 1810, and later on Tortoni, the inventor of the famous tortoni ice cream, opened an establishment that has remained famous to this day. Unfortunately, Tortoni committed suicide because of unrequited love. In these ice-cream parlors, one would eat delicious pastries and ice cream in a brilliant setting of flowers, chandeliers, and individual marble tables. It was a favorite haunt of many famous figures of the day, especially Victor Hugo, Balzac, and de Musset.

Mousse Glacée à l'Ananas

FROZEN PINEAPPLE MOUSSE

Procope, who owned the famous coffee shop in Paris, created *mousse glacée* in 1720 for a special party given at the Château de Chantilly in the outskirts of Paris. The dessert was called *glace à la Chantilly* and immediately became extremely fashionable. *Mousse glacée* is a frozen mixture which is not churned. This simple recipe uses pineapple flavoring, but many different flavorings may be used.

1 cup confectioners' sugar, sifted   *4 servings*
4 ounces frozen pineapple juice, defrosted
1 cup heavy cream

1. Mix together the sugar and the undiluted pineapple juice.
2. Whip the heavy cream until it holds a peak, then add the pineapple juice. Transfer to a plastic container and freeze.

◆   U N D E R   T H E   C O O K ' S   H A T   ◆

This ice cream does not freeze to a hard consistency, therefore pipe it out of a pastry bag fitted with a large rosette, into Champagne glasses. Top with a small piece of candied red or green cherry.

◆   ◆   ◆

Until World War I, important and substantial dinners were interrupted in the middle of the meal with a fruit sorbet flavored with alcohol. This practice was called the *trou* or *coup du milieu* (the hole or punch in the middle). Sorbets cooled the palate and the alcohol stimulated the digestion, preparing the guests for the rest of the meal. As people began eating simpler meals, this custom was discontinued, and the sherbets were served at the end of the meal as a refreshing final touch.

Sorbet à l'Ananas et à l'Orange
PINEAPPLE AND ORANGE SHERBET

This sherbet is ideal as a summer dessert.

3¼ cups water   *6 servings*
1¼ cups sugar
½ cup light corn syrup
¼ teaspoon salt
1 tablespoon unflavored gelatin
1 can (6 ounces) frozen orange juice, defrosted
1 can (6 ounces) frozen pineapple juice, defrosted
1 tablespoon lemon juice
3 tablespoons dark rum
3 tablespoons Grand Marnier liqueur
3 maraschino cherries, halved

1. Combine 3 cups water, the sugar, corn syrup, and salt in a saucepan. Boil for 5 minutes, then remove from the heat.
2. Soften the gelatin in ¼ cup water. Stir into the syrup until dissolved. Let cool to room temperature.
3. Add the orange, pineapple, lemon juices, rum, and Grand Marnier. Pour into freezer trays. Freeze for several hours, stirring vigorously every 30 minutes with a whisk to give a snowy texture.
4. Serve in sherbet or Champagne glasses, topped with half a maraschino cherry.

Bombe aux Framboises

MOLDED RASPBERRY ICE CREAM

Ice cream flavored with liqueur was introduced for the first time in 1779 at the Café au Caveau in Paris.

1 quart vanilla ice cream

6 servings

2½ cups heavy cream

Confectioners' sugar

¼ cup kirsch liqueur

1 pint fresh raspberries, or 1 package (10 ounces) frozen
    raspberries, thawed

1. Place the vanilla ice cream in the refrigerator for several hours to soften.

2. Whip 1 cup of the cream and sweeten with confectioners' sugar to taste. Reserve half for garnish. Combine the kirsch and raspberries. Let stand for 10 minutes.

3. Combine the ice cream, whipped cream, and fruit. Pour the mixture into a 6-cup mold, lightly oiled with a flavorless oil. Cover with foil, and freeze for several hours, until firm.

4. One hour before serving, dip the mold into hot water for a few seconds and unmold onto a chilled serving plate. Refrigerate. Just before serving, decorate with whipped cream piped from a pastry bag fitted with a star tube.

• *Chocolate* •

Chocolate originated in Mexico, where the Indians drank it at their feasts as a cold refreshing drink.

In the sixteenth century the drink became indispensable to the Spanish conquistadors. Philippe Dufour wrote in 1685, "I have seen in a seaport where we landed to draw water a priest who told us the Mass like an Apostle, but who was obliged by necessity, being very fat and very tired, to sit down in a pew before the thanksgiving after communion, and there was a servant holding a vessel full of chocolate which he drank and God gave him the strength to finish the Mass after he rested."

The Spaniards returned to Europe with chocolate. It was introduced in France when Marie-Thérèse, daughter of Philip IV of Spain, became the wife of Louis XV in 1660.

Doctors prescribed chocolate as a medicine for convalescents, and some apothecaries sold purgative chocolate or aphrodisiac chocolate!

During the sixteenth and seventeenth centuries, chocolate became the favorite beverage of ladies and the clergy. Because of the fondness of the latter for chocolate, a theological debate arose. Was it a food or a beverage? Was it a sin to drink it during the frequent fasts? An ounce of cacao was thought to be as nourishing as a pound of beef. Toward the end of the seventeenth century Cardinal Stefano Brancaccio wrote a dissertation to prove that drinking chocolate did not break a fast.

A seventeenth-century recipe for making chocolate:

Mix 2 pounds of cocoa, hulled, with 11 pounds of sugar, 1 ounce of powdered vanilla, 3 drachms powdered cinnamon, powdered clove, pepper of India, 8 grains of ambergris, and 4 grains of musk.

Soufflé au Chocolat
CHOCOLATE SOUFFLÉ

¾ cup milk   *4 servings*
1 tablespoon cornstarch
⅓ cup cocoa powder (not a mix)
2 teaspoons instant coffee
1 cup confectioners' sugar
Pinch of salt
3 egg yolks, lightly beaten
3 tablespoons butter
1 teaspoon pure vanilla extract
7 egg whites

1. Combine first 6 ingredients in a heavy saucepan. Cook until mixture starts to thicken. Remove from heat.

2. Let stand until just warm and then add egg yolks, butter, and vanilla.

3. Beat egg whites until stiff. Fold one-quarter of the whites into the chocolate mixture thoroughly enough so that no streaks of white will show. Gently fold in the remaining egg whites.

4. Pour into a generously buttered 1½-quart soufflé dish and bake in a preheated 375°F. oven for 30 minutes. Sprinkle with confectioners' sugar and serve immediately with a sauceboat of sweetened whipped cream, if desired.

Mousse au Chocolat

CHOCOLATE MOUSSE

4 eggs, separated   *6 servings*
¾ cup confectioners' sugar
12 ounces semisweet chocolate bits
5 tablespoons cold water
Pinch of salt
1½ cups heavy cream
2 teaspoons pure vanilla extract

1. Beat the egg yolks and sugar until thick and lemon-colored.
2. Melt the chocolate with the water in a baking dish in a 350°F. oven for a few minutes. Do not stir the chocolate until it is creamy. Add the egg yolks and sugar while the chocolate is warm.
3. Beat the egg whites with a pinch of salt until stiff. Fold the chocolate mixture into the egg whites, using a large spatula, until there are no light or dark streaks.
4. Whip the cream and add vanilla. Fold cream into the chocolate mixture. Spoon into a crystal bowl or individual cups. Chill for at least 4 hours.

◆   UNDER THE COOK'S HAT   ◆

Sprinkle chocolate curls on the mousse. Use a vegetable peeler to scrape the side of a chocolate bar. If too cold, the chocolate will shave instead of curling. Place in a tepid oven just long enough to bring the chocolate to the right temperature.

Chocolate mousse can be frozen in a lightly oiled mold. Use an unflavored oil.

It is delicious served like an ice cream.

Leftover mousse can be used as a filling for a chocolate layer cake.

Wine must not be served with a chocolate dessert. The chocolate kills the wine.

◆   *Variation*   ◆

For Chocolate Mousse with Grand Marnier, add ½ cup of Grand Marnier or other orange liqueur to recipe.

• *On the Use of Coffee* •

About 1643, in a shop owned by a Levantine, coffee beans were sold for the first time in Paris—but without much success. Several Armenians tried to popularize the use of coffee in their shops, with even less success until the arrival in Paris of Soliman Aga Mustapha Raca, sent by Mahomet IV in 1669 as the Turkish Ambassador to Louis XIV.

He was received with great pomp at Versailles by Louis XIV in the Gallerie des Glaces, which was ablaze with hundreds of candles. Overnight, the Ambassador became the talk of the town. He followed the Turkish custom of greeting his visitors with a cup of coffee from his reclining position on a carpet. Coffee was served in fine china cups and accompanied with little damask napkins bordered with gold fringes. To tempt his visitors, he added sugar to the coffee, a custom that scored an immediate success.

Two years later, the first coffee house, then owned by the Armenian Pascal, stood on the Saint-Germain fairground. Several other coffee shops opened, but they were similar to taverns—dark, dirty, grim places—and were poorly frequented.

In 1680, a coffee merchant, Procope, changed all this by opening a luxurious establishment decorated with mirrors and chandeliers, an elegance unknown in a public place until then. Located at 13 rue de l'Ancienne Comédie and still flourishing today, this coffee house was staffed with waiters in Armenian costumes, presumably to represent the country best known for making good coffee. The court and its followers made it the fashion to have lackeys dressed as Armenians serve coffee in a special room reserved for this delightful new custom. The "fumoir," or smoking room, may be a remnant of this period.

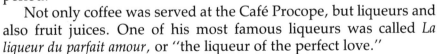

Not only coffee was served at the Café Procope, but liqueurs and also fruit juices. One of his most famous liqueurs was called *La liqueur du parfait amour,* or "the liqueur of the perfect love."

One of the first clients of the Café Procope was the fabulist La Fontaine. It also became the favorite rendezvous of actresses and their admirers, when the Comédie Française was built five years later on the same street. Women of society were not to be seen in such a setting but would have their coffee brought in silver cups to their stagecoaches in front of the Café Procope. This often created terrible traffic jams in this narrow street.

Coffee was considered more a drug than just a drink and became the panacea of all ailments; it reduced the fat, fattened the skinny, and accomplished whatever else was needed.

But soon the adversaries of coffee became numerous. Coffee was accused of causing stomach ailments, of darkening the skin, and making man impotent! To save coffee from discredit, Dr. Aliot, one of Louis XIV's doctors, thought of adding milk and sugar to it. Coffee started a comeback and became the famous *café au lait* or breakfast coffee of the Parisians, which sold for two sols per cup. Early in the morning, street merchants would go through the city, with fountains made of tin on their backs, calling, "Café, café!"

Dorine, Madame Du Barry's little dog, sipped her coffee daily from a golden saucer.

Procope's son had the brilliant idea of posting the news of the day on the stovepipe that warmed the room of his shop. This was the beginning of the literary and political coffee shops that held such an important place in the life of the French in the nineteenth century.

Famous clients of the Café Procope were Racine and later Voltaire, who spent two hours every day in the café. His favorite drink was *choca*, a mixture of coffee, chocolate, and milk. It was also a favorite rendezvous for such revolutionaries as Marat and Robespierre. About 1780, when he was a diplomat in Paris, Benjamin Franklin often went there. A later visitor was Bonaparte, who once had to leave his hat as security when he was unable to pay his bill.

During the blockade of 1808, when Bonaparte was Emperor, chicory was added to coffee to make it stretch further. This flavor is still held dear by the French.

In the nineteenth century, the Café Procope continued to be the favorite rendezvous of the Romanticists: George Sand, accompanied by Frédéric Chopin, Alfred de Musset, Balzac, Victor Hugo, and many others.

Noir comme le diable,	Black as the devil,
Chaud comme l'enfer,	Hot as the inferno,
Pur comme un ange,	Pure as an angel,
Doux comme l'amour.	Mellow as love.

—TALLEYRAND (1754–1838)

• *Brandy* •

Nearly every province of France makes some kind of brandy or *eau de vie*. Alsace produces the best fruit brandy—Kirsch (black cherries), Mirabelle (plums), and Prunelle (sloes). Calvados is made of apples from the Calvados region of Normandy.

But the king of brandy is Cognac, called the monarch of liquids by Brillat-Savarin, and made from distilled wine in Cognac in the Charente region of western France. The knights de la Croix Marron, who lived in the sixteenth century, were the first to distill wine from their grapes. Armagnac, named for a town in Gascony, is in the same class as Cognac. Both are matured in oak casks. Armagnac was first made in the thirteenth century and was used as a medicine during the fourteenth century.

A great debate at that time arose over the proper method of finding an honest *eau de vie*. There were two foolproof tests:

Dip a flag in it and flame it. If the flag burns, it is not good enough; if it dries without burning, it is good. In quite another way, take a tablespoon of the *eau de vie* and throw it in the air. Place a sheet of paper underneath and if it falls on the paper, it is not good; if it stays in the air it is good.

To bring out the full body of most fruit brandies, serve in a chilled glass, but for grape brandy, warm the glass in your hand.

Mousse au Café
COFFEE MOUSSE

3 eggs, separated   *6 servings*
1½ cups plus 2 tablespoons confectioners' sugar
Pinch of salt
1 tablespoon unflavored gelatin
7 tablespoons water
2 to 3 tablespoons instant coffee powder
2 tablespoons Cognac
2 teaspoons vanilla extract
1½ cups heavy cream

1. Beat egg yolks, 1 cup of sugar, and a pinch of salt with an electric mixer until thick and lemon-colored.

2. Sprinkle gelatin in 3 tablespoons of water to soften.

3. Heat remaining 4 tablespoons of water to a boil and remove from the heat. Stir in the coffee powder and softened gelatin until both are completely dissolved. Add to the egg-yolk mixture. Stir in the Cognac and vanilla; mix well. Refrigerate until almost set.

4. Beat egg whites until stiff. Add ½ cup sugar. Fold into the coffee mixture until no trace of egg whites remains.

5. Beat 1 cup heavy cream until stiff and fold into the coffee mixture. Spoon mousse into a crystal bowl and chill for at least 4 hours.

6. Whip remaining cream and sweeten to taste. Decorate the mousse with the whipped cream.

◆   *Variation*   ◆

For *mousse au café pralinée* (coffee-praline mousse), reduce the quantity of sugar to ½ cup and add ½ cup Praline Powder (see Index) to the eggs. Serve as soon as set, or the caramel will dissolve in the mousse.

Mousse au Citron

LEMON MOUSSE

4 large eggs, separated   *8 servings*
1 cup confectioners' sugar
1 teaspoon vanilla extract
Grated rind of 2 lemons
2 or 3 drops of yellow food coloring
1 tablespoon unflavored gelatin
6 tablespoons lemon juice
2 tablespoons water
1¾ cups heavy cream
Sauce Melba (see Index) (optional)

1. Beat the egg yolks with ¾ cup of the confectioners' sugar in a large bowl until light and lemon-colored. Add the vanilla, lemon rind, and food coloring.

2. Soften the gelatin in lemon juice and water in the top pan of a double boiler over simmering water. Heat, stirring constantly, until gelatin is dissolved and hot. Gradually add to the egg-yolk mixture, then cool.

3. Beat egg whites until stiff. Fold into the lemon mixture.

4. Whip the cream until stiff. Add remaining ¼ cup sugar, then fold into the lemon mixture. Spoon the mousse into a lightly oiled 6-cup ring-mold. Chill for several hours or overnight. Unmold and serve with Sauce Melba, if desired.

◆ *Variation* ◆

Sprinkle fresh strawberries with sugar and let stand for 1 hour. Fill the center of the lemon mousse with the strawberries. Decorate around the border with whipped cream piped from a pastry tube with a decorative tip. Garnish with whole strawberries.

Sauce Melba

RASPBERRY SAUCE

Defrost a 10-ounce package of frozen raspberries. Combine with 1 tablespoon cornstarch, ½ cup raspberry or currant jelly, 1 teaspoon lemon juice, and ⅓ cup sugar. Bring to a boil and simmer until clear. Strain and chill.

◆ ◆ ◆

The mother of Brillat-Savarin loved custards. When in her nineties, just after having supper in bed, she had a premonition that her last hour was coming.

Urgently she asked her maid to rush and bring her favorite dessert, a custard. After she died, Brillat-Savarin said his mother had had coffee in heaven.

Crème Renversée au Caramel

CARAMEL CUSTARD

Condensed milk makes an exquisite custard that is smoother and more delicate than one made with fresh milk.

1 cup sugar   *6 servings*
4 tablespoons water
1 can (14 ounces) sweetened condensed milk
6 eggs
1 tablespoon vanilla extract
Few drops of lemon extract
Pinch of salt

1. Boil the sugar and water in a small saucepan over moderate heat, without stirring, until the syrup is golden (do not brown it or

it will have a bitter taste). Pour immediately into a 5-cup round mold, 8½ inches in diameter and 2 inches deep, or into a ring mold. Tilt mold in all directions to cover the bottom and sides with caramel. Set aside for the caramel to cool and harden.

2. Pour the condensed milk and 2 cans of cold water into a large bowl. Add the eggs, vanilla, lemon extract, and salt. Beat with a hand eggbeater until smooth.

3. Pour the custard into the prepared mold. Set the mold in a pan of very hot water that reaches halfway up the sides. Bake in a preheated 325°F. oven for 1 hour, or for 45 minutes if in a ring mold, or until a knife inserted in the center comes out clean. The center of the custard should move slightly when the pan is shaken but will become firm as it cools. When cooled to room temperature, refrigerate.

4. To serve, run a knife around the edges and turn onto a flat serving dish with a low border, to hold the caramel sauce.

◆   *Variations*   ◆

For a caramel custard with rum, add ⅓ cup dark rum to the milk-and-egg mixture before baking.

Custard can be flavored with 3 tablespoons coffee extract or ¼ teaspoon orange extract in addition to the vanilla.

◆   UNDER THE COOK'S HAT   ◆

Three cups of fresh milk mixed with ⅔ cup sugar can be substituted for the condensed milk.

A custard must be smooth, without the little holes that would indicate it has been overcooked.

If you use individual custard cups, reduce the baking time to 20 to 30 minutes. Round or oval metal molds of ½-cup capacity, made for eggs in aspic, are ideal for individual custards.

Do not stir the pan when preparing caramel; the sugar will crystallize and become white.

To clean the pan in which the caramel was made, fill it with hot water and boil until caramel dissolves.

Le Pudding à la Diplomate

BAVARIAN CREAM WITH GLACÉED FRUITS AND KIRSCH

This was the creation of Montmireil, chef for Chateaubriand and later for the Comte de Marcellus, a diplomat for whom this dessert was named in 1856.

½ cup finely diced mixed glacéed fruits   *6 servings*
4 tablespoons kirsch
2 teaspoons unflavored gelatin
1½ cups milk
6 egg yolks
Pinch of salt
¾ cup sugar
½ teaspoon cornstarch
2 tablespoons pure vanilla extract
1 cup heavy cream, whipped
12 ladyfingers, split

1. Quickly rinse the glacéed fruits under cold water, unless they are imported. Pat dry, and combine with the kirsch. Soften the gelatin in ¼ cup of milk.

2. Beat the egg yolks, salt, sugar, and cornstarch with an electric beater until pale yellow. Bring remaining milk to a boil in a saucepan. Slowly add the milk to the egg mixture, then return the mixture to the pan and set over a Flame-Tamer. Cook over medium heat, stirring constantly with a whisk, until slightly thickened. Do not boil. Remove from the heat and add vanilla.

3. Stir the gelatin into the mixture. Set the pan in a bowl half full of cracked ice and stir until cool and thickened.

4. Fold in the whipped cream with the drained glacéed fruits. Use the kirsch drained from the fruits to moisten the split ladyfingers, and break in two pieces.

5. Spoon some of the Bavarian cream into a 6-cup decorative mold, then alternate layers of the cream with the ladyfingers. Finish with the cream. Cover the mold with plastic wrap and refrigerate for 4 to 5 hours, or overnight.

6. Unmold and serve with an apricot or raspberry sauce, flavored with kirsch.

◆ ◆ ◆

Ritz remembered Marnier Lapostolle. . . . When the fussy little man with a tremendous sense of his own dignity had arrived one day at the Savoy with a bottle of liqueur of his own invention, he asked my husband for his opinion of it. Ritz tasted it, found it excellent, and said so. Whereupon the gratified wine merchant

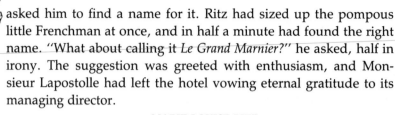

asked him to find a name for it. Ritz had sized up the pompous little Frenchman at once, and in half a minute had found the right name. "What about calling it *Le Grand Marnier?*" he asked, half in irony. The suggestion was greeted with enthusiasm, and Monsieur Lapostolle had left the hotel vowing eternal gratitude to its managing director.

—MARIE LOUISE RITZ,
César Ritz: Host to the World

Mousse au Grand Marnier
GRAND MARNIER MOUSSE

This mousse was a great favorite when served on the French liner *Île de France*.

1 tablespoon unflavored gelatin	*6 servings*
½ cup Grand Marnier liqueur	
3 eggs, separated	
½ cup sugar	
1 cup heavy cream	
12 ladyfingers, split	

1. Soften the gelatin in the Grand Marnier.
2. Drop the egg yolks and sugar into a small bowl placed over hot water. Beat with a mixer for 5 minutes, until thick and pale yellow. Stir in the gelatin mixture.
3. Beat the egg whites until stiff. Fold into the gelatin mixture.
4. Beat the cream until stiff. Fold into the mousse. Line a bowl or individual cups with split ladyfingers. Spoon in the mousse. Cover with plastic wrap. Chill for 6 hours or overnight.

Pudding de Pain
BREAD PUDDING

5 cups diced stale French bread	*4 servings*
2 cups milk	
⅓ cup raisins	

4 tablespoons rum or kirsch
4 eggs, separated
¾ cup sugar
1 tablespoon vanilla extract
Butter

1. Soak the diced bread in the milk for 30 minutes. Soak the raisins in rum or kirsch.

2. In a mixing bowl combine the egg yolks, sugar, raisins, rum, and vanilla. Mix in the soaked bread.

3. Whip the egg whites and fold into the mixture. Spoon into a buttered 6-cup soufflé dish or charlotte mold. Set the mold in a pan of hot water and bake in a preheated 350°F. oven for 45 minutes to 1 hour.

4. When cold, unmold and cover entirely with a chilled Vanilla Custard Sauce (see Index), well flavored with vanilla. Serve the rest of the sauce separately.

◆ UNDER THE COOK'S HAT ◆

Never throw bread away! Any leftover French bread should be wrapped in a wet towel and placed in a 350°F. oven for 5 to 10 minutes, depending on the dryness of the bread. Unwrap and return to the oven for a few minutes to get back its crispness and fresh taste.

◆ *Vanilla* ◆

A member of the orchid family, vanilla is a long podlike seed capsule that has been used in Mexico as a flavoring since pre-Columbian days. After the bean has been cured, it becomes black and emits a delicious aroma.

When Anne of Austria (daughter to the King of Spain) married Louis XIII, she brought vanilla beans from Mexico as part of her trousseau.

To monopolize the vanilla market for their perfumes, the perfumers spread a rumor that vanilla was poison. Therefore, it was only a little over a century ago that vanilla began to be used extensively in desserts and pastry. Before that, the main flavoring was orange-blossom water, which is still used occasionally.

Crème à l'Anglaise

VANILLA CUSTARD SAUCE

5 egg yolks   *Makes 3 cups*
Pinch of salt
⅔ cup sugar
¼ teaspoon cornstarch
2 cups milk
1 tablespoon pure vanilla extract
2 tablespoons rum or kirsch (optional)

1. In a mixing bowl combine the egg yolks, salt, sugar, and cornstarch. Beat with an electric mixer until thick and lemon-colored. Reserve.

2. Bring the milk to a boil. Slowly pour milk into the egg mixture, stirring constantly.

3. Transfer the mixture to the top pan of a double boiler set above simmering water in the lower pan. Stir constantly with a whisk until the mixture is thick enough to coat a spoon. When cooled, add the vanilla and rum or kirsch. Serve at room temperature or chill.

◆   UNDER THE COOK'S HAT   ◆

This sauce is excellent spooned over stewed fruits.

Riz à l'Impératrice

RICE PUDDING WITH GLACÉED FRUITS
AND APRICOT SAUCE

This classic French dessert is named for Empress Eugénie, wife of Napoleon III.

½ cup finely diced mixed glacéed fruits   *6 servings*
4 tablespoons Cognac
½ cup raw unconverted short-grain rice
2 cups milk, boiling
2 tablespoons unsalted butter
1⅓ cups sugar
Pinch of salt

1 tablespoon unflavored gelatin
2 tablespoons cold water
4 egg yolks
1 tablespoon vanilla extract
1 cup heavy cream
Angelica and glacéed red cherries

APRICOT SAUCE
1 cup apricot jam
3 tablespoons sugar
5 tablespoons water
2 tablespoons Cognac

1. Rinse the glacéed fruits briefly under cold water (not necessary if fruit is imported). Combine them with Cognac. Reserve.

2. Rinse the rice under cold water. Place the rice in a large pan almost filled with cold water. Bring to a boil and cook for 8 minutes. Drain and rinse under cold water. Place rice in a baking dish.

3. Add milk, butter, ⅓ cup sugar, and salt to the rice. Cover the baking dish tightly and place in a preheated 350°F. oven. Bake, without disturbing, for about 40 minutes or until soft and tender. Drain the rice thoroughly and reserve the milk.

4. Soften the gelatin in 2 tablespoons cold water.

5. Beat the egg yolks with 1 cup sugar until thick and lemon-colored. Bring ¾ cup of the reserved milk to a boil in a heavy saucepan and slowly add to the egg mixture, stirring well. Return the mixture to the saucepan, stirring over low heat until thickened. Do not allow to boil.

6. Stir the softened gelatin thoroughly into the custard mixture. Remove from the heat and add the vanilla. Combine custard mixture with the rice. Chill until mixture begins to thicken.

7. Whip the heavy cream until stiff. Fold into the rice mixture. Add the glacéed fruits and Cognac. Pour into a lightly oiled 5-cup ring mold or other decorative mold. Chill for at least 6 hours, or overnight.

8. Combine the sauce ingredients in a small saucepan and simmer until liquefied. Chill.

9. To serve, run a sharp knife around the edges of the mold. Dip the mold into hot water for a few seconds before unmolding on a serving plate.

10. Decorate the top with angelica cut into diamond shapes, and glacéed red cherries. Pour a little of the apricot sauce around the base of the rice and serve remaining sauce separately.

◆ *Variation* ◆

Melt red currant jelly instead of apricot jam for the sauce and substitute kirsch for Cognac.

◆ *Charlotte Russe* ◆

In 1802, Carême created the *Charlotte russe* at his restaurant on the
rue de la Paix. He originally called it *Charlotte à la parisienne* but later
dedicated it to his employer, Russian Emperor Alexander, and it
became *Charlotte russe.*

An earlier charlotte was made with bread slices and apples. The
name refers to any dessert made with bread or cake lining a mold
and filled with Bavarian cream.

Charlotte Russe aux Abricots

CHARLOTTE RUSSE WITH APRICOTS

This is a spectacular dessert that is as good as it looks. Ladyfingers
form a circle around a filling of Bavarian cream.

1 cup dried apricots   *6 to 8 servings*
1½ cups sugar
3 tablespoons kirsch
6 egg yolks
1½ cups milk
¾ tablespoon unflavored gelatin
3 tablespoons water
2 tablespoons pure vanilla extract
1 cup heavy cream
24 ladyfingers
Kirsch syrup, made by combining 1 tablespoon sugar, dissolved
    in 2 tablespoons water and 2 tablespoons kirsch

1. In a small saucepan cover the apricots with water and simmer
for 25 minutes. Add ½ cup of the sugar and cook for 10 minutes.
Purée apricots in a blender or food processor, or push through a
sieve. Add the kirsch. Reserve.

2. Lightly oil an 8-cup charlotte or soufflé mold. Line the bottom of the mold with a circle of unoiled wax paper.

3. Prepare the Bavarian cream: Beat the egg yolks with 1 cup sugar until pale yellow. Boil the milk in a heavy stainless-steel or enamelware saucepan. Slowly add a little of the milk to the yolks, then mix in the remaining milk, stirring constantly. Return the mixture to the pan. Cook, stirring constantly with a whisk, until custard is slightly thickened or until the spoon is well coated. Do not boil.

4. Soften the gelatin in 3 tablespoons water. Stir the gelatin mixture into the custard, then add the apricot purée and 1 tablespoon vanilla. Cool the mixture over a bowl of ice water.

5. Whip half the cream and add remaining 1 tablespoon vanilla. Fold cream into the cooled custard.

6. Cut enough ladyfingers diagonally to fill the bottom of the mold, and press them together. Sprinkle with kirsch syrup. Press remaining ladyfingers all around the mold, with the curved side against the surface of the dish. Fill the mold with the Bavarian cream. Chill for at least 6 hours.

7. When ready to serve, trim the tops of the ladyfingers to make them even with the surface of the cream. Slide a knife around the mold and unmold the charlotte on a serving plate lined with a paper doily. Remove the wax paper.

8. Whip the rest of the heavy cream for decoration and sweeten to taste. Spoon the cream into a pastry bag and decorate the top of the charlotte and the grooves between the ladyfingers.

◆   UNDER THE COOK'S HAT   ◆

Spread the split part of commercial ladyfingers with some of the Bavarian cream before lining the mold so they will unmold in one piece.

Place a plate inside the mold, on top of the filling, to prevent the ladyfingers from rising slightly during the chilling process. Remove plate after 1 hour.

Pudding Nesselrode

NESSELRODE PUDDING

This exquisite dessert was created by the French chef to Count Nesselrode, the Russian statesman, in the middle of the nineteenth century. It consists of custard blended with a purée of chestnuts and whipped cream. Contrary to popular opinion, candied fruit is not an ingredient in this classic pudding.

⅓ cup sugar *6 servings*
4 egg yolks
1 teaspoon cornstarch
1 cup milk
2 cans (8¾ ounces each) sweetened chestnut purée
1½ cups heavy cream
1 tablespoon vanilla extract
2 tablespoons rum
1 cup candied chestnuts, cut into pieces

1. Beat sugar, egg yolks, and cornstarch together. In a heavy stainless-steel or enamelware saucepan, bring the milk to a boil. Slowly pour the milk into the egg mixture, stirring constantly. Return the mixture to the pan and bring almost to a boil, stirring with a whisk until slightly thickened. Remove from the heat.

2. Mix in the chestnut purée. Let cool.

3. Whip 1 cup of cream until stiff, then add the vanilla and rum. Fold the cream, a few tablespoons at a time, into the purée to keep the mixture light. Chill.

4. Whip remaining heavy cream and sweeten to taste.

5. Serve in sherbet glasses topped with rosettes of the sweetened whipped cream and garnished with candied chestnuts.

• *Meringues* •

Meringues, a light and delicate confection of egg whites, are thought to have been invented by a Swiss pastry cook named Gasparini in 1720. They are named after the small town of Meiringen in the Aar valley of Switzerland, where Gasparini practiced his art.

The first meringues served in France were at the court of Stanislas, ex-King of Poland, in Nancy. The King's daughter, Marie Leczinska, wife of Louis XV, passed her fondness for meringues on to Marie-Antoinette, her granddaughter by marriage. Marie-Antoinette frequently made her own meringues at the Petit Trianon at Versailles.

Meringues Chantilly

MERINGUES WITH WHIPPED CREAM

Sweetened, flavored whipped cream is called crème Chantilly, after the beautiful Château of Chantilly, where Vatel, the *maître d'hôtel* to the Prince de Condé, created it. Any dessert with the name Chantilly in its title has sweetened whipped cream as a major ingredient.

6 egg whites, at room temperature
1 teaspoon baking soda
1 teaspoon vanilla extract
¾ cup granulated sugar
¾ cup confectioners' sugar
Crème Chantilly (1 cup heavy cream, whipped with 1 teaspoon vanilla extract and sugar to taste)
Toasted sliced almonds

12 servings

1. Beat the egg whites with the baking soda until stiff. Add the vanilla extract and both sugars very slowly, beating constantly until the mixture is stiff and glossy and the whites hold their peaks when you lift the beater straight up.

2. Spoon the meringue into a pastry bag fitted with a plain tube. Pipe out 3-inch round or oval shapes onto lightly buttered and floured nonstick baking sheets.

3. Bake in a very slow (225°F.) oven for 2 hours. The shells should be white, crisp, and slightly sticky inside.

4. When cold, sandwich in pairs with sweetened whipped cream flavored with vanilla. Decorate the top with more whipped cream piped from a pastry bag. Sprinkle with sliced toasted almonds. Place the meringues in fluted white paper cups to serve.

Cold chocolate sauce can be served separately.

If the egg whites are not beaten stiff enough to hold a peak before sugar is added, they will be soft and won't keep their shape even after much beating.

Do not attempt to make meringue on damp days.

For small individual meringue nests, pipe the meringue in an ever-widening spiral, beginning in the center. Pipe a rim around each base, measuring 1 to 2 inches high. Bake as instructed. Serve these nests with pipe rosettes of sweetened whipped cream on the border, filled with ice cream, strawberries, or a mousse.

If meringues start to brown, cover loosely with tissue paper.

Les Crêpes

DESSERT CRÊPES

Dessert crêpes should be made as thin as possible. They are delicious just sprinkled with sugar, or dusted with vanilla-flavored confectioners' sugar. Fold the crêpes in half and then in half again, or roll them up. Serve on very hot plates and provide dessert knives and forks.

Serve a semidry Champagne.

2 whole eggs   *12 to 14 crêpes*
2 extra egg yolks
2 tablespoons sugar
Pinch of salt
1 teaspoon vanilla or lemon zest
1½ cups milk
½ cup water
6 tablespoons unsalted butter, melted and cooled
1 tablespoon unflavored oil
1¼ cups flour

1. With a hand eggbeater, lightly beat together all the ingredients except the flour. Sift the flour into a large mixing bowl. Make a well in the center. Slowly add the batter and with a whisk, stir in the flour gradually until all has been absorbed. Beat until smooth, but do not overbeat or the crêpes will be rubbery once cooked.

2. Strain the batter through a fine sieve. Let stand for 1 hour at room temperature. On hot days, omit the butter and refrigerate the

batter. Before using the batter, bring it to room temperature, then add the butter.

3. Heat a 7-inch crêpe pan over medium-high heat. If a few drops of water dropped on the pan sizzle and evaporate immediately, the pan is ready to use.

4. Pour about 2½ tablespoons of batter from a ladle into the pan. Tilt the pan quickly in a circular motion to cover the surface evenly with a thin layer of batter. When the edges are golden brown, about 1 minute, flip the crêpe or turn over with a round-edged metal spatula. Cook for 20 to 30 seconds, or until speckled golden brown underneath. Turn crêpes out onto a warm plate, one on top of another, and cover.

◆ UNDER THE COOK'S HAT ◆

Use two crêpe pans to save time and keep them hot.

Crêpes aux Fruits Confits
CRÊPES WITH GLACÉED FRUITS

For 12 crêpes

Prepare Pastry Cream (see Index). When the pastry cream is tepid, add 4 ounces glacéed fruits that have been steeped in 4 tablespoons Cognac. (If fruits are domestic, rinse under cold water briefly.) Fill each crêpe with about 3 tablespoons of the mixture, spread along the center line. Roll, then sift vanilla-flavored confectioners' sugar over each crêpe.

◆ UNDER THE COOK'S HAT ◆

When filling a crêpe, the speckled side should be on the outside. Crêpes can be kept warm on a covered plate set over a pan of hot water.

◆ *Variations* ◆

Crêpes à la Confiture, CRÊPES WITH JAM Heat any jam of your choice—apricot, peach, raspberry, etc.—until warm. Spread about 1½ tablespoons of jam on each warm crêpe, then roll or fold into quarters. Sift a little confectioners' sugar over each crêpe. Heat ¼ cup kirsch or rum, ignite, and pour over the crêpes.

Crêpes Pralinées, CRÊPES WITH PRALINE CREAM Make Pastry Cream (see Index) flavored with 2 tablespoons rum and only

¼ cup sugar. Fold in ¾ cup whipped cream and ½ cup Praline Powder (see Index). Spread 2 to 3 tablespoons of the mixture on each crêpe. Sift vanilla-flavored confectioners' sugar on each crêpe.

Crêpes aux Bananes, BANANA CRÊPES Slowly sauté firm bananas in butter until golden, then sprinkle with sugar, rum, and lemon juice. Place bananas on crêpes and roll. Add 2 to 3 tablespoons rum to the frying pan. Ignite the sauce and pour over the crêpes.

• *Crêpes Suzette* •

The creator of the famous crêpes Suzette was Monsieur Joseph, who was in charge of the restaurant Paillard in Paris in 1889. At that time, these crêpes were spread with a sugar-orange-butter sauce and were nameless, although a specialty of this restaurant. Later, when Monsieur Joseph opened his own restaurant, the Marivaux, he continued to serve these crêpes with the orange sauce.

In 1897, at the Comédie Française, an actress playing the role of a lady's maid, Mademoiselle Suzette, had to bring crêpes onstage to be eaten by the actors at an intimate dinner. Every day these crêpes would be brought from the restaurant Marivaux nearby. One day, Monsieur Joseph, who prepared them, decided to break the monotony of these daily crêpes by serving them warm and flaming, and he named his creation "Suzette" in honor of the actress.

The simple orange sauce for crêpes Suzette was later replaced with one made with tangerines and Curaçao liqueur. And as for flaming, it is unnecessary as it accentuates the flavor so that it tastes "like an apéritif or a digestif," as Chef Raymond Grangier of the S.S. *France* told me with wit.

Crêpes Suzette

It is the sauce that distinguishes these crêpes from all others. Prepare the Dessert Crêpes (see Index) ahead of time; sprinkle them lightly with sugar and keep warm. Flavor the dough of the crêpes with lemon zest, vanilla, or Grand Marnier.

SAUCE FOR APPROXIMATELY 12 CRÊPES
⅓ cup granulated sugar
8 tablespoons (1 stick) unsalted butter
1 large orange or 2 tangerines
⅓ cup orange or tangerine juice
¼ cup Cointreau or orange liqueur
¼ cup Grand Marnier

1. The sauce can be made ahead of time to improve the flavor or it can be made at the table in a chafing dish. Bring the crêpes to the table. Melt the sugar with 4 tablespoons of the butter, stirring from time to time to prevent the mixture from burning.

2. Grate the rind of the orange or tangerines over the sugar mixture. Add the orange or tangerine juice. Bring almost to a boil. Add the rest of the butter in bits and add the liqueurs.

3. Reheat the sauce gently until hot. Using a fork and a spoon, dip the crêpes on both sides into the sauce, one at a time. Fold the crêpes in half and then again in half, ending with the speckled side up. Place on hot individual plates, 2 crêpes per serving. Serve immediately.

Crêpes Soufflées au Grand Marnier
SOUFFLÉ CRÊPES WITH GRAND MARNIER

This festive dessert can be prepared 2 to 3 hours ahead, to be baked just before serving.

6 Dessert Crêpes (see Index)   *6 servings*
3 eggs, separated
½ cup sugar
Grated rind of 1 large orange
1 tablespoon Grand Marnier liqueur
2 tablespoons vanilla extract
¼ cup flour, sifted
½ cup milk
Grand Marnier Sauce (recipe follows)
Confectioners' sugar

1. Prepare the crêpes.
2. Beat the egg yolks, sugar, grated orange rind, Grand Marnier, and vanilla in a small bowl with a whisk for 2 to 3 minutes. Add the flour, stirring well.

3. Boil the milk in a small heavy pan. Pour into the egg mixture, stirring with the whisk. Pour the mixture back into the pan and cook without boiling, over medium-high heat, stirring constantly until very thick, about 2 minutes. Remove from the heat and cool until tepid.

4. Whip the egg whites until stiff. Fold the cooled mixture into the egg whites, but do not blend thoroughly.

5. Fill the center of each crêpe with approximately 3 large soup spoons of the soufflé batter. Fold 1 side of the crêpe on top, then fold the other side loosely because these crêpes will expand, like a soufflé, to twice their original size. Place the crêpes, folded side down, in a buttered baking dish, leaving ½ inch of space between them. At this point the crêpes can be set aside for 2 or 3 hours.

6. Brush the crêpes with some of the sauce before baking in a preheated 400°F. oven for 15 to 20 minutes. Pour remaining sauce over, dust with confectioners' sugar, and serve at once.

GRAND MARNIER SAUCE
¼ pound unsalted butter
4 tablespoons sugar
Grated rind of 2 small oranges
6 tablespoons Grand Marnier liqueur

1. Slowly melt the butter with the sugar and orange rind. Stir in the liqueur.

A FEW
CONFECTIONS
❖ ❖ ❖

*Confectionery is the **DESSERT** of the dessert.*
—CHÂTILLON-PLESSIS, in 1894

Sugar was brought to Europe from the Orient by the Crusaders. Until then, honey was the only sweetener. Sugar was called "Indian salt" at first, because its origin could be traced back to India. It was considered a spice and a complement to salt. Sugar helped season meat as well as fish.

Sugar was very expensive; it was thought of as medicine, a help in digesting the spicy food of that time. It could only be bought at an apothecary's shop and was sold by the ounce. The apothecary also had the sole right to sell jelly, candy, fruit syrups, and liquor, which were then looked upon more as remedy than tasty delicacy.

During the Renaissance, sugar in the form of candy became the rage. The lords of the French court would carry candy boxes of great value, decorated with precious stones, in their pockets. Henri IV always had his pocket full of candies so that he could offer them to the ladies.

Because of the continental blockade, Napoleon wished that a new way could be found to extract sugar from indigenous plants to replace the sugar that came from the French colonies. He was extremely pleased when Parmentier, who helped introduce the potato to France, discovered grape syrup as a replacement for sugar in 1809. The following year this could be read in the newspaper *Intérieur:* "Paris, March 10, 1810—Mr. Collin, first 'Chef d'Office' of his Majesty the Emperor, served him ice cream sweetened with grape syrup which had been sent to his Majesty by Parmentier. It was as perfect as if it had been prepared with the most refined of sugar."

This new substitute for sugar was used for two years, during the continental blockade, until Benjamin Delessert built a factory in Passy, near Paris, that produced sugar from beets. Napoleon made an official visit on January 2, 1812, and was given two beet sugar loaves by Delessert. Overjoyed, the Emperor removed his own decoration of the Légion d'Honneur to pin on Delessert, and gave him the title of Baron.

When beet sugar continued to be used even after the blockade was over, Lamartine, the well-known poet, went to the Chambre of Deputies in 1843. He asked for a law to banish the sugar-beet industry, which was ruining the sugar-cane industries of the French colonies. His request was defeated by only four votes and beet sugar was here to stay, along with cane sugar.

Écorces d'Oranges Confites
CANDIED ORANGE PEELS

Peels of 4 oranges, preferably thick-skinned
1 tablespoon coarse salt
2 cups granulated sugar
6 tablespoons white corn syrup
1 cup water
Confectioners' sugar

1. Soak the peels overnight in cold water with the coarse salt. Drain and remove the white pith. Cover the peel with water and boil for 20 minutes. Drain and repeat this step twice. In the last cooking period, cook until tender. Cut the peel into ¼-inch strips.

2. Combine the granulated sugar, corn syrup, and 1 cup water in a saucepan. Bring to a boil, then add the orange strips and simmer until translucent, about 1 hour. Do not allow the syrup to caramelize.

3. Remove the peels with a skimmer and let them drain on a cake rack. Roll in confectioners' sugar while still hot. Let them rest on the cake rack to dry for 24 hours. Store in glass jars.

◆   UNDER THE COOK'S HAT   ◆

The syrup used in the preparation of the orange peels makes a refreshing drink with the addition of club soda, citrus juice, and a little grenadine syrup.

◆ ◆ ◆

Knight Paul . . . owned, near Toulon, a very beautiful garden filled with orange trees . . . Being informed that King Louis XIV was coming to look at them, he had the idea of candying part of the oranges on the trees. The King and his court, who did not expect this gallantry, were agreeably surprised by it.

These candied oranges mixed indistinctly with others which were not, made a number of the ladies of the court believe that oranges in Provence came already candied on the trees.

—ALEXANDRE DUMAS, FILS,
Grand dictionnaire de cuisine

Les Aiguillettes d'Orange au Chocolat
CHOCOLATE-COVERED ORANGE PEELS

Melt 16 ounces semisweet dark chocolate bits over barely simmering water. Using a fork, dip the candied orange peels into the chocolate. Drain on a metal cake rack placed over wax paper. Press the prongs of a fork along each strip to make the traditional design. Dry for about 6 hours.

◆   U N D E R   T H E   C O O K ' S   H A T   ◆

When working with chocolate, make sure that the weather is not too humid or too warm.

A special candy-making chocolate is available at candy stores. It is high in cocoa butter and less sweet.

◆ *Praline* ◆

Pralines originated in Montargis, in Burgundy, about 1560 and were sold in the confectionery shop of Simon Ingon.

In the eighteenth century, these candies, still supplied by the same shop, were introduced to the French court by the Duc de Praslin. He gave them so lavishly to the ladies that soon both the candy and the confectioner's shop became known by his name. The shop is still in existence under the name Au Duc de Praslin.

Poudre de Pralin

PRALINE POWDER

Makes about 2 cups

¾ cup filberts (hazelnuts) or slivered almonds, ground
1 cup sugar
6 tablespoons water
1 teaspoon pure vanilla extract

1. Place the nuts in a nonstick skillet. Sauté over medium heat until golden brown.
2. Combine sugar and water in a saucepan and cook without stirring until the syrup is golden brown. Immediately add the vanilla and the nuts. Pour the praline onto a piece of foil; let cool until hardened.
3. Crush the praline in a mortar, electric blender, or food processor. The powder should be fine but still retain some of its texture. Store leftover powder in a glass jar in the freezer.

Truffles au Chocolat Pralinées

PRALINE CHOCOLATE TRUFFLES

¾ cup blanched almonds
¾ cup plus 1 tablespoon sugar
1 tablespoon pure vanilla extract
½ cup heavy cream
1 tablespoon instant coffee powder
12 ounces semisweet Swiss chocolate bars
1 tablespoon unsalted butter

1. Coarsely grind the almonds with 1 tablespoon sugar in a blender or food processor.
2. Combine ground almonds, ¾ cup sugar, and the vanilla in a heavy nonstick saucepan. Cook over moderate heat, stirring constantly, until the mixture is caramelized or golden. Let cool in the pan until hardened.
3. Pound the mixture in a mortar or grind to a powder in a blender. Measure out ½ cup of the powder and reserve the rest.
4. Heat the cream, stir in the coffee powder, and reserve.
5. Place the chocolate in a heatproof bowl and melt in a 350°F. oven until barely warm. Stir in the butter, the ½ cup praline pow-

der, and the coffee-cream mixture; mix thoroughly. Cover with plastic wrap and put in a cool place until firm, about 2 hours.

6. Sprinkle the reserved praline powder in a deep plate. With a small spoon, scoop out cherry-size pieces of the chocolate. Roll between the palms of your hands to form smooth balls. Roll each ball in praline powder until coated. Place in tiny fluted foil or paper cups. Store in a cool place.

◆ UNDER THE COOK'S HAT ◆

If your hands are too warm to shape the truffles, dip them into ice water first, or cool them by holding a plastic bag filled with ice cubes.

◆ *Jam* ◆

The first book on jam was published in 1555 in Lyon and was written by Nostradamus, the Latin name for Michel de Nostre-Dame. He was born in France in Saint-Rémy. He became an astrologer and was famous for his prophecies.

In old cookbooks, two kinds of jam are mentioned: liquid jam, which is our present-day jam, and dry jam, or candied fruits. These were both served as desserts until the twentieth century.

The famous currant jelly of Bar-le-Duc is made today in exactly the same way as it was in the thirteenth century. The seeds are still removed by hand with the help of a goose feather carved into a point. Mary Queen of Scots was very fond of this jam and called it "a ray of sunshine put into pots."

Confiture de Fraises

STRAWBERRY JAM

This simple way of making jam brings out all the flavor of the fruits.

Hull ripe and flavorful strawberries. Crush them with a fork. For each cup of strawberries, add 1¼ cups of sugar. Combine and let the mixture stand, covered, for several hours.

Put the mixture in an enamelware pan and bring slowly to a boil. Cook over low heat, stirring frequently, for about 5 minutes, depending on the quantity. Do not make more than 4 cups at the same time. Let the pan stand overnight, at room temperature, adding 1 tablespoon of lemon or lime juice for every 2 cups of jam.

Next day, boil the jam until it sheets from a spoon. Skim off foam from on top of jam. Pour into sterilized glasses and seal.

Confiture de Pêches

PEACH JAM

Immerse the fruits in boiling water for a minute, peel them, and remove the stones.

Follow instructions for making strawberry jam. Peach jam requires a little longer cooking time than strawberry jam.

If the jam sets when a little is poured onto a plate, it is ready. Seal when jam is cool. Keep the jars of jam under refrigeration.

Confiture de Marrons

CHESTNUT PURÉE

This is a simple procedure for making sweet chestnut jam at a fraction of the cost of purée bought in cans.

1½ pounds large chestnuts *Makes about 3 cups*
2½ cups sugar
1 cup water
¼ teaspoon salt
2 vanilla pods, split, or 2½ tablespoons vanilla extract

1. My own method for peeling chestnuts does not require cooking. Soak the chestnuts for at least 2 hours in a solution of sweetened water, made up of ¼ cup sugar for each quart of water. The peel will come off easily.

2. Place the peeled chestnuts in cold water, bring to a boil, and cook for about an hour at a point just below boiling. Remove the inner skin. Put the chestnuts through a vegetable mill or potato ricer twice.

3. Combine the sugar, water, salt, and vanilla pods. Boil for 10 minutes without stirring. (If using vanilla extract, add it at the end.) Add the chestnut purée and cook, stirring continuously, for 5 to 6 minutes.

4. Pour into sterilized jars and keep under refrigeration.

◆   *Variation*   ◆

Serve with sweetened whipped cream flavored with vanilla, and vanilla ice cream; with warm chocolate sauce; in meringue nests; or as a spread for layer cakes, glazed with a coffee icing.

13. *La Pâtisserie*
PASTRY AND CAKES

⚜ ⚜ ⚜

A good pastry chef easily becomes a capable cook while one never sees a cook become a great pastry chef!
—JULES GOUFFÉ, *Le Livre de Pâtisserie,* 1867

Is it not through pâtisserie that all, or almost all, of us learned our art? Is it not an incontestable fact that a cook cannot become celebrated unless he has an exact knowledge of pâtisserie and has acquired the rudiments of the art as a young man?
—TAVENET, *L'Art culinaire,* 1884

The importance of pastry is reflected throughout French history; it is first mentioned in a charter from King Louis le Débonnaire in 822. As sugar became more widely available during the Renaissance, a great variety of pastry developed. In the sixteenth century, the practice of pastry making was an acknowledged French art and the Maréchal de Vieilleville said, "All the foreign princes send to France to seek their pastry makers and cooks."

332

By the seventeenth century, each city displayed a banner bearing the coat of arms of its pastry cooks. During the eighteenth century their meeting place for the pastry cook's guild was the Sainte-Chapelle in Paris, but it was not until the beginning of the nineteenth century that the illustrious Carême brought a new precision to the art of pastry. He haunted museums for inspiration and made beautiful etchings that were copied in pastry. Carême left valuable books on pastry making, filled with sketches for large decorative pieces to be served at royal feasts, diplomatic receptions, and other important affairs.

"The fine arts are five in number, to wit: painting, sculpture, poetry, music, and architecture, whose main branch is pastry," said Carême.

The town of Melun in the region between the Seine and Marne rivers elected its mayor during the nineteenth century based on a cooking contest. The best baker won.

It was during that time that a great many classics of French pastry were created and *pâtissiers* were developing house specialties. The three Julien brothers invented the Savarin, Chiboust created the gâteau Saint-Honoré, and Rouget made a specialty of the mille-feuille (napoleons). It was the golden age of pastry making.

Until the beginning of the twentieth century, pastry held a very important place in a meal. Traditionally, at both ends of the table, high and voluminous set pieces were placed, standing on pedestals made of brioche, meringue, or pastry dough—often decorated with inedible ornaments. This area of French gastronomy, pastry, has no equal in the world and goes hand in hand with the art of French cuisine.

The basic pastry doughs are: *pâte à choux, brioche* and *baba, pâte feuilletée, biscuit de savoie, génoise,* and *pâte brisée.* Most French pastries are variations of these, and all are included in this chapter.

◆　◆　◆

Butter is the soul of pastry.
—MARIN, 1740

◆ *Tips for Preparing Pastry* ◆

Nothing compares with the flavor and quality of freshly baked pastry. Because of the high content of butter, French pastry must be eaten the day it is made. Here are a few simple rules for pastry making.

• Measure all ingredients accurately. Ingredients in measuring spoons should be leveled.

• Only unsalted butter should be used in pastry.

• Butter should be at room temperature except for puff pastry.

• All eggs in the following recipes are large.

• Do not roll very chilled dough or it toughens.

• When placing yeast dough in a bowl to rise, mark the inside of the bowl to show how high the dough should rise.

• To unmold a cake, invert the mold on a plate and place a thick towel over the mold for 5 minutes.

• If yeast dough rises in a too warm place or for too short a time, an unpleasant yeasty flavor develops.

• If edges brown too much during second baking, in a tart such as a quiche made of puff pastry, cover the edge with a strip of aluminum foil.

• Unless otherwise noted, all pastry recipes are for a French 10-inch pie ring with 1-inch fluted sides and a detachable bottom.

• *Cream Puffs* •

Choux à la crème is one of the oldest favorites of French pastry, so named because it looks like a *chou* or cabbage. Already mentioned about 1560 in the cookbook *Ménagier de Paris*, these *petits choux*— along with other pastries in vogue at the time—were sold in the streets of Paris by the *oubloyers* (street vendors of pastry), who shouted: "Here is your pleasure!"

Edmond Rostand must have been very fond of *choux* as they are mentioned in *Cyrano de Bergerac* several times. The baker Ragueneau says he paid for his theater ticket with four custards and fifteen *choux* puffs. The author has Cyrano ask the duenna if she likes the pastry called *petit choux*. She replies, "Yes, when they are made with cream."

Pâte à Choux

CREAM-PUFF DOUGH

This is a delicate, versatile dough used in many desserts such as cream puffs, petits choux Saint-Honoré, and éclairs. It is also used in savory dishes such as quenelles and gnocchi.

½ cup water
4 tablespoons unsalted butter
Pinch of salt
½ teaspoon sugar (if used for desserts)
½ cup flour, sifted, plus 1 tablespoon
3 medium eggs

1. Bring the water, butter, salt, and sugar to a fast boil in a heavy saucepan. Remove from the heat and add the flour all at once, stirring vigorously with a wooden spoon. Place pan over low heat, and beat until the batter leaves the sides of the pan and forms a smooth, shiny ball.
2. Remove pan from the heat and transfer batter to a bowl. Let it cool slightly. Beat in 1 egg until well blended. Beat in the second egg, then add the third egg. Beat until the dough is smooth.
3. Follow the individual recipes for shaping and baking the dough.

Choux à la Crème

CREAM PUFFS

1 recipe Cream-Puff Dough (preceding recipe)
Crème Chantilly (see Index) or Pastry Cream (see Index)
Vanilla-flavored confectioners' sugar

1. Prepare the cream-puff dough.
2. Drop the batter onto a lightly greased baking sheet from a small spoon, pushing the dough off with your finger. The size should be about 1¼ inches in diameter. Space dough balls 2 inches apart.
3. Bake in a preheated 425°F. oven for 10 minutes, until well puffed but not colored. Lower the heat to 325°F. and bake for 20 minutes longer, until golden beige. Do not open the oven during baking. Remove puffs from the oven and let them cool.
4. When puffs have cooled, cut into the top third with a serrated knife, but do not detach the hat completely.
5. Fill the puffs, using a small spoon or a pastry bag filled with Chantilly cream or Saint-Honoré cream. Sift confectioners' sugar over the top, and place in small white fluted paper cups.

◆ UNDER THE COOK'S HAT ◆

For making cream puffs in quantities, use a pastry bag fitted with a plain ¾-inch tube.

Preheat oven for 10 minutes, or the first batch will be smaller than later batches.

◆ *Variation* ◆

Before baking the puffs, brush them with beaten egg and cover generously with sliced almonds.

Crème Pâtissière

PASTRY CREAM

1½ cups milk
4 egg yolks
½ cup plus 2 tablespoons sugar
2 tablespoons flour
2 tablespoons cornstarch
1 tablespoon vanilla extract

1. Scald the milk in a heavy saucepan (not aluminum).
2. In a bowl, beat the egg yolks and sugar until a ribbon is formed when the whisk is lifted. Sift the flour and cornstarch into the mixture, mixing just long enough to blend. Gradually stir in the scalded milk until the mixture is smooth.
3. Pour this mixture into the heavy saucepan. Cook the custard over low heat, whisking it constantly with back and forth strokes, until it has boiled for 1 minute. Add the vanilla.
4. Pour the cream into a bowl and cover with a buttered piece of wax paper.

◆ *Variations* ◆

The Italian Marquis Frangipani, who lived in Paris at the time of Louis XIII, was the inventor of a perfume to scent gloves. During the eighteenth century, *crème pâtissière*, with the addition of powdered almonds to flavor it, was named crème Frangipane after the Marquis.

To make a Saint-Honoré Cream, add 4 stiffly beaten egg whites with the addition of ⅓ cup sugar to the *crème pâtissière*, while it is still hot.

Profiteroles au Chocolat

CREAM PUFFS WITH CHOCOLATE SAUCE

Using the basic Cream-Puff Dough (see Index), spoon it into a pastry bag fitted with a large plain tube (no. 6) or ½-inch opening. Make the puffs the size of a large cherry. Without a pastry bag, drop the dough from a teaspoon onto a lightly greased baking sheet. Follow instructions for Cream Puffs (see Index).

Make a small hole in the bottom of the puffs and pipe in sweetened whipped cream flavored with vanilla, or split open the upper part and fill them.

Pile the puffs in a pyramid shape on a serving dish. Sift confectioners' sugar over them. Serve with hot Chocolate Sauce (see Index).

• *Gâteau Saint-Honoré* •

Saint-Honoré was the patron saint of bakers and pastry makers because he baked his own bread when he was the Bishop of Amiens in A.D. 660. On the Paris street named in honor of Saint-Honoré was a pastry shop owned by Monsieur Chiboust. In 1864 Chiboust created a great classic of French pastry called gâteau Saint-Honoré. The first versions were made with biscuit dough, but cream-puff dough was later substituted. Every Sunday Chiboust sold 200 of his beautiful creations.

Gâteau Saint-Honoré has a base of pâte brisée surrounded by a crown of 14 to 16 caramelized cream puffs. The center is filled with cream Chantilly or Saint-Honoré cream. The latter was invented by Monsieur Chiboust, too. Because of the time consumed in making this famous cake, often the *petits choux* alone are served.

Les Petits Choux Saint-Honoré

CARAMELIZED CREAM PUFFS

1 recipe Cream-Puff Dough (see Index)
1½ cups sugar
Saint-Honoré Cream (see Index) or Crème Chantilly (see Index)

1. Prepare the cream puffs according to the basic recipe. Bake and cool them.

2. Prepare a syrup: Combine the sugar with just enough water to moisten it in a saucepan. Do not stir or move the pan around. Cook over medium heat until the syrup is straw-colored and beginning to caramelize.

3. With tongs, dip each puff top halfway into the syrup. Place on foil to cool. If the syrup hardens too fast, return to the heat until the right consistency is reached.

4. When the puffs have cooled, slice off the tops with a serrated knife. Fill the puffs, using a small spoon or pastry bag filled with Saint-Honoré cream or cream Chantilly. Replace their tops and put into fluted white paper baking cups.

◆   UNDER THE COOK'S HAT   ◆

Set the pan of caramel syrup in a pan of hot water to keep it from hardening too fast.

◆ *Croquembouche* ◆

Croquembouche, which means "crackle in the mouth," is a pyramid of about 75 caramel-coated cream puffs, topped with an ornament, spun sugar, or a figurine. It is often topped with the figures of a bride and groom when used as a wedding cake.

A great classic of French pastry, *croquembouche* is an elegant dessert for a buffet or special festive occasion such as a wedding or christening.

The great chef Carême devoted fifteen pages of his classic book on pastry, *Le pâtissier royal parisien*, to the *croquembouche*.

Croquembouche

PYRAMID OF CARAMELIZED CREAM PUFFS

1. Make a 9-inch-round flat base of Sweet Short-Crust Pastry (see Index).

2. Make Caramelized Cream Puffs (see Index), *except that:* (a) You should double the recipe; (b) in making the syrup, you should add a good pinch of cream of tartar to the sugar; and (c) you should fill the puffs (with crème Chantilly or pastry cream) from the bottom

rather than from the top. Make a pencil-size hole in the bottom and fill from a pastry bag fitted with a no. 3 tube.

3. Build the puffs in a pyramid shape on the pastry base. The puffs should stick to each other. Place a few caramelized, glacéed cherries or a few crystallized violets here and there and decorate with points of whipped cream.

Paris-Brest

CROWN OF PUFF DOUGH WITH PRALINE WHIPPED CREAM

To celebrate the first European bicycle race, which was held between Paris and Brest in 1912, Monsieur Brestois, a pastry chef, invented this delicious and glamorous dessert.

Butter and flour for baking sheet
1 recipe Cream-Puff Dough (see Index)
1 egg, beaten
¼ cup almonds, thinly sliced
1½ cups heavy cream
Sugar
2 teaspoons vanilla extract
1 cup Praline Powder (see Index)
Vanilla-flavored confectioners' sugar

6 servings

1. Butter a large nonstick baking sheet, dust lightly with flour, and shake off the excess. Using a 7-inch plate or circular mold, mark an outline of it on the baking sheet.

2. Prepare the cream-puff dough. Spoon it into a pastry bag fitted with a large plain tube. Pipe the dough in a 1-inch-wide circle, following the outline on the baking sheet. Pipe a second circle, touching the first one, around the outside. Pipe a third circle on top and in the middle of the other two circles.

3. Brush with the beaten egg.

4. Push one-third of the almonds into the dough, then sprinkle the remaining almonds on the top.

5. Bake the ring in a preheated 400°F. oven for 20 minutes, then reduce the heat to 350°F. and bake until pastry is firm to the touch, about 25 minutes. Do not open the oven during baking. Cool the ring on a wire rack.

6. Whip the cream until stiff, then add sugar to taste, the vanilla, and praline powder.

7. Slice a lid off the upper part of the cake. Fill the bottom half with the praline cream piped from a pastry bag. Replace the lid. Sift confectioners' sugar over the top. Transfer the cake with 2 spatulas onto a round serving dish lined with a doily.

Éclairs au Café
COFFEE ÉCLAIRS

The name *éclair* means lightning and probably comes from the shine of the icing on top of the pastry. French éclairs are much smaller than the American version.

1. Make a coffee-flavored Pastry Cream and prepare Cream-Puff Dough (see Index for recipes). The recipe should make about 18 éclairs.

2. Fit a pastry bag with a round plain tube with a ½-inch opening (no. 6). With the help of a rubber spatula, fill the bag with the batter. Holding the pastry bag at an oblique angle, pipe 3½- to 4-inch sticks, about ½ inch wide, onto an ungreased nonstick baking sheet. Finish each stick with a backward motion and flatten each tiny peak with a wet pastry brush.

3. Bake in a preheated 425°F. oven for about 12 minutes until puffed up and golden beige all over. Reduce the heat to 350°F. and bake for about 10 minutes longer. The éclairs should be rather firm to the touch.

4. When cool, take a serrated knife and slit one side open the entire length of the éclair, following the natural ridge. Fill both sides with the pastry cream. Dip each éclair into the icing so that it is coated halfway down. Allow to harden on a wire rack.

Fondant ICING

The invention of the original icing is attributed to a foreman named Gillet of the pastry house Lemoine in Paris in 1824. Here is a simpler version of the time-involving recipe he originated. (Do not prepare icing in advance.)

2 cups confectioners' sugar
1 tablespoon light corn syrup
5 tablespoons coffee extract (or 2 tablespoons instant coffee
   diluted in 5 tablespoons water)

1. Combine the confectioners' sugar, light corn syrup, and coffee extract in a heavy-bottomed saucepan. Beat with an electric beater until smooth.

2. Place the pan over very low heat and stir constantly until the icing is just tepid. At intervals, dip your finger in to test the temperature. If the icing becomes warmer than tepid, it will lose its sheen and cannot be used.

The icing should coat the éclairs in one dipping. If it is too thin, add a little confectioners' sugar, and if too thick, add a few drops of water.

◆ *Beignets* ◆

Pâte à choux was originally called *pâte à chaud* because it is the only French dough that must be cooked before using. It is baked for cream puffs and deep-fried for beignets—the fritters that originated in the Arabic world. In one of the early references, the chronicler Jean de Joinville (1224–1317) recounts how Saint Louis and his knights "gracefully" received fritters from the Saracens while giving them back their freedom.

Beignets Soufflés
SOUFFLÉ FRITTERS

Spun sugar was created by Sabatier to decorate these soufflé fritters, in 1772, when he was *Chef de Bouche* to Louis XV.

1. Prepare Cream-Puff Dough (see Index) using just 3 tablespoons butter, but adding either ½ teaspoon of vanilla or grated lemon rind and 1½ tablespoons sugar.

2. With the help of your forefinger, drop small balls of batter (about ½ tablespoon) into moderately hot deep fat (350°). Increase the heat until the fat is hot (375°). When the *beignets* stop turning over and are uniformly golden, remove with a slotted spoon.

3. Drain fritters on paper towels and roll in vanilla-flavored confectioners' sugar. Pile the *beignets* in a pyramid on a serving plate lined with a doily. Serve with hot Apricot Sauce (see Index).

• *Pâte Feuilletée* •

A leaved cake *(feuillés)* was mentioned in a charter drawn up by the Bishop of Amiens in 1311. It was not *pâte feuilletée* as we know it today, but it resembled a flaky dough that is still used in southwestern France for a cake called *pastis*. This dough is made with eggs and stretched gently in all directions until paper-thin. Brushed with oil and flavored with rosewater, it is rolled and baked in a mold between embers. This flaky dough, which resembled phyllo pastry and strudel dough, was a gift of the Arabs who occupied the south of France until they were driven out by Charlemagne.

The true *pâte feuilletée*, which is the base for such outstanding creations as *vol-au-vent* (patty shells), *mille-feuilles* (Napoleons), and *chaussons* (turnovers), was the invention of Claude Gellée (1600–1682) and is the subject of a fascinating tale. Better known as Le Lorrain, he is one of the great masters of French painting, referred to sometimes as "the Raphael of landscape."

When Claude Gellée was young, he was too poor to paint so he was apprenticed in a pastry shop in his native city of Champagne in the Vosges. One day he created a loaf of bread for his sick father by adding butter and folding the dough about 10 times. It rose to considerable height when baking and his father enjoyed the bread so much he asked for it again and again.

In 1635 Claude Gellée moved to Paris and worked for an obscure pastry shop owned by Monsieur Ratabout. Gellée made the shop famous because of his special gift for pastry making, and meanwhile he was perfecting his *pâte feuilletée*.

There he met another pastry cook, Mosca Luigi, who persuaded him to go to Italy to work for Luigi's brother in Florence. There, Claude Gellée made his creation such an outstanding success that two more pastry shops were opened within a year.

Mosca was extremely jealous of Gellée and made him work in a cellar, pretending that he himself was the originator and baker of *pâte feuilletée*. After discovering the secret of the dough, the Mosca brothers locked Gellée in for three months. Finally Gellée escaped and took refuge for five years in Naples at the home of a German painter, where he improved his painting skills.

Gellée returned to Florence to resume his old trade. He found that the house of the Mosca family had burned to the ground and the entire family had perished in the fire. All that remained was a fire-blackened sign that read *Fabrica di Pasta Sfogliata e Altre Pasticceria—Mosca Angelo Inventore* (Manufacturers of Puff Paste and Various Pastries—Angelo Mosca, Inventor).

Claude Gellée was avenged. He spent the rest of his life painting, living to the ripe old age of 82.

This dough remains one of the outstanding French pastry doughs, and one of the hardest to master.

Pâte Feuilletée

PUFF PASTRY

This method for making *pâte feuilletée* is a variation of the classic recipe; it is easier to make and gives the same results.

    2 cups unbleached flour, sifted and chilled, plus additional
        flour as needed
    1 cup pastry flour
    2 teaspoons salt
    2 teaspoons sugar (for sweet pastry)
    ¾ pound (3 sticks) unsalted butter, chilled
    Generous ¾ cup cold water, depending on the dryness of the
        flour

1. Combine the two kinds of flour. Mix 2¾ cups flour, the salt, and sugar if used, together in a large bowl. Dip 6 ounces (1½ sticks) of the butter into the dry ingredients. With a sharp knife, chip off small pieces of flour-covered butter, the size of large peas. Repeat

dipping and chipping until the whole 6 ounces of butter is in small pieces.

2. Sprinkle on the water a little at a time, and mix quickly with a spoon, until the flour and butter are bound together. Shape into a smooth ball; the dough will be fairly soft. Dust lightly with flour and wrap in a plastic bag. Refrigerate for 1 hour.

3. Place the remaining butter between 2 sheets of plastic and beat with the rolling pin until pliable.

4. Work ¼ cup flour into the butter. Roll the butter into a thin sheet between the 2 pieces of plastic. The butter and the dough (*détrempe*) must be *exactly* the same temperature and consistency.

5. Place the dough on a lightly floured work surface. Dust the dough and the rolling pin lightly with flour. Roll the dough from the center toward the top or bottom into a large *neat* rectangle, approximately 8 by 18 inches.

6. Cover the upper two-thirds of the dough with butter, leaving a ¾-inch border around 3 sides. Starting with the lower, unbuttered portion of the dough, fold the rectangle in thirds as for a letter. Press the edges firmly to seal.

7. Turn the dough clockwise so that the open side is on your right. Roll the dough again into a large, neat rectangle. Fold into thirds again, repeating this step of turning, rolling, and folding once more. This is known as two turns. Wrap the dough in plastic or foil and refrigerate for 1 hour.

8. Repeat rolling, turning, and folding four times with a 30-minute (or longer) resting period between turns. The dough will be too elastic and will shrink if it does not rest long enough. Chill the dough for at least 1 hour before using. If not used right away, cover with plastic wrap or foil and refrigerate. Puff pastry will keep in the refrigerator for 1 or 2 days or in the freezer for up to 1 month.

◆　　U N D E R　T H E　C O O K ' S　H A T　　◆

Most important, do not work this dough unless you have a cool kitchen.

Always remove excess flour from the dough with a brush, especially after each turn; otherwise, the dough will harden. The best brush is a thin clothes brush with natural bristles.

After each turn, make an indentation in the dough by pressing it slightly with your finger so you can keep count of the number of turns made.

Four turns makes a very adequate *pâte feuilletée*.

If the dough springs back and is difficult to roll, turn it over or let it rest for 10 to 20 minutes.

Never grease the baking sheet when using *pâte feuilletée*, but sprinkle it with water, which will hold the dough and prevent it from shrinking while baking.

Never glaze the cut part of the dough or it won't rise properly.

The baking time for *pâte feuilletée* is about 20 minutes in a preheated 400°F. oven, unless filled.

It is best to use some pastry flour with the unbleached flour to make a workable dough and a flakier pastry. Pastry flour—not to be confused with cake flour—is available at specialty shops or at your local bakery.

Mille-Feuille

NAPOLEON

Mille-feuille, which means "a thousand leaves," perfectly describes the flaky layers of this delicious pastry.

François Marin, in his book *Les dons de Comus* (1758), gave the recipe for *gâteau de mille-feuille*. It was made with 5 or 6 layers of puff pastry with white icing all over it and garnished with cutouts of candied lemon peel, or currant jelly.

Puff Pastry (see Index)
Pastry Cream (see Index)
1 cup sweetened whipped cream
Confectioners' sugar

1. Roll out the dough on a lightly floured surface into a large rectangle ⅛ inch thick. Let the dough rest for 30 minutes. Drape dough over the rolling pin and unroll on a moist baking sheet. Prick the surface of the dough at 1-inch intervals with the tines of a fork.

2. Bake the pastry in a preheated 400°F. oven for 25 minutes, or until light golden. Cool on a rack.

3. With a pastry wheel, cut the pastry into 3 lengthwise strips, about 4½ inches wide. Spread pastry cream combined with whipped cream on two of the strips. Place one strip neatly on top of the other. Invert the third and place on top of the top layer of pastry cream. Press down slightly, so that when the three slices are cut, they will not tend to separate.

4. Cut the strips into 1½-inch portions with a serrated knife.

Dust generously with vanilla-flavored confectioners' sugar. Serve immediately.

◆　*Variations*　◆

Spread strawberry jelly on two of the layers of puff pastry. Scatter fresh strawberries on top, then spread sweetened whipped cream over all.

For another unusual combination, spread each layer with honey and then 1½ cups whipped cream mixed with 2 stiffly beaten egg whites. Dust the top with confectioners' sugar.

PIE SHELL OF PUFF PASTRY

1. On a lightly floured surface, roll out Puff Pastry (see Index) into a large circle, ⅛ inch thick. Let the dough rest for 15 minutes.

2. Lightly moisten a baking sheet. Roll up the dough on the rolling pin and unroll on the baking sheet.

3. Cut the dough into a square, rectangle, or circle, using a ruler or the bottom of a pie ring as a guide.

4. Turn the dough in to make a 1-inch border all the way around. Raise this border to make a standing rim. With a sharp knife, make diagonal slashes half-way through the dough, about every half inch; this will help the sides of the pie to rise and form a border. Chill 30 minutes.

5. Prick pastry all over the bottom, so it won't puff up too much. Line the shell with wax paper and fill with dried beans and bake in a preheated 400°F. oven for 10 minutes. Remove wax paper and beans and bake for another 10 to 15 minutes, or until the dough is light golden.

Tarte Feuilletée aux Poires

CARAMELIZED PEAR PIE

½ recipe Puff Pastry (see Index)　　　　　　*6 servings*
6 large ripe pears
1½ cups sugar
1 cup water
2-inch pieces of lemon rind, without white portion
1 teaspoon vanilla extract
Confectioners' sugar

1. Prepare and bake a pie shell of puff pastry.

2. Peel the pears and cut into halves. Core with a melon-ball cutter and cut out the fibers with a knife.

3. Combine the sugar, water, and lemon rind in a saucepan. Stir over low heat until the sugar is dissolved.

4. Poach the pears in the syrup over low heat until tender but still firm. Add the vanilla and let the pears cool in the syrup.

5. Cut the pear halves into ¼-inch slices across, and keep the slices close together. Transfer the pears with a spatula to the pie crust. Fan the slices by pressing each pear half gently toward the border, so you have a row of overlapping slices.

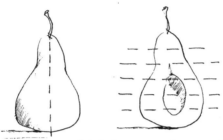

6. Reduce the syrup over high heat until very thick and almost caramelized. Pour the syrup over the pears.

7. Heat the pie in a preheated 550°F. oven for a few minutes. Remove from the oven and sprinkle with confectioners' sugar. Serve warm.

◆   *Variation*   ◆

Warm a few spoonfuls of the caramelized syrup with 1 cup of orange marmalade. Glaze the tart with this mixture.

Tarte Galette Feuilletée aux Pommes

APPLE PIE WITH PUFF PASTRY

This thin pie with its light, crisp pastry covered with sliced apples represents a fruit tart at its best. It is served warm.

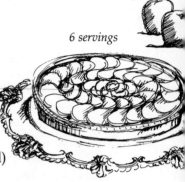

½ recipe Puff Pastry (see Index) *6 servings*
5 or 6 large flavorful apples, peeled, cored,
    and cut into ½-inch-thick slices
3 tablespoons unsalted butter
2 teaspoons lemon juice
2 teaspoons pure vanilla extract
Granulated sugar
Vanilla-flavored confectioners' sugar (optional)

1. Prepare the pastry. Roll out the dough ⅛ inch thick into a 12-inch circle. Let the dough rest 15 minutes. Drape the dough over the rolling pin and invert on a dampened baking sheet.

2. Fold the dough up all around to make a 6-inch raised rim. Chill the dough for 30 minutes.

3. With the blunt edge of a knife, make straight cuts halfway through the thickness of the border of dough so that it will rise.

4. Arrange the apples in one layer, starting near the edge of the crust, to form a circle of closely overlapping slices. Make a second row, touching the first but facing the other direction. Fill the center with a rosette of apple slices.

5. Melt the butter, then add the lemon juice and vanilla extract. Brush the apples with this mixture and dust generously with granulated sugar.

6. Bake the pie in a preheated 450°F. oven for about 25 minutes, without peeking. It is done when the edges of the apples are golden brown. Serve while warm as is or sift vanilla-flavored confectioners' sugar all over.

◆   UNDER THE COOK'S HAT   ◆

For more than 6 servings, use a rectangular baking sheet 15½ by 10½ inches.

◆ *Tarte Tatin* ◆

Tarte Tatin was accidentally created in the late 1800s by Caroline and Stephanie Tatin, owners of a hotel that still exists across from the train station in Lamotte-Beuvron in Sologne.

Caroline, the younger sister, managed the family inn, which became popular with hunters who stopped to taste the famous pie created and cooked by her sister, Stephanie, who reigned over the kitchen.

The invention of the pie was the result of clumsiness; the pie was dropped, then was picked up and served upside down with the crust on top. It was such a hit that they began to prepare it that way on purpose. It was the famous gastronome Curnonsky who, in 1926, discovered the Tatin sisters' inn and their delicious apple pie and made its reputation.

Tarte des Demoiselles Tatin

UPSIDE-DOWN CARAMELIZED APPLE PIE

½ recipe Puff Pastry (see Index)   *6 servings*
1 cup sugar
¼ pound unsalted butter
1 tablespoon vanilla extract
10 large flavorful apples, peeled, cored, each cut into 8 pieces
Crème Fraîche (see Index), or equal parts of heavy cream and
    sour cream mixed 12 hours ahead

1. Prepare the pastry. Roll dough into an 11-inch round about ¼ inch thick. Chill for 30 minutes.

2. In a small heavy pan cook ¾ cup of the sugar with just enough water to moisten until it is a golden caramel color. Pour immediately into a 10-inch white porcelain quiche pan, tipping so the bottom is covered with caramel.

3. Melt the butter in a large skillet. Add the vanilla. Sauté the

apples for 2 or 3 minutes, then add remaining sugar. Turn with a spatula once or twice, without crushing the apples.

4. Make 2 layers of apples in the caramelized pie pan, building up slightly in the center. Place the dough over the hot apples, tucking 1 inch inside the pan all around the edge. Prick the dough in a few places with a knife.

5. Place the pie pan on a baking sheet and bake on the lowest shelf of a preheated 450°F. oven for about 25 minutes, or until the crust is golden brown. Cover loosely with foil and bake for 10 more minutes.

6. Remove the pie from the oven and set aside for 10 minutes. Place the pie on a Flame-Tamer over high heat for exactly 1 minute. Invert the pie onto a serving dish so the crust is on the bottom and the caramelized apples are on top. Serve with a bowl of *crème fraîche*.

◆   ◆   ◆

Curnonsky, the pseudonym for Maurice-Edmond Sailland, was elected the "Prince of Gastronomes" in 1927. A few years earlier, Curnonsky had traveled all over France by car in search of fine inns and restaurants that served the masterpieces of provincial cooking.

Following his extensive tour, he published a guide for each province that featured regional cooking, such as *quiche lorraine, choucroute alsacienne,* and *tarte Tatin.* This gave birth to a third cuisine, *cuisine régionale,* as *haute cuisine* and *cuisine bourgeoise* already were recognized. Curnonsky summed it up when he said, "Regional cookery reflects the climate, the manner of living, the spirit of a country."

Allumettes Glacées

ICED MATCHSTICK PASTRIES

These delicious *petits fours* originated in Dinard in the middle of the last century. Monsieur Planta, a pastry cook at a loss as to what to do with some leftover icing, spread it on thinly rolled puff pastry. Afterward he cut it into small strips and baked them. These *allumettes* were an immediate success.

1. Roll the puff pastry to a long strip, a scant ¼ inch thick. Using a ruler as a guide, cut the strips 4½ inches wide with a pastry cutter. The length depends upon the number of *allumettes* desired. Let the dough rest for 30 minutes.

2. Spread the icing thinly and evenly with a rounded spatula over the top of the dough. Let it rest for 8 minutes. Cut the band across in strips 1½ inches wide and transfer these one by one to a moist baking sheet. Make sure that the icing does not go on the cut part, which would prevent the dough from rising properly.

3. Bake on the middle shelf in a preheated 375°F. oven for about 20 minutes, or until the *allumettes* are raised and the icing is a deep and even beige.

Glace Royal

WHITE ICING

Beat with a mixer 1 egg white with 1½ cups confectioners' sugar until stiff. Add a few drops of lemon juice, a pinch of salt, and ½ teaspoon vanilla extract.

• • •

Noël, the French cook of Frederick II of Prussia, invented the pastry wheel at the beginning of the eighteenth century. He originally used the spur of a horseman, supposedly that of the king. The pastry wheel as we know it today has evolved from this.

Fleurons

PUFF PASTRY CRESCENTS

Fleurons are little crescents made of *pâte feuilletée* and used as a garnish for elegant dishes. They were already being served at the court of the Grand Dukes of Tuscany in the fifteenth century for decorating spinach. They are attractive served with fish in cream sauce.

Fleurons can be made with leftover puff pastry or commercial patty shells.

To make *fleurons:* Roll the pastry a scant ¼-inch thick. With a 2½- to 3-inch fluted round pastry cutter, cut out neat crescent shapes by placing the pastry cutter 1 inch above the previous fluted outline. Keep cutting half-moons, working from the bottom toward the top. Allow the crescents to rest for about 30 minutes.

Place the crescents on a baking sheet sprinkled with cold water.

Brush the tops lightly with an egg yolk mixed with 2 teaspoons water, taking care that the egg does not drip down the sides or they won't puff. Bake in a preheated 400°F. oven for 15 to 20 minutes, or until puffed up and golden.

◆   UNDER THE COOK'S HAT   ◆

To keep a supply of crescents on hand, place the unbaked crescents on a lightly greased baking sheet. Freeze, then slip them into a plastic bag and store in the freezer.

◆ *Vol-au-Vent* ◆

Carême was making a *tourte* (covered tart) at Allain, the confectionery shop on rue Gaillon in Paris, when he omitted the traditional band that surrounds a *tourte*. He cut 2 rounds of dough to exactly the same size, fitted one on top of the other, and cut a circle of dough from the center of the upper layer.

When the ovenkeeper, Fournier, saw it come out of the oven, he said, *"Antonin! Elle vole au vent!"* (She flies in the wind.) Its light, high appearance made it an immediate success and *vol-au-vent* (patty shell) soon replaced the *tourte*.

Petits Vol-au-Vent

PATTY SHELLS

Puff Pastry (see Index)
1 egg yolk, beaten with 1 tablespoon cold water

1. Roll out puff pastry to ¼-inch thickness. Let the dough rest for 30 minutes.
2. Cut circles 3 to 3½ inches in diameter with a fluted or plain round pastry cutter.
3. Cut out the center of half of these circles with a 1½-inch-diameter pastry cutter. The rings will form the borders and the small rounds will be the tops.

4. Brush all around the surface of the solid circle with water. Place the ring on top and press slightly.

5. Lift the circles onto a dampened baking sheet. Brush the tops of the circles and the small rounds with the egg wash. Be careful not to let egg wash run down the sides or dough will not rise properly. Allow the pastry to rest for 1 hour.

6. Bake in a preheated 425°F. oven for 18 to 20 minutes, or until golden brown. The shells are now ready to be filled. After filling, top with the small rounds.

♦   UNDER THE COOK'S HAT   ♦

In order to prevent the shells from becoming lopsided while baking, cover with two layers of foil.

♦   ♦   ♦

In 1683 Vienna was the last rampart in Europe against the Turks. The Austrians resisted the Turkish siege heroically. One night the Turks began to tunnel under the city. The bakers of Vienna, who had started to work at dawn, heard the sounds of the picks and gave an alert. The Austrians were then able to capture their enemies, thanks to the bakers.

In honor of their heroism, the bakers' guild was given the privilege of making rolls in the shape of a crescent moon, which is the Turkish emblem.

Les Croissants

CRESCENT ROLLS

It was at the turn of the century that French bakers started to use this dough, a combination of raised dough and puff pastry dough. It should be started the day before the croissants are to be served because the dough must be refrigerated overnight.

¼ ounce active dry yeast   *Makes about 8 croissants*
1 cup spring water, lukewarm
1 tablespoon sugar
4 tablespoons instant dry milk
1 teaspoon salt
2 cups plus 3 tablespoons bread flour and additional flour as
    necessary
6 ounces (1½ sticks) unsalted butter
1 egg yolk beaten with 2 teaspoons water

1. In a large bowl, dissolve the yeast in the lukewarm water. Let stand 10 minutes, then add the sugar and dry milk.

2. Stir salt into the 2 cups of flour and add to the yeast mixture. Stir with a wooden spoon until all the liquid is absorbed. Shape quickly into a smooth ball, adding more flour if too sticky. The dough should be quite soft. Place in a buttered bowl, cover with a towel, and let the dough double in volume in a warm place such as an oven with a pilot light or preheated for 1 minute (80–85°F.) Refrigerate the dough for 2 to 3 hours.

3. Place the butter between 2 plastic sheets. Beat with a rolling pin until it is softened and pliable. Work the 3 tablespoons of flour into the butter and then flatten and roll it between plastic sheets.

4. Gently punch down the dough with floured hands. Add just enough flour so that the sticky dough may be easily handled. Roll it out on a lightly floured surface into an 8- by 16-inch *neat* rectangle.

5. Dot two-thirds of the dough with the flattened butter, cut into small pieces, leaving a 1½-inch margin on 3 sides. Fold the unbuttered third of the dough up over half of the buttered part. Fold again over the rest of the buttered third part of the dough like a business letter. Press down the edges.

6. Give it a quarter turn to the right, so that the open side is on your right. Roll the dough into a large, neat rectangle. Fold into thirds again and repeat this step again. This is known as two "turns." Wrap the dough in plastic and refrigerate for 30 minutes.

7. Repeat the rollings and foldings twice again. Wrap the dough tightly in plastic and refrigerate overnight.

8. Roll the dough into a large rectangle on a lightly floured surface, 1/16 inch thick. Let the dough rest for 15 minutes.

9. With a pastry wheel, cut into two strips, then into 8-inch squares. Cut each square into two triangles. Loosely roll each triangle from the wide end, stretching it slightly, toward the point. Place the croissants on a lightly buttered baking sheet with the point touching the surface (but not tucked underneath). Curve the ends into a crescent shape. Let the croissants rise in a warm place until almost double in size.

10. Brush the croissants lightly with the egg wash, being careful not to touch the cut edges. Place the croissants in a preheated 400°F. oven. Throw 3 ice cubes in the bottom of the oven. (The melting ice cubes will create steam and will make the croissants crisp.) Bake for 20 minutes or until the croissants are golden brown. Cool on wire racks. They are at their best eaten lukewarm.

◆ UNDER THE COOK'S HAT ◆

Croissants can be frozen. To heat them, place still frozen in a pre-heated 400°F. oven. Throw 3 ice cubes in the bottom of the oven to crisp the croissants.

This recipe, adapted for home bakers, was given to me while watching the famous croissants being made at three o'clock in the morning on board the S.S. *France*.

Work in a cool kitchen. A plastic sheet placed on the dough is helpful in rolling the dough and prevents the addition of extra flour, which hardens it.

Powdered milk, thought of as a rather recent invention, was the staple diet of the Tatars, in the thirteenth century. After removing the cream, which was made into butter, the milk was put in the sun to dry. When going on expeditions, the Tatars would each take 10 pounds of this powdered milk and churn it in leather bottles with water to make a pap; this was their meal.

Pâte Brisée

TART OR FLAN PASTRY

For a 9-inch pastry shell or 7 tartlet shells

1 cup plus 2 tablespoons all-purpose flour, sifted
¼ cup plus 2 tablespoons cake flour
1 teaspoon sugar (1½ tablespoons for dessert tarts)
½ teaspoon salt
6 tablespoons unsalted butter, at room temperature
2 tablespoons solid shortening
3 tablespoons cold water, approximately

1. In a large mixing bowl, combine the flours, sugar, salt, butter in bits, and shortening. Mix lightly with both hands, rubbing the flour and fat together until crumbly. Add just enough water to hold the mixture together. Knead the dough quickly until it can be gathered into a ball. Dust with a little flour and cover with plastic wrap. Chill for 2 hours.

2. Roll out the dough to a thin sheet between 2 pieces of plastic wrap. Remove the top sheet of plastic and invert the dough onto a French fluted metal flan ring with a detachable bottom. (For a larger pie crust, roll up the dough on the rolling pin and unroll it on a baking sheet.) Ease the dough into the flan ring without stretching or it will shrink when baked.

3. Roll the rolling pin across the top to cut away excess dough.

Gently press the dough against the sides of the ring with your fingers. The dough around the sides should be thicker than that on the bottom. Or press the dough against the sides of the ring firmly enough to raise it ¼ inch above the rim, and then, with a pastry crimper, pinch the dough to make indentations on the bias every ½ inch. If you do not have a pastry crimper, use the dull edge of a knife to make indentations in the edging of the dough in the same way.

4. Line the dough with wax paper, extending it 1 inch above the rim, and fill with raw rice or dried beans. Place on a baking sheet and bake in a preheated 400°F. oven for 10 minutes. Remove the wax paper and rice, then return to the oven for 10 to 15 minutes, or until light golden. Cool the shell in the pie ring.

5. Place the pie tin on a small bowl and let the rim slide down. With a spatula, slide the pie shell onto a serving plate.

♦   UNDER THE COOK'S HAT   ♦

If the crust is going to be filled with a creamy filling, brush the dough with an egg yolk beaten with 1 tablespoon cold water. Return to the oven for 5 to 8 minutes, or until set.

Dough for a piecrust must be worked very rapidly, using the tips of the fingers. The longer it is worked, the tougher the dough becomes. The flaw ring should be liberally buttered.

Baking sheets must be in first-class condition for best results. Therefore it is necessary to replace them as they show signs of wear.

Keep a jar of raw rice or dried beans for baking crusts. The same rice or beans can be used over and over again.

Pâte à Foncer Sucrée

SWEET SHORT-CRUST PASTRY

Similar to a cookie dough, *pâte sucrée* is used for fruit pies and tartlets.

1½ cups sifted flour   *For a 9-inch pastry shell or 7 tartlet shells*
4 tablespoons sugar
¼ teaspoon salt
¼ pound unsalted butter, at room temperature, cut into pieces
2 tablespoons shortening
Few drops of vanilla, lemon, or orange extract
2 egg yolks

1. Combine in a bowl the flour, sugar, and salt. Add the butter and shortening. With fingertips, rub the flour, butter, and shortening together until the texture resembles coarse cornmeal. Do not overmix or the pastry will toughen.

2. Add the flavoring and egg yolks. Knead the dough just long enough to incorporate the yolks and to form dough into a ball. Cover with plastic wrap, and refrigerate for 2 hours.

3. This dough is hard to roll and if pieced together it will separate once baked. Place the dough between 2 pieces of plastic wrap. Roll the dough into a ⅛-inch-thick round. Transfer to pie pan and then proceed as for Pâte Brisée (preceding recipe), step 3, except that there is no need for the lining of wax paper and the rice.

Tarte Bourdaloue

PIE BOURDALOUE

Tarte Bourdaloue is known around the world. Its invention is attributed to Briam, owner of a pastry shop on the rue de Bourdaloue in Paris at the end of the last century. His establishment was named Pâtisserie Bourdaloue after the street that honored Louis Bourdaloue, a celebrated clergyman of the seventeenth century who preached at Versailles.

The pastry shop is still flourishing today, where copper molds stamped with the name Briam can be seen.

6 servings

1. Make a Puff Pastry shell or 1 recipe Sweet Short-Crust Pastry (see Index).

2. Half fill with Pastry Cream (see Index) flavored with kirsch.

3. Arrange half pears cooked in syrup (or canned) on top of the pastry cream, placing the pointed ends toward the center. Glaze with strained, warm apricot jam.

◆   *Variation*   ◆

Halves of apricots or pineapple garnished with candied red cherries can be substituted for the pears.

◆   ◆   ◆

When Richard the Lion-Heart was Duke of Guyenne in 1175, he issued this decree: "Whoever takes a bunch of grapes from the vineyard of his neighbor must pay 5 *sous* or lose an ear."

Tarte aux Raisins

GRAPE PIE

1 recipe Sweet Short-Crust Pastry (see Index)   *6 servings*
½ cup sugar
⅓ cup water
3 cups green seedless grapes
⅓ cup apricot preserves

1. Mix the pastry. Roll it out and fit into a 9-inch pie pan. Bake in a preheated 425°F. oven until golden.
2. Combine the sugar and water and cook to the soft-ball stage (230°F. on a candy thermometer), about 5 minutes.
3. Cook the grapes in the syrup for 2 to 3 minutes. Transfer with a skimmer to the piecrust. Arrange the grapes in a single layer touching each other.
4. In a small saucepan, combine the apricot preserves with 3 tablespoons of the syrup. Cook until bubbles form around the edges of the pan. Brush the grapes and the edges of the piecrust with the preserves. Serve at room temperature, or reheat the pie briefly before serving.

◆   *Variations*   ◆

Fill the baked shell with fresh raspberries, close together. Brush fruits and border with raspberry glaze. Decorate the top with a lattice design of sweetened whipped cream piped from a decorative tube.

Arrange 1 quart fresh strawberries points up, close together, in one layer on the baked shell. Brush the fruits and border with raspberry glaze mixed with 1 tablespoon kirsch. Serve a bowl of sweetened whipped cream, flavored with vanilla.

Cook 4 cups fresh blueberries with 1 cup of sugar until berries are soft. Combine 1½ tablespoons cornstarch, 1 tablespoon each of water and lemon juice, and a pinch of salt. Add to the blueberries and stir until the juice is thick and clear. Cool. Pour into the pie shell. Glaze fruits and border with raspberry glaze.

RASPBERRY OR CURRANT GLAZE

To give a glaze and professional finish to pies with red fruits, combine ¾ cup raspberry or currant jelly with 3 tablespoons sugar and

2 tablespoons water. Boil over low heat, stirring until the syrup sheets from the side of a spoon. For light fruits (apple, pineapple, pear, peach, apricot), use an apricot glaze.

Gently coat the surface of the fruits and pie border with the hot glaze, using a flat pastry brush.

La Brioche

BRIOCHE

Brioche is one of the oldest French bread cakes, dating back to the Middle Ages. Brie cheese, from which brioche took its name, was originally one of its ingredients but was later replaced by butter.

By the middle of the eighteenth century, Gisors and Gournay were especially known for their fine brioches. Today, throughout France, it is one of the best-loved bread cakes, and an individual brioche served with butter for breakfast is considered the most delicious way to start the day.

This dough is usually prepared a day ahead of baking and works best if made in large quantities. The following recipe makes enough for two large brioches (*brioches à tête*); if only one is required, half of the dough may be frozen and kept for as long as a month before using. Thaw for 24 hours under refrigeration before baking.

½ ounce fresh yeast in cakes or 2 packages (¼ ounce each)
    active dry yeast
⅓ cup lukewarm milk
About 3½ to 4 cups bread flour
6 large eggs, lightly beaten, at room temperature
2 tablespoons sugar
2 teaspoons salt
A generous ¼ teaspoon lemon extract
2 sticks or 8 ounces softened unsalted butter
2 egg yolks beaten with 1 tablespoon water

1. Soften the yeast in the milk for 10 minutes.
2. Warm up a large bowl with hot water; then dry.
3. Sift 3 cups of the flour into the bowl, and make a well in the center. Pour the yeast mixture in the middle. With a fork, stir just enough flour into it from the sides to make a very soft mush, leaving the rest of the flour untouched. Dust the top of this batter lightly with the surrounding flour. Cover the bowl with a cloth and put it

in a warm place, such as an oven with a pilot light or an electric oven preheated 1 minute (80–85°F.).

4. When the dough has doubled in volume (1 to 1½ hours), add the eggs, sugar, salt, and lemon extract. Stir with a wooden spoon until all is roughly blended. Knead the very soft and sticky dough in the bowl with your hands while sifting in the remaining flour a little at a time. Draw the dough up high and slap it down again and again for about 5 minutes. Then remove and work the dough on the table for 10 more minutes or until the dough separates easily from your hands like putty.

5. Break the butter into small pieces on top of the dough. With your hands, work the butter into the dough quickly, no longer than 3 minutes. It does not matter if some butter remains unblended. Place the dough in a large, buttered bowl. Cover with a cloth and let it rise in a warm place for 1 to 1½ hours, or until the dough has doubled in bulk.

6. Flatten the dough with floured fingers, then stretch it two or three times. Because the dough is so rich in butter, it cannot be shaped while warm. Therefore, cover and refrigerate the dough and let it rise a second time all day if made in the morning or overnight if made in the afternoon.

SHAPING THE DOUGH (for *brioche à tête*)

For one brioche, use half of the dough and reserve the rest for later. On a floured surface, divide this amount of dough into 2 balls —one a little more than three-quarters, for the base, and one a little less than one-quarter, for the head. Place the larger ball into a well-buttered brioche mold that measures 6½ inches across the top and 3¾ inches at the bottom. The dough should fill it about half full. With two fingers dipped in flour, make a small conical hole 2 inches deep and 2 inches wide in the center of this ball. Form the smaller piece of dough into a pear-shaped ball. Insert it, pointed end down, into the hole. The top of this ball should be level with the top of the mold. Then, with a sharp knife dipped in water, make 6 slashes in the dough around the base of the head. It will make the head stand out while baking. Brush the dough with the egg glaze (except where the head joins the base), being careful not to let it drip down the mold. Preheat the oven and a baking sheet to 425°F. Place mold on baking sheet and bake 30 minutes or until the brioche is a deep, rich brown in color. Test by inserting a thin knife into it. If it comes out dry, the brioche is done. Unmold. Serve warm or reheat before serving.

Petites Brioches
SMALL BRIOCHES

Small brioches are shaped the same way as *brioche à tête*, and baked in small fluted brioche molds, in a preheated 425°F. oven for about 15 minutes. Brioche dough can also be baked in a generously buttered loaf mold in a preheated 375°F. oven for 40 minutes or until deep brown.

Brioche en Couronne
BRIOCHE RING

In the South of France, a ring-shaped brioche replaces the more usual Galette for the feast of Twelfth Night.

Add to the dough an additional ¼ cup of sugar. Flavor with 1 tablespoon of orange-blossom water or 1 teaspoon pure orange extract. Flatten the dough. Spread the top with ½ cup candied fruits (rinsed thoroughly if not imported) that have been soaked several hours in ¼ cup Cognac. Shape the dough into a ball. With two fingers dipped in flour, make a hole in the center of the ball, turning the dough around your fingers to enlarge the hole to 7 inches in diameter. The dough should have the same thickness all around. Place on a large, slightly buttered baking sheet. Insert a dry white bean inside and underneath the dough if served for Twelfth Night. Let the dough rise to a little more than double in bulk. Glaze gently. With scissors dipped in water, cut 1½-inch slices on a slant, 1 inch deep all around the crown at an interval of 1½ inches. Garnish with candied cherries and angelica. Spread coarse crystallized sugar over all and bake on the middle shelf of a preheated 425°F. oven for about 25 minutes. Cover loosely with foil if it becomes too brown.

◆ UNDER THE COOK'S HAT ◆

Brioche dries out quickly so store it in a plastic bag.

◆ *Variation* ◆

Brioche ring is delicious made with the addition of 1½ cups diced Swiss cheese and ½ cup grated Parmesan. This is a specialty of the province of Auvergne, where it is made with Cantal cheese.

• *Galette des Rois* •

Galette des rois (Three Kings' Cake) is one of the oldest French cakes. It is served on Epiphany, the Feast of the Three Kings, which is celebrated in France, especially in the South.

Since 1874 a bean, or a tiny metal doll, representing the infant Jesus has been inserted into the dough before baking. The recipient of the bean is crowned King or Queen and is toasted by everyone at the table.

Originally Epiphany was celebrated with a simple *galette*, a word derived from *galet* (pebble) because of its flat, round shape. It was an unleavened bread made for the use of sailors.

In the ninth century, on Epiphany, Louis III annually chose the poorest child in Paris, dressed him in royal clothing, invited him to eat at the royal table, crowned him the King of Twelfth Night, and gave the child money for an education.

During the Revolution, Epiphany was declared "the feast of the good neighborhood," and the *galette des rois* was renamed "the cake of equality."

General Charles de Gaulle faithfully celebrated the Feast of the Three Kings with his family. He observed it three times at the Hôstellerie de l'Abbaye de la Celle in Provence, where the *galette* is a brioche crown decorated with candied fruits. Three beans were placed in the cake for the General's three children. When his sister-in-law remarked that it was not the custom, the General replied gallantly that "one was for the King, one for the Queen, and another for his favorite . . ."

Until the First World War, it was the custom for pastry makers to give the *galette des rois* to their customers in celebration of the day.

• *Baba au Rhum* •

The invention of *baba au rhum* is attributed to Stanislas Leczinski, King of Poland; after he was driven from Poland, he was made Governor of Lorraine by his son-in-law, Louis XV. A great reader of *A Thousand and One Nights*, Stanislas gave the name of its hero, Ali Baba, to this creation which later was shortened to Baba.

While residing in the city of Nancy, Stanislas had the idea of soaking a Kugelhopf, a specialty of Strasbourg and similar to a *brioche*, in a syrup of Málaga wine—his invention. Later the Málaga wine was replaced with rum; thus was born the Ali Baba au Rhum.

Baba au Rhum

0.6 ounce fresh yeast in paste or ¼ ounce active dry yeast
½ cup plus 1 tablespoon tepid milk
2 cups sifted bread flour
3 eggs, at room temperature
5 tablespoons unsalted butter
1½ tablespoons confectioners' sugar
½ teaspoon salt
½ cup dried currants
¼ cup golden raisins
Butter for mold

RUM SYRUP
1¾ cups water
1½ cups sugar
½ cup dark rum

1. Soften the yeast in the milk.
2. Warm up a large bowl under hot water, and then dry it.
3. Sift the flour into the bowl and make a well in the center. Pour the yeast mixture into the middle. Stir in enough flour from the sides with a fork to make a very soft mush, leaving the rest untouched. Dust lightly with flour and set the bowl in a warm place, such as an oven with a pilot light or an oven preheated for 1 minute (80–85°F.)
4. About 40 minutes later, or when the top of the soft dough has cracks and has doubled in volume, add the eggs, slightly beaten. Stir with a fork, then with your hand, adding the surrounding flour to form a smooth dough. Transfer to a greased bowl. Cover and put it in a warm place until the dough is double in bulk or about 1 hour.
5. Melt the butter with the sugar and salt until tepid. Pour over the dough. Beat the dough, lifting it high and dropping it in the bowl, for about 10 minutes, or until the dough detaches itself in one mass, and is very elastic. Add the currants and raisins.

6. Put the dough into a generously buttered baba or Kugelhopf mold. It should be one-third to half full. Let the dough rise in a warm place until it reaches the brim of the mold.

7. Immediately set the mold on a baking sheet and bake in a 375°F. oven for about 40 minutes, or until a skewer inserted in the center comes out clean. After 15 minutes of baking, cover loosely with a piece of foil the size of the mold.

8. When the cake is done, invert the mold on a wire rack and place a thick towel over the mold. After 10 minutes, loosen the edge of the cake carefully with a sharp knife, and unmold. Cool until it is warm.

9. Prepare the syrup. Bring the water and sugar to a boil and simmer until dissolved. When the syrup is tepid, add the rum and pour it in the baba mold. Slowly replace the cake. This procedure will allow the baba to wait for several hours without getting dry.

10. Unmold on a serving plate and serve with a bowl of sweetened whipped cream, flavored with vanilla.

◆   U N D E R   T H E   C O O K' S   H A T   ◆

For individual babas, butter the molds generously and fill halfway up with the dough. Let the dough rise to the brim and bake for 20 to 30 minutes. These small babas treated as savarin are very attractive. Brush them with an apricot glaze; top with a large rosette of sweetened whipped cream and a red candied cherry in the center. Put a piece of angelica cut in a diamond shape on both sides. A 6-cup ring mold can be used, decorated the same way, with rosettes around the bottom edge of the baba.

◆ *Savarin* ◆

Savarin, a variation of the baba, was the creation of Auguste Julien, *Maître Pâtissier* at the pastry shop of Monsieur Chiboust in Bordeaux in 1845. Julien kept secret the syrup recipe used on his Savarin.

His creation was dedicated to Brillat-Savarin, but the first part of his name was dropped so that it became simply "Savarin."

Savarin à la Chantilly
SAVARIN WITH WHIPPED CREAM

Make a baba dough (see Index), omitting the raisins. Place dough in a generously buttered savarin mold or a 6-cup rounded ring mold. Proceed as for the baba recipe. Unmold immediately after baking.

Just before serving, brush the savarin with ¾ cup apricot jam, boiled and strained through a fine sieve. Pipe 2 cups of heavy cream whipped, sweetened, and flavored with vanilla, into the center of the savarin in a round-topped pyramid. In the middle of the cream place a red candied cherry between 2 small pieces of diamond-shaped angelica. Use the same motif all around the top of the savarin, spacing each design a few inches apart.

◆   *Variations*   ◆

Pineapple pieces can be added to the whipped cream. Or flavor the syrup with kirsch. Macerate strawberries with sugar for 1 hour and mix with the whipped cream. Garnish the base of the savarin with strawberries, centered in rosettes of whipped cream.

La Bûche de Noël

YULE LOG

The *bûche de Noël* in France is an extra large log, which traditionally burns all through Christmas Eve.

French pastry shops always have a replica of this log at Christmastime. This symbolic cake is an important part of the Christmas Eve supper, or Réveillon.

BISCUIT DE SAVOIE   *10 servings*
5 eggs, separated, at room temperature
¾ cup confectioners' sugar, plus extra for dusting towel
1 teaspoon pure vanilla extract
2 tablespoons granulated sugar
½ cup cake flour

1. Preheat oven to 375°F. Line a baking sheet, 15½ by 10½ inches, with 1-inch rim all around, with wax paper. Do not butter or flour the pan or paper.

2. Combine egg yolks, confectioners' sugar, and vanilla in a large bowl. Beat with an electric mixer at low speed for about 4 minutes.

3. Beat egg whites until they form soft peaks. Add 2 tablespoons granulated sugar and beat until stiff.

4. Sift the cake flour over the egg whites and at the same time carefully fold both, a little at a time, into the yolk mixture with a large spatula, as for a soufflé.

5. Pour the batter into the prepared pan and spread evenly with a spatula. Bake for 14 to 18 minutes without opening the oven door, or until the cake springs back when touched lightly.

6. Turn out the cake on a towel that has been dusted generously with confectioners' sugar. Peel off wax paper and roll towel and cake together lengthwise.

MOCHA-RUM BUTTERCREAM

6 ounces (1½ sticks) unsalted butter, at room temperature
¾ cup sugar
⅓ cup water
4 egg yolks
1 tablespoon instant coffee powder, dissolved in 2 teaspoons hot water
1 teaspoon vanilla extract
2 tablespoons rum

1. Cream the butter with an electric beater until light and fluffy.

2. Combine the sugar and water to make a syrup and let the syrup boil for 8 to 10 minutes, or until it forms a thread when dropped from a spoon (219°F. on a candy thermometer).

3. Beat the egg yolks for 1 minute, then pour in the syrup in a thin stream, beating constantly. Set the bowl of egg yolks in a pan of cold water and beat until the mixture reaches *exactly* the temperature of the butter. Add the butter in bits to the egg-yolk and syrup mixture, beating constantly until the mixture is firm enough to hold its shape. Add all flavorings.

4. If the buttercream should curdle, set the bowl in a pan of hot water and beat until smooth again.

CHOCOLATE BUTTERCREAM

6 ounces (1½ sticks) unsalted butter, at room temperature
6 ounces semisweet chocolate
⅓ cup milk
3 egg yolks
1 cup confectioners' sugar
1 tablespoon pure vanilla extract

1. Cream the butter. Combine the chocolate and milk in a saucepan and set over low heat, stirring until the chocolate is melted. Off the heat, add the egg yolks and butter and mix with an electric beater.

2. Add sugar and vanilla to the mixture and beat until creamy smooth. Chill until firm, but still of a spreading consistency.

MERINGUE MUSHROOMS

1. Beat 1 egg white until very stiff. Add 3 tablespoons sugar and beat again until very stiff. Reserve a little uncooked meringue.

2. With a pastry bag fitted with a no. 7 tube, or ½-inch round opening, press out the meringue onto a baking sheet lined with foil, holding the pastry bag vertically. Pull the meringue up to a point to make mushroom stems. Make 3 different-size round mounds, 1 to 1¼ inches in diameter, which will make the caps. They can be lightly dusted with a little cocoa powder before being baked.

3. Bake mushrooms in a 225°F. oven until dry but not colored. They must remain white.

4. Make a small hole in the bottom of each cap. Put a little uncooked meringue on the point of each stem and insert it into a mushroom cap. These meringue mushrooms can be made several days in advance. Store in a dry place.

TO ASSEMBLE THE LOG

1. Unroll the cake and spread the mocha-rum buttercream evenly on it, reserving some for ends and tree "knots." Roll up cake like a jelly roll, with the cut edges underneath. Cut off the ends diagonally. Use the cut-off portion to make knots. Place them near the ends of the log, using some of the buttercream underneath. Spread the surface of the knots as well as both ends of the log with remaining buttercream. Transfer the log to a large serving plate lined with paper doily.

2. Spread the chocolate buttercream thickly over the log with a large rounded knife or spatula. With a thick wooden fork, make ridges in the buttercream, the length of the log and up the knots, to simulate bark. Mark the knots and ends also with a silver fork so it will look like bark.

3. Sprinkle green crystal sugar partly on the knots to give the illusion of moss, and add a cluster of little meringue "mushrooms." Or decorate with marzipan holly leaves and candied cherries. Serve on a silver dish lined with a lace paper doily.

Biscuit Roulé

JELLY ROLL

6 to 8 servings

1. Prepare a Biscuit de Savoie (see Index). Line a baking sheet, 10½ by 15½ inches with a 1-inch rim all around, with unbuttered wax paper.

2. Spread batter in the prepared pan and bake the cake in a preheated 375°F. oven for 10 to 12 minutes, or until a knife inserted in the center comes out clean.

3. Dust a kitchen towel with confectioners' sugar. Turn the cake out onto the towel. After 10 minutes, remove the wax paper.

4. Heat strawberry, raspberry, or apricot jam until liquefied and spread a thin layer on the warm cake. Gently roll up the cake, and then sift vanilla and confectioners' sugar all over the cake.

◆   *Filling Variations*   ◆

Sprinkle the cake with raspberry brandy or kirsch, then spread on a layer of sweetened whipped cream. Put fresh raspberries on top, pressing them slightly into the cream. Or spread Pastry Cream (see Index) on cake layer, top with ground toasted almonds and roll up. Sift vanilla confectioners' sugar abundantly on all sides. Serve on a silver dish lined with a lace paper doily.

◆   UNDER THE COOK'S HAT   ◆

Do not open the door while the cake bakes; it will not rise properly.

Gâteau le Moka

MOCHA LAYER CAKE

Made with *génoise* dough, mocha cake was the creation of a pastry chef, Guignard, who in 1857 was located at the carrefour de l'Odéon in Paris.

Génoise, the basic dough for literally hundreds of varieties of French cakes and *petits fours*, was made famous by a pastry cook, Auguste Julien, in the middle of the nineteenth century. After seeing it made in Bordeaux by a Genoese pastry maker, Auguste

Julien brought it to Paris and named it *génoise* (from Genoa) for this baker.

Mocha is the name of the port city in Yemen from which the extremely strong, flavorful South Arabian coffee, rich in caffeine, was exported in past centuries. The city gave its name to the coffee. The *génoise* batter for this cake is flavored with mocha, which implies in France pure coffee. When a combination of beans is blended, it is simply called "coffee."

GÉNOISE BATTER
Butter for pans
6 eggs, at room temperature
1 cup sugar
Pinch of salt
2 teaspoons instant coffee powder, dissolved in 2 teaspoons hot
    water
1 teaspoon pure vanilla extract
1 cup cake flour
6 tablespoons Clarified Butter (see Index)

1. Preheat oven to 350°F. Butter and flour the sides only of 2 round cake pans, 8 inches across and 1½ inches deep. Line the bottoms with wax paper.

2. Place the eggs, sugar, and salt in a large bowl set in a larger container of warm water. This will help the eggs to whip to a greater volume. Beat with an electric beater for about 15 minutes, or until almost triple in volume. Add coffee essence and vanilla.

3. Sift the flour, in small amounts at a time, over the batter, at the same time folding thoroughly but gently with a spatula. Fold in the clarified butter.

4. Pour the batter into the prepared cake pans. Bake in the preheated oven for 25 to 30 minutes, or until the cake has shrunk slightly from the sides of the pans.

5. Turn the cakes immediately onto wire racks. When cool, gently remove the wax paper and make a small notch on the side of the cake from top to bottom so it can be correctly re-formed.

KIRSCH SYRUP
¼ cup water
¼ cup sugar
¼ cup kirsch

1. In a small heavy saucepan, boil the water and sugar for 5 minutes. Remove from the heat and add the kirsch.

MOCHA BUTTERCREAM

¾ pound unsalted butter, at room temperature

1½ cups sugar

⅓ cup water

5 egg yolks

2 tablespoons instant coffee, dissolved in 1 tablespoon hot
water

1 teaspoon pure vanilla extract

1. Cream the butter with an electric beater until light and fluffy.

2. Combine the sugar and water to make a syrup, and let the syrup boil for 8 to 10 minutes, or until it forms a thread when dropped from a spoon (219°F. on a candy thermometer). Cool to warm.

3. Beat the egg yolks for 1 minute, then pour in the syrup in a thin stream, beating constantly. Cool the mixture over a bowl of ice water until it reaches *exactly* the temperature of the butter.

4. Add the butter in parcel to the egg-yolk and syrup mixture, beating constantly until the mixture is firm enough to hold its shape. Add the flavorings.

5. If the buttercream is not to be used immediately, leave in a cool place but do not refrigerate or it will harden too much. If the buttercream should curdle, set the bowl in a pan of hot water and beat until smooth again.

TOASTED ALMONDS

⅓ cup blanched almonds

1. Chop the almonds in an electric blender or food processor.

2. Spread almonds in a large nonstick skillet. Cook slowly, stirring until light golden.

TO ASSEMBLE THE CAKE

1. Cut each cake horizontally in two, to make 4 layers. Brush 3 layers (all except the top one) with warm kirsch syrup.

2. Spread layers with mocha buttercream and reshape the cake, using the underside of the cake for the top, matching the notches carefully.

3. Spread the sides and the top with more mocha buttercream, smoothing it with a metal spatula knife dipped into hot water.

4. Lift the cake with a spatula and place your left hand underneath, tilting it on its side. Press chopped toasted almonds on the frosting all around the sides.

5. Decorate the top layer with a circle of rosettes of mocha buttercream touching one another, and place several in an attractive design in the center, or make a lattice design. Serve on a silver dish lined with a lace paper doily.

♦   U N D E R   T H E   C O O K ' S   H A T   ♦

This cake improves with a day of mellowing. Keep under refrigeration and bring to room temperature before serving.

♦   ♦   ♦

Dietetic meals are like an opera without the orchestra.
—PAUL BOCUSE

Biscuit Roulé aux Noix

WALNUT SPONGE ROLL

This exquisite light and delicate cake is simple to make.

7 eggs, separated, at room temperature   *10 servings*
2½ cups confectioners' sugar
¼ teaspoon orange extract
4 tablespoons cornstarch
1½ cups shelled walnuts or pecans, ground
2 cups heavy cream
1½ teaspoons instant coffee powder

1. Line with wax paper a baking sheet 10½ by 15½ inches with a 1-inch rim all around.
2. Beat the egg yolks, 1 cup confectioners' sugar, and the orange extract with a mixer until thickened.
3. Fold in the cornstarch, then add the ground nuts.
4. Beat the egg whites until soft peaks form. Gently fold in the nut mixture with a large rubber spatula.
5. Spoon the batter into the prepared baking sheet. Bake in a preheated 375°F. oven for 12 to 14 minutes without peeking. When a knife inserted in the center comes out clean, it is ready.
6. Dust a kitchen towel with confectioners' sugar. Turn the cake out onto the towel. When cool, remove the wax paper.
7. Whip the cream. When it begins to thicken, add the remaining confectioners' sugar and continue whipping until very thick. Reserve 2 cups of the cream for frosting.

8. Spread a thick layer of cream on the cake, then gently roll lengthwise. Cut a slice off each end on the bias.

9. Dissolve the instant coffee powder in 1 teaspoon hot water. Combine with the reserved cream. Spread the cream on the cake except for the ends. Make swirls with a fork, then dust with confectioners' sugar. With a spatula under each end, lift the cake onto a serving plate lined with a paper doily.

◆ UNDER THE COOK'S HAT ◆

To remove walnuts easily from their shells, soak them overnight. This will also prevent the shells from shattering. For each quart of water, add ¼ cup sugar.

Gâteau pour le Thé

TEA CAKE

This tea cake is simple to make and can be kept for a week. Its delicate flavor improves as the days pass. Serve thinly sliced with unsalted butter.

¼ pound unsalted butter
4 eggs
¾ cup sugar
Generous ¼ teaspoon lemon or almond extract
¼ teaspoon salt
⅓ cup milk
1 tablespoon double-acting baking powder
2 cups sifted flour

1. Melt the butter. Do not let it get hot. Set aside.

2. In a large bowl mix together the eggs, sugar, lemon extract and salt until just blended. Beat in the melted butter and the milk, then the baking powder mixed with the flour. Mix quickly until well blended.

3. Pour the batter into a buttered and floured narrow cake mold, 8½ by 3 by 3 inches. The batter should reach a little more than halfway up the sides of the mold.

4. Bake in a preheated 375°F. oven for about 45 minutes, or until a knife inserted in the middle comes out almost dry.

❖ *Pain d'Épices* ❖

Pain d'épices (spiced honey loaf) probably originated in the Near East. It was introduced in France by the hermit bishop Gregory about A.D. 992, when he came from Armenia. An eleventh-century manuscript from the Abbey of Micy relates that the hermit settled in a cavern two kilometers from the city of Pithiviers. Gregory shared his meals with priests and "devoted laymen to whom he would not only serve food for the body but also for the soul. With his own hands he made a cake using honey and spices, in the manner of his country, offering it with a smile on his lips after meals, during the singing of hymns and canticles. His guests, while eating it with pleasure, believed that they tasted all the delights of Paradise."

During the Middle Ages, *pain d'épices* was a favorite delicacy of Agnès Sorel, the mistress of Charles VII. His son, Louis XI, is thought to have poisoned her with it.

Pain d'Épices

SPICED HONEY LOAF

½ cup honey
⅓ cup sugar
½ cup water
2 teaspoons baking soda
1 teaspoon ground cinnamon
¼ teaspoon ground ginger
¼ teaspoon anise extract
½ teaspoon salt
2 cups medium rye flour (not rye meal)

1. Butter a loaf pan, 8 by 3 by 3 inches. Line with wax paper.
2. In a large saucepan, stir together the honey, sugar, and water over medium heat until sugar is melted. Do not boil. Off the heat, add the baking soda, spices, and salt. Stir in the flour, 1 cup at a time, until well blended.
3. Turn the batter into the prepared pan and let it rest overnight.
4. Wrap the pan in a double thickness of foil to keep the cake from rising while in the oven. Bake in a preheated 325°F. oven for 1

hour. Cool for 15 minutes in the pan, then turn out onto a wire rack. The flavor is even better if allowed to develop for a day before serving, thinly sliced, and spread with unsalted butter.

♦   UNDER THE COOK'S HAT   ♦

If honey is too thick to measure, place the jar in hot water until liquefied.

♦   *Variations*   ♦

Decorate the loaf with blanched almond halves before baking. Add ½ teaspoon pure orange extract. Or top with a white icing, made with confectioners' sugar and water or rum, when cool.

Madeleines

These small ridged cakes date back to the Middle Ages. They are made in shell shapes to commemorate the pilgrimage of those returning from Santiago de Compostela who stopped on their way home in Illiers. Madeleines were immortalized by Marcel Proust in *Remembrance of Things Past*.

3 eggs, at room temperature
⅔ cup sugar
½ teaspoon lemon extract
½ teaspoon vanilla extract
Pinch of salt
⅔ cup cake flour
½ cup (1 stick) Clarified Butter (see Index)

Makes 36 cookies

1. Warm a large bowl in hot water.
2. Beat the eggs, sugar, lemon extract, vanilla, and salt with a mixer at high speed for 10 minutes, until the batter has almost tripled in volume.
3. Sift the cake flour, ⅓ cup at a time, over the batter, folding gently each time with a large rubber spatula. Fold the butter, 1 tablespoon at a time, into the batter.
4. Generously butter and flour 2 sets of madeleine molds. Spoon about 1 tablespoon of batter into each shell, or until three-quarters

filled. Bake in a preheated 400°F. oven for 10 to 15 minutes, or until golden brown. Turn over to cool on a wire rack. Madeleines dry out fast. When cool, store immediately in a tightly covered container.

Tuiles aux Amandes

ALMOND WAFERS

These are probably the best-loved French cookies, light in consistency and easy to prepare. They are called *tuiles* (tiles) because the cookies look like the curved roof tiles on some French houses.

3 egg whites
½ cup plus 2 tablespoons sugar
¼ teaspoon salt
½ teaspoon pure vanilla extract
6 tablespoons flour, sifted
3 tablespoons Clarified Butter (see Index)
1 tablespoon heavy cream
1 cup shelled almonds, sliced or slivered

Makes 24 cookies

1. Combine the egg whites, sugar, salt, and vanilla with a fork until blended. Add the flour and mix well.
2. Stir in the butter and cream. Fold in the almonds.
3. Drop scant tablespoons of batter on a liberally buttered non-stick baking sheet, spacing the mounds about 3 inches apart. Flatten by using the back of a spoon to a circumference of about 2 inches. Bake 5 or 6 cookies at a time in a preheated 350°F. oven for 8 to 10 minutes, or until ½ inch of the edges is golden brown.
4. Remove the cookies with a round-ended spatula, turning them quickly onto a long piece of foil. Place another piece of foil on top. Roll the foil and cookies together around a French rolling pin or a cardboard cylinder 2 inches in diameter, until a curved shape is formed. This step must be done quickly while the cookies are hot and pliable so they will not break. Leave until cooled. Keep dry and crisp in a tightly sealed container.

◆   UNDER THE COOK'S HAT   ◆

If the cookies harden too fast, return to the oven until soft enough to bend.

◆ *Macaroons* ◆

The little round almond cookies with crisp crusts and chewy centers, known as macaroons, originated in the twelfth century in the city of Nancy.

During the French Revolution three nuns took refuge with a private family on the rue de la Hache in Nancy. While there, they continued to bake such delicious macaroons that their fame spread far beyond the neighborhood.

The cookies were called *macarons des soeurs* and still are, and the sisters were affectionately called *soeurs macarons* (macaroon sisters).

Macarons

MACAROONS

6 ounces almond paste, in can or bulk   *Makes 36 cookies*
1 cup sugar
3 or 4 egg whites
1 teaspoon vanilla extract

1. Knead the almond paste until softened and in small pieces. Add sugar, 3 egg whites, and the vanilla, and beat with a mixer until smooth. If the batter is too stiff, add half of another egg white. If not thick enough to hold its shape, add ¼ to ½ cup confectioners' sugar.

2. Line a baking sheet with parchment paper. Fill a pastry bag fitted with a plain tube with the mixture. Squeeze out a generous teaspoon for each macaroon, spacing the mounds about 2 inches apart.

3. Bake in a preheated 300°F. oven for 15 to 20 minutes, or until golden brown. Remove from the oven and place the parchment paper on a wet towel. Let cool, then pull the paper from the macaroons. Store in a tightly closed container in a dry place.

14. *Les Fromages et les Vins*
CHEESE AND WINE

⚜ ⚜ ⚜

Pour qui mange du fromage
Jamais santé ne fait naufrage.
—old French saying

He who eats cheese
Will always be healthy.

France produces some of the best-known cheeses in the world, due to the skill and knowledge accumulated over the centuries, and to the great care taken in its preparation. Pliny the Elder praised the cheese of the Gauls in the first century A.D. In the Middle Ages, when Christians fasted Wednesday as well as Friday and Saturday, cheese was sometimes their only food. Cheese is still an important part of a meal in France. It is often served in place of dessert with a selection of fresh fruits and fine bread. Brillat-Savarin said, "A dessert omitting cheese is a beautiful girl who is missing one eye."

Cheeses take their names, character, and flavor from the places where they are made. Climate, soil, pastures, time of year, and water are all influential factors. In addition to the widely known cheeses such as Camembert and Roquefort, there are numerous local cheeses that should be tasted in the regions where they originate. Summer and fall are generally the best seasons for cheese.

The best French cheeses are labeled *Les Fromages Fermiers* (cheeses from the farms), but because they are made from unpasteurized milk they are not imported into the United States. The flavor of those such as Camembert and Brie changes when pasteurized for export and becomes neutered. Then, too, salt is sometimes added as a preservative and cheeses such as Roquefort become too salty. Some, such as Petit-Suisse, are frozen for shipping and this changes the texture. Therefore, you will understand why some imported cheeses do not taste as good as those sampled in France.

Cheese is a living substance constantly in the process of change. It should be treated with care. Most cheeses continue to ripen even when refrigerated. Ideally, cheese should be served the same day it is purchased. To bring out the full flavor and aroma, cheese should be served at room temperature. As for goat cheese, try placing it under the broiler for a few minutes to heighten the flavor. Remove soft cheeses from the refrigerator one hour before serving and hard cheeses two hours ahead. Cover with a damp cloth.

For a variety of textures and tastes for a cheese tray, select three or four cheeses ranging from mild to strong; soft, semisoft, and hard; cow, goat, and blue cheeses. The quality is more important than the quantity.

Cheeses should be presented on a marble, glass, wicker, or wooden tray, but never on a plate. Always provide appropriate knives in sufficient quantity to prevent conflict of tastes.

Crusty French bread is the best accompaniment for cheese, although very bland unsalted crackers can be served with goat cheeses or pressed cheeses such as Gruyère. With the bread, serve unsalted butter, which goes well with the drier and strong cheeses, although it is never served with Roquefort.

The crust of soft-ripened cheese such as Camembert and Brie is often eaten, but a true cheese lover will discard it.

General Charles de Gaulle once quipped, "How can you govern a country that has three hundred forty-six cheeses?" Because of that wide variety, here are just a few of the most popular French cheeses.

BRIE   This is one of the most celebrated cheeses of France, named after the ancient province of Brie, where the cheese was first made.

Brie has been a great favorite since 774, when Charlemagne tasted it at the priory of Rueil in Brie.

To break the monotony of serious debate during the Congress of Vienna, which was convened in 1814 to reorganize Europe after the downfall of Napoleon, each delegate presented the best cheese of his country. Brie was shipped to Talleyrand and was unanimously voted the king of cheeses.

Brie is made with cow's milk. It has a flat, round shape, 7 to 14 inches in diameter and 1¼ inches thick. Of the main varieties, Brie de Meaux is the most classic, Melun and Provins are slightly smaller, and Brie de Coulommiers (often simply called Coulommiers) is only 5 inches across. The crust is white with traces of reddish pigmentation. The interior should be a glossy, buttery yellow from top to bottom and *never* runny. A layer of dry, chalky paste in the middle indicates the cheese is not yet ripened, and it will not ripen once sliced.

CAMEMBERT It is hard to guess which French cheese is the best known, but Camembert is certainly one of the best loved. Made in the village of Camembert in Normandy, it is a soft cheese with a white crust flecked with reddish pigmentation and indented with marks from the straw mats used during the curing period. Do not get a Camembert if the crust is all white or all red. It is at its peak when it yields to the fingertip with the same softness all over. It is past its prime if there is an ammonia smell, if it has shrunk in the chipwood box, or if it is runny.

Camembert was known in the twelfth century but its reinvention was attributed to Madame Harel, about 1791. Her daughter, Marie Harel, developed the manufacture of this famous cheese, and a statue of her was erected in Vimoutiers in 1928, five kilometers from Camembert, where she lived. It was destroyed in an air raid during World War II. In 1953 another statue of Marie Harel was given to the city by 400 dairy farmers of Van Wert, Ohio. Napoleon III is said to have kissed the waitress when he tasted this local cheese for the first time, and named the cheese "Camembert" after its home village. He had this cheese sent to the Tuileries and soon it became famous. So that the cheeses could be shipped to markets throughout most of the world, a circular chipwood box was invented by Monsieur Rivel in 1890. Until that innovation, Camembert had been wrapped in straw.

CHÈVRES France produces two-thirds of the world's goat cheeses. These delicious cheeses are an acquired taste for some, especially when the cheese is well aged in the drying process.

Some of the best chèvres include the small, cylindrical Saint-Maure; the pyramid-shaped Levroux, Chabichou, Valençay covered with pulverized wood ashes; the small chestnut leaf-wrapped Banon of Provence, and the Crottin de Chavignol.

COMTÉ OR FRENCH GRUYÈRE The word Gruyère comes from *gruyers* or inspectors who traveled through the mountains to collect levies when Switzerland was part of Gaul. Very similar to Swiss Gruyère, Comté has been made since the fourteenth century in the Jura and Haute-Savoie, across the border from Switzerland. This Gruyère is a superb cheese, frequently used for cooking, but better for eating alone. Comté should not be confused with Emmental, which has perfectly round, big holes. Oviform holes signify irregular fermentation, a tasteless and rubbery cheese.

FONTAINEBLEAU This unsalted fresh cream cheese is mixed with whipped cream during its preparation until it reaches the consistency of a light mousse. Fontainebleau is often eaten for dessert with *crème fraîche* and sugar. It is particularly delicious with fresh raspberries.

MAROILLES This square cheese is produced in several sizes. The monks of the Abbey of Maroilles in the province of Flandre first made it around 960.

Maroilles has a strong flavor, a soft and creamy texture, and a smooth, shiny reddish-brown rind that is brushed with beer during its curing. Because of its powerful aroma, it is called *Vieux Puant* (old stinker).

MUENSTER This round cheese originated in the Münster valley in Alsace in the seventh century. It has a very strong flavor, a creamy semisoft texture, and a high proportion of fat. It is sometimes flavored with cuminseeds or caraway seeds.

PETIT-SUISSE This double-cream cheese is made by adding cream to the curds of whole milk. The process is said to have been developed by a Swiss cowherd in 1850, who worked for a farmer's wife, Madame Héroult, in Villers-sur-Auchy in Normandy.

It is unsalted, slightly tangy, and is available in small cylindrical forms, individually wrapped.

PONT-L'ÉVÊQUE In medieval times, this cheese was called Angelot because it was stamped with a gold coin by that name. The coin bore the image of Saint Michael with the dragon under his feet. This cheese later came to be called Pont-l'Évêque, named after that town in Normandy, where it is made.

Pont-l'Évêque has never been duplicated elsewhere because of a fungus, *Monilia candida,* found only in the cellar where the cheese is cured; this fungus affects the flavor.

This soft fermented cheese is square, has a rich creamy yellow texture with tiny holes, and a reddish-gold crust. It is not ripe if the center is hard. It comes packaged in a light chipwood box.

PORT-SALUT   In 1233 Thibault de Mathefelon, Lord of the commune of Entrammes in Mayenne, gave away the small farm of Port-Rheingeard to monks belonging to the congregation of Sainte-Geneviève of Paris. He established a monastery for them, specifying that they should have six monks there "to serve God to perpetuity, for me, my forefathers, and my descendants." The church is still standing.

The monks were expelled from France during the Revolution. When they came back from exile, in 1815, they changed the name of Port-Rheingeard to Nôtre Dame de Port-du-Salut, or Our Lady of the Port-of-Salvation.

It was about 1850 that this highly reputed French cheese, Port-Salut, which until then was made only for the monks' consumption, started to be sold, first to nearby Laval, then to Paris. In 1860, 300 cheeses of 4 pounds each were sold daily. This production reached such proportions that the monks sold the cheese dairy in 1960, as well as the trade name of "Port-Salut," registered in 1878, to the *Société des Fermiers Réunis.*

Since then the monks have been producing, on a small scale, an unpasteurized cheese of the highest quality, sold under the trade name "Fromage de l'Abbaye."

A slow-ripening cheese, creamy-yellow though firm, Port-Salut's flavor varies greatly with age from very mild to very robust in taste. Its shape is thick and round with a hard thin rind. If the top is rounded, it indicates a bitter taste. This holds true for all the hard and semihard crusted cheeses.

SAINT-NECTAIRE   The cows' milk used in this cheese is produced from the rich high pastures of les Monts-Dore in Auvergne.

A semihard, uncooked pressed dough, this cheese has a mild taste with an aromatic flavor.

Maréchal de Saint-Nectaire made the cheese famous when he had it served at the tables of Louis XIV.

SAINT-PAULIN   A Trappist cheese, very similar to Port-Salut, originated at the Abbey of Mont-des-Cats in the north of France. It is now made all over France.

REBLOCHON   One of France's best-liked cheeses, it appeals to all tastes. This cheese has been made in the mountains of Haute Savoie for many centuries. Its name comes from the local dialect, *reblocher*, which is the day's second yield of ewes' milk, although Reblochon is made with cows' milk. Round and flat, its soft, buttery consistency resembles a Camembert.

ROQUEFORT   Long recognized as the King of Cheeses, Roquefort has been known for nearly 2,000 years; it is the oldest of all the blue cheeses. Originating in the Aveyron area of southeastern France in a small town called Roquefort-sur-Soulzon, it is made of ewes' milk.

Roquefort is inoculated with *Penicillium roqueforti* made with mold from rye bread crumbs and the presence of the mold is visible in the green streaks called *persillé*, characteristic of this cheese. It ripens for three months in the damp, drafty limestone caves of the Monts of Cambalou. This exposure gives the cheese its incomparable pungent flavor, imitated but never duplicated.

When Charlemagne was the guest of the monks of Saint-Gall, he was served Roquefort. He removed the *persillé*, but was told by the prior that it was the best part of the cheese. Charlemagne agreed and Roquefort became his favorite cheese. Two cases were sent to his palace at Aix-la-Chapelle every year.

Roquefort was used as a dressing for wounds during the Middle Ages, long before it became known that *Penicillium roqueforti* in the cheese, a cousin of penicillin, was a healing agent.

Charles VI made a law in 1411 specifying that it would be illegal to use the name "Roquefort" for any cheese made outside of the Roquefort area. He gave to the people of Roquefort "the monopoly of refining the cheese manufacture for time immemorial in the caves of this village." This charter was renewed many times, and again, internationally, in 1951. Roquefort has a distinctive wrap of metal foil that is stamped with a ring of red sheep.

Other worthy blue cheeses include Bleu d'Auvergne, Bleu de Bresse, and Bleu des Causses, made with cows' milk.

TRIPLE-CRÈME   This type of soft cheese, with 72 percent fat content, is a newcomer, compared to the double cream, which has 60 percent. Some of the popular triple-crèmes include Boursault,

Boursin, and Fin-de-Siècle. Aromatic seasoning and herbs are often added.

WINE

Wine is an integral part of French cuisine and is worth a story all by itself.

Wine making goes back many thousands of years. Recently, a beautiful amphora still filled with wine and dating back to 900 B.C. was discovered in Cyprus.

Hippocrates, in referring to wine, described it as "this drink admirably appropriate to man."

Wine, a symbol and sacrament in the Christian religion, was necessary for Mass and other religious needs during the year. It was imperative that a sufficient supply of wine be made annually. Therefore, we owe a great deal to the Cistercian monks who, during the thirteenth century, developed the great wines of Côte d'Or, and the Chablis of Burgundy. All excess wine was sold to benefit their religious orders, because they were forbidden to drink it. For the same reason, the great wines of Châteauneuf-du-Pape of Avignon were produced and sold. Gradually, as a result of the sale of the excess production, the wine industry developed.

For those occasions when several wines are to be served, the lighter wines should be served first and then, gradually, the more full-bodied wines, to prevent their being detrimental to each other.

White wine and rosé wine should be chilled for 1 hour before serving. Red Bordeaux is served *chambré* (room temperature), or around 65°F. Burgundy is served cool. Champagne is served cold, but not *frappé,* or it loses its taste and aroma. Champagne can be drunk throughout a meal or at its end. Traditionally, it is served in a *flûte* (long-stemmed glass), a shape that dates to Dom Pérignon.

◆ *A Toast* ◆

During the Middle Ages and into part of the Renaissance, *porter un tostée* (to toast someone) was a custom meant to honor a special guest.

A slice of toast was placed in the bottom of a glass, which was then filled with wine. The glass was passed around, and when it reached the guest, he would finish the wine and eat the *tostée* (toast) lying in the bottom of the glass. This custom resulted in two quite dissimilar meanings for our word *toast*—both the bread itself and the act of drinking to a guest.

◆ *On Wine and Cheese* ◆

*L'homme, pour accompagner le fromage, n'a encore rien trouve
de mieux que le vin.*

Man has never yet found anything better than wine
to accompany cheese.
—PIERRE ANDROUET
Guide du Fromage, 1971

Most authorities feel that cheese and wine are an ideal combination, although a few are convinced that wine removes the delicate aroma of cheese and vice versa. In any case, water must never be drunk with cheese.

A general rule is to avoid serving a strong, full-bodied wine with a delicate cheese or serving a wine that is light and subtle with a fermented cheese. French cider can be served with cheese from Normandy; beer can be served with goat cheeses. Any local cheese should be enjoyed with the local wine.

This is only a suggested list of wines and cheese combinations; it is a matter of personal taste.

Fresh cheeses: Boursin, Petit-Suisse: white or rosé wines; light Beaujolais or Loire Valley wines.

Roquefort and other blue cheeses: strong, full-bodied red Burgundy (Pommard); Beaujolais (Moulin-à-Vent); Côtes du Rhône (Châteauneuf-du-Pape).

Cooked and uncooked cheeses: Gruyère, Port-Salut, Saint-Nectaire: delicate wines such as white or red Graves, Bordeaux or Loire, Médoc and Chinon.

Soft cheeses: Livarot, Pont-l'Évêque: the same wines for fresh cheeses. Muenster: an Alsatian beer or a wine such as Gewürztraminer.

Goat cheeses: light red or rosé wines such as Côtes du Rhône (Tavel), or Burgundy (Mâcon), or Beaujolais.

Fromage! Poésie!	Cheese! Poetry!
Bouquet de nos repas	Crowning glory of our meals,
Que sentirait la vie	How would life taste
Si l'on ne t'avait pas!	If we didn't have thee!

GLOSSARY

Bain-marie: A double boiler for slow cooking or keeping foods warm; the top pan must not touch the water. Or a hot-water bath used to hold the baking dish for a delicate custard or other dish; or used to keep sauces or egg dishes warm. In such a hot-water bath the top pan sits in the water, which is kept at a constant temperature.

Baking sheet: Keep these in first-class condition for best results. Replace them whenever they become battered, stained, or warped.

Baste: To moisten foods with a marinade, pan drippings, fat, or liquid while cooking. Basting prevents drying and adds to the flavor.

Batter: A soft, smooth semiliquid mixture usually containing eggs, flour, milk, and seasonings, as crêpe batter.

Bay leaves: One of the traditional herbs of a *bouquet garni.* This aromatic herb is the leaf of the laurel tree or shrub. Emperors and dictators and victors in the games were crowned with laurel wreaths in ancient Greece and Rome. Bay leaves were thought to be good for the health and a protection against thunder and lightning. Pulverize a bunch of dried bay leaves in a blender and bottle. This is simpler than extracting a whole leaf from a pan after cooking.

Beurre manié: A mixture of softened butter and flour used to thicken sauces or stews. *Beurre manié* can be made of equal amounts of butter and flour, or of more of one or the other, according to the recipe. To make, mash the butter and flour together thoroughly with a fork. Dot the sauce with bits of the *beurre manié* and swirl the pan until the mixture has blended and thickened the sauce to the desired consistency. Do not boil after adding *beurre manié.*

Blanch: To boil vegetables briefly in a large quantity of water so as to reduce a bitter or too strong flavor, to remove excess salt, or to facilitate peeling.

Blender: For a quick blender cleanup, add water and detergent to the jar, cover, and whirl the contents for a few seconds. Refill with clean water and again turn motor on and off to rinse out any detergent.

Blending: Thoroughly mixing two or more ingredients.

Bouquet garni: A small aromatic nosegay of parsley, thyme, and bay leaf, occasionally celery, tied together with string. Remove the little bundle from the finished dish before serving.

Braise: To cook slowly with a little liquid in a covered dish in the oven or on top of the stove.

Butter: Butter is salted to increase its shelf life. It keeps for months and tastes like it; moreover, salted butter burns after 5 minutes of cooking. Use unsalted butter for the recipes in this book; it keeps in the refrigerator for at least 2 weeks. To make unsalted butter, whip 1 cup heavy cream in a chilled blender until firm. Add ¾ cup ice water and 1 ice cube. Blend on high speed for a few minutes until the butter rises to the surface. Strain through a *chinois* or strainer. Press the lump of butter under cold water to wash and remove any milk left in it. Shape and chill. Yield: about 7 tablespoons.

Caramelize: To heat sugar until it forms a golden syrup. To caramelize a 1½-quart mold, combine 1 cup sugar and 4 tablespoons water. Place over moderate heat and boil until golden, then quickly coat the mold. If syrup is too dark, it will impart a bitter taste. Do not stir or touch the pan or the sugar will crystallize. To clean the pan, add water and boil until the caramel has dissolved.

Cauliflower: When cooking cauliflower, place a piece of stale bread crust in the liquid. It will take away the strong odor.

Chervil: This herb is used extensively in French cooking for sprinkling on soups, as a garnish for salads, and one of the *fines herbes.* Pliny in the first century recommended it as a cure for hiccoughs.

Cheese: Do buy cheese from a cheese store. The flavor of these cheeses is far superior to prewrapped pieces of cheese, which are often tasteless and rubbery in texture. Remember that the Swiss Emmental cheese has large holes and is best uncooked. Swiss Gruyère, with fewer and small holes, has a stronger, full-bodied taste and is preferable for cooking. If you like the effect of stringy cheese in onion soup or in a gratin dish, then use Emmental. A quarter pound of cheese will give you 1 cup of grated cheese. A special small gadget designed for grating cheese is a great saver of time and cheese ends.

Cheesecloth: Be sure the cheesecloth has not been chemically treated. Have on hand for straining stock.

Chinois: A conical strainer that looks like an old Chinese hat. Indispensable for straining sauce.

Cocotte: A round or oval casserole with a cover, usually made of enameled cast iron. Individual dishes of ovenproof china used for baking and serving eggs.

Court-bouillon: The name means "short-bouillon" because the cooking time is short. It is a flavorful liquid for poaching fish and poultry.

Cream: Use only a hand rotary beater for whipping cream. It produces more volume and the cream keeps better. Refrigerate the beater as well as the bowl before whipping cream during the summer months.

Heavy cream that is at least 1 day old is best for whipping. Avoid the ultrapasteurized cream, or "whipping cream," as it becomes watery, especially when squeezed from a pastry bag.

To maintain whipped cream firmness for decorating desserts, add a teaspoon of gelatin dissolved in 2 teaspoons of hot heavy cream into a cup of cold heavy cream just before whipping it.

Crème Chantilly: Beat 1 cup heavy cream, add 1 teaspoon pure vanilla extract, and sugar to taste.

Crème fraîche: Pasteurization prevents heavy cream from thickening as it kills the lactic acid. Prepare a substitute by combining 1 cup heavy cream and ½ cup dairy sour cream. Blend thoroughly. Heat until lukewarm. Let stand at room temperature for 12 hours, or until it develops the consistency of mayonnaise. It will keep refrigerated for several days.

Crème Saint-Honoré: Make a Pastry Cream (see Index). While hot stir in 1 tablespoon unflavored gelatin softened in 2 tablespoons water. Fold in 4 egg whites, whisk to a very stiff peak, then whisk again with ⅓ cup sugar.

Croutons: Remove the crusts from slices of good-quality bread. Cut the bread into ½-inch cubes. Melt unsalted butter with 1 teaspoon oil in a skillet. Add the bread cubes, cover, and brown slowly, shaking the pan often. For hearty soups, cut ½-inch slices of French bread. Brown under a broiler or fry in a combination of oil and butter. Rub the croutons with a garlic clove while hot.

Cube: To cut meat or vegetables into 1-inch cubes.

Cutting board: To eliminate the odor of onion or garlic from a wooden cutting board, rub the surface with a sliced lime.

Deglaze: To dissolve flavorful drippings and brown particles from a roasting pan by adding stock, wine, or water, and scraping the bits over heat.

Degrease: To skim off excess fat from the surface of liquid.

Dice: To cut meat or vegetables into ¼-inch cubes.

Dry vegetables: Dry vegetables should be cooked in cold water with a lid.

Dust: To sprinkle lightly with flour or sugar.

Eggs: Eggs should be removed immediately from their carton, except if it is made of plastic, and placed in a bowl. Eggshells are porous and absorb any strong smell.

  If eggs are needed immediately after removing them from the refrigerator, warm them to room temperature in tepid water.

  Eggs for these recipes should be large unless otherwise specified.

  For boiled eggs, lower the eggs, one at a time, on a spoon, into boiling water. For large quantities, use a wire basket. Let the water come to a boil before timing, then reduce the heat to a simmer. Cook for 3½ minutes for soft-cooked eggs, 6 to 8 minutes for *oeufs mollets,* and 10 minutes for hard-cooked eggs. Add salt to water to prevent eggs from running if they have a slight crack.

  When the egg in its shell is done to your needs, tap gently to crack the shell, plunge into cold water for 5 minutes, and peel.

Egg whites: Beat whites slowly at first, with a hand eggbeater, then increase the speed. When stiff, turn the whites over four or five times, using the hand eggbeater in place of a spatula. This will stabilize them. Leftover whites may be frozen in tiny individual plastic cups for soufflés, to lighten whipped cream, for meringues, etc.

Egg yolks: To keep unused egg yolks, drop them into a small jar of cold water and refrigerate.

Fines herbes: Finely chopped or cut with scissors mixed herbs such as parsley, chives, tarragon, and chervil.

Fish fillet: The right side to fold a fillet of fish is the side that had the skin on, or which is less white and smoother. Do not season that side as salt will make the fillet render water, and if stuffed, the stuffing will not stick to it. Roll fillet by the small end.

Flake: To separate into small pieces with a fork.

Flambé: To flame a dish or a food with alcohol. Warm a metal soup ladle under hot water, add the alcohol, ignite, and pour it flaming into the dish or over the particular food.

Fleurons: Decorative crescents of puff pastry used to garnish fish, chicken, or spinach dishes.

Floral arrangements: It is important that the fragrance of a floral arrangement for a dinner party should not overpower the aroma of the food. Be particularly cautious about such flowers as tuberoses or carnations.

Flour: The use of the right flour is very important in baking. In raised dough, bread flour is essential. Many supermarkets now carry bread flour. Pastry flour, a low-gluten flour, is not to be confused with cake flour, which is a soft wheat flour. Pastry flour is available in specialty food shops, at your pastry shop, and by mail order.

Fold: To incorporate a delicate mixture gently into a heavier mixture, using a large spatula, so the air will not be lost and the ingredients will be evenly blended.

Frozen foods: One of the most famous French chefs, Alexandre Dumaine, called frozen foods *nourriture morte* (dead food). For best results, buy only the freshest food.

Fumet: A rich concentrated stock made with fish trimmings, bones and white wine.

Garlic: The Parisians in the sixteenth century never failed to eat garlic with butter during the month of May, and were convinced that it would bring them health for the rest of the year. Today, garlic is seldom used, except in the South of France. Do not use a garlic press, but mince the garlic clove finely with a knife.

Garnish: To decorate a dish just before serving with colorful accents such as parsley, watercress, croutons, or grooved lemon slices.

Glaze: To place a dish under the broiler just before serving to produce a golden color, or to make the food opaque.

Herbs: Date your herb and spice jars when you buy them. Throw out after 6 months because the flavor will be gone. Fresh herbs are less strong in flavor than dried ones. Double their amount in recipes.

Julienne: Long, thin strips of food, ⅛ inch to ¼ inch wide. This appellation first appeared in a cookbook, *Le cuisinier Royal,* in 1722.

Knives: Why are table knives rounded on the end? Because Cardinal Richelieu was annoyed by his guests who used their knives as toothpicks, as was the custom of the day. The Cardinal ordered that all the knives, except those used for carving, have the points rounded off. The Court followed suit.

Treat your kitchen knives with constant, loving care. Use carbon steel knives. Keep sharpened at all times. Never immerse knives in the dishpan. Dry them promptly and thoroughly after washing under running water. Stains can be removed with a steel-wool pad and scouring powder or with white malt vinegar.

Leeks: A must in many French dishes, leeks look like huge overgrown scallions; 1 inch in diameter is the best size. A very important flavoring agent, especially in soups.

Lemon: The best lemons have a fine-textured skin. Rough-looking ones have thick skins and are less juicy.

Lobster: To remove cooked meat from the lobster's tail section, break the tail off with the back up. Break off the flippers at the end of the tail, then slide the meat out whole.

Macédoine: A mixture of cubed or diced vegetables or fruits.

Macerate: To place fruits in a flavorful liquid.

Mandoline: An implement with a blade for fine slicing and making julienne strips.

Marinade: A seasoned liquid, with an acid, cooked or uncooked, in which food is steeped. It seasons and tenderizes the food.

Marinate: To soak food, especially meats, in a marinade to season or tenderize.

Measurements: All recipes in this book call for level spoonfuls and level cups.

Measuring cups: Have enough measuring cups and spoons on hand so you do not have to keep washing them while preparing an elaborate recipe.

Meat: Season large pieces of meat when halfway cooked. This method does not toughen the meat as easily as it would if you added seasoning at the start; and it prevents extra loss of juice. Allow meats and fowls to "rest" 10 minutes after cooking. This retains the juices and makes the carving task easier.

Milk: When boiling milk, rinse the pan under cold water and do not dry before adding milk. This will prevent the milk from scorching.

Mirepoix: This culinary base is the creation of the cook of the Duc de Lévis-Mirepoix, Maréchal de France of Louis XV. A mixture of carrots, onions, celery, sometimes ham, cut into ¼-inch cubes, with bay leaf and thyme; the mixture is cooked slowly in butter, then added to a sauce or dish to enhance the flavor. Also used as a bed for braising meats or poultry.

Mushrooms: The Greeks claimed that mushrooms were the food of the gods. Buy mushrooms with tightly closed caps. As mushrooms age, the caps open and they lose their fragrance and freshness. Never peel mushrooms. Wash them only if they have dirt particles. Do this step quickly and dry the mushrooms thoroughly. Cut off part of the stem tips. For garnish, slice off the stems on a level with the caps. A sprinkling of lemon juice while cooking will keep them white. Never buy prepackaged, prewashed mushrooms that are chemically bleached white with sodium bisulphate. This camouflages discoloration and stickiness of poor mushrooms.

Olive oil: French olive oil has a delicate flavor that is not as overpowering as Spanish, Italian, or Greek products. Virgin olive oil is the best quality to buy. Odorless peanut oil is almost exclusively used in France, when oil is required for cooking and frying.

Pan: Do not use a cast-iron pan if wine is used, or it will alter the flavor. Never use a nonstick pan to sauté meat or vegetables as they boil in their juices and have no flavor.

Parmesan cheese: Buy Parmesan in a block from a reputable cheese store and grate it just before you use it. Already grated cheese is much less flavorful and almost always more expensive.

Parsley: The ancient Greeks wore crowns of parsley at banquets as a preventative against drunkenness. Parsley was used as early as the second century as a flavoring in salads. The stems of parsley hold a great deal of flavor; use them in court-bouillon, stocks, or chopped with their leaves for salads.

A special small gadget for mincing parsley (parsley mouli) is a great saver of time. Parsley will retain its freshness if kept wrapped in foil under refrigeration.

Pastry bags: Two pastry bags with a selection of tubes are essential for decorating dishes or for pastry making. In an emergency, a plastic bag with a corner clipped off can be used, with a rubber band to hold the tube in place.

Pepper: White pepper is similar in taste to French pepper; it is preferred in white or delicate sauces and for chicken or egg dishes.

Petits fours: These small delicate pastry were created by Carême (1784–1833). The oven could not be regulated, and when the fire was becoming extinct, the cookies were placed at a lower temperature, which explains *petit four* (slow oven). Petits fours are usually served at teatime or as an accompaniment for ice cream or a mousse.

Pickled white onions: A perfect accompaniment for pot-au-feu or any cold meat. Cover 2 pounds of tiny white onions with cold water. Bring to a boil and boil 7 minutes. Strain and peel. Place in a bowl and cover them with boiling fine red wine vinegar (preferably French). Next day, strain the onions and place in a glass jar or stoneware pot. Reserve the vinegar, then bring to a fast boil with 1 tablespoon coarse salt and pour over the onions, reaching 1 inch above them. Add 1 or 2 sprigs each of thyme and tarragon (or ½ teaspoon dry tarragon), ½ bay leaf, ¼ teaspoon peppercorns, and 2 cloves. Seal the jars hermetically as vinegar evaporates quickly. The pickled onions are ready to use in a month.

Plates: Use warm plates for hot food, but not so hot that you can't handle them. Use cold plates for cold foods.

Poach: To cook gently in simmering liquid so the surface of the liquid barely quivers.

Potato-ball cutter: A potato-ball cutter, a special gadget to make balls, is indispensable, since tiny new potatoes are seasonal. Potato balls make any meat or fish dish more attractive and refined. Allow 6 to 7 balls per serving.

Potatoes: Potatoes will stay white, firmer, and retain their shape if, after they are peeled, they are placed in cold water for several hours. This method is especially fine for parsleyed potatoes and potato balls in butter.

Poultry: For a more flavorful bird, season inside the cavity, never on the outside. Salt on raw meat produces dampness and prevents a good browning.

Ramekin: Often made with cheese and eggs, this is baked and served in small dishes. One of the small ovenproof dishes for cooking and serving individual portions.

Ravier: A shallow dish made in various shapes, used to serve *hors-d'oeuvre*.

Reduce: To boil a liquid rapidly so as to thicken, concentrate, and intensify the flavor of the sauce or soup.

Salad: It is handy to keep a small plastic pan under the sink just for washing greens.

Salt: "If salt has lost its taste, how shall its saltness be restored?" Matthew 5:13. Salt has a taste of its own and enhances food. Coarse salt (*gros sel*) is always used in French cooking because it gives more flavor to food. It is excellent for salads because it does not wilt the greens as quickly as fine salt. Some fine salt has up to seven different additives. Besides, it tastes only salty without giving any flavor. Use it for its quick dissolving quality for preparing eggs and pastry. Kosher salt is an acceptable substitute for *gros sel*.

Sauté: To cook quickly in a very small amount of butter or fat, in a skillet or *sauteuse*.

Sauteuse: A round shallow pan, with sloping sides and with a long handle, for quick frying of food in a small amount of fat.

Sautoir: An indispensable large round shallow, straight-walled heavy pan for sautéing food in a small amount of fat, at high temperature.

Shallots: A pungent bulb related to onion, shallots are almost always used cooked. Shallots have been used extensively in French cookery since the Crusaders brought them back to Europe. Do not let shallots brown too much or they will impart a bitter taste.

Shoestring potatoes: The same as French fried, but cut like matches.

Sift: To put through a sifter or a fine sieve so as to remove lumps, making the ingredient (flour, for instance) lighter and fluffier.

Simmer: To cook just below the boiling point or to cook gently in liquid over low heat.

Steak: When panfrying a steak, add a few drops of oil to the butter to prevent it from burning.

Stews: When liquids are added to stews, they should be hot. Cold water toughens meat and vegetables.

Tarragon: A highly aromatic herb, tarragon is used for salads and seems to have a special affinity for chicken dishes. Since early days tarragon has been a very distinctive French flavoring and it remains one of the country's best-loved herbs.

Thyme: Hippocrates, the "father of medicine," wrote a treatise on thyme as an all-inclusive therapeutic herb. Roman soldiers bathed in water infused with thyme to gain courage and strength.

Tomato paste: To keep unused tomato paste, spoon it into a small jar, smooth the top with a knife, and cover with a film of olive oil to seal out the air.

Toss: To mix ingredients so as to combine them without crushing or breaking them.

Truffles: Truffles, one of the most costly of the luxury food items, can be purchased in large department stores. They can be purchased at less cost directly from France, since truffles originate there: La Maison de la Truffe, 19 Place de la Madeleine, Paris, France.

Vegetables: Green vegetables in France are cooked in a large pot of boiling water, seasoned with coarse (kosher) salt, *uncovered.* Place the strainer with the vegetables in ice cold water to set the color. Drain and place the vegetables in a *sauteuse.* Stir around until they have lost all their moisture and steam is no longer visible. Add unsalted butter in parcels, white pepper, and sauté or shake the pan until the vegetables are well coated. Serve immediately on a heated serving plate.

When green vegetables have to wait before serving, after they have been refreshed or dipped in ice cold water, place them in boiling salted water just long enough to warm them up. Drain and proceed as above.

Vinaigrette: A basic dressing for salads and vegetables made with 3 parts oil and 1 part French vinegar (4 parts oil for American vinegar because of its acidity) and salt and pepper. Mustard, herbs, shallots, and garlic can be added.

White sauces: Never guess at the proportions for a white sauce. For a medium consistency, use 2 tablespoons butter, 1½ tablespoons flour, and 1 cup liquid. For a very thick white sauce, use 2 tablespoons butter, 2 tablespoons flour, and 1 cup liquid.

Yogurt: Yogurt is the Turkish name for fermented milk. It was introduced into France when it was used to cure François I of intestinal troubles. The doctor of the Grand Turk Suleiman I was called upon, and he responded by bringing a herd of sheep across all of Europe so that he could make and give his patient fresh yogurt. The doctor would never reveal his secret recipe. On his journey back to Turkey, he lost most of the herd due to the hardships met along the way.

Making yogurt is a simple process: Bring 4 cups milk to a full boil, transfer to a bowl, and cool to *lukewarm*. Remove skin formed on the top. Stir in 3 tablespoons commercial yogurt. (Keep some of your own for later batches.) Pour into 5 or 6 small bowls and place on a tray in a gas oven. The pilot light will keep the heat at the right temperature. Or put an electric oven on warm. Cool to 105°F., or until oven feels barely tepid to your hand. *Do not touch* for 5 to 8 hours, until yogurt is completely set. During the process turn on the electric oven again for ½ minute.

Let the yogurt mature for at least 12 hours. The longer you keep yogurt under refrigeration, the more pronounced the tart taste becomes. True yogurt is never sour.

Yogurt cheese: Yogurt cheese is delicious, low in calories, and simple to make. Make yogurt in a bowl instead of individual containers. Let the yogurt mature for one day. Stir in 1 teaspoon of salt, or to taste. Pour the yogurt into a colander lined with two thicknesses of cheesecloth. Let stand undisturbed for 12 hours to drain, but not under refrigeration. This yogurt cheese will have the consistency of a very fine cottage cheese. Chill several hours before serving at room temperature with French bread. If the taste seems too sharp, add an equal amount of cream cheese or whatever proportion seems right.

Wine: Do not hesitate to use the best wine for cooking. The results of your dishes will be comparable to the quality of the wine. The wine can be chosen to complement the food, or the food can be planned around a great wine. If the main dish is cooked with wine, the same wine should be served as its accompaniment.

Tips on wines that may prove useful: True Sauternes, a French wine, is spelled with an *S* at the end. The shape of a bottle of Bordeaux wine has a shoulder, while Burgundy wine has none. "Aroma" refers to white wine, "bouquet" to red wine.

Wine becomes red when you crush the red grape skins, which are left in the vat with the juice. The pigment in the skin, after several days of fermenting, results in the red color.

White wine is white because the skins are removed before the fermentation.

Rosé wine is made with black grapes, with white juice. Its color is found in the skin of the grapes during a short maceration of the must.

BIBLIOGRAPHY

Ali-Bab. *Gastronomie pratique*. Paris: Flammarion, 1923.

L'Almanach de Cocagne. Paris: Sirène, 1920–1921.

Amsertam, A. *Le Pâtissier François*. Chez Louys and Daniel Elzevier, 1655.

Amunategui, Francis. *L'Art des mets ou traité des plaisirs de la table*. Paris: Arthème Fayard, 1959.

———. *Le Plaisir des mets*. Paris: Au Fil d'Ariane, 1964.

Andrieu, Pierre. *Fine bouche*. London: Cassell, 1956.

Androuet. *Guide du fromage*. Paris: Stock, 1971.

Apicius. *The Roman Cookery Book*. London: Peter Nevill, 1958.

Appert, François-Nicolas. *L'Art de conserver*. Paris: Patris & Cie, 1810.

———. *Le Livre de tous les ménages*. Paris: Barrois l'Aine, 1831.

Aron, Jean-Paul. *Essai sur la sensibilité alimentaire à Paris au 19ᵉ siècle*. Paris: Colin, 1967.

Athenaeus. *Les quinze livres des Deipnosophistes d'Athénée*. Paris: Langlois, 1680, written first in A.D. 228.

Audot, Louis Eustache. *La cuisinière de la campagne et de la ville*. Paris: Librairie Audot, 1875.

Aulagnier, A. F. *Dictionnaire des Substances alimentaires*. 2 vols. Paris: 1830.

Auriscoste de Lazarque, Ernest. *Cuisine Messine*. Nancy: Sidot, 1898.

Beauvillers. *Le Bon et Parfait Cuisinier universel*. Paris: Lebigre Frères, 1837.

Beauvilliers, Antoine. *L'Art du cuisinier*. 2 vols. Paris: Pilet, 1814.

Berchoux, Joseph de. *La gastronomie*. Paris: Giguet, 1801.

Bernardi, T. *L'Écuyer tranchant*. Paris: Gustave Barba, 1845.

Blond, Germaine et Georges. *Histoire pittoresque de notre alimentation*. Paris: Arthème Fayard, 1960.

Bonnefons, Nicholas de. *Les Délices de la campagne*. Paris: Antoine Cellier, 1662.

Boulestin. *The Best of Boulestin*. Elvira and Maurice Firuski, eds. Canada: Ambassador Books Ltd., 1951.

Bourgeat, Jacques. *Les Plaisirs de la table en France des Gaulois à nos jours*. Paris: Hachette, 1963.

Bouzy, Michel. *Les Poissons, coquillages, crustacés*. Paris: Impression Blondel la Rougery, 1929.

Brillat-Savarin, Jean Anthelme. *Physiologie du goût*. Paris: Charpentier, 1858.

Burnet, M. *Dictionnaire de cuisine et d'économie ménagère*. Paris: Librairie Usnelle, 1836.

Carême, Marie-Antoine dit Antonin. *Le Pâtissier pittoresque*. Paris: Imprimerie de Fimmin Didot, 1828.

————. *Le Maître-d'hôtel.* Paris: Renouard, 1842.

Castelot, André. *L'Histoire à table.* Paris: Librairie Plon, Librairie Académique Perrin, 1972.

La Chapelle, Vincent. *Le cuisinier moderne.* 1733.

Courtine, Robert J., et Desmur, Jean. *Anthologie de la poésie gourmande.* Paris: Édition Trévisse, 1970.

Curnonsky. *Recettes des provinces de France.* Paris: Les Productions de Paris, n.d.

————. *La Table et l'amour.* Paris: La Clé d'Or, 1950.

———— et Derys, Gaston. *Anthologie de la gastronomie française.* Paris: Librairie Delagrave, 1936.

———— et Rouff, Marcel. *La France gastronomique.* 25 vols. Paris: F. Rouff, 1921–1928.

De Croze, Austin. *What to Eat & Drink in France.* London: Frederick Warne, 1931.

Dentu, E. *La Cuisine classique.* Paris: n.d.

Derys, Gaston. *L'Art d'être gourmand.* Paris: Albin Michel, 1929.

Des Ombriaux, Maurice. *L'Art de manger et son histoire.* Paris: Payot, 1928.

Dictionnaire de l'académie des gastronomes. Paris: Aux Éditions Prisma, 1962.

Dion, Roger. *Histoire de la Vigne et du Vin en France.* Paris: 1959.

Dufour, Philippe Sylvestre. *Traitez du café, du thé et du chocolate.* La Haye: Adrian Moetjens, 1685.

Dumas, Alexandre [fils]. *Grand dictionnaire de cuisine.* Paris: Alphonse Lemerre, 1873.

Dumas, F. G. *Almanach des gourmands.* Paris: Nilsson, 1904.

Dumenteil, Fulbert. *La France gourmande.* Paris: Librairie Universelle, 1906.

Durand, Charles. *Le Cuisinier Durand.* Nîmes: Imprimerie de P. Durand-Belle, 1830.

Émy, M. *L'Art de bien faire les glaces d'office.* 2 vols. Paris: Librairie Le Clerc, 1768.

Escoffier, Auguste. *Les Fleurs en cire.* Paris: L'Art Culinaire, 1910.

————. *Ma cuisine.* Paris: E. Flammarion, 1934.

Escudier. *La Véritable Cuisine provençale et niçoise.* Toulon: Éditions Provencia, 1967.

Fabre, Joseph. *Dictionnaire universel de cuisine pratique et alimentaire et d'hygiène alimentaire.* Paris: Chez tous les librairies, 1891.

Finebouche, Marie-Claude. *La Cuisine de madame.* Paris: Gallimard, 1932.

Francisque, Michel, et Fournier, Édouard. *Le Livre d'Or des Métiers.* Paris: Librairie Historique, Archéologique et Scientifique de Sère, 1851.

Franklin, Alfred. *La vie privée d'autrefois: arts et métiers, modes, moeurs, usages des Parisiens, du XIIᵉ au XVIIIᵉ siècle.* Paris: Édition Plon, 1888.

Gouffé, Jules. *Le Livre de cuisine.* Paris: Hachette, 1867.

Grimod de la Reynière, Alexandre. *Almanach des gourmands.* Vols. 1–8. Paris: Maradan, 1803–1812.

Guégan, Bertrand. *La Fleur de la Cuisine Française.* Paris: Sirène, 1920.

————. *Le Cuisinier français.* Paris: Émile-Paul, 1934.

Guy, Christian. *Une Histoire de la cuisine française.* Paris: Les Productions de Paris, 1962.

Jacques, Marie. *Colette's Best Recipes.* Boston: Little, Brown, 1923.

Lallemand, Roger. *La Vraie Cuisine d'Anjou et de Touraine.* Paris: Quartier Latin, 1969.

————. *La Vraie Cuisine du Nord de la France.* Paris: 1973.

La Mazille. *La Bonne Cuisine du Périgord.* Paris: E. Flammarion, 1929.

La Varenne, François Pierre de. *Le Pâtissier françois.* Paris: Jean Gaillard, 1653.

————. *Le Vray cuisinier françois.* Lyon: Léonard de la Roche, 1667.

Lebas, J. *Festin joyeux ou la cuisine en musique.* Paris: Lesclapart, 1738.

Lebault, Armand. *La table et le repas*. Paris: Lucien Laveur, 1910.

Lémery, Louis. *Traité des aliments*. Paris: J. B. Cusson et P. Witte, 1702.

Lune, Pierre de. *Le cuisinier*. Paris: Pierre David, 1656.

Manant-Ville. *Cours gastronomiques ou les diners de Manant-Ville*. Paris: Capelle et Renand, 1809.

Marin, François. *Les dons de Comus*. Paris: Veuve Pissot, 1758.

Ménagiers de Paris (written in 1392). 2 vols. Paris: Crapelet, 1846.

Menon. *La science du Maître d'Hôtel cuisinier*. Paris: Paulus-du-Mesnil, 1749.

Montagné, Prosper. *Larousse gastronomique*. Paris: Librairie Larousse, 1938.

Moura, Jean, et Louvet, Paul. *Le Café Procope*. Paris: Librairie Académique Pérrin, 1929.

Nostradamus (Michel de Nostre-Dame). *Excellent et moult utile opuscule à tous nécessaire qui désirent avoir connaissance des plus exquises recettes . . .* Lyon: Antoine Volant, 1555.

Nigon, Édouard. *Les Plaisirs de la table*. Paris: Piazza, 1933.

Pomiane, Édouard de. *Code de la bonne chère*. Paris: A. Michel, 1924.

Reboul, J. B. *La Cuisinière provençale*. Marseille: Édition Tacussel, n.d.

Ritz, Marie Louise. *César Ritz: Host to the World*. Philadelphia: J. B. Lippincott, 1938.

Saint-Ange, Mme D. *Le Livre de cuisine de Madame Saint-Ange*. Paris: Librairie Larousse, 1927.

Salaman, R. N. *History and Social Influence of the Potato*. Cambridge, England: Cambridge University Press, 1949.

Saulnier, Louis. *Le Répertoire de la cuisine*. Paris: Dupont et Malgat, 1923.

Sévigné, Mme. de. *Lettres*. Paris: Hachette, 1950. (Letters date from 1664 to 1696.)

Story, Sommerville. *Dining in Paris*. New York: Robert M. McBride, 1924.

Taillevent, Guillaume Tirel dit. *Le Viandier* (circa 1490). Paris: J. Pichon, 1892.

Tendret, Lucien. *La Table au pays de Brillat-Savarin*. Paris: Alphonse Lemerre, 1892.

Urbain-Dubois, Félix. *L'École des cuisinières*. Paris: Flammarion, 1926.

In addition to this list of books, numerous others as well as reviews, such as *Revue Culina*, Paris, Librairie des Publications Nouvelles, issues from 1911 to 1939, and *Cuisine et Vins de France*, magazine founded by Curnonsky in 1950, have been used in the historical research.

INDEX

⚜ ⚜ ⚜